The Massacre of Political Prisoners in Iran, 1988: An Addendum

Witness Testimonies and Official Statements

Drawing by Sudabeh Ardavan, a prisoner in Evin Prison, a composite of various sections of the prison, including the interrogation corridors, the Amuzeshgah, and wards 216 and 325, from her book *Memories from Prison*.

THE MASSACRE OF POLITICAL PRISONERS IN IRAN, 1988: An Addendum

Witness Testimonies and Official Statements

Abdorrahman Boroumand Foundation

About the Abdorrahman Boroumand Foundation

The Abdorrahman Boroumand Foundation (ABF) is a non-governmental, non-profit organization dedicated to the promotion of human rights and democracy in Iran. ABF is an independent organization with no political affiliation. It is named in memory of Dr. Abdorrahman Boroumand, an Iranian lawyer and pro-democracy activist who was assassinated in Paris on 18 April 1991, allegedly by agents of the Islamic Republic of Iran. ABF believes that promoting human rights awareness through education and the dissemination of information is a necessary prerequisite for the establishment of a stable democracy in Iran. ABF was founded in 2001 by Ladan and Roya Boroumand, the daughters of Dr. Boroumand. In 2009 they were awarded the Lech Walesa Institute Foundation Prize in honor of their work promoting human rights, freedom of expression, and democracy in Iran.

ABF is committed to the values enshrined in the Universal Declaration of Human Rights and in other internationally recognized human rights instruments. ABF seeks to ensure that human rights in Iran are promoted and protected without discrimination. Guided by the belief that impunity and unremedied human rights violations are major obstacles to the establishment of a stable democracy, ABF is committed to the rights of all victims of human rights abuse to justice and public recognition.

The work of ABF is enabled through the support of a diverse range of funders, including private foundations in Europe and the U.S. and individual donors. It has received funding from the National Endowment for Democracy (NED), which is funded by the U.S. Congress but is governed by an independent Board of Governors.

On the front cover: Photographs of some of the victims of the 1988 massacre, from the Omid memorial on the foundation's website (www.iranrights.org). The photographs were supplied by families and friends; some were taken from newspapers and others from Internet sites, including Facebook and the sites of various political parties.

On the back cover: top, photograph of a gathering on 2 September 2005 commemorating the victims of the 1988 massacre at the gravesites in Khavaran Cemetery, Tehran; below, left to right, a newspaper photograph of a pro-Khomeini demonstration on 23 November 1978, from the Pars News Agency; Khomeini's fatwa ordering the execution of Mojahedin prisoners; a doll Fatemeh Zare'i, one of the victims, made for her daughter while she was imprisoned; letters and receipts from prison from Shahram Shahbakhshi, a victim of the massacre. Photographs of the Zare'i doll and Shahbakhshi letters and receipts are from the exhibition *Omid ist mein Name*, held at the Anne Frank Educational Centre, Frankfurt, in 2012, and are reproduced courtesy of the exhibition curators.

Frontispiece: Sudabeh Ardavan's book *Memories from Prison* was published in Laholm, Sweden by Trydells Tryckeri AB in 2003; the drawing is reproduced with the artist's permission.

Contents

Acknowledgments • 9

Introduction • 11

Executive Summary, by Geoffrey Robertson • 15

Witness Testimonies

Mohammad Reza Ashough • 39

Hamid Ashtari • 48

Mehdi Aslani • 51

Monireh Baradaran • 62

Hossein Behbudi • 76

Jahangir Esma'ilpur • 92

Manuchehr Esshaqi • 96

Ebrahim Fatemi • 110

Mersedeh Ghaedi • 116

Rahmat Gholami • 122

Mehrdad Kavousi • 133

Hossein Maleki • 144

Seifollah Mani'eh • 159

Mohammad Reza Matin • 174

Iraj Mesdaghi • 183

Rezvan Moghaddam • 198

Ebrahim Mohammad Rahimi • 209

Ahmad Najarha • 215

Mehrdad Neshati Malekians • 225

Maryam Nuri • 239

Ebrahim Rastak • 252

Mihan Rusta • 260

Banoo Saberi • 272

Fariba Sabet • 283

Reza Shemirani • 298

Shahab Shokoohi • 316

Soraya Zangebari • 330

Fatemeh Zare'i: *Three Witnesses*

Hassan Makaremi • 344

Aziz Zare'i • 351

Chowra Makaremi • 360

Official Statements

1 Imam's last warning to the conspirators, 17 August 1979 • 46

2 Prosecution of dissident educators and teachers; Islamic education and pardons for Kermanshah Prison inmates, 23 September 1979 • 61

Official Statements

3 Message to the Iranian people on the subjects of dealing with strikers, the necessity of a Cultural Revolution, and the role of the press, 22 March 1980 • 74

4 Ten-point statement on freedom of the press and association, 8 April 1981 • 90

5 Hashemi Rafsanjani's opinion about the MKO and its leaders, 24 April 1981 • 108

6 Government's position vis-à-vis political groups and parties, 1 May 1981 • 121

7 On the dangerous nature of the MKO and the necessity for the whole people to be [members of] the intelligence organization, 2 July 1981 • 130

8 Those municipal public prosecutors who are lenient toward corruptors [on earth] will be punished themselves, 18 September 1981 • 142

9 Killing rebellious hypocrites is justice par excellence, 25 September 1981 • 158

10 Who is an apostate and what is his sentence in Islam? 19 October 1981 • 172

11 What to do about the political groups who confront the Islamic Republic, 29 November 1981 • 182

12 On dispensing justice in Islam and the spiritual guidance of prisoners, 14 December 1981 • 197

13 Open discussion on issues raised by Evin prisoners, January 1982 • 207

14 Whoever disobeys the government is disobeying the command of God and His messenger, 7 January 1983 • 213

15 On university admission requirements, 3 January 1987 • 223

16 Eligibility requirement for pardons, 27 January 1988 • 251

17 On pardon eligibility requirements for prisoners, 29 January 1988 • 259

18 On confronting the deviant mini-groups and on campaigning against corruption and drug addiction, 13 July 1988 • 271

Official Statements

19 Courts to act with greater resolve in confronting *mohareb* and drug traffickers, 1 September 1988 • 282

20 The danger from the hypocrites has not been completely removed, 23 September 1988 • 297

21 The students' question and answer session with the president regarding human rights, the difficulties experienced by students, and economic issues, November 1988 • 314

22 Divine government, non-divine or human governments, and due process of law, 20 January 1989 • 328

23 Ayatollah Khomeini's classified death fatwa against the Mojahedin, 21 August 2004 • 343

Appendices

Appendix A
Brief Chronology • 367

Appendix B
Glossary • 376

Appendix C
Political Parties and Religious Denominations Referred to in the Witness Testimonies • 385

Victims who were remembered by name by the witnesses • 395

Group photograph of the witnesses • 398

Acknowledgments

They volunteered to bear witness to the unspeakable; they were willing to revisit their traumatic memories for the sake of truth and justice; with patience and understanding they submitted to the time constraints of their interviews; they summarized their many years of suffering, sometimes in less than 30 minutes, while every minute of their experience should have been given unlimited time to be recorded. Listening to them tell their stories and working with them was a humbling experience for the editors and the ABF staff. We would like to express our profound gratitude to all the witnesses whose testimonies made the publication of this volume possible. We are especially indebted to two of the witnesses, Monireh Baradaran and Iraj Mesdaghi, both of whom are former political prisoners and survivors of the prison massacre. Since relocating to Europe, Monireh Baradaran and Iraj Mesdaghi not only have published their prison memoirs but also have indefatigably fought against oblivion and for making the truth known.

Monireh Baradaran's numerous interviews with other survivors, published in Persian on the Bidaran website, have enriched the body of evidence pertaining to the 1988 prison massacre. She also helped ABF obtain the authorization to publish in this book the photographs of prisoners' belongings, writings, and artifacts that come for the most part from a remarkable exhibition, *Omid ist mein Name—und der steht für Hoffnung* (Omid Is My Name—and It Stands for Hope), held in the Anne Frank Educational Centre in Frankfurt from 10 March to 31 October 2012. ABF is grateful to the organizers of the exhibition for graciously allowing the publication of these photographs that bear witness to how, in an isolated world dominated by evil and death, prisoners heroically and ingeniously try to bring back life, hope, love, and beauty.

We will never adequately thank Iraj Mesdaghi, whose numerous publications on the situation of political prisoners during the 1980s constitute an important source for any research on this subject. We benefited from his assistance throughout Geoffrey Robertson's investigation and the publication of both volumes concerning the 1988 prison massacre. Without Mr. Mesdaghi's support, ABF would not have been able to connect with many of the witnesses who agreed to testify for the first time and authorized the publication of their testimonies. He has graciously permitted the publication, in this volume, of the photographs of the victims' gravestones, from his book *Raqs-e Qoqnus-ha Va Avaz Khakestar* (Dance of the Phoenixes and Song of the Ash), which is dedicated to the 1988 prison massacre and was published in 2011 in Stockholm.

Once again we would like to thank Geoffrey Robertson for his interest and his remarkable legal opinion on the 1988 prison massacre. Our special thanks to Jennifer Robinson, Geoffrey Robertson's collaborator, who spared no effort toward the completion of this project's research and dedicated hours to listening to the many witnesses and survivors she interviewed. The design and copy-editing of this volume benefited from the work of Marilan Lund; we are grateful for her support and dedication.

Finally, we would like to thank all ABF staff and volunteers, often prison survivors themselves, who worked tirelessly on this project and without whose devoted commitment this publication would not have been possible.

Introduction

EVERY YEAR SINCE THE LATE 1990S, ON THE LAST FRIDAY OF AUGUST OR first Friday of September, a group of people has gathered at Khavaran Cemetery, located in the southeastern outskirts of Tehran, to commemorate the victims of a secret execution of several thousand political prisoners that took place in Iranian prisons in the summer of 1988. The victims of this mass execution were, for the most part, political prisoners who had been previously tried and sentenced to prison terms. While some of them were serving their sentences, others had completed their sentences, yet continued to be arbitrarily detained. Relatives of the victims were not informed until several months after the executions took place. The bodies of the executed were never returned to their families. Some families were told about a burial place, but most were not.

Soon after the massacre, while searching for the burial places of their loved ones, victims' relatives found mass graves in Khavaran Cemetery where, they believed, the bodies of some of the executed prisoners had been hastily interred. Over the years, and in defiance of the authorities, victims' relatives have been trying to mark the ground in Khavaran Cemetery, to plant flowers and trees there, only to see their loved ones' makeshift tombs be destroyed. By refusing to publicly acknowledge the truth about the executions and return the bodies of the victims, the authorities deprive the families of coming to terms with the tragic and violent disappearance of their loved ones.

Khavaran is only one of the burial grounds of the victims of the 1988 clandestine mass executions; many others are buried across the country, in different cemeteries, in anonymous mass graves, or in individual graves marked with their names. But over the years, Khavaran has become the symbolic place for the commemoration of the victims of the 1988 mass executions. Each year, braving police harassment and arbitrary arrest, survivors and relatives attempt against considerable odds to commemorate the killing of their loved ones. On 29 August 2007, for instance, relatives of the victims gathered at Khavaran Cemetery to commemorate the 19th anniversary of the mass executions. Seven participants, including Ali Saremi, who spoke at the event and was subsequently executed (on 28 December 2010), were arrested. This violent reaction is a clear indication that, rather than acknowledging the truth, the authorities aim at erasing it from the nation's collective memory—by intimidating relatives and survivors and preventing them from commemorating it. In 2008, victims' relatives could not gather at Khavaran, their cars were stopped before they reached their destination, and they were forced to abandon the commemoration.

In late 2008, aware of the plight of the victims' families, and as a first step in securing their right to truth, justice, and reparations, the Abdorrahman Boroumand Foundation (ABF), which has, for years, documented the stories of the victims of the 1988 mass executions, brought the body of evidence it had gathered and archived to Geoffrey Robertson, QC, the respected international legal authority, and commissioned him to investigate the case and provide an independent legal opinion on the crime. ABF considered that the qualification of the crime is the *sine qua non* for seeking justice and reparation. Such an investigation had become all the more urgent when reports from Iran indicated that, between 9 and 16 January 2009, the numerous ad hoc grave markings made by the families of some of those executed had been destroyed by bulldozer. The site was at least partially covered by soil and trees were planted. The authorities' initiative was yet another step toward annihilating the forensic evidence and preventing the families from ever recuperating the remains of their loved ones and providing them with proper funerals.

In May 2010, ABF published the first electronic edition of Geoffrey Robertson's *The Massacre of Political Prisoners in Iran, 1988, Report of an Inquiry* (later made available in print on Amazon), in which he qualifies the crime as a crime against humanity and even suggests that it may arguably be qualified as genocide. To substantiate his legal opinion, Geoffrey Robertson profusely quotes Iranian authorities and former prisoners who survived the massacre, and who either wrote their memoirs or were interviewed by him or by Jennifer Robinson, his collaborator in this investigation.

For, indeed, with the invaluable help of two former political prisoners and survivors of the massacre, Monireh Baradaran and Iraj Mesdaghi, ABF was able to facilitate meetings of the two legal experts with more than thirty survivors and provide them with interpreters and translation services. The interviews took place in person in London, Amsterdam, Paris, Frankfurt, Berlin, and Washington, D.C., as well as over Skype or by telephone in other cities and countries of Europe and the United States. In addition, ABF provided the investigators with English translations of relevant excerpts from published prison memoirs, as well as translations of over a decade of official statements by Islamic Republic authorities, which reveal the ideological underpinnings of this massacre. It is this body of evidence consisting of witnesses' testimonies and official statements that is published in the present volume, along with a summary of Geoffrey Robertson's report.

The thirty witness statements are the edited and at times abridged versions of the statements Geoffrey Robertson explored during his investigation. The statements are not only from former political prisoners who survived the massacre but also from their relatives, parents, and spouses, who were victims of terrible and offensive treatment only because they were trying to get information on the whereabouts of their loved ones. The twenty-three official statements that are interspersed between the witness statements, in chronological order, are only a partial selection of what was provided to Geoffrey Robertson for his investigation. The appendices include a brief political chronology, a glossary, and a list of political parties and religious denominations relevant to the witness testimonies, for readers who may be less familiar with Iran's contemporary history.

Initially, it seemed that an addendum to *The Massacre of Political Prisoners in Iran, 1988, Report of an Inquiry* was needed to furnish the international legal community and the court of international public opinion with access to the body of evidence upon which Geoffrey Robertson based his legal opinion, qualifying it as a crime against humanity, because, once committed, a crime against humanity concerns not only the victims and the state within whose boundaries the crime is committed, but also and more importantly the international community as a whole. For the international community becomes the ultimate recourse for the victims, when and if their governments remain impervious to their calls for truth, justice, and reparation. From that original impetus to set forth the evidence, the publication of this companion volume to the Robertson report sprang.

The witness testimonies, however, are endowed with an intrinsic value that goes far beyond their relevance in an inquiry regarding a crime against humanity. Each witness's background provides a window into the political history of Iran in the late 1970s and 1980s and sheds light on the characteristics of the emerging Islamic state. The carceral universe depicted in the testimonies offers invaluable keys to the mindset of a regime that considers itself godly and that strives to recreate man according to its own values. Similar in that they report on the same crime, the testimonies are different in that they recount the life, experience, and suffering of one individual, unlike any other. However, one common thread runs throughout all the testimonies: the prisoners' intense desire to protect their human dignity. The closing witness statement of this volume is signed by the daughter of one of the victims. She depicts what the children of the victims have experienced in the absence of public acknowledgment of the crime and when justice is denied to the survivors. She also reports on the police harassment and discrimination that plague some of the lives of the victims' closest relatives, for the sole reason that they are the children or spouses of an executed person.

Reading the victims' stories constitutes an existential experience. Revisiting in memory the labyrinth of evil in which they were trapped for so many years leaves no one unscathed. One feels and shares the burden of the survivor's guilt that has kept each of the survivors from living a normal life ever since his or her release from prison. Survivors and victims' relatives are trapped in the memory of a crime committed 25 years ago, as if caught in a bubble let loose in an oblivious world.

The ongoing agony of the relatives and survivors, the harassment and discrimination that plague the lives of the survivors, and, more tragically, the execution of someone like Ali Saremi constitute a challenge to the conscience of humanity, a challenge whose substance is made of human suffering, and which indisputably confirms the veracity and pertinence of Geoffrey Robertson's con-clusion:

> As long as the graves of the dead remain unmarked and relatives are forbidden
> from mourning, Iran will continue to contravene the rule of international law,
> which its leaders so brutally defied in 1988.

A quarter of a century ago in Iran, several thousand political prisoners were executed in a deafening silence for the sole crime of their opinion. To mark this anniversary, the Abdorrahman Boroumand Foundation echoes the voices of the victims, hoping that they will be heard by the international community, that it might take up the challenge and ensure that the victims of this tragedy can exercise their long overdue right to Truth, Justice, and Reparation.

LADAN BOROUMAND
ROYA BOROUMAND

Geoffrey Robertson, QC

The Massacre of Political Prisoners in Iran, 1988: Report of an Inquiry

Executive Summary

Late in July 1988, as the war with Iraq was ending in a truculent truce, prisons in Iran crammed with government opponents suddenly went into lockdown. All family visits were cancelled, televisions and radios switched off and newspapers discontinued; prisoners were kept in their cells, disallowed exercise or trips to the infirmary. The only permitted visitation was from a delegation, turbaned and bearded, which came in black government BMWs or by helicopter to outlying jails: a religious judge, a public prosecutor, and an intelligence chief. Before them were paraded, briefly and individually, almost every prisoner (and there were thousands of them) who had been jailed for adherence to the Mojahedin Khalq Organization—the MKO. This was a movement which had taken its politics from Karl Marx, its theology from Islam, and its guerrilla tactics from Che Guevara: it had fought the Shah and supported the Revolution that brought Ayatollah Khomeini to power but later broke with his theocratic state and took up arms against it, in support (or so it now says) of democracy. The delegation had but one question for these young men and women (most of them detained since 1981, merely for taking part in street protests or possession of "political" reading material), and although they did not know it, on the answer their lives would depend. Those who by that answer evinced any continuing affiliation with the Mojahedin were blindfolded and ordered to join a conga-line that led straight to the gallows. They were hung from cranes, four at a time, or in groups of six from ropes hanging from the front of the stage in an assembly hall; some were taken to army barracks at night, directed to make their wills and then shot by firing squad. Their bodies were doused with disinfectant, packed in refrigerated trucks and buried by night in mass graves. Months later their families, desperate for information about their children or their partners, would be handed a plastic bag with their few possessions. They would be refused any

15

information about the location of the graves and ordered never to mourn them in public. By mid-August 1988, thousands of prisoners had been killed in this manner by the state—without trial, without appeal, and utterly without mercy.

The regime did not stop at this extermination of Mojahedin supporters. The killings were suspended for a fortnight's religious holiday but began again when the "Death Committee" (as prisoners would later call the delegation) summoned members of other left-wing groups whose ideologies were regarded as incompatible with the theocratic state constructed by Imam Ruhollah Khomeini after the 1979 Revolution. These groups included the Communist Tudeh Party, aligned with Moscow, the Marxist/Leninist Fadaiyan Khalq (which had split into Majority and Minority factions), Peykar (orthodox Marxist/Leninist), Trotskyites, Maoists, and any remaining liberals who had supported the Republic's first short-lived president, Abolhassan Banisadr. Their interviews were longer, trickier, and the chance of survival (albeit in most cases after torture) somewhat higher. This time the issue was not their political affiliation, but their religion and their willingness to follow the state's version of Islam: in short, whether they were apostates.

This time there was a kind of brief trial, ending with a sentence of death for those atheists and agnostics whose parents were practicing Muslims, while women in that category and others from secular families were instead ordered to be whipped five times a day until they agreed to pray, or else died from the lash. So there followed, in late August, September, and October a second wave of executions, genocidal in intention (because the victims were selected on religious criteria) although more confused and arbitrary in implementation, with torture as an alternative sentence. This second wave of killings was accompanied by the same secrecy that had attended the extermination of the Mojahedin—families were not informed for several weeks and sometimes months, and were not told where their sons and husbands had been secretly buried. There was a news blackout over all these prison executions: the regime controlled all media.

Nevertheless, mass murder will out. Reports of an increase in political executions in Iran appeared in the *Financial Times* and the *New York Times* in mid-August 1988, and on 2 September 1988 Amnesty International put out an Urgent Action telegram evincing its deep concern that "hundreds of political prisoners may have been executed."[1] There was no conception of the scale of

1. Amnesty International, *Iran: Political Executions*, UA235/88 (MDE 13/14/88, 2 September 1988).

the massacres, but in September, the Human Rights Commission's Special Representative for Iran, the El Salvador Professor Reynaldo Pohl, was deluged with oral and written complaints about a "wave of executions." He raised this with Iran's permanent representative at the UN, at a meeting on 29 September 1988, only to be told that the "killings" were merely those which had occurred on the battlefield after the Mojahedin's small Iraq-based army had attempted to invade Iran in mid-July (in the final incursion, called by the Mojahedin Operation Eternal Light, regime forces routed the MKO in a counter-attack that they called Operation Mersad). Iran's position was complete denial, with a refusal to answer Pohl's questions on the grounds that his information had been provided to him from Mojahedin sources and was therefore unreliable propaganda.[2] Pohl nonetheless published in October credible allegations that 860 bodies of political prisoners had been dumped in a mass grave in a Tehran cemetery between 14 and 16 August 1988. (This interim report may have prompted the speaker of the Parliament, Ali Akbar Hashemi Rafsanjani, to admit unguardedly in February 1989 that "the number of political prisoners executed in the last few months was less than one thousand"[3]—a number he appeared to think was commendably low.)

Prime Minister Mir Hossein Musavi (who twenty years later would be the defeated candidate in the 2009 Presidential elections) was asked in December 1988 by an Austrian television reporter what he had to say about the allegations made by the western media concerning the Mojahedin killings: incautiously, he tried to defend them with the dishonest response that "they [i.e. the MKO prisoners] had plans to perpetrate killings and massacres. We had to crush the conspiracy. . .in that respect we have no mercy." In February 1989, Khomeini delivered an "historical message" about his former left-wing supporters: "We are not sorry that they are not with us. They never were with us. The Revolution does not owe anything to anyone." He inveighed against "the liberals" who had criticized him for "enforcing God's sentence" against the Mojahedin, whom he described by using the Persian word *monafeqin* ("hypocrites") and he warned

2. See Reynaldo Galindo Pohl, Interim Report Annexed to Note by the Secretary General, ECOSOC Report, "Situation of Human Rights in the Islamic Republic of Iran," A/43/705, 13 October 1988, 43rd Session, Agenda Item 12 (hereafter referred to as Pohl, *Interim 1988 Report*), Section II.

3. Iran Research Group, Iran Yearbook 89/90 (MB Medien & Bücher Verlagsgesellschaft, 1989).

against feeling pity for "enemies of God and opponents of the regime." He went on, "as long as I exist I will not allow the regime to fall into the hands of liberals. I will not allow the hypocrites of Islam to eliminate the helpless people."[4] Although the Iranian stance at the UN was to deny all allegations about prison executions, these veiled but menacing under-statements by its leaders, for home consumption, can in retrospect be interpreted as a defiant justification for mass murder.

———————

It is important to appreciate that the UN was well aware of the massacres (if not that its victims were numbered in thousands) shortly after they had commenced and before they had concluded. Its Human Rights Commission had appointed an El Salvador law professor and diplomat, Reynaldo Galindo Pohl, in 1986 as its Special Representative to report regularly upon the situation in this country, with particular concern to investigate the credible reports of executions and torture of political prisoners and the brutal repression of those who followed the Bahá'í Faith.[5] His first report, in 1987, confirmed the widespread use of *bastinado* and other torture techniques (medical examinations of escaped and released political prisoners had put this beyond doubt) but did no more than call on the Iranian government to set up a human rights commission to reply to what he described as "allegations" of mistreatment and summary executions, and to allow him into the country. The government declined to address any of the allegations and instead diverted the professor by raising academic questions about the compatibility of Shari'a law with international human rights law and historical quibbles about whether there had been sufficient input from Islamic jurists in the drafting of the Universal Declaration of Human Rights. Pohl was more than happy to ponder these questions at length in his report in 1988: he made no effort to calculate the number of political prisoners in Iranian jails, who had by this stage run into many thousands, and he dropped his request to visit prisons (despite his awareness of information that "some prisoners were in danger of execution"). He merely suggested that "the government may wish to initiate an

4. *Kayhan*, 25 February 1989, 16.

5. See Bahá'í (the religious denomination) in "Political Parties and Religious Denominations Referred to in the Witness Statements," Appendix C, below.

urgent investigation of these complaints in order to take measures of redress."[6] The measures of redress the government wished to take, namely the murder of all prisoners associated with the opposition, began in late July 1988 and lasted until November.

On 26 August 1988, Pohl received information that 200 Mojahedin prisoners had been hanged in the assembly hall at Evin Prison. But not until 28 September ("having received information about a wave of executions that was allegedly taking place since the month of July 1988") did he write to Iran's Permanent Representative, inviting the government's comments. He did, however, make an interim report to the General Assembly on 13 October 1988, in which he clearly set out information that "a large number of prisoners, members of opposition groups, were executed during the months of July, August, and early September"[7] and reported that on 5 August the Chief Justice of Iran (Ayatollah Musavi Ardebili) had announced that the judiciary was under pressure from public opinion to execute all members of the Mojahedin, without exception and without trial, and had added a threat that more members of that organization and "other groups" of oppositionists would be executed.[8] The UN Special Rapporteur on Summary Executions had already telegrammed the Iranian Minister for Foreign Affairs to the effect that the state was breaching Article 14 of the International Covenant on Civil and Political Rights by executing prisoners after "extremely summary, informal and irregular proceedings, failure to inform defendants of specific accusations against them, lack of legal counsel, absence of any instance of appeal and with irregularities that contravene international standards of fair trial."[9] It is therefore quite clear that, notwithstanding Professor Pohl's failure to take any urgent action during the massacre period, the General Assembly was provided on 13 October 1988 with evidence of mass murder in Iranian prisons. It did absolutely nothing, and neither did the Security Council.

Thereafter, credible and persistent reports of the "wave of killings" continued to reach Pohl. In his next report in January 1989, he appended a list of the names

---

6. Pohl, *Report on the Situation of Human Rights in the Islamic Republic of Iran*, E/CN.4/ 1988/24, 25 January 1988.

7. Pohl, *Interim 1988 Report*, see above, note 2.

8. Reported in *Kayhan*, 6 August 1988, 15.

9. Pohl, *Interim 1988 Report* (see above, note 2) at paras 69 and 71.

of over 1,000 alleged victims and noted that his sources indicated that there had been several thousand, mostly from the Mojahedin but also from other left-wing groups. Many of the victims "had been serving prison sentences for several years, while others are former prisoners who were arrested and then executed. . . . [P]eople witnessed large numbers of bodies being buried in shallow graves."[10] Mr. Pohl concluded:

> The global denial [by the Iranian Government] of the wave of executions which allegedly took place from July to September of last year. . .is not sufficient to dismiss the allegations as unfounded. . . . [T]he allegations received from several sources, including non-governmental organizations, and reported in the media, referred to summary executions in places that were not affected by military operations. . . .[11]

Notwithstanding this knowledge, Professor Pohl became lost in admiration for the ceasefire (he records "immense satisfaction and deep appreciation" to the Iranian government), which he is sure "will soon turn its positive attention to human rights problems" and will investigate abuses of power. With astonishing naïveté, he assumed in this crucial report that the Iranian government would investigate its own abuses, despite meetings with the Iranian representatives to the UN who, with utter dishonesty, had assured him that all the Mojahedin deaths had occurred on the battlefield.[12]

No truthful information from the Iranian government was ever supplied to the UN Special Representative about the 1988 massacres. Mr Pohl is partly to blame: although his mandate was renewed by the Human Rights Commission, he made no real investigation of the massacre allegations, and at this stage (one year after the killings) the regime had not even permitted him to visit the country.

10. Reynaldo Galindo Pohl, *Report on the Situation of Human Rights in the Islamic Republic of Iran* (UN Commission on Human Rights, E/CN.4/1989/26, 26 January 1989), paras 15–18. Hereafter referred to as Pohl, *Human Rights in Iran* (1989).

11. Pohl, *Human Rights in Iran* (1989), para 68.

12. The Iranian diplomats who blindsided Pohl in this period were Ambassador Ja'far Mahallati in New York and Ambassador Sirous Nasseri in Geneva. The latter is now a businessman in Europe and the former resides in the US; they may have a case to answer. See Pohl, *Human Rights in Iran* (1989), Section II: Contacts and Communications with the Government of the Islamic Republic of Iran.

By the time of Pohl's 1990 report, the government's campaign of assassinating its critics had achieved its terrorist purpose, and the murder in Switzerland of Mr. Kazem Rajavi, representative of The National Council of Resistance (led by the Mojahedin) at the UN, and of other dissidents in Europe had chilled criticism and deterred potential witnesses. So had the outrageous death sentence fatwa which Supreme Leader Khomeini had pronounced on author Salman Rushdie in February 1989. The government felt sufficiently confident of Mr. Pohl to allow him a six-day visit, with five days of meetings with its officials and a half-day visit to Evin Prison, where he was welcomed with a band concert (a tactic used by the Nazis for foreign visitors at Terezin and Auschwitz)[13] but denied access to the prisoners he requested to see.[14] They paraded before him instead some alleged inmates—they may not have been prisoners at all—who told him that "their treatment was satisfactory and the food superb"[15] and some stooges from state-backed women's organizations who explained that "women enjoyed freedom in absolute terms and without any limitations."[16]

It is clear that the UN Human Rights Commission and the General Assembly had some evidence of the massacres shortly after they commenced, but no effective investigation was undertaken at that time or subsequently. Astonishingly, Professor Pohl's reports from 1991 onwards do not even mention them (although they note that execution of political prisoners without fair trial continues).[17] By this time, the reports are more concerned with Iran's overseas

13. Ervand Abrahamian, *Tortured Confessions: Prisons and Public Recantations in Modern Iran* (University of California Press, 1999), 221.

14. One prisoner (and one of the witnesses in this book), Monireh Baradaran, in her memoirs *The Plain Truth: Memoirs of the Prisons of the Islamic Republic of Iran* (Independent Association of Iranian Women, 2006), 543-4, tells how she later met Pohl and discovered that he had been introduced to fake "prisoners" in Evin, who had (unsurprisingly) praised their humane treatment. Other witnesses suggest that the professor had been deceived, although the naïveté shown in his reports does suggest that he lacked the experience and instinct to be an effective human rights investigator.

15. Reynaldo Galindo Pohl, *Report on the Situation of Human Rights in the Islamic Republic of Iran*, 6 November 1990, 90-28544-1985-86e(E), para 230. Hereafter referred to as Pohl, *Report* (1990).

16. Pohl, *Report* (1990), para 240.

17. Professor Pohl seems to lose interest in the massacres: his report on 13 February 1991 makes no reference to them, despite the fact that Amnesty International had published its de-

assassination campaign against its opposition leaders (the Shah's last Prime Minister, Shapour Bakhtiar, was killed in France, and other dissidents died in a hail of bullets in Germany, Switzerland, and Turkey) and with the murder of Salman Rushdie's translators following the bloodthirsty call by the new (and current) Supreme Leader, Seyed Ali Khamene'i, for Muslims throughout the world to carry out the fatwa on all connected with the publication of *The Satanic Verses*. There can be little doubt that the Islamic Republic was emboldened to flout international law so outrageously as a result of the way in which it was able to avoid accountability, or even criticism, at the UN, for the brutal extermination of thousands of its prisoners. Why was it permitted to get away with the worst violation of prisoners' rights since the death marches of Allied prisoners conducted by the Japanese at the end of the Second World War? This was, of course, 1988—five years before international tribunals were established to punish crimes against humanity in the former Yugoslavia and Rwanda. In March of that year Saddam Hussein had gassed the Kurds at Halabja, and had suffered no UN reprisals. The end of the Iran-Iraq War later in August 1988 produced a political climate in which other diplomats and UN officials wanted to give both countries the benefit of any doubt. But what they gave Iran was impunity and the message that goes with it: if you can get away with murdering thousands of your prisoners, you can get away with other breaches of international law, like assassinating your enemies in other countries and even, eventually, with building nuclear arsenals. In 1988, the Islamic Republic of Iran learned the easy way, from the failure of the UN and its Commissions and its member states to investigate mass murders in Iranian prisons, that international law had no teeth for biting, or even for gnashing.

---

tailed report just two weeks previously. See Pohl, *Report on the Human Rights Situation in Iran*, 13 February 1991. In 1992, Pohl reports that 164 executions of political prisoners have taken place in 1992: see Pohl, *Final Report on the Situation of Human Rights in the Islamic Republic of Iran*, E/CN.4/1993/41, 28 January 1993, para 281. At one point, the Iranian government officials realized that Pohl was obtaining his information on political executions from the local media, which had been reporting the boastful statements of judicial authorities. So they took action to curtail reporting—a leaked government document expressed satisfaction that "one of the sources used by Galindo Pohl to provide documented and irrefutable reports was therefore neutralized," Note by the Secretary General transmitting the Pohl Report to the General Assembly, A/48/526, 8 November 1993, para 92.

There are, of course, non-legal mechanisms available at the United Nations —it has "Special Rapporteurs" on extra-judicial killings and on torture who might be prevailed upon to pick up the baton dropped by Professor Pohl and to conduct a proper investigation. Iran might be required to cooperate by the Human Rights Council, which purports to guard the ICCPR and has replaced the Human Rights Commission, which so dismally failed to call Iran to account in 1988. It has to be said that the UN human rights mechanisms are highly politicized, as well as underfunded, and tend to be reserved for inquiries into recent atrocities (for example, the Alston Inquiry into the Kenyan election violence and the Goldstone Inquiry into the Gaza war).

My opinion on the facts and the international law issues to which they give rise may be shortly stated. Iran in 1988 was a nation of 40 million people (as of this writing, it has 73 million), with prisons in over 100 cities. At least 20 of those prisons held political prisoners incarcerated for membership in groups opposed to the Islamic Republic. On 20 July 1988 Ayatollah Khomeini, the Supreme Leader, reluctantly "drank the cup of poison" and accepted the UN ceasefire in the war with Iraq. One week later, a small force of Mojahedin with Iraqi air cover mounted an attack over the border. After an initial success, they were routed on 29 July 1988. The previous day, Khomeini had issued a fatwa ordering a death sentence for all imprisoned Mojahedin, and this was put into immediate operation through three-man "Death Committees" who confirmed the identity and "steadfastness" of Mojahedin prisoners prior to sending them for execution. By mid-August, up to 3,800 of them had been killed. There was a lull in executions for ten days, but on 26 August a second wave broke, entailing brief trials of all "leftist" prisoners for the religious crime of apostasy. Those men from Muslim families who declined to say Islamic prayers were sent for execution, while female non-believers were tortured until they agreed to pray, and this torture was inflicted, more severely, on men who did not come from a devout Muslim family. The prison massacres stopped by November, when relatives began to be notified, in a cruelly slow and bureaucratic way, of the fact of a child or spouse's death, but they were refused any information about the place of burial and were forbidden to mourn. This prohibition is still enforced today.

I find that the state of Iran has committed four exceptionally serious breaches of *jus cogens* rules of international law, which entail both state responsibility and individual accountability for war crimes and crimes against humanity, *viz*

1. The arbitrary killing of thousands of male and female prisoners, pursuant to a fatwa that held them collectively responsible for the Mojahedin invasion, notwithstanding that they had been in prison and *hors de combat* for years, serving fixed term sentences for relatively minor offenses. This was not the execution of a lawful sentence, because there was no trial, no charge and no criminal act other than adhering to a particular ideological group. It was dishonest of Iranian leaders to pretend that the executed prisoners had all been given death sentences and had refused an opportunity to reform: this was a lie. So too was the suggestion that they had rioted or that they were all "terrorists and spies." None of those whom I interviewed had been charged with terrorism offenses or with espionage, and most had been in prison since 1981–83. The immediate trigger for the massacre was tit-for-tat retaliation for the "Eternal Light" invasion and the pain of agreeing to a ceasefire, but the medieval defence of "reprisal" has long been abolished. The right to life, guaranteed by customary international law, by treaties to which Iran is a party, and by the Geneva Conventions, was quite deliberately and barbarically breached, and all who bear international law responsibility for this mass murder should be prosecuted. An obligation to prosecute may also arise from the Genocide Convention, since the reason why MKO members were condemned as *moharebs* ("warriors against God") and exterminated was that they had adopted a version of Islam which differed from that upheld by the State.

2. The second wave of apostate killings was also a breach of the right to life, as well as the right to religious freedom. The male prisoners who were executed were given some kind of trial, but it was wholly deficient in compliance with legal safeguards and massively unfair. They were offered no time or facilities to prepare their defense and were taken by surprise by questions, the implications of which they did not understand. They were executed for a crime of

conscience in that their only offense was to refuse to adopt the religious beliefs, prayers, and rituals of the state. There is force in the argument that in this sense they comprised a distinct group exterminated not because of their left-wing political leanings but because of their beliefs about religion: they were, in consequence, victims of genocide. Apostasy in any event is not a crime for which the death penalty is permissible in international law—a position taken by most states a few months later when Khomeini purported to pass that sentence on Salman Rushdie. They were not, as the government later alleged, spies or terrorists or prison rioters. They were executed for no better reason than to rid a theocratic state of ideological enemies in post-war circumstances that could not possibly give rise to a defense of necessity or to any other defense.

3. The beatings inflicted on leftist women and on other men who were regarded as capable of religious compliance satisfied the definition of torture, which is absolutely prohibited even if it is consonant with national law. The beatings by electric cable on the soles of the feet, five times a day for weeks on end, together in many cases with beatings on the body, were calculated to and did cause excruciating pain and extensive suffering as well as humiliation and degradation. The mental anguish was heightened by the fact that the beatings were inflicted not for the purpose of punishment, but to make the prisoners adopt a religion that they had rejected, and thus surrender their freedom of conscience. Again, no defense of necessity can possibly arise: the only object of the beatings was to break their will and their spirit and to make them more amenable to the state's version of Islamic governance.

4. Finally, the rights to know where close relatives have been buried and to mourn their deaths have been and still are being denied by the state. These rights are implied from the right to life and (more logically) from the right of innocent families not to be treated inhumanely or cruelly. There is no possible justification, today, for denying information about burial locations or for prohibiting gatherings of mourners: there is no evidence to suggest that these gatherings would cause public disorder or breaches of the peace.

What is being denied, two decades after the deaths, is the right of parents, spouses, and siblings to manifest their feelings of devotion in respect of the memory of a family member: this is a denial of their rights to respect for home and family life (an aspect of privacy) as well as a denial of the right to manifest religious beliefs. It also amounts to discrimination, since no other class or category of the bereaved has been denied the opportunity to mourn. The refusal to identify mass graves implicitly involves a refusal to prevent DNA testing (which has proven reliable in war crimes investigations as a means of identifying the remains in mass graves) and, in consequence, the prevention of a proper burial.

So far as the state of Iran is concerned, these breaches of its treaty and customary law responsibilities have no criminal consequence. States cannot be subjected to a penal sanction. But these breaches do give rise to two obligations: the state must cease the wrongful conduct and must make full reparation for the injury caused by its act.[18] Reparation should include damages where appropriate, which will be compensatory but not punitive.[19] The beneficiaries of holding Iran to these obligations would be relatives of the deceased, but action by them or by another state on their behalf would obviously have to be taken in a forum outside Iran. The difficulty will be in finding such a forum: the International Court of Justice might be activated by a UN organ or by a member state, but Iran would refuse to cede jurisdiction to it.

That would not matter if the General Assembly or another UN organ were to seek an advisory opinion (e.g. on whether the prison killings amounted to genocide or to a crime against humanity): in such a case, the consent of Iran would not be required—the reason why Israel could not stop the ICJ from deciding the issue of the Palestinian wall. The prospect of a claims tribunal, or any other form of arbitration or negotiation under UN auspices, depends upon *realpolitik*. It may, for example, be urged that any concession to Iran in regard to its nuclear facilities should be contingent upon its atoning for past human rights

18. *International Law Commissions, Articles on Responsibility of States for International Wrongful Acts* (2001) Articles 1, 30, and 31.

19. In *Velásquez Rodriguez v. Honduras*, the Inter-American Court of Human Rights held that international law did not recognize the concept of punitive or exemplary damages (Series C No.7 1989). See also *Letelier v. Moffitt*, (1992) 88 ILR 727.

abuses by providing information and compensation to survivors and relatives of those it has unlawfully massacred, and in opening mass graves so that DNA testing may establish and identify the remains.

The individuals against whom there is a *prima facie* case for prosecution for crimes against humanity, torture, genocide, and war crimes are those in the chain of command, from Supreme Leader to hangman. At the middle level, the members of the Death Committee are well known, as are the senior prison officials who organized and authorized the executions, and no doubt those Revolutionary Guards who acted as hangmen, firing squad members, and gravediggers can also be identified. There is however, a good deal of opacity at the higher level: it is unclear to me, for example, which leaders were involved in advising Imam Khomeini to issue the fatwa on 28 July 1988 and which officials were involved in transmitting that decree to the prison governors and arranging the logistics of the first wave of executions. Different ministries would have had to give approvals and directions, most importantly the Ministry of Information, whose officials conducted interrogations, set questionnaires, and kept tabs on every prisoner. There is evidence that, at some prisons, warders were supplanted by Revolutionary Guards who carried out the killings. When relatives were eventually notified, they were not in most cases informed by the prison authorities, but by Revolutionary Guards. There is a real mystery over the authority for the "second wave" of leftist/apostate executions, which were beyond the terms of the 28 July fatwa: was there another secret fatwa, as Montazeri suggests, in the first weeks of September, or was this a decision taken by the political leadership under pressure from hardliners in Qom and communicated through the Supreme Court to the Death Committees? These questions must be answered before there can be any authoritative identification of all those criminally complicit in the massacres.

That said, the identification of some of those who directed the victims to the slaughterhouse in Tehran prisons is very plain. The fatwa was directed to Hossein'ali Nayyeri,[20] a religious judge at the time and, as of this writing, Deputy Chief Justice of the Supreme Court. He was identified as presiding over Death Committees in Tehran prisons by many survivors permitted to take their

---

20. Iranian law reports often refer to Hossein'ali Nayyeri, whom some of the political prisoners called, incorrectly, "Ja'far" Nayyeri.

Khomeini's fatwa ordering the execution of all Mojahedin prisoners, probably on 28 July 1988:

In the name of God, the Compassionate, the Merciful,

Since the treacherous *monafeqin* do not believe in Islam and whatever they say stems from their deception and hypocrisy, and since according to the claims of their leaders they have become renegades, and since they wage war on God and are engaging in classical warfare on the western, northern, and southern fronts with the collaboration of the Baathist Party of Iraq, and also they are spying for Saddam against our Muslim nation, and since they are tied to the World Arrogance and have inflicted foul blows on the Islamic Republic since its inception, it is decreed that those who are in prisons throughout the country who remain steadfast in their support for the *monafeqin* are considered to be *mohareb* (waging war on God) and are condemned to execution. The task of implementing the decree in Tehran is entrusted to Hojjat ol-eslam Nayyeri, the religious judge; Mr. Eshraqi, the Tehran prosecutor; and a representative of the Intelligence Ministry. Even though a unanimous decision is better, the view of a majority of the three must prevail. In prisons in the provinces, the views of a majority of a trio consisting of the religious judge, the revolutionary prosecutor, and the Intelligence Ministry representative must be obeyed. It is naïve to show mercy to *moharebs*. The decisiveness of Islam before the enemies of God is among the unquestionable tenets of the Islamic regime. I hope that you satisfy almighty God with your revolutionary rage and rancor against the enemies of Islam. The gentlemen who are responsible for making the decisions must not hesitate, nor show any doubt or concerns with detail. . . .To hesitate in the judicial process of revolutionary Islam is to ignore the pure and holy blood of the martyrs.

RUHOLLAH MOUSSAVI KHOMEINI

On the back of the original fatwa, Khomeini's son,
Haj Ahmad, wrote:

My pre-eminent Father. . . [Chief Justice] Ayatollah
Musavi Ardebili has telephoned to raise three questions
about your. . .recent decree. . . :

1. Does the decree apply to those who have been in
   prison who have already been tried and sentenced
   to death, but who have not changed their stance
   and for whom the verdict has not yet been carried
   out, or are those who have not yet been tried also
   condemned to death?

2. Those *monafeqin* prisoners who have received
   limited jail terms, and who have already served part
   of their terms, but continue to hold fast to their
   support for the *monafeqin*, are they also condemned
   to death?

3. In reviewing the status of the *monafeqin* prisoners
   in counties that have an independent judicial body,
   is it necessary to refer their cases to the independent judiciary in provincial capitals or can the
   counties' judicial authorities [Death Committees]
   act autonomously?

Underneath the questions, Khomeini replied:

In the name of God, the Most High,

In all the above cases, if the person at any stage or at any
time maintains his support for the *monafeqin*, the
sentence is execution. Annihilate the enemies of Islam
immediately.

As regards the cases, use whichever criterion speeds up
the implementation of the verdict.

Ruhollah Moussavi Khomeini

[his seal]

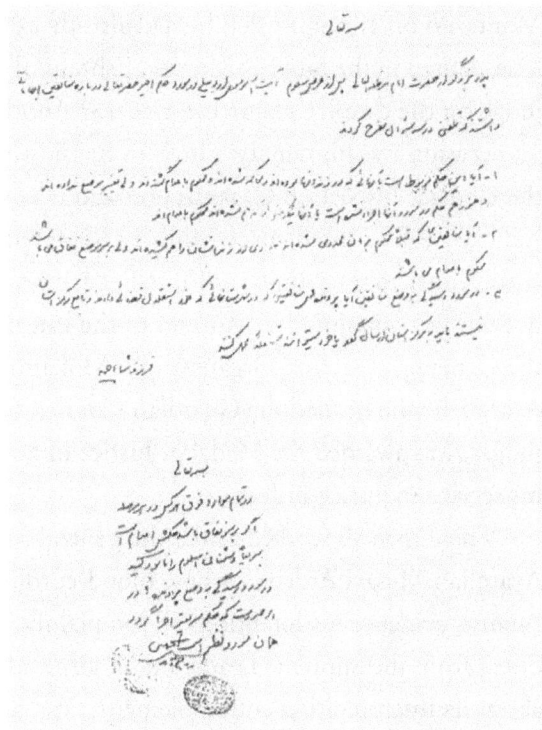

blindfolds off when attending the committee, because he had presided over their earlier cases or was well known from television appearances. He admitted to Montazeri on 13 August that he had already executed 750 prisoners in Tehran. Also named in the fatwa is Morteza Eshraqi, the Tehran Prosecutor and now a judge on the country's Supreme Court.[21] Another prosecutor who took his place on occasion was his deputy, Ebrahim Ra'isi, who went on to become the Head of the General Inspection Organization and is now the Deputy Head of the Judiciary.[22] The Intelligence Ministry Representative on the Tehran committee and Deputy to the Minister of Intelligence was Mostafa Pourmohammadi,[23] who in 2005 was appointed as Minister of the Interior.[24] He is currently the Head of the General Inspection Organization. Mohammadi Gilani, the outspoken Ayatollah who headed the Guardian Council and supervised Tehran's religious judges, was awarded the Medal of Justice in 2009 by President Ahmadinejad for his service to justice in Iran.

These men all worked under the general supervision of Chief Justice Ayatollah Musavi Ardebili, whose blood-curdling Friday sermons, as early as 4 August, evidence his intentions all too plainly.[25] He certainly received the fatwa direct from the Supreme Leader on 28 July and immediately raised questions about its interpretation and implementation, and he must have transmitted that interpretation to all members of the Death Committees. As head of the judicial system he presumably appointed the religious judges who headed the Death Committees in the provinces. Ayatollah Musavi Ardebili is, as of this writing, an influential religious leader in Qom who is competent to issue fatwas. Another

21. He also has his own law firm on the corner of Vila and Sepand Avenue, Tehran.

22. Information provided by Iraj Mesdaghi, 11 March 2010.

23. During the Khatami period he was forced to resign from the Ministry because he was implicated in the "Chain Murders" (death squad murders of intellectuals and journalists), but he was taken under Khamene'i's protection until he could return to work for Ahmadinejad and became a cabinet minister.

24. Human Rights Watch Briefing, *Ministers of Murder: Iran's New Security Cabinet*, December 2005.

25. He made a radio broadcast on 6 August 1988 saying "The Judiciary is under great pressure . . . . there are questions about why these people are not executed. They must all be executed. We will no longer have trials or bother with the dossiers of the convicts." See NCRI (National Council of Resistance of Iran), *Crimes Against Humanity*, 56.

influential political jurist, who succeeded Musavi Ardebili in 1989, was Mohammad Yazdi. He later became the Head of the Judiciary and is currently deputy chairman of the Assembly of Experts (which appoints the Supreme Leader) and is a member of the Guardian Council.

All these individuals appear to have been directly responsible for approving the death and torture sentences, which they must or should have known to have been contrary to international law. On the well-known principle established by the Nuremberg case of *US v. Joseph Altstoetter and others* (the "Justice Case" dramatized in the film *Judgment at Nuremberg*), judges who contribute to crimes committed in the guise of legal process cannot themselves escape prosecution. As the Nuremberg prosecution put it, "men of law can no more escape. . .responsibility by virtue of their judicial robes, than the General by his uniform." Those defendants were convicted for "administering legislation which they must be held to have known was in violation of international law."[26]

In considering the complicity of professionals in crimes against humanity, there is no good reason to exclude diplomats who, knowing the truth, nonetheless lie about them to UN bodies to whom they owe a duty of frankness. Iran's UN ambassador, Ja'far Mahallati, consistently denied the massacres and claimed the allegations were propaganda; so did the Geneva representative Sirous Nasseri in his meetings with the UN Special Representative.[27] Mahallati is said to be living in the US, where he may be liable to civil action for aiding and abetting torture under the Alien Tort Claims Act. Nasseri, a businessman who lives in Europe, might be liable to prosecution on the same basis under the laws of some European countries.

Other individuals who feature in the witness statements as key figures in the interrogations and executions are senior prison officials, most zealously Naserian (real name Mohammed Moghisei), then the governor of Gohardasht, and his

26. See Philippe Sands, *Torture Team—Deception, Cruelty and the Compromise of Law* (Allen Lane, 2008) 30.

27. See Pohl, *Human Rights in Iran* (1989) report and Kaveh Shahrooz, "With Revolutionary Rage and Rancor: A Preliminary Report on the 1988 Massacre of Iran's Political Prisoners," *Harvard Human Rights Journal* volume 20 (2007), 227, 241. Shahrooz points out that another massacre denier at this time was Abdullah Nouri, Minister of the Interior, who a decade later became a leader of the reform movement and was jailed by the regime he had so enthusiastically served.

Head of Security Davoud Lashkari (real name Taghi Adeli). Eyewitnesses tell grisly stories of both men enthusiastically supervising the death sentences and the tortures. They are described as bringing prisoners before the Death Committees and sometimes making critical remarks about them to the judges and are accused in a few cases of putting prisoners they disliked in the wrong queue for execution. Naserian is accused by several witnesses of actually hanging prisoners and participating in their torture. He is currently serving as Head of Branch 28 of the Revolutionary Courts in Tehran, which is responsible for sending those arrested during the 2009 demonstrations to prison. Similar allegations are made against Sayed Hossein Mortazavi, the Deputy Governor of Evin Prison, who is said to have personally supervised the executions there, and the Ministry of Intelligence official known as Zamani (real name Mehdi Vaezi) who collected much of the intelligence upon which the Death Committees acted. If these allegations are proved—and the consistency and credibility of the witnesses who make them does amount to a *prima facie* case—then they are accountable on the same legal basis as prison guards at Omarska and at Nazi camps, convicted by the International Criminal Tribunal for the former Yugoslavia and the Nuremberg tribunals respectively.

There have been a number of high-echelon figures accused by Mojahedin organizations of advising and supervising the implementation of the fatwa, although the evidence is sketchy. Ahmad Khomeini, the powerful but now deceased son of the Supreme Leader, wrote out the fatwa and was responsible for its delivery. Mohammadi Reyshahri, the Minister of Intelligence, must have played a role, at least to appoint his ministry's representatives on the Death Committees (until late 2009 he was the Supreme Leader's representative for the pilgrimage to Mecca). His autobiography makes no reference to these events, despite his obvious knowledge of them. So too would Mohammad Moussavi Khoeniha, the General Prosecutor of Iran, be responsible for appointing his Death Committee representatives. He has turned reformer and is now known as a spiritual advisor of the reform movement.

Ali Khamene'i, as President of the Republic, had been closely involved in advising acceptance of the UN ceasefire resolution and must be presumed to have played the same advisory role a week or so later with respect to the fatwa. His statements in December 1988 can be read as enthusiastic support for its implementation, and in that month he refused permission for Professor Pohl, the

UNHRC Special Representative, to enter Iran to investigate. As Iran's current Head of State (he is now Supreme Leader) he would, of course, have immunity from prosecution in any court other than in one set up by the Security Council.

Ali Akhbar Hashemi Rafsanjani was the "inner circle" member whom the Supreme Leader came to rely upon most.[28] He was Acting Commander and Chief of the Armed Forces and another key advisor of the ceasefire: he would have been responsible for the Revolutionary Guard detachments sent to the prisons and would have authorized the firing squads which in some provinces conducted the executions. He also led the Friday sermons in Tehran around this time, in which he led crowds in chanting slogans such as "Death to the *monafeqin* prisoners." In December 1988, he too defended the executions, while pretending that "fewer than a thousand" prisoners had died. He is now Head of the Expediency Council and the Assembly of Experts, and these positions may not be sufficiently ministerial to attract the immunity approved by the ICJ in *DRC v. Congo*. Command responsibility might fall on Mohsen Rafiqdust who was Commander of the Revolutionary Guards at the time. He is now a frequently traveling businessman who comes on occasion to the UK.

There is more doubt over the role of Mir Hossein Musavi who was Prime Minister at the time and in consequence held some ministerial responsibility for the prison system. He joined the leadership chorus in December 1988 which sought to justify or ameliorate the massacres, speaking to Austrian television as if he had insider knowledge of them. Some students were heard to chant "Eighty-eight" at his 2009 election meetings, but he has not given any account of his role at the time or his reaction to it today.[29] Musavi responded to student questions about the massacres during his election campaign by stating that the executive branch had nothing to do with "trials." His struggle, since being denied the Presidency after the disputed election in June 2009, has won international admiration, but he cannot expect true respect unless and until he gives a full account of his conduct from July to November 1988, as the Prime Minister on whose watch barbarism became state policy. Now that Montazeri, the man of

28. Baqer Moin, *Khomeini: Life of the Ayatollah* (Thomas Dunne Books, 2000), 263.

29. Although Musavi's wife, Zahra Rahnavard, has vigorously condemned the Mojahedin Khalq as terrorists and traitors at meetings with students after the 2009 demonstrations. See Maziar Bahari, "Who is behind Tehran's Violence?" Newsweek Web Exclusive, 17 June 2009.

undeniable courage, can no longer testify in person, Musavi must stand in his shoes to explain exactly what was done by senior officials around Khomeini, who implemented his fatwa and then covered up the crime.

The situation in Iran today illustrates the consequences of impunity for crimes against humanity that have never been properly investigated or acknowledged. Some of the perpetrators and their acolytes remain in powerful positions in the judiciary and the state, whose Supreme Leader Ali Khamene'i has in the past year called upon the Revolutionary Guards to use violence against peaceful protests with the support of Ayatollah Mesbah Yazdi, who threatens that "[a]nybody resisting against the ruling system will be broken."[30] Those staged television show trials of the 1980s, with televised "confessions" by leftist prisoners wracked by torture and fear for their families, re-emerged in 2009, this time featuring "Green Movement" reformists confessing to participation in an international conspiracy devised by the US and the British Embassy in collaboration with the BBC, Twitter, Facebook, George Soros, Human Rights Watch, and Amnesty International. Once again, dissidents are being prosecuted for being *moharebs* ("warriors against God") and some are being sentenced to death.[31] Evin Prison, scene of mass murder in 1988, remains a brutal environment for blindfolded prisoners picked up for no more serious offense than attending student demonstrations or contacting NGOs concerned about human rights.[32] There have been many casualties over the past year, and many ironic reminders of 1988, the year of impunity. Hundreds of protestors, including Ayatollah Khomeini's granddaughter, have been detained. Mir Hossein Musavi's own cousin was shot and killed by Revolutionary Guards. One of Grand Ayatollah Montazeri's very last acts was to call on Iranians to accord three days of mourning to Neda Agha-Soltan, the young woman student shot dead by forces loyal to Ahmadinejad; and

30. "Meet the Ayatollahs," *New Statesman*, 10 August 2009, 30.

31. See Catherine Philip, "Iran executes alleged dissidents 'to warn opposition,'" *The Times* (of London), 29 January 2010, 9.

32. See Haleh Esfandiari, *My Prison, My Home: One Woman's Story of Captivity in Iran* (Ecco, 2009). Esfandiari, an Iranian turned American who directs the Middle East Program at the Woodrow Wilson Center in Washington, DC, was arrested on a visit to her mother in Tehran and incarcerated in Evin for some months in 2007. Her account is important evidence of the mindset of the Intelligence Ministry and its current establishment, which has convinced itself that the "Green Movement" is really an emanation of a Zionist and Western conspiracy.

to support other victims of the repressive state which he helped to create, but then came to condemn.

The government of Iran was confident enough to table a massively dishonest "periodic review" report to the Human Rights Council in November 2009,[33] on the strength of which it sought election to the Council, a result which would have seriously damaged the Council's credibility had its candidacy not been withdrawn. The sanctions that have been applied to Iran in recent years have all been in response to its determination to develop nuclear power—a right that is in principle hard to deny, since many other nations use nuclear power for peaceful purposes, and some—Israel, India and Pakistan, for example—have already developed nuclear weapons.[34] Further sanctions are under discussion, although some proposed by the US (for example, on unrefined petroleum products) would hurt ordinary citizens while others (on communication technology) would actually have the result of inhibiting the organization and reporting of protests. Europe (which does 24% of Iran's trade) has been slow to show support for these measures. There have been recent calls for "targeted" sanctions on members of the elite, especially on the Revolutionary Guards, whose leaders have been enriched by a grateful government and allowed to take shares worth millions of dollars in privatized industries,[35] but who have no direct role in nuclear policy-making.

It would be more sensible to impose sanctions for the crimes against humanity that occurred in 1988, so long as they go uninvestigated and unpunished, than it would to impose them for alleged moves towards uranium enrichment. Given the evidence of international crimes, including one which the 1948 Genocide Convention imposes a duty to investigate and punish without limit of time, the Security Council would be perfectly entitled under its Chapter VII powers to establish an international court with a prosecutor who can quickly collect the incriminatory evidence and obtain access to the relevant state witnesses and records. After all, the most reasonable objection to Iran developing nuclear power for peaceful purposes is the fact that it is a regime that has already granted itself impunity for mass murder, and may do so again.

33. Iran National Report, 18 November 2009, A/HRC/WG.6/7/IRN1.

34. "Iran: Barricades and the Bomb," *The Economist*, 13 February 2010.

35. "US sees opportunity to press Iran on nuclear fuel," *New York Times*, 3 January 2010.

International law obliges all states to acknowledge and comply with their obligations under a human rights law which is fundamental and universal. It abominates systematic torture and summary executions—but that is what happened in the prisons of Iran in the middle of 1988. In the annals of post-war horrors, the killings compare with the 1995 massacre at Srebrenica in terms of the vulnerability of the victims, and they exceed it when measured by the cold-blooded calculations made at the very pinnacle of state power. As long as the graves of the dead remain unmarked and relatives are forbidden from mourning, Iran will continue to contravene the rule of international law which its leaders so brutally defied in 1988.

WITNESS TESTIMONIES

and

OFFICIAL STATEMENTS

Mohammad Reza Ashough

ARRESTED: June 1981
DETAINED IN: Revolutionary Guards Detention Center, Andimeshk,
              and Unesco Prison, Dezful
RELEASED: 1984
RE-ARRESTED: June 1986
DETAINED IN: Unesco Prison, Dezful
ESCAPED: August 1988

1. My name is Mohammad Reza Ashough. I was born in southern Iran, in Khuzestan Province. I was trained in paramedical studies and while a student I also worked as a food and hygiene inspector, until I was arrested in 1981. I was then 26 years old. I left Iran in 1988, and applied to the UN for political asylum in the United Arab Emirates. I live in the Netherlands.

2. I make this statement in support of an investigation into the mass execution of political prisoners in 1988 in Iran.

3. This statement is true to the best of my knowledge and belief. Except where I

indicate to the contrary, I make this statement on the basis of facts and matters within my own knowledge. Where the facts and matters in this statement are within my own knowledge they are true. Where the facts and matters are not within my own knowledge, I have identified the source or sources of my information, and I believe such facts to be true.

Pre-arrest Activities

4. I was born in 1955 in Andimeshk, in Khuzestan. When I was a student, different political organizations were active in the university. I was a sympathizer of the Mojahedin (MKO) and I attended their meetings. I was a fan of MKO militants who had been arrested in previous years [under the former regime]; they were my friends.

5. A year before the Revolution, in 1977, I was spending my compulsory service time in the Development Corp (Sepah Tarvij). During the Iran-Iraq War [1980–1988], Iraqi soldiers came within 20 kilometers [12.4 miles] of Andimeshk. I was against the war.

6. Under these circumstances, I became attracted to the MKO because they had political experience [dating back to the struggle against the Shah] and they were Muslims. Some of them [imprisoned under the Shah] had just been released from prison. They were very active [politically]. We wanted to protect the Revolution and stabilize the revolutionary government. I didn't take the clergy seriously; to me they were ignorant in both the sciences and politics. My fellow MKO sympathizers and I were against their reactionary ideas. We were for individual freedoms and against the mandatory veil. We opposed the restrictions that were slowly being imposed upon social freedoms. So, naturally, we were attracted to democratic parties. Furthermore I was an athlete, playing soccer for the Khuzestan team, and the MKO militants were also young and athletic. We were from the same generation; we understood each other.

First Arrest and Trial

7. I was a third-year university student and had been working at the same time as a food and hygiene inspector when I was first arrested in 1981. It was just after the June demonstration organized by the MKO; I was 26 years old at the time. I was kept for two weeks in the Revolutionary Guards Detention Center in Andimeshk, where I was interrogated several hours each night for ten nights, and then I was transferred to Dezful, where I was again interrogated.

8. I was detained for 11 months before I was brought to court in 1982. The trial looked more like an interrogation session than a

trial. The judge was a clergyman by the name of Eslami. He is still working as a judge in the city of Qom. I was blindfolded, and could see the judge only for two to three minutes. Then they read the verdict to me. I received a two-year sentence, in addition to a ten-year suspended sentence, but there was no judgment in writing. I insisted that I needed some proof. He just wrote the sentence on a piece of paper and gave it to me. But it didn't seem to be a very official kind of document as it was handwritten. I threw it out of the window. I served my two-year sentence and was released after pledging I would not get involved in politics anymore.

Re-arrest

9. Upon my release from prison in 1984 I was notified that I had been banned from the university and could not continue my studies. I filed a complaint with the Ministry of Education, but they also wouldn't let me return to the university. They said that I could go back to my previous job but that I could not serve in any management capacity. It took a year of paperwork and going through the administrative court in order for me to obtain the authorization to go back to work. Finally, in early 1986, I returned to my previous job.

10. Before the war between Iran and Iraq started, different political organizations had rebelled against the regime. The government had banned all [independent] political activism. Political activists like us had no choice other than to carry on their struggle clandestinely. The MKO people

moved first to Iranian Kurdistan and then to Iraq.

11. During the Iran-Iraq War, I was in touch with an MKO contact person. He would commute from Pakistan to Iran and organize the transfer to Iraq of volunteers who wanted to fight the regime. I didn't want to go to Iraq. The volunteers were people who had been arrested once, or were friends and relatives of MKO members. In 1985 the MKO contact person was arrested at the Pakistani border. Soon after he was arrested, all the people he had been in touch with—about 50 people—were also arrested. In June 1986, I was arrested for the second time, at my workplace.

12. Unesco Prison in Dezful was dedicated to hosting ordinary criminals (as opposed to political prisoners). The prison is called "Unesco" because it was built for educational purposes by Unesco, during the time of the Shah. After the Islamic Revolution it was turned into a prison, but they kept the name, so it's known as the Unesco Prison. After a while, when a lot of political activists were arrested, all its cells were full. Soon they built three additional rooms [a political ward] near the prosecutor's office and transferred all the political prisoners [from the general ward], about 30 to 40 people, there. Some time later, people who had been arrested in other cities were also transferred to Unesco Prison, and kept in the general ward for a few days, and then they were transferred to the political ward. They were 27 to 28 people who were arrested in Ahvaz, Andimeshk, Dezful, Shush, Haft Tappeh, and Masjed Soleyman.

Altogether there were approximately 65 of us [political prisoners].

13. I was tortured for about a year. Unesco Prison has an underground area, just below the court, called the Tamshit Room, which still exists. There they would lay the prisoner down and tie his hands and feet and start flogging. The prisoner was interrogated and beaten once a week. I did not accept the charges levelled against me [intending to go to Iraq to wage war against the regime] because I really never intended to go to Iraq. But still, every week they would interrogate me and beat me with blows and kicks for the same charges.

14. I was interrogated ten times in Andimeshk and ten times in Dezful, but I denied all the charges levelled against me. . . .

15. I was taken six times to the religious judge Hojjat ol-eslam Ahmadi. Because I would not say anything about my political activities, the interrogators would demand that the judge issue a "confession flogging" verdict. So each time Ahmadi would order, "Beat him until he speaks or he dies." So the interrogators would come into the room where I was being flogged to get confessions. During the flogging blood would gush everywhere.

16. When a prisoner's feet were swollen and injured they would lash another part of the body, to avoid skin tears. My feet and body were injured and in terrible shape. My skin was all broken. My feet were deformed. They would give three or four blows, then the interrogators would start questioning me, and if they didn't hear the response they were expecting, they would hit me

again. Thirty or 40 blows—sometimes up to 60, until they would get tired and I would pass out.

Second Trial

17. The second time I was arrested, my interrogator in Unesco Prison, in Dezful [Khuzestan region], was a man by the surname "Kazemi." He was also the interrogator at the prosecutor's office. Kazemi brought the MKO contact person [who had been in touch with me] from the Sistan Baluchistan region [where he had been arrested] to Khuzestan [where I was being held]. This person had denounced me. Kazemi told me that he knew I was a member of that group [MKO] and that there was no need for me to confess. I was sentenced to a ten-year imprisonment then.

Events Surrounding 1988

18. When the Iran-Iraq War ended we were told, by the families who were visiting, that a delegation would be coming to consider pardons for the prisoners. After a while rumors about Khomeini's pardon intensified as the war was ending. One day during the very last days of the war, the prison guards brought a television into the ward and it showed the Mojahedin attacking Iran. About five days after the end of the war, we were told that the pardon committee had arrived at our prison.

19. From that day on visitations were suspended. When the pardon committee arrived, the guards told us to leave our belongings. We were all blindfolded and lined up. I couldn't count everybody but there were

about 60 or 70 of us, [which means that] they had brought [MKO] prisoners from the ward where ordinary criminals were kept. This line-up was of MKO sympathizers only. They took us to court eight at a time, where Ahmadi was sitting. Ahmadi was the religious judge, and Kazemi, the interrogator, was also there. There were three other people in the room: Ava'i (currently a prosecutor in the Tehran Public Court), Hardavaneh (the head of Unesco Prison), and Kafshiri (Commander of the Revolutionary Guards in Dezful). I knew Kafshiri, because he had been one of the people flogging me in 1983 when I was first arrested [in 1981]. And there was also an intelligence officer [present]. We were all blindfolded. When we were questioned by the judge, we were told to take our blindfolds off for a moment and look at the judge and then to put the blindfolds on again. We would take the blindfolds off only when they asked us a question.

20. The judge asked me: "Would you fight the Mojahedin or not?" I tried to avoid giving a positive response. I said, "Well, I'm not a fighter. I work for the Department of Hygiene. If there is anything to do with hygiene and there is a need, I will do it." But they kept saying, we only need one answer, "Would you fight [against the MKO] or would you not?" I evaded the question, again by saying that fighting is not my job. And then the religious judge and the interrogator started to debate over my case. I said: "I don't believe in Saddam and I will not go to Iraq [to join the MKO forces]." The judge asked me, "Would you die for Iran and Islam?" And I said, "I

would. If it's necessary to die, I would die."
The judge asked, "Would you step on a
mine [for the sake of the Islamic regime]?"
I replied "why should I have to step on a
mine? One who is a supporter should go
on a mine."* The intelligence officer said,
"Add his name to the list of executions."
Then the religious judge asked one more
time if I would walk [on a mine] or not"
and I said I wouldn't. He said no more.

21. In his [4 August 1988 complaint] letter [to
Ayatollah Khomeini, about the ongoing
unfair procedures] Montazeri quotes the
same religious judge, who had reported to
him that he had told the interrogator and
the intelligence officer that I should not
be executed, but he could not convince
them, because the decision was based on
a majority vote. As they were trying us
one by one, they told each of us: "he too is
one who will be executed." Some [prison-
ers] said that they would not fight against
the MKO. Among the eight of us, only
two said that they would fight against the
Mojahedins. Their names did not appear
on the list of executions. They separated
them from us and we later heard they had
been spared, and were released about three
to four months later. One was about 15 to
16 years old and the other around 20 or 21.

22. We stood in line, eight by eight. It was a
long line. The trial of 60 people had lasted
less than one hour. Then we were taken
back to the ward. In the evening, they
came and said, "Take your belongings. We
are taking you to Ahvaz." It was after
dinner, around 10 p.m. They told us,
"You'll go to the prosecutor's office first,
which is right there." There was a room,
[where] they told us, "Put your bags here."
They took us in one by one to another
room, where there was a table facing the
wall. There they sat me on the chair
behind the table and told me, "Write your
will." I said, "I won't. I have to see to my
family." Kazemi, the interrogator, told me,
"You have ten minutes to write your will.
You need to have written your will when I
come back." When they came back, I still
had not written it.

23. They put the blindfold on me, tied my
hands, and beat me up. They took me to
the prison courtyard. When I looked from
below the blindfold I could see that all of
the prisoners sitting in that open area were
blindfolded. Every one of them had written
his will. I said, "I need to go to the bathroom." I looked again beneath the blindfold, and I saw two ambulances and two
minibuses, a couple of Land Rovers from
the Revolutionary Guards. They dragged
me to the bathrooms and brought me back
to the same place.

24. It was around 1 a.m. when they put us
in the minibuses. They told us that they
were taking us to Ahvaz, but once we were
on the minibuses and could look around,
we all realized we were not going towards
Ahvaz. It was the wrong direction. We
were going toward Dehloran, toward Iraq.

---

*"Step on a mine": a reference to a tactic commonly used by the Revolutionary Guards in the Iran-Iraq War, in
which waves of boy soldiers were sent across minefields to clear the way for the Guards' advance. Hundreds of thousands
of young Iranians perished in these "human wave" attacks.

It was completely the opposite direction. Two Revolutionary Guards were at the front of the bus, and all the cars were following each other. The two buses were in the front, and, behind them, other cars. We were taken to the area where the Vali Asr Garrison is located. In this garrison there was a bathroom. The Guards told us to go there and do the *ghosl* [cleaning ritual—religious cleaning—for the dead]. An old man who used to bring food to the prisoners was there in the garrison giving us some white fabric to use as shrouds. We were also given camphor. They told us, "go wash, use the camphor, and put the white cloths around yourself."

25. I said, "I don't want to wear that." Kazemi came back with two Revolutionary Guards and told me, "You have to wear this. I will be back in ten minutes, and you'd better be ready." I took a quick shower and put my own clothes back on. It was a tense atmosphere. They tied my hands and put a blindfold on me and started to beat me up; I was screaming and fell on the floor. Other prisoners started to scream. And we could hear women washing themselves, waiting to be executed too. And everyone was giving their names out loud, because I guess they wanted someone to tell their families, so that people would know who had been taken.

26. I finally understood they were serious and all this was for real. But some of the prisoners still had doubts. I was on the ground; everyone else had their shrouds on. Kazemi said: "Take him and execute him as he is." They threw me on the minibus and told me to go and sit in the back seat. I sat on the right-hand side of the bus, and everyone came in white. Everyone hands tied with plastic rope. Everyone blindfolded. But my rope had loosened while they beat me up. It was dark. Prisoners were tired. The guards were also terrified. Everyone was screaming. Mostly, they were insulting Khomeini. I tried to move the blindfold a little with the help of the seat. I told Sadeq, a person who was sitting next to me, that I could get out of the handcuffs, and that I was going to escape. Even in the shower, I had looked to see if I could escape, but it didn't look like a safe place to try. The buses were going slowly, because it was a war zone, and it's really not very even—the road was bad. And there was dirt everywhere. There were other cars passing by as well. I opened the window and took my shoes off. I told Sadeq that I was going out. Once I decided to jump out of the window, I saw my cousin sitting just in front of me. So they took him too to be executed.

27. I noticed the noise and tumult in the bus. There were two Revolutionary Guards in the front of the minibus. I was lucky that I could open the window. I thought: if they don't shoot at me within ten minutes after I throw myself out, my escape will be successful. I slowly put my hands on the edge of the seat and stood up and threw myself out of window. I fell on the ground on my back. The air was very dusty, I waited for a couple of seconds, nothing happened. Then I ran for between 200 and 500 meters [200–500 yards], only to realize that I was still within the garrison precinct and had just reached the barbed wire. I climbed up the barbed wire and threw myself to the

other side. Only the next day did I realize how much blood I had lost. After 20 years I still have the scars from the injuries.

28. I was hardly a kilometer away [from the barbed wire] when I heard bursts of machine gun fire, followed by single gunshots. It was late at night and in the silence of the night I could hear the sound of the gunshots. They executed the prisoners. And they looked around with lights [trying to find me]. I could see the moving lights. I continued walking away until I got to the Karkheh River, and I could see where I was. There are hills on the other side of the Karkeh bridge called "Ali Gorize." I had gone hunting there before so I knew the area very well. I headed north. By morning I was quite far from the garrison.

29. They didn't bury all the executed ones in one place. They scattered their bodies into six different remote cemeteries. Some were buried in the deserts. Later, when the families went to the graves, wishing to exhume the bodies, they opened the graves and found out they were empty.

30. The day after my escape my father was summoned to court. The religious judge, Ahmadi, told him, "You must turn Mehdi in," and my father said, "But you have him.

I don't have him." My father didn't know I had escaped. And they told him, "No, no, no, we don't have him," and they told them, "If he comes to ask for money, or anything else, don't give it to him."

31. I fled to the mountains. Two days later, in the mountainous war zone, I found a pair of military boots [which I put on] and I started walking toward Andimeshk. On the road to Andimeshk, I hitchhiked and a car gave me a ride. I got off near Andimeshk. I was covered with dust, very hungry and in very bad shape. I went to the house of an acquaintance. There I was informed that the security forces had broken into the house of one of my relatives to look for me.

32. So, I left town on foot and walked north until the next morning—two train stations away. I took the train to Tehran; it was crawling with Basij militia returning from the war.

33. I hid in Tehran for a while and [after that] I returned to Ahvaz, and from there I fled to the United Arab Emirates. I still have the plan of the prison with me. I drew it 20 years ago when I escaped. I was very agitated. I couldn't sleep for months.

Amsterdam, June 2009

OFFICIAL STATEMENT • 1

كيهان

Subject :   Imam's last warning to the conspirators
The official: Founder and Supreme Leader of the Islamic Republic of Iran, Ayatollah Ruhollah Khomeini
The occasion: Speech delivered to hundreds of thousands of pilgrims at the holy city of Qom
Date: 17 August 1979
Source: *Kayhan, 18 August 1979*

We Made an Error by Not Acting in a Revolutionary Manner.
If the corrupt don't return to the people's fold, by God we will become more revolutionary.

Qom—*Kayhan*'s reporter: Yesterday afternoon, in the presence of hundreds of thousands of Qom residents and pilgrims who had converged on the city from all over Iran, Imam Khomeini, the leader of Iran's Islamic Revolution, delivered an important speech on the country's problems and the role of Islam in the world. The following is the text of the speech:

... If we had acted in a revolutionary fashion since day one when we brought the corrupt regime to its knees and tore down this evil barrier [to our salvation], and had closed down the mercenary and corrupt newspapers and magazines and tried their editors; if we had banned all corrupt parties and punished their leaders; if we had erected gallows on every street and gotten rid of the corrupt and the corruptors, we would not be inconvenienced in this way. I apologize to almighty God and to our dear people for our errors. We were not revolutionary leaders; our government is not a revolutionary government [allusion to Mehdi Bazargan's government, the liberal Islamist Prime Minister designated by Khomeini to head the post-revolutionary provisional government]. Our armed forces are not revolutionary. Our rural police forces are not revolutionary. Our Revolutionary Guards are not revolutionary either. I, too, am not revolutionary. If we were, we would not have allowed them [our opponents] to even manifest themselves and speak; we would have closed down all political parties, banned all political fronts, and created only one party, the Hezbollah, the party of the downtrodden. I ask forgiveness for the errors that we have made. I warn the corrupt elements still in our midst, wherever they are, that if they don't stop challenging us we shall deal with them in a most revolutionary manner, as God has instructed us. Our master, Ali, the commander of all devout Muslims, the embodiment of knowledge, the epitome of a true human being, the most faithful of God's followers, the most devout among Muslims, treated the downtrodden with mercy and kindness

46

but faced the exploiters and conspirators with his drawn sword. It is said that he slaughtered 700 Jews of the Bani Qarantiah [tribe], who just might be the kin of present-day Israelis, in one day. God almighty is merciful when mercy is due and vengeful when vengeance is needed. So was the Imam of all Muslims. We are not intimidated by what they write about us in pre-revolutionary newspapers or in the foreign press. We are not seeking popularity in Iran, in the Muslim world, or in foreign countries. We strive to act according to God's instructions, and we shall. Treat the infidel harshly and act mercifully with your brethren. The conspirators are from the ranks of infidels. The plotters in Kurdistan and other provinces are no more than infidels. They should be treated in the harshest possible fashion. The government should act mercilessly against them. The rural police force must deal with them severely. So should the armed forces. If they do not act as they must, we will deal with them harshly, and without charity. There is a limit to leniency. There is a limit to the desire for public approval. I shall not allow the interests of Muslims to be ignored because of such consider-ations. The Revolutionary Prosecutor is duty bound to close down all publications that conspire and agitate against the interests of our people and should summon their writers to account for their actions and prosecute them [in the courts]. He must similarly prosecute and try the leaders of those conspiratorial groups that characterize themselves as political parties. . . .

Hojjat ol-eslam Sadeq Khalkhali, Chief Justice of the Revolutionary Court, interrogating a defendant in the Kurdish city of Paveh—
Ettela'at, 19 August 1979

Hamid Ashtari

ARRESTED: April 1981
DETAINED IN: Evin, Qezel Hesar, and Gohardasht Prisons
RELEASED: February 1989

1. My name is Hamid Ashtari. I have been a refugee in England since 2006. I was a political prisoner in Iran for eight years, from 1981 to 1989, during which time I was kept in Evin, Qezel Hesar, and Gohardasht Prisons. I was released a few months after the mass executions in 1988.

2. I make this statement in support of an investigation into the mass executions of political prisoners in 1988 in Iran.

3. This statement is true to the best of my knowledge and belief. Except where I indicate to the contrary, I make this statement on the basis of facts and matters within my own knowledge. Where the facts and matters in this statement are within my own knowledge, they are true. Where the facts and matters are not within my own knowledge, I have identified the source or sources of my information, and I believe such facts to be true.

Arrest and Torture

4. I was arrested in April 1981. I was arrested when I was collecting the Mojahedin Khalq's (MKO) printed newsletters from the Sahab printing house. My brother had been a member of the MKO and had been arrested during the time of the Shah. After he was released, I began to sympathize with his political ideas. We were only teenagers then. I started to work actively with the MKO in 1979.

5. I was tried twice. The first time was in December 1981. The second time was in December of 1982, and I was sentenced to ten years' imprisonment for being an MKO sympathizer.

6. I was in Evin from April 1981 until November 1982. I was interrogated in Evin. My arrest took place before the MKO military phase started. Before these events, conditions in Evin Prison were not terribly bad. After I was sent to Evin, I was charged with being an MKO sympathizer. I was not interrogated or tortured at that stage. But after June 1981, things changed.

7. In December 1981 my interrogations started, and from then on I was tortured many times. The most common type of torture was their flogging me with an electrical cable while I was tied to a bed. Another form of torture they used is called *qapani* in Persian (Palestinian hanging), where one of my hands was bent back over my shoulder, as if to touch my back, while the other hand was pulled down and the elbow bent so my hands could almost reach each other behind my back. My hands were handcuffed in this awkward position. Then they hung me from the handcuffs, which would usually dislocate your shoulders and often broke prisoners' shoulder blades and elbows. They applied *qapani* on me once. I have since had to have two operations on my elbow because of this torture. As a result of this torture my body still cannot function completely normally.

8. These tortures were applied to us particularly during our interrogations, but other types of torture, such as group beatings, or making us stand for hours, or depriving us of fresh air, taking showers, or using the toilet, etc., were used on us routinely.

Events Surrounding 1988

9. In Gohardasht, several months before the mass executions started, the transfer of prisoners to various other wards was taking place, and we could not figure out the reason for the transfers. They transferred me, for example, four times to different wards.

10. Shortly before the mass executions started, around 150 prisoners (I cannot give the exact figures) of different political persuasions were brought to the jihad ward. This ward contained several workshops. It seems to me that Davud Lashkari, the deputy head of the prison, had intentionally transferred those prisoners in order to prevent them from being executed.

11. Also around that time, prison conditions changed. Prisoners had started to go on strike; they were bolder in expressing their demands. For example, prisoners brought into the jihad ward refused to eat after they arrived. They asked about the reason for being transferred to the jihad ward. The jihad ward was known as the repenters ward, and they did not want to be considered repenters.

12. In 1988 I was being held in Gohardasht Prison in the jihad ward. I remember that things changed in the summer of 1988. It was about the time that we heard about the MKO attack. Some prisoners in my ward were working in other wards of the prison during the day, as mechanics or builders inside the prison. I worked as a carpenter within my own ward. When these prisoners were no longer taken out of their cells during the day to work we realized that something had changed. All of a sudden, all of the security procedures and the guards changed. All of the old guards that we knew were transferred somewhere else and new guards were brought in. There was also one noteworthy case: one of the officers responsible for our ward had told some prisoners that the situation was deteriorating badly and that widespread executions were being carried out and that we had better not antagonize the authorities. He also

recommended to the prisoners that they answer any questions in the way favored by the authorities.

13. One day, during the mass executions, we were taken, blindfolded, to the office of the ward, and were questioned one by one. They asked me three questions:

> Do you still agree with the *monafeqin* (MKO)?
>
> Will you go on television and give a public confession?
>
> Do you accept the validity of the Imam's orders and decrees?

I answered no to the first question and yes to the second and third questions. I was blindfolded the entire time and could not see the judges. I recognized the voice of Lashkari asking me questions.

14. I was then taken to the ward. From our ward we could see that in the yard near the office, there were two lines of prisoners. One line was sent to their cells, and the other one was taken out of the ward. We later heard that the second line was taken to the Hosseinyeh and there they were all hanged. In the Hosseinyeh there was a stage with five or six ropes in a line. They would line the prisoners up, make them stand on the stage, place the rope around their necks, and then kick them off the stage.

15. I was told this by several different prisoners who had been taken to the Hosseinyeh either to be threatened and warned, or to

be killed, but who had been saved at the last minute by a friendly prison guard. For example, Lashkari, the deputy head of the prison, had known many of these kids for a long time; some of them he had known since before he became a Revolutionary Guard—so he would protect them. ["Kids" is a familiar way of referring to a group of people that the speaker feels close to.] For example, Lashkari liked a kid by the name of Shapur Irantalab, who had been to interrogation and answered "no" to each of the questions. Lashkari took him into the Hosseinyeh, showed him what was happening to scare him, and then took him back to the court room telling him, "now say yes." Lashkari had himself taken another of the kids from the Fadaiyan Khalq (FKO) Minority, Majid Ehsasian, out of the court room and had beaten him with a cable and forced him to write on a piece of paper that he is a Muslim and that he prayed. When Lashkari finally got the confession on paper from Majid, he took him back into the courtroom, gave him the written confession, and Majid was saved. Majid told me this when we went back to our cell.

16. I never saw any dead bodies. I only heard news of the executions from other prisoners, and then from visiting relatives once our visitations started again. I never saw many of my friends after that event.

London, June 2009

Mehdi Aslani

ARRESTED: February 1985
DETAINED IN: Gohardasht Prison
RELEASED: February 1989

1. My name is Mehdi Aslani. I was arrested in February 1985 (Bahman 1363) and was a political prisoner in Iran for more than four years. I was sentenced to five years imprisonment. I was serving my sentence in Gohardasht Prison during the massacre of political prisoners in 1988.

2. I make this statement in support of an investigation into the mass execution of political prisoners in 1988 in Iran.

3. This statement is true to the best of my knowledge and belief. Except where I indicate to the contrary, I make this statement on the basis of facts and matters within my own knowledge. Where the facts and matters in this statement are within my own knowledge they are true. Where the facts and matters are not within my own knowledge, I have identified the source or sources of my information, and I believe such facts to be true.

Arrest and Detention

4. I was affiliated with the Fadaiyan Khalq Organization (FKO), followers of the 16 Azar (December 7th) Congress. Our group was a small group within the FKO Majority (Aksariat) Organization that opposed the latter's alliance with, in fact dissolution within, the [pro-Soviet Communist] Tudeh Party. We split from the Aksariat Organization on 7 December 1981.

5. On a cold February day of 1985, a clean Renault car with two young passengers, rather well dressed, passed by me while my friend and I were walking toward a newsstand at the Golkar crossroads in Tehran. One of the young men seemed to be looking for an acquaintance; he gazed at me for a moment. I saw a hunter's glint in his eyes and he said something to the driver. Ignoring the car, I stopped at the newsstand and started to browse the newspapers. The Renault stopped when I stopped walking. The two young men in the car did not

match the image of political police I had in mind. In the car I saw a big open photo album between the driver and the front seat. One of the agents got out of the car, came to me, and said, "Be quiet and get in the car." I raised my voice and said loudly: "Didn't the authorities say this year was dedicated to the rule of law and we should confront lawlessness?" I wanted to alert the bystanders to my arrest, so that they could give the news to my family. A few people noticed the brawl and started to gather around us. I started to consider the option of fleeing. The young agent realized what was going on and showed me the firearm he was carrying under his overcoat. When I saw the firearm, I decided against fleeing. But I shouted, "Doesn't this country have laws? You cannot arrest whoever you want in the middle of the day without a warrant!!!" The agent said, "Keep quiet and get in the car or else I will break your teeth." The number of people gathering around us was increasing. Suddenly the agent screamed, "You rascal son of a dog, you ruin young people's lives. You filthy drug dealer, you are distributing drugs in this neighborhood." I shouted: "Everyone knows me in this area, drug dealer yourself." An old woman of our neighborhood came forward and said, "We know his family, I am sure you are mistaking him for someone else. Furthermore, you yourself look more like a drug addict." I became more confrontational. The agent felt that the situation was getting out of control, the driver of the Renault joined him and the two of them tried to force me into the car. I resisted and asked for their i.d. cards. I was trying to make sure that my fam-ily would learn of my arrest. I shouted, "I have to bring medicine to my old mother who lives a block away at 68 Shahin Street. She is waiting for her medicine." Then I turned toward the crowd and said, "I beg you, don't give her the news brutally; she may have a heart attack." Meanwhile, my companion, who had continued on his way, unaware of what was happening, noticed the brawl and hurried back to the scene. I tried to warn him with signs, but to no avail. He thought I was fighting with a bystander and rushed to one of the agents. The first agent shot his gun in the sky to disperse the people in the street. Then they took us [me along with my friend] to a nearby carpentry shop and called the revolutionary committee's patrol for help. The patrol arrived and they threw a military blanket over our heads and forced us into the committee's patrol car and took us to the detention center.

6. The two young agents who arrested me were members of Tehran's prosecution team. My arrest was accidental. At the time I was under the Ministry of Information watch and they didn't plan to arrest me then [for they wanted to find as many as possible of my fellow militants and arrest a great number of us at the same time]. In fact before the creation of the Ministry of Information in the summer of 1984, all the issues related to arrests, detentions, and interrogations were under the control of the prosecutor's office and the intelligence branch of the Revolutionary Guards. Between 1981 and 1984, Lajevardi, Tehran's Revolutionary Prosecutor, and his team had the upper hand in all matters related to intelligence and arrests. During the

transition and the transfer of responsibilities to the Ministry of Information, there was some overlapping of jurisdiction [with the prosecutor's office and the Ministry of Information each pursuing its own agenda], of which my untimely arrest [was an example], but after that every similar matter was under the control of the Ministry of Information.

7. I call my blindfold my "travel mate." In the early days of the Revolution, the interrogators were called the "Ku Klux Klan" because they wore hoods. But later, most of the time, it was the prisoners who were wearing the blindfolds, and wearing them made us confused and disoriented.

Events Surrounding 1988

8. In the fall of 1987, about ten months before the massacres of 1988, there was a general reclassifying and relocating of prisoners in Gohardasht Prison. The prison was divided into two distinct sections, separating religious and non-religious prisoners. There was this redistribution and questions and answers that felt like an inquisition. The questioning was less about our political stands and more about our ideology.

9. In addition to this faith-based redistribution, prisoners were also divided based on the length of their sentences. Those sentenced to fewer than ten years were held in a ward; and those sentenced to between ten and twenty years, in another location. Prisoners sentenced to more than twenty years were moved to Evin Prison in a process that lasted a few months. Almost all those who were transferred to Evin, except for a

handful, were hanged during the summer of 1988.

10. Another notable point was the interrogation around mid-fall 1987, during which Naserian, the Assistant Prosecutor, and Lashkari, the prison guard, asked inquisitorial questions. For example, "Do you pray"? Previously, after an interrogation, prisoners were taken back to their wards, which enabled them to inform their fellow prisoners of the tone of the interrogation. This time however, after questioning, prisoners were held in the administrative part of the ward so that they couldn't communicate with other prisoners. The Hosseinyeh was also in the same administrative section, as were the offices of Naserian and Lashkari. At the time of the questioning we were not paying much attention. It was only later that we thought about all these issues. At the time, we didn't know what was happening and we were not thinking of a hidden agenda. Generally since 1987 the prison situation had been pretty good because the regime was getting weaker on all fronts, on the war front and the political front. The number of *mellikesh*, those who would not agree to be interviewed in order to obtain their release, was increasing regularly, and so did the prisoners' demands.

11. Several incidents occurred in 1988 [before the prison massacres] that lifted the prisoners' morale and in particular gave MKO sympathizers courage and made them more resistant.

12. Before the 1988 massacres, the Liberation Army of the Mojahedin Khalq Organization carried out two important military

operations in the western part of the country: Operation Aftab and Operation Chelcheragh. During the Chelcheragh Operation, the town of Mehran was occupied by the Mojahedin for a few days. This is the origin of the [MKO] slogan "Today Mehran, tomorrow Tehran." During the same period [two other noteworthy events occurred: first], the chemical bombing of Halabcheh, an Iraqi Kurdish region occupied by Iran, took place, causing the death of 5,000 people; and later [on 3 July 1988] an Iranian Airbus, a civilian jetliner carrying passengers from Bandar Abbas to Dubai, was hit by the Americans [USS *Vincennes* (CG-49)] in the [Persian] Gulf. All 300 passengers [and crew] of the plane were killed. These events testified to the weakness of the Iranian regime on the front and boosted the prisoners' will to be defiant.

13. Another reason I think the killing had been planned [in advance] was what happened during the Ramadan period in 1988. In previous years, during the Ramadan fasting month, they [prison guards] would bring breakfast before sunrise. The Mojahedin [who fasted] would eat breakfast [before sunrise] and the leftists would keep it and eat it for lunch [since no lunch was served at noon]. Because we had no refrigerators in the ward and the food could go bad, the leftists always asked the guards to have warm meals and the guards always reacted strongly. Surprisingly, during Ramadan 1988 (which was in the spring and thus the weather was not very hot), the guards did not react and responded positively to the leftist prisoners' request. In fact, in doing so, they acknowledged our

identity as leftists. At the time we totally missed the meaning of [their reaction]. For Ramadan, regardless of the political angle, is also a matter of values and beliefs, and [it was strange that] a regime that publicly lashed ordinary people for eating in public during the fasting period would allow the prison guards to serve Marxist prisoners three warm meals a day. In previous years [during the month of Ramadan], food caused confrontations between prison guards and prisoners. In fact, the regime made us draft our own indictments because in the summer of 1988 they killed leftist prisoners for apostasy. For according to Shari'a law and Islamic jurisprudence, there are four ways to prove apostasy, the most important of which is the accused's own confession. In fact, with our behavior [eating during Ramadan], we had exposed our leftist identity [and therefore the fact that we were non-believers]. The authorities encouraged us to do so. They were opening the path, or to be more specific, a one-way highway leading to a dark tunnel ending in the cemetery, and they gave us space to drive at the maximum speed.

14. They [the authorities] were looking for an appropriate excuse to justify the physical elimination of 1988, which was not a massacre in the classical sense. As I said, for the leftists, the excuse for the execution was apostasy, meaning turning back from God; for the Mojahedin, it was waging war on God. Before the period leading to the summer of 1988, no Mojahed had the right to call his or her organization "Mojahedin." If any of them did so, they would smash his/her teeth. But in 1988, they [the guards]

didn't mind. When asked about their charge, the Mojahedin prisoners would use the word "Organization." And prison guards would not react. Then, the prisoners took one step forward and fearlessly said "Mojahedin." Some even said, "the Proud and Respected People's Mojahedin of Iran Organization," but the prison guards had been ordered to let them be. The prison guards' lack of reaction was a trap set for prisoners, who were later executed on that charge. This was the great treachery [that facilitated] the killings.

15. The Mojahedin used the excuse of religious holidays to organize events. Before 1988, if the prison guards got wind of the Mojahedin having celebrations, they would confront them seriously. But at that time [1988], not only did they not prevent them from doing so, they encouraged them. Iraj Mesdaghi, a surviving Mojahed, has written in his book, Khalil Al Wazir was killed in the Palestinian-occupied territories. The Mojahedin declared silence in the ward and then started to chant a hymn. First they did so quietly and when nothing happened, they sang louder and still no reaction. They regularly organized protests using the excuse of religious events and nothing happened. In Gohardasht Prison, Naserian, the Assistant Prosecutor, was the de facto manager of the prison. He had been there since 1986 (1365).

16. In prison, twice a day, at 8 a.m. and 2 p.m., they turned the radio on for half an hour so that we could listen to the news. At 2:00 p.m. on 18 July 1988, they announced in the news that Iran had accepted the conditions of the United Nations Resolu-

tion 598 to end the war. The news had been announced by the then-President Ali Khamene'i to Javier Pérez de Cuéllar, the UN Secretary-General. Two days later, on 20 July, we heard of Khomeini's officially accepting the Resolution and "drinking the poison." We could not contain our joy when we heard that Khomeini had accepted the Resolution. The prison exploded from happiness that day. We had two reasons [to rejoice]; first, our biggest enemy had been humiliated; second, the society was going to be free from the misery of war. What we didn't know was that for the little sip of poison that Khomeini drank they were going to force us to drink buckets of poison.

17. Normally, daily chores in the prison were done by Afghans and the ordinary [nonpolitical] prisoners. The Islamic Republic was exploiting the Afghans. During the three weeks of the killings, that is from the time the television was taken away, the Afghans didn't come and the guards brought the food themselves. Before the Afghans disappeared, one of them had tried to warn prisoners by making signs that a cleric has come and he is killing prisoners. But the prisoners did not understand his signs and did not get his message.

18. They turned the radio off on 26 or 27 of July, but the television was still there. Fridays were exciting because feature movies were aired on public television in the afternoon. But on 29 July, an hour before the movie was scheduled to air, they took the television away. That day, the ward's guard brought the food on a cart to the door himself and left the cart there. An

hour later, the same guard came back and went straight to the television, unplugged it and put it on the cart to take it out. We protested, saying, "Why are you taking the television now?" They said, "We need to fix these and bring a color television." Some said: "how about taking it in a few hours so that at least we get to watch the Friday movie?" He responded, "I have orders. I have to take it now." We told the guard, "the news was not broadcast from the radio." He said "the guard probably forgot to turn it on." It had happened before that the guards would forget to turn it on, but not several times in a row. It meant they had cut it off. [That Friday], there were quasi-inaudible radio sounds coming from *zir hasht* [the administrative section of the ward]. The Friday Sermon Imam had become the conductor of the "must be executed" orchestra and the prayer attendants were chanting "the armed hypocrite must be executed."

19.   [The guard] was clearly lying. That day, all prison televisions were taken away. The next day, 30 July, was our turn to get fresh air in the morning. At 8:00 a.m., after breakfast, the guard was supposed to open the door [to let us out]. Sometimes our time was switched with that of ward 7. Surprisingly, neither of the wards was allowed out. There was no sign of the 8:00 a.m. radio news. The two morning newspapers, *Jomhuri Eslami* and *Sobh Azadegan*, were cut off, as were the two afternoon papers, *Kayhan* and *Ettela'at*.

20.   The next day, Sunday, 31 July, was our ward's visitation day. But there was no visitation. Some banged at the door to protest.

They said, "We are remodeling the visitation room and there will be no visitations until further notice." During those days, they did not mistreat prisoners. They only cut off all our means of communication. Cutting off all means of communication without a punishment context was out of the ordinary. Among all the restrictions imposed on us, banning visitations seemed strange considering that the regime had no desire to alienate families. We saw in this a sign of the regime's weakness.

21.   Based on the news we heard later, we realized that in July the leadership of the Mojahedin had mobilized its forces from countries around the world for a final attack against a regime that, they believed, was collapsing. But this political adventurism lasted three days. A great number of the Mojahedin were burned, hanged, or arrested in the western towns of Iran, and some of them managed to escape. We learned of this attack a few days later when the state television showed the MKO's burned tanks, the militants' dead bodies, and the POWs. The Mersad or Forugh Javidan operation provided the regime with the excuse to implement a plan that it had prepared before this operation and not because of it.

22.   We didn't know at the time that, starting the last week of July, the Death Committee nominated by Ayatollah Khomeini had started the killing of the Mojahedin. We had no information whatsoever about the Mojahedin because they were held in another wing of the prison. The Mojahedin were kept in the left wing of the prison and the leftists in the right side. From ward 8,

where I was held, we had a partial view of the prison's administrative area. One night in early August, we stayed awake and managed to push the blind up slightly [giving us a view out of the window] in the ward's last cell. We saw a number of masked people loading and unloading a refrigerated truck for meat. We used the last cell in our ward as a kitchen. This room overlooked the lower section of the prison administration's parking area. Looking out through the blind, we recognized prison guards from their green Revolutionary Guard outfits, but their faces were covered by masks. The guards were sanitizing that area. Each of us had a different interpretation, but no one was thinking about death. Later we learned that when they hanged people, the smell of feces and urine on the execution site took over the whole area. Apparently, because of the extreme heat of August and to fight the stench, they felt sanitizing was necessary.

23. A prisoner who was a member of the Tudeh Party, Mohammed Zahedi, who survived and now lives in Belgium, could hear the sound of something being thrown into the truck. He says that he heard that sound 20 to 25 times every day. But this may have been the sound of the first bodies hitting the truck's floor. The rest of the bodies falling on the previous ones did not produce any sound. This usually happened after sundown. We all had different interpretations. One person said, "maybe they are planting flowers and are using pesticides." Another person said: "I read in the news that rotten chicken has been distributed in the city. What if they are trying to make us eat it?"

24. Some prisoners with good taste had planted flowers in the garden. Since we were not allowed out, there was no one to water the flowers in the heat of August. Prisoners kept calling the guards and told them, "since you don't let us go out, water the flowers yourself." A guard called Seyyed Morteza told them angrily, "are you thinking of the flowers? You should be thinking about yourselves." We didn't understand why we had to worry about ourselves. They were slaughtering people two feet away from us and we really had no idea.

25. What I, in ward 8, and other inmates in ward 7 and the subsidiary ward, realized was that the killing of MKO affiliates took approximately 20 days (the last week of July and the first two weeks of August). Later when we read Ayatollah Montazeri's book, we realized that on 15 August, the first day of the holy month of Moharam, the killing of MKO affiliates in Gohardasht and Evin prisons had ended. Owing to the insecurity in important cities such as Kermanshah [caused by the war with Iraq and the fact that the MKO had occupied the western city of Mehran for 72 hours, beginning on 19 June 1988, during its Operation Chelcheragh], some of the MKO prisoners in Dizelabad Prison (in Kermanshah) had been transferred to the subsidiary ward in Gohardasht, and most of the inmates in that ward were hanged in the summer of 1988. Furthermore, between 15 and 22 August, for a week, the Death Committee did not come to Gohardasht Prison. There was a one-week gap between the MKOs' killing and the leftists' killing.

26. For a couple of weeks the prison was calm. On 27 August the killing of the leftists in Gohardasht Prison began. We had no idea about the ongoing calamity. Even when we were standing before the Death Committee, we didn't know why we were there. It was all deception and lies. On 28 August (it was still in the month of Moharam), guards wearing black came to our ward, ward 8. They took us all—there were 80 inmates in our ward. That day there were not enough blindfolds; usually the guards brought the blindfolds. So we had to use towels or anything at hand to cover our eyes. We were not even given enough time to put on our slippers.

27. They sat us on the two sides of the hallway in the administrative section of the prison. A quick interrogation took place in two separate offices. Lashkari was in one office, and Naserian was in the other. One by one, we were taken in very quickly and asked our name, charges, group, if we prayed, if we were Muslim, what we thought of our group, if we would denounce our group, if we would give an interview. It happened very fast and we were not beaten and didn't experience any pressure. From those 80 people, only 17 were separated from us. Apparently these people had given responses that showed that they were not as stubborn.

28. As we were waiting in the hallway, the guards wearing black reappeared carrying their whips. They put us in line and started to lash us on our backs and push us toward the left part of the prison where there were three cells. They squeezed the 63 of us into three rooms and sent the other 17 prisoners back to the ward.

29. We were put in a room without a window. At last, at sunset on the 28th of August, the door opened with difficulty (as the room was filled with people), and a guard appeared with a handheld transceiver. He started to scream violently: "Ten people to the committee." This was the first time we were hearing about the committee. They didn't even call it "court." Before we had time to react, the guard picked ten of us. I was one of them, the last one who was selected and so I was the first one on the line. Lajevardi, the butcher of Evin, was right when he said, "the prisoners analyze any meaningless fact." Later when we, the survivors, tried to figure out what the guard's criteria were for choosing us, we couldn't find any common denominator except our physical corpulence. They took us to the lower level. The delegation was on the ground floor. We had our hands on each other's shoulders and we were blindfolded. We couldn't imagine what fate awaited us. Like robots we were following the guard's orders. At some point I made a mistake and turned in the wrong direction.

30. As a result, the initial order of the line was disrupted. And in the new order, Jahanbakhsh Sarkhosh, an FKO (Minority) affiliate, became the first in line. He had served almost all his sentence; just a few months were left. We were led to the lower level of the prison, near the room where the Death Committee was officiating. They made us sit and wait.

31. Jahanbakhsh was the first to be called in; his ward mates called him Jahan ("world" in Persian). The seconds were slow to pass. A few minutes later, Jahan came out of the

room grumbling. Naserian entrusted him to the guard and said, "Take him to the left." That was the last time anyone saw Jahan. We didn't know that a few minutes later, Jahan's honey-colored, gentle, and kind eyes—the eyes of someone who wanted nothing but the happiness of all the world's (Jahan's) inhabitants—would be closed forever. In every prison, it is customary to give a moment to the condemned to say goodbye to his cellmates. But we were not even allowed to hug and kiss Jahan. Jahan was destined to the left and a hanging noose kissed his valiant neck. Had I turned in the right direction given by the guard in the corridor of death, today you would be taking Jahan's testimony.

32. Among the ten of us, Mehrdad Neshati was the second one to be called before the Death Committee. He was an FKO (Minority) sympathizer. He too had almost finished serving his term. He was born to a Christian father, but because of a problem in his file, they considered him a Muslim. Nayyeri couldn't declare Mehrdad an apostate [because of his father's religion]. Some other prisoners also did not accept being Muslim, but since they didn't defend their ideology, their apostasy could not be proven. So Islam was to be introduced to them with the help of a cable. Naserian had told them, disappointedly, "It is a pity there is only one signature [of one of the committee members] missing for you [to be executed]." However the prisoners didn't know, at this point, the price they would have to pay for not praying.

33. After Mehrdad, Akbar Alyin was called in and came out with the same verdict as Mehrdad, "Beat him until he prays." It was then my turn, on 28 August 1988. As I entered the room the Death Committee was in, I was ordered to take off my blindfold and respond to the religious judge. I was facing three members of the committee who were sitting behind a big desk. From right to left: Morteza Eshraqi, the prosecutor; Hojjat ol-eslam Hossein'ali Nayyeri, the religious judge, and head of the Committee; and Mostafa Pourmohammadi, the representative of the Ministry of Information. Nayyeri posed the first question: "Are you a Muslim or a Marxist?" During all these years I had tried to elude the question.

34. I have to say that during my detention (1985 to 1988), we had some margin to maneuver (in our Q and A) that prisoners didn't have in 1981 to 1984. But with the Death Committee, there was no way I could equivocate. So I responded, "I was born to Muslim parents, but philosophically speaking I consider myself neither Muslim nor Marxist." The judge said, "but you are charged with being a member of a Marxist group." I replied, "I was attracted to the FKO pro-justice slogans but not to their philosophy." He said, "Cut the crap, as if only Marxist movements are promoting justice in this country!"

35. I was standing and responding to questions, when the phone on the desk rang. The religious judge spoke very respectfully with his interlocutor on the phone. Then he hung up and, with his hands, he signaled to his fellow committee members that they had to go. He told Naserian, take him away for now, we will see [him] later. For the first time I got lucky.

36. The Committee left Gohardasht Prison, to come back only three days later, on 31 August. I was led out of the room and joined the six people who remained from our group of ten prisoners. They took us to a big cell. One of the mysteries of the 1988 killings was why the Death Committee stopped working in Gohardasht on 29 and 30 August. As far as I know, no one was called before the committee during these days. Until now, we have been only conjecturing about it.

37. On 31 August, about noon, they took us to the corridor of death. I went in. Hojjat ol-eslam Nayyeri posed his customary questions about my identity and my charges and then asked the key question, "Are you Muslim or Marxist?" I replied, "I am Muslim." He then asked, "Do you pray?" I said, "Haj Aqa! Up until now, like many other Muslims, I have not prayed. I think if I feigned praying I would be disrespectful to you. Morteza Eshraqi said to Naserian, "Take him away. He will damn well pray!" As I was trying to insist on not praying, Eshraqi said, "A born Muslim must pray. Take him out and shave his mustache. He will pray." Naserian took me by my shirt and brutally dragged me out of the room. Nayyeri told Naserian, "He needs to sign the form first and then be shaved and start to pray. And if he refuses to pray, beat him until he starts praying."

38. A mustache is very valuable among Iranian men, and in particular within leftist circles. Well aware of this point, these male chauvinist dispensers of death ordered my mustache to be shaved. At the very doorstep, Adel the evil [guy] responsible for the prison store, shaved half of my mustache and then gave me the form to sign.

39. There were a few paragraphs on this form. I had to acknowledge that I was a Shi'a Muslim and pledge that I would do my religious duties, in particular the prayer. I crossed out the last paragraph and signed the form. Those who signed the form would be taken to their wards. But Naserian got angry when he saw what I had done with the form. He tore up the form and punched and kicked me into a cell where a few *mellikesh* resided.

40. In the cell, I was informed that some of the *mellikesh* had been called that same day before the committee. Luckily, they had been warned through Morse code messaging before their hearing. All those thrown in that cell had refused to pledge to pray. After a few hours, Naserian came with two guards carrying whips. With his languid red eyes, he looked at us and asked, "Why didn't you fill out the form the way it was?" And then he signaled to the guards to start beating us, and so they did. After the beating, we were returned to ward 8 and started to ask after our friends. Where is Ahmad? Darius? Mahmud? Homayun? We were all downcast, tears in our eyes, trying to swallow an explosive anger. *They had simply stopped being, and we were, not so simply, still being.*

Frankfurt, July 2009

OFFICIAL STATEMENT • 2

کیهان

Subject:	Prosecution of dissident educators and teachers; Islamic education and pardons for Kermanshah Prison inmates
The official:	Kermanshah's Chief Shari'a Judge, Mohammad-Ali Razizadeh
The occasion:	The first day of the academic year
Date:	23 September 1979
Source:	*Kayhan*, 24 September 1979

"Kermanshah Education and Learning [Ministry] authorities have the duty to report the [names of] teachers and educators who speak in opposition to Islamic interests, providing us with clear evidence [of that], so that [a proper] decision may be made in their regard. . . . We are fully aware of the current atmosphere and conditions of Kermanshah's schools and intend to identify and prosecute whoever prevents children from studying or speaks against the interests of Islam." He also explained the condition of Kermanshah's prisoners, saying that the facilities that have been created for them and the procedures that have been put in place for their medical care in different prison sections will be improved daily. The Chief Shari'a Judge added, "The religious and Islamic education of the Dizelabad prisoners and setting up meetings and speeches to guide them are among our urgent plans. Through these methods, we try to introduce them to their duties." Regarding the question of a general amnesty for prisoners, he stated, "We will release those prisoners whose crimes are subject to pardon and who are [mainly] Democrats [members of the PDKI—Democratic Party of Iranian Kurdistan], as well as others, upon obtaining a signed statement of a pledge and guarantee [of good conduct]. But regarding a general pardon for those whose cases are not fully clear, and about whom we have received new reports, we will pay closer attention and will proceed with greater caution."
. . . In closing, the [Chief] Shari'a Judge stated: "For those who are not familiar with the [Shari'a] Court's procedures, I must point out that, contrary to the Ministry of Justice judges [who are modern university-educated, secular judges who render decisions on the basis of established rules of civil and criminal procedure], we rule [solely] on the basis of witness testimony, [circumstantial evidence, and] inferences of facts based on judicial determination of certain events. This enables the Shari'a Court to render verdicts expeditiously in each prisoner's case.

Monireh Baradaran

ARRESTED: October 1981
DETAINED IN: Eshratabad Revolutionary Committee, Evin and Gohardasht Prisons
RELEASED: October 1990

1. My name is Monireh Baradaran Khosroshahi. I was born in 1954 in Tabriz, but I went to school in Tehran. I got a B.A. in sociology from the University of Tehran. I continued my studies in Germany after I left Iran, and I have a master's degree in social sciences from the University of Hanover. I was a political prisoner, detained in Evin Prison, during the 1988 massacres of political prisoners.

2. I make this statement in support of an investigation into the mass execution of political prisoners in 1988 in Iran.

3. This statement is true to the best of my knowledge and belief. Except where I indicate to the contrary, I make this statement on the basis of facts and matters within my own knowledge. Where the facts and matters in this statement are within my own knowledge, they are true. Where the facts and matters are not within my own knowledge, I have identified the source or sources of my information, and I believe such facts to be true.

Arrest and Detention

4. I was arrested once before the Revolution and was in prison for six months [June to December 1978]. I was released from the Shah's prison when the people called for the release of political prisoners.

5. The second time I was arrested was in October 1981, on the same day my brother and sister-in-law were arrested. Forty days after his arrest, my brother was executed. Under the Shah, he had been in prison for eight years. I was in prison for nine years, until October 1990.

6. When I came to Germany after I was released, I decided to focus on prison and focus my activities on fighting against torture and the death penalty. I wrote my memoirs of my time in prison in three volumes. The work was translated into German, Dutch, and Danish. In 1999, I received the Medal of Karl von Ossietzky

[of the International League for Human Rights] as a sign of gratitude for my work in writing the book. I wrote two more books relating to prison. One is about the psychology of torture, based upon my own experience. The other is about truth commissions in other countries.

7. I was acquainted with political issues because both my brother and sister were arrested during the time of the Shah. All my cousins were in prison. One of my cousins committed suicide under the Shah after being tortured in prison. My house was filled with political discussions. Naturally, when I entered university at the age of 19, I was drawn to political activities. I was not really affiliated with any particular group. The reason I was arrested under the Shah was because I was trying to smuggle in a communiqué to my brother, who was being held in prison. I was held for six months at that time. I was very active during the Revolution.

8. After the Revolution, I was active because I did not believe that the new situation reflected the principles upon which the Revolution was based. In particular, I disagreed with the compulsory veil, the increased role of the clerics in the courts and Parliament, as well as the censorship of the press, which had led to the banning of most of Iran's newspapers.

9. I became active with a Marxist group, Revolutionary Workers Organization [Rah-e Kargar], and was in this group for about a year and a half before being arrested. The activities were above-ground. We had a student cell, which distributed leaflets in the street about our group's ideals, and we started debates and discussion of important issues in the street and we recruited new members. Our group never believed in armed struggle.

10. I was arrested only because I was known as a leftist in the university.

11. I was first taken to Eshratabad Revolutionary Committee. It was like a military barracks. I was there for about ten days. Then I was taken to Evin, where I was tortured. They were beating me in prison to find out which group I belonged to and what I did for them. Everyone was being beaten because they used to arrest people randomly and did not have information on them. They were beating us so that we would confess. Sometimes detainees would confess to things they had not done, just to escape being tortured.

12. For several days we were held in the hallways outside the prison cells and torture rooms so we could hear people being tortured. We could hear moaning, and there were groups of people everywhere. The rooms were full, overflowing. We were wearing blindfolds, but if you dared to lift your blindfold you could see that people had bandages around their heads, their feet. In the hallways there were both men and women. But in the cells the male and female wards were separate.

13. I was in the hallway for five days. I think that my interrogation and torture lasted altogether seven hours. The torture was beating and flogging the soles of my feet, which was customary at that time. They also flogged my back. There was another

torture that they used at the time: *qapani.*
It often caused problems with the shoulder;
it would dislocate it. They did not hang me
by my shoulder, but they did so to others.
My fingers were numb at first, but after a
few weeks it went away. However, I still
have pain and discomfort in my shoulder.

Trial and the Prison Conditions

14. They did not know anything about me
when I had my trial a year later [October
1982]. I think the religious judge was Mobasheri. They do not introduce themselves,
but from the description of other friends,
I gathered it was Mobasheri. We were not
blindfolded in the trial. He was alone—
there was no prosecutor and there were
only the two of us in the room. It lasted
no more than five minutes. He told me
that I had been accused of demonstrating
in front of the U.S. Embassy. This was the
sort of thing I had acknowledged during
my interrogation, because I thought it was
harmless. I was also charged with being a
Marxist and reading leftist literature. The
religious judge also asked if I would do
an interview and I refused. Two to three
weeks later they showed me a paper on
which it was written that I was sentenced
to three years in prison. A short while later
I was transferred to Qezel Hesar Prison.

15. One year after my trial, they learned more
about me. I was returned to Evin and taken
to solitary confinement, interrogated for
six months, and I had another trial, on a
Thursday in the fall of 1983. The religious
judge and one other person were present.
At my second court [trial], not only was I
charged with my former political activities
but also with organizing protests within

the prison. The second trial lasted a bit
longer than the first one, twenty minutes,
and it was interrupted by the call to noon
prayer. The judge left and didn't come
back. The next day was Friday [Fridays are
a religious holiday], so I had to wait until
Saturday. These two days were difficult
because I thought I might be executed, and
I wanted to get it over with.

16. The charges brought against me were not
true. The judge would cut me off and
ask me personal questions. I had a fiancé.
He would ask me whether I had met his
family, whether they had given me any
gifts—women were asked a lot of personal
questions meant to humiliate them. They
wanted to know if I would give an interview and if I was going to reject my group.
Every person was asked: "Are you going
to denounce your group?" "Are you going
to give us an interview?" Little mattered
that you were not part of any group; they
would ask you, "Would you denounce ALL
groups?" Sometimes it was funny—they
had arrested an Iraqi who they thought was
a spy. They found out he was innocent,
and decided to release him. But before being released he was asked to make a public
denunciation. His interview was broadcast
at the Hosseinyeh, for all the prisoners.
The Iraqi prisoner asked: "What should I
denounce?" The person in charge of the
interview hesitated a moment and said,
"Well, you have to denounce Saddam."

17. I was sentenced to ten years. At the time,
the sentences started when they were issued. They would not count your imprisonment beforehand. So it would have been
13 years for me. I was happy I did not get
the death sentence. When I had this second

Embroidery made by Monireh Baradaran, after the prison massacre. She wrote: "I sewed it in a solitary cell, while I was still under the shock of the killings and overwhelmed by the memory of my young cellmates who had been killed. . . . I was anxious to hide my work from the guards, for having a thread and needle was forbidden, and in solitary confinement we were not allowed to do any crafts. . . . The flowers are the symbols of youth and purity; perhaps they represent my executed cellmates. The sun always represents the truth for me, and the person on the boat represents us, the survivors, who have stayed to tell the story."

trial, Lajevardi [the prosecutor for Evin Prison] had already left the prison—it was the fall of 1984. I think that if I had been caught with the same things two years earlier I would have been executed for what I had done. This time it was a bit better.

18. I was then taken to Qezel Hesar again. A year after I got my ten-year sentence, in 1985, I was pardoned by the Montazeri committee. Many people were released at that time. The first group was the repenters and also people in prison who were passive—they were not really politically active. I was very surprised that I was pardoned after all the punishment and additional sentencing I had received while in prison.

One of the people who came to talk to me about the pardon was from Tabriz and knew my family. He told me that he wanted to get me released. But the head of the prison, Meysam, wanted me to give an interview in front of the prisoners or be videotaped. I refused so they reduced my sentence to three years [instead of releasing me]. About the same time I was transferred to Evin Prison.

19. I had a third trial in Evin in the summer of 1987. Because I refused to give the interview, they gave me a new sentence of ten years. I spent two months in solitary confinement. Then I was taken to the *sar-e moze'i* [i.e. prisoners who defended their

political opinions and remained steadfast] ward, with the other women who refused to give up their views. That summer I was in a very nice ward. I had been there while in prison under the Shah. The people who had been there before us were those who did not have very serious charges. It had a little garden and trees. There were two levels. The doors were open and we had limited access to the garden during the day for specific hours.

20. In early fall, maybe September or October of 1987, they took everyone out of that ward. They took us to the Amuzeshgah [building]. These wards are at the top of Evin hill. They did not exist under the Shah. They had made prisoners themselves construct these buildings. They are very big and I think there were perhaps six wards with three levels, and there were a lot of solitary cells there. I was taken to one of those wards. We were in ward 3, on the third floor. Each of these wards had three levels. We were on the top level. The majority of us were leftist *sar-e moze'i*. There were 40 to 50 MKO *sar-e moze'i* as well. There was also a room of Bahá'ís, maybe 20 or 30 Bahá'ís.

21. More moderate MKO and leftist prisoners, along with some repenters, were held on the second floor. They were not as hardcore. The number of repenters had diminished compared to the years before, because most of them had been released. The first floor where the doors were closed [also called the "solitary" ward, because it had no communication with other wards] was mostly MKO and some leftists. They had brought these prisoners back from

Gohardasht. I do not know why the doors were closed, but I know they had been taken to Gohardasht as a punishment.

22. During the time of Lajevardi, group activities were really prohibited. Any communal life, even eating together, was prohibited. In our lessons in the Hosseinyeh, when we were receiving ideological training or teachings, the idea was that you had to get closer to God, and in order to get closer to God you had to be on your own. Therefore being together with friends would distract us from God. This psychological torture was inspired by the archaic idea that the lonelier the prisoner is, the more prone he/she is to forget everything and doubt his or her beliefs. When you isolate someone, there is an unsettling of ideas; the ideas are confused and you are more open to being influenced by the prison authorities.

23. Most MKO *sar-e moze'i* believed at that time that there should be a very serious and strong distinction between them and the repenters. So, for example, when the repenters brought food for the ward, they would not take the food from them. In practice they were on a hunger strike, because they would not take the food. Most of us, the leftists, were opposed to this kind of behavior. For us it did not make a difference whether the food was brought by the guards or the repenters. The MKO prisoners would also exercise in a group, which was prohibited. Each time the wardens caught them while exercising in a group they would beat them right away. There were permanent clashes between prisoners and the prison guards.

24. Around the end of fall, November or December 1987, we were seeing videos of interviews with prisoners. Since we refused to go to the Hosseinyeh to watch them, they would broadcast them over the loudspeaker so you had to listen to them. These were mostly high-ranking leaders of leftists, mostly the Tudeh members. Mostly these interviews aimed at tarnishing people who had already been executed or people who had refused to take part in the interview. Again it was mostly about the higher-ranking people. In one interview the husband of our cellmate Parvin Goli Abkenary was accused of having collaborated with the regime. He had not given an interview before he was executed, but, nevertheless, the authorities put out the story that he had collaborated. After hearing this, his wife committed suicide by eating depilatory cream. This was one example of a person who was dragged through the mud. It was very hard in the ward, because she had been with us for so long. This event affected us all a lot.

Events Surrounding 1988

25. In February 1988, a representative of the Ministry of Information was in Evin—we knew him as Zamani. He called the whole ward and there was an office and he took the prisoners one by one into his office. He asked two questions, about "the Islamic Republic" and "Islam." He would then say with a sarcastic smile, "This is a democracy, so you can say whatever is on your mind." But most of us said this is an inquisition and I am not going to respond. He would not argue with us, he would just take notes. Some people openly expressed their views. It was surprising that he would neither argue with us nor threaten us for what we were saying. This was totally unprecedented. Before, for a similar response during an interrogation, there would have been punishment. But it was very unusual for a whole ward to be taken and asked about their views.

26. Furthermore, theoretical debate occurred only during the trial, before the prisoner was issued a sentence. But in the winter of 1988, Zamani [representative from the Ministry of Information] had not come to try us. Nothing changed in prison after his visit. And that was unprecedented. We thought these questions and answers were strange and mysterious: first, because we had been already tried and sentenced, and second, because the prison environment had changed a lot. It was not as oppressive. It was much more open; we could protest more easily. We were still being punished if we protested, but still the situation was better. Before we had been forced to call the guards "sister" or "brother." But by now we no longer did this, and the nature of the relations between the inmates and the wardens had changed. We did not feel compelled to follow to the letter all the rules and regulations.

27. Actually, there was no parallel between what was happening outside and what was happening inside. During the 1980s, our society was under a very harsh and oppressive rule. It is true that around the mid-80s there were some openings on the cultural front, but it had nothing to do with the political situation. Ordinary people had re-

nounced political struggle and were trying to live their lives. The opposition groups had been weakened by repression and executions, whereas, we, the political prisoners, were continuing to protest. There was no correlation between what was going on outside in the society and what was going on in the prisons. The war, in spite of its heavy cost for the regime, had no impact on us inside the prisons, at least for us the leftist prisoners. The creation of the MKO army [in Iraq] may have lifted the moral of the MKO prisoners, but not ours. We did not agree with the MKO ideas, and they never spoke to us about their organization's situation. In the early 80s, many of them had decided to keep a low profile and feign repenting. But the leftist prisoners kept resisting and, for instance, refused to pray or to attend the "educational programs" at the Hosseinyeh. The resistance in Qezel Hesar [in the early 80s] led to harsh punishment such as the "boxes" or "the coffins." This was the darkest period of our prison time.

28. I think that around the spring of 1988 (after the New Year, 21 March), there were some changes in the structure of the wards. People who had served their sentences but were kept in prison, the *mellikesh*, some of them were transferred to solitary cells and some to the closed cells (not solitary) downstairs. The Bahá'ís stayed in our ward, ward 3. We knew this because, when we went to the courtyard to get fresh air, there were holes in the windows downstairs, and we could communicate and get information by talking through these holes, exchanging short written notes, or lip reading.

29. From that ward, where the doors were closed, they put some of the MKO in solitary confinement. But one of them, Raf'at Kholdi, had a life sentence and, psychologically, she was really gone, so they took her from our ward to a ward where moderate prisoners were held. Many of her family members had been executed—at least two of her brothers. I don't remember very well. In the summer of 1988, in the midst of the massacres, she also committed suicide by swallowing depilatory cream.

30. There was a closed room in our ward that was an office for the guards, but they never used it. One time, a three-member delegation came there that was called the "pardon delegation." I don't remember the details. I even remember the face of one of them, but nothing more. This happened either shortly before the massacres or shortly after they had started. They called us all and asked if we were praying or if we were willing to write a letter denouncing our group.

31. They [a second delegation] came again. It was about lunchtime when they came in. They came to the rooms, actually. They also said they were the "Pardon Delegation." I think it was late July. I remember clearly; he asked if we were willing to write a letter denouncing [our group]. We were asked to introduce ourselves and respond to the questions. I don't remember if they were taking notes. As far as I remember only one person agreed to do so. She wanted to be released. I remember she said with intense anger, "Yes. I will." Some of the delegation members looked familiar; they had been part of the delegation that Montazeri had sent to the prison. But I am

sure that this delegation had nothing to do with the Death Committee. No one was pardoned after this visit.

32. After that visit, the *mellikesh* were taken away. The atmosphere in our room had changed.

33. I am not sure when this second delegation came—after they took the televisions away or before—but I am not sure when.

34. One night we heard shooting and some noise and commotion. That night, three leftists were executed, and I know their names—they had death sentences. That night the prison environment was especially tense. Two or three days later, visitations were suspended. Each ward had one day of the week for visitations. Some of our cellmates went to visit their brothers or husbands [who were also prisoners]. It was during this visit that they were told visitations were suspended. That same evening, two female guards took the television that we had in the ward. All this happened between 26 and 28 July 1988.

35. That same night, or the following night, at 10:30 p.m, they came and called three MKOs. It was strange; it was not for interrogation—they just told them to come. In a very short period of time afterwards they took several other groups of MKOs. In a few days, from a total of 40 to 50 MKO sympathizers, only 15 were left in our ward.

36. Before, if someone was not well, they would be taken to the prison infirmary—but at that time the guards would not take anyone. They wouldn't bring newspapers, etc., so our relationship with the outside was completely cut off.

37. About five days after they took the first group of MKOs, we were out in the courtyard getting fresh air when an MKO member, who had recently been taken away from our ward, returned and joined us in the courtyard. She was completely pale and did not look normal. She ran towards her MKO friends who were sitting in a corner in the courtyard; during those days no one was in the mood for walking or exercising—people were keeping to themselves. She went to them and told them some things. We felt that in the MKO group there was suddenly some fear, shock, and surprise. We could sense the change of feeling in the group. Later, we heard that she had been taken to ward 209 for interrogation and that the hallways were filled with prisoners—men and women—and they were given a questionnaire to be filled out. They had to respond to the questions prior to the interrogations. And then they were going to a room for interrogation. In the courtyard it was just a few minutes before a Revolutionary Guard came and said, "Why are you here?" and took her away. But the girl had not come on her own. I still don't know why they brought her there for a few minutes. I think that they wanted someone to let the others know what was happening. She was called Zahra (Farzaneh) Mirza'i and was executed the same summer.

38. One day they took the group of 15 MKOs that was left there—they called all of them together. They brought them back around noon to the ward. The group told us that their turn had not come up. They also said there were a lot of people there. I do not know if they were given the paper or not.

They were still in the ward for a few days, still disoriented and waiting—they knew they had to go but no one came for them. I think that around the second half of August they took them too. This was the last MKO group. They never came back. There was one member of that group left. She was an MKO but did not pray. She had distanced herself from the group. She had been in prison for seven years. She was uncomfortable and uneasy and very upset that they had not taken her as well. She was even willing to tell the guards, "You have forgotten me." But they finally called her too and she never came back. Her name was Mahin Qorbani.

39. I think about 40 to 45 MKOs were taken from our ward. No one came back. Their bags and belongings were left all over the rooms. The rooms were empty. In the fall they slowly informed their families and took away their belongings from the ward. At the same times that MKO people were taken from our ward, other MKOs were also taken from ward 1—they were the ones who had been sent to Gohardasht for punishment and brought back to Evin afterward—and MKOs were taken from among the *mellikesh* ward. From these two wards they took all the MKOs who never came back. From ward 2—the more moderate prisoners—they also took the MKO sympathizers. Only a few of them survived. We came to know this because we communicated through the windows while we were in the fresh air.

40. We heard at that time that one woman who was a repenter (and her husband was also a repenter) had seen the execution of some MKO girls from her own ward. I did not hear this from the repenter in person, but she was intentionally taken to observe the executions. She was not among the ones to be executed. She had seen the MKO girls who had been hanged and she had seen how they made a knot of the chador around their necks, but it was knotted around their neck so it would not fall off. They didn't want to execute her, but they wanted her to see the executions. The repenter's husband had been executed too. I am not sure if she had seen her husband's execution, but she was devastated. Even before that, she was not very psychologically stable, but after this she was really not well—she was screaming every night in her sleep.

41. [During the killings,] they took one of our wardmates, Fatemeh (Fardin) Modaress Tehrani, to ward 209 for interrogation. When she came back a few days later, she had turned into an old woman. She told us that there, in ward 209, there were many MKO men who perhaps knew they were going to be executed, but they were in good spirits and were talking and singing together. From there, they were taken to the gallows. Fardin was not an MKO affiliate, and they didn't execute her then. She was a Tudeh affiliate; she was forty and had a daughter. In a few days all her hair turned grey like an old woman's. They executed her in late March 1989. Six months later, I was sent to a solitary cell [because I still refused to sign the paper they required from us before releasing us]. There, I found a coded note carved in the wall by Forouzan Abdi Pirbazari (she was the head of the

[Iranian] volleyball team). She had served her sentence and was a *mellikesh*.

42. Based on what we, women prisoners, sensed at the time, which was confirmed later by the accounts and the memoirs of male prisoners, in mid-August the killing of MKO sympathizers ended. By early September it was time for the leftists. The execution of the men started then. We know that in four or five days many were executed. These were mostly in Gohardasht but some were in Evin Prison. We think that in Evin Prison, whether MKO or leftist, very few survived this process. I think the executions continued through the end of October 1988. Most of the prisoners were executed.

43. Parallel to the execution of male prisoners, as we learned later, the flogging of female leftist prisoners began. We heard this news from a young Bahá'í woman who had been arrested at that time and was in a solitary cell and had been brought to our ward from there. We heard from her that, at each time when it was praying time, there was a call for prayer, and they would take them from their cells and then flog them. We did not know who they were—we learned later that these women were our friends and leftist ward mates, taken to solitary confinement some time before. The first group were leftist *mellikesh* women. Every day they were flogged for refusing to pray. Those who accepted praying were returned to ward 2.

44. Then it was our ward's turn. They took ten to fifteen inmates to court [Death Committee]. The first group that went to court was brought back to the ward shortly afterwards. They told us that in court they had asked them, "Are you Muslim? Do you pray?" I think they may have asked them if they believed in their political groups or not. I think they all said no—except that they said that they still believed in their groups, the groups that had supported the Islamic Republic. [During their trial] these people claimed they had done nothing wrong, because their groups supported the Islamic Republic. They were told they were nonetheless sentenced to flogging because they refused to pray. They were told that their sentence was an "unlimited number of lashes until they either accept praying or die." These people had told the court at that very moment that they were protesting these sentences and they would go on a hunger strike. Two other groups were taken to the court and they had also protested against a similar sentence by going on a hunger strike.

45. By noon, when the call for noon prayer started, the guards came to our ward and took the first group with them. After several days and, for some, after several weeks, a number of the prisoners accepted praying, because they could not bear being flogged for an unlimited period of time. I heard that many of them were trying to find ways to commit suicide. One of them cut her vein, but the guards found her, and they saved her. Later, they brought her back and flogged her.

46. One of them, Soheila Darvish Kohan, died in a solitary cell, but I do not know exactly how. There are two possibilities: she either hanged herself with her chador in her cell, or, since she had some kind of heart

ailment, her heart may have given up under the floggings. I am not sure what explanation was given to her family. For the families of these people who wanted their death certificates, they had marked natural causes. Someone else whose husband was killed in 1988—she had gone to get a certificate—she told me that the death certificate said he had died in his home. It was not unusual for the executed to have fake reasons listed as the cause of death. It would never be marked "execution." I have not heard of any instances where the death certificate said "execution."

47. I think that there were time restrictions on the guards for the floggings—everyone had to be flogged individually and in the half hour within the prayer call. With the large number of inmates refusing to pray, there was a waiting list for the people to be flogged. Only when some prisoners agreed to pray was there room for new ones. We were just waiting our turn. We were sure it was going to come to us too—we were teasing each other about how we could limit the impact of the floggings. One would say, "I would put a platter under my chador on my back; then they would flog me and it would make a noise and they would think they would be doing so well that it makes this noise." One would say she would put a pillow [under her chador] and then we said that they would tell her, "Well, you have never had a hunchback!" She said she would reply, "Oh you know I have always had it, you just never noticed." Psychologically, we needed to make fun of events. At the beginning, Mojtaba Halva'i, the famous torturer, was flogging female inmates himself. But later, female guards took over, and they were flogging the prisoners. They used to flog on the back and so [the prisoners] had black and blue bruises on their backs; sometime after they were returned to the ward, the bruises started to heal.

48. In late September 1988, a man by the name of Forutan became the new head of the prison. He had also been the head of the prison for a short period after Lajevardi left in 1984. He gathered us all together, and he introduced himself and asked if we had any requests. Obviously, no one even raised his head to respond to him. He said that the visitations are going to start, again, so you can give the phone number of your house to the guards. About a week later there were visitations. Forutan had also gone to the solitary cells and told the recalcitrant prisoners that the flogging was over, "So break your hunger strike." The women had asked, "How can we be sure?" He told them, "It is over, I tell you, I am the new head of the prison." First, the prisoners didn't believe him, but when they saw that the flogging had, in fact, stopped, they stopped their hunger strike. Two of them had been on hunger strike for 21 or 22 days while being flogged several times a day. They were brought back to the ward ten days after they had stopped their hunger strike. They still looked like the dead—when we saw them, we started to cry. Not only had they lost a lot of weight, but they also were peeling because of dehydration. They could not walk straight, and I think they probably had marks from the floggings, but in prison we did not necessarily show these things to each other.

49. The visitations started. That is when we learned about the scope of the killings. Our families came into the visitation rooms crying because outside large numbers of people discovered that they had no one to visit, and the guards kept telling them, "Wait here, you do not have anyone to visit." They did not really give them the news there. They would send them to a district revolutionary committee—there they would get their loved one's bags. They would not tell everyone at the same time—[informing them] happened over a period of two months.

50. In each visitation, we would hear the names [of executed prisoners] from our families, because our families had known each other, because they had been visiting their prisoners together for years. We estimated that from the female wards—and the ones below—between 200 and 250 women had been killed. I couldn't estimate how many men were executed. Our ward mates who had brothers or husbands in prison came back, and most of them said that their relatives had been executed.

51. In October 1990, I was finally released. Six months after the killings, they had started to release everyone else. The men were released before the women. In the women's ward we were still there for a few years. Some of us were released and some others were sent on leave from prison. They sent them on leave and brought them back repeatedly, and eventually they let them stay out permanently.

52. Naserian himself threatened me that if I refused to recant they would either kill me or leave me forever in a solitary cell. He sent me to solitary confinement where I was kept for six months.

53. Even the families were treated with the utmost cruelty. After the massacres, many of us had visitations with our families in a room without the glass [partition], in the presence of Naserian himself. They used this situation to put pressure on the inmates' families and force them to pressure us to give in and recant. At that time, both my parents had passed away. My sister had come to visit me; I was still in solitary confinement then. Before bringing her in, they had asked her to stand aside, because they wanted to tell her something. And then they had told her that her hijab was not appropriate. This was exactly how they had treated the executed prisoners' relatives in the previous months: using false excuses to make them wait. My sister thought that I had been executed. She fainted. There were no women there, so there was no one who could slap her. The men would not touch her, so they threw a bucket of cold water over her. When my sister came in and I hugged her, she was all wet, and she was blue. When we met, I asked her, "Why are you wet?" She told me to be careful and take care of myself. Naserian would say, "Tell her to repent." My sister said, "She has done nothing. Why are you keeping her?" This was two weeks after Khomeini's death. She was very brave, but she did not understand what she was saying. "Now that Khomeini is dead why are you still keeping her?" Naserian said, "You too are an anti-revolutionary! Get out!"

Frankfurt, July 2009

OFFICIAL STATEMENT • 3

Subject: Message to the Iranian people on the subjects of dealing with strikers, the necessity of a
               Cultural Revolution, and the role of the press [excerpts]
The official: Founder and Supreme Leader of the Islamic Republic of Iran, Ayatollah Ruhollah Khomeini
The occasion: The beginning of the Iranian New Year
Date: 22 March 1980
Source: *Sahifeye-nur* [The Book of Light], Tehran, Ministry of Culture and Islamic Guidance, 1982,
               Volume Twelve, p. 19–24

5. The government is responsible for providing workers, farmers, and laborers with the necessary means and tools of production. In return, they should be aware that strikes and deliberate slow-downs will not only strengthen the superpowers, but will also cause the rising downtrodden people of the world, in both Muslim and non-Muslim countries, to lose heart and hope. Whenever the workers of a plant go on strike in any city, the citizens must immediately meet with them in order to find out what their complaints or demands are. They must identify all anti-revolutionary elements [who incite strikes] and denounce them to the people. The noble people of Iran can no longer pay wages to the godless in their midst [allusion to socialist militants working in factories]. . . .

11. There must be a fundamental [cultural] revolution in all Iranian universities, in order to purge all professors and lecturers who hew to the East or the West. The university must thus become a healthy atmosphere for the teaching of advanced Islamic sciences. We must fully discard the flawed educational policies and programs for higher education created in the pre-revolutionary regime. They have been the main cause of all the calamities that befell Iranian society in that era. Had a principled

university system been in place, we would never have faced a class of intellectuals who, in the most critical hour of our history, were rent by internecine dissention and disagreements, alienated from their own people and so oblivious to what was taking place in their country as to seem to be living in another world. Every failure and setback that we have suffered has been caused by the failure of our university-educated intellectuals to correctly understand our Islamic society, a failure that continues to plague us even today. Most of the fatal blows to our society have come from these same intellectuals who have always considered themselves, and still consider themselves, superior and who are engaged in a discourse understandable only to their peers, leaving ordinary Iranians in the dark. What is not important to them is the people of Iran, for these intellectuals are completely self-absorbed. They were raised in the Shah's flawed educational system and have absorbed its false teachings and thus never had any respect for the downtrodden and, unfortunately, still don't. . . .

Seminary and university students must pore over the basic Islamic tenets and abandon the slogans offered by deviant groups and replace all false values and ideas with those of our revered Islam.

They should know that Islam is a rich creed and, therefore, never in need of incorporating alien tenets. All of you must know that eclecticism is tantamount to a grave betrayal of Islam and Muslims. The undesirable consequences of such eclecticism will appear in later years. Unfortunately, as the result of a faulty and inaccurate understanding of Islam, some have combined Islamic principles with Marxist ideas and created an amalgam that is completely alien to the progressive laws of Islam. Dear students! Do not tread the deviant paths chosen by uncommitted [to the Islamic Revolution] university intellectuals, lest you alienate your own people. . . .

12. Another issue concerns the press. . . . Once more, I call upon you, the members of the Iranian press, to unite and write freely, but do not engage in conspiracies. . . . I have repeatedly reiterated [my belief] that the press should be free and independent. Unfortunately, and surprisingly, however, I have noticed that some newspapers have unfairly helped, and are still helping, to realize the evil objectives of the left and the right in Iran. In every country, the press performs an essential task in creating either a healthy or unhealthy atmosphere. I hope that our press will move to serve both God's will and the people's interests.

A newspaper photograph of a pro-Khomeini demonstration on 23 November 1978—
Pars News Agency

Hossein Behbudi

ARRESTED: 1976
RELEASED: October 1978
RE-ARRESTED: October 1983
DETAINED IN: Evin and Gohardasht Prisons
RELEASED: February 1989

1. My name is Hossein Behbudi.* I was born in the city of Rasht in 1954. I was a political prisoner held at Gohardasht Prison during the 1988 massacre of political prisoners in Iran.

2. I make this statement in support of an investigation into the mass execution of political prisoners in 1988 in Iran.

3. This statement is true to the best of my knowledge and belief. Except where I indicate to the contrary, I make this statement on the basis of facts and matters within my own knowledge. Where the facts and matters in this statement are within my own knowledge, they are true. Where the facts and matters are not within my own knowledge, I have identified the source or sources of my information, and I believe such facts to be true.

Background Information
Prison Conditions and Torture Under the Shah

4. The first time I was arrested, it was under the Shah, when I was an industrial engi-

neering student and was in my fourth year at Tehran University of Technology. I was charged with actively supporting the Fadaiyan Khalq Organization (FKO). Though I was openly supporting the FKO, I was not armed. I was arrested in 1976 and was in prison until the Revolution. I was released in October 1978.

5. Under the Shah's regime [as political prisoners] we were under pressure during the interrogation. Physical and psychological pressure aimed at forcing us to give out information regarding the organization. We were tortured. The worse kind of torture, as far as I was concerned, was flogging on the soles of the feet with a cable. During the Shah's era it was called flogging; in the Islamic Republic it was called *ta'zir* (Islamic punishment). Many of your nerves go through the soles of your feet, and the foot is stronger and it can resist longer so they can beat you for a longer period of time. It does not leave a trace and disappears pretty fast. They would beat you until your feet were swollen and the skin would crack and they would continue beating it. Because the blood

---

*The witness used the name Akbar Sadeqi in homage to his friend, who was executed in 1988, in the companion volume by Geoffrey Robertson.

coagulates in those areas, the kidneys cannot refine the blood, and it can kill the prisoner. At this point the interrogators would take you to the infirmary and "dialyze" you, in order to clean the blood, so that they could carry on the flogging and the interrogation [without killing the detainee]. Under the Shah, I was not flogged so bad that I needed dialysis, but under the IRI, I had to be transferred to the infirmary and stayed there for several days.

6. Both under the Shah and under the IRI, members of groups engaged in armed struggle were treated more harshly and subjected to more torture than members of non-violent opposition groups. Ill-treatment aimed at breaking the detainees quickly and extracting information about their next organizational [clandestine] meeting. Under the Islamic Republic, the MKO sympathizers, in particular, were under more pressure than the others, followed respectively and decreasingly by the FKO (Minority), Peykar, Rah-e Kargar, and then only the FKO (Majority) members.

7. I had a court hearing during this first detention under the Shah. It was an in-camera court proceeding, held in a room. During the Shah's time, they [the authorities] would provide the defendant with a lawyer. I was given the choice between two lawyers designated by the authorities. After eight months in solitary confinement and having no idea that I was about to be tried, right before the trial I talked to my lawyer and realized that I was being taken to court. The lawyer did not really defend me, rather he encouraged me to ask for a

pardon. My charge was being involved in activities for the FKO and acting against national security: organizing and partici-pating in demonstrations and distributing [pro-FKO] leaflets in the university. I was sentenced to six years in prison.

8. One year after I was sentenced to prison, the situation in prison improved. I was released on 1 October 1978 [a few months before the victory of the Revolution], and rejoined my organization. I was released with one thousand other political prisoners in Iran, and the newspapers reported that, as well.

9. After the Revolution, precisely after June 1980, the FKO split into two main groups—the Majority and the Minority. The Minority thought they had to oppose the Islamic Republic of Iran (IRI), because they [the IRI] were against the people. The Majority thought the IRI "anti-imperial-ist," they should have an alliance but be critical at the same time—to tell them [the IRI] their problems but support them. I was a member of the FKO (Majority).

10. After my release in 1978, I took a job as a cartographer in a company. But this was not my main activity; I had become one of the full-time [professional] cadres of our organization. The FKO (Majority) was not a guerrilla group anymore and had expanded. I believe it was the biggest leftist political organization in the country. Both in terms of membership and influ-ence, it had surpassed the Tudeh Party. I was in charge of the organization of the FKO (Majority) in one of Tehran's districts and a member of the larger Tehran region's committee, but this [my responsibilities

within the organization] was not uncovered during the interrogations. So, along with my work in the organization, I had also kept my normal job. And hence, if we had a financial problem, the organization would help us. My wife was also working for the FKO (Majority). Besides working at the organization, she was a high school teacher. I was active in the party until I was arrested in 1983.

Arrest and Detention after the Islamic Revolution

11. In October 1983, I was arrested in the street, by chance. Perhaps the Revolutionary Guards were following someone else, their behavior was very strange, so I do not know whether they were following me or whether they found me accidentally. It appeared to me that it was an accident, because, at the time, my political activism was underground.

12. When, in 1983, the Tudeh Party was outlawed and the authorities started to arrest its members, we, the main cadres of the FKO (Majority) were ordered to go into hiding. When Kianuri [Tudeh's secretary general] was arrested, it became clear that all political activists close to Tudeh [such as members of the FKO (Majority)] were at risk. Therefore, and in particular after the televised confessions of Kianuri were broadcast, our cadres were hastily transferred to safe houses and were given pseudonyms and forged ID cards. But [at the time of my arrest] I still hadn't received my pseudonym and my fake ID. The Guards stopped me and asked for my ID, I showed them my real ID, the one I used for

my work. Perhaps they became suspicious by just looking at my demeanor, although they had no reason to be suspicious; I had no beard (like the Hezbollahi) and no mustache and eye glasses (like the MKO affiliates), I just looked like an ordinary civil servant, so there was no need to arrest me. At the time, random arrests were made based on how people looked, for people's physical appearance was a sign of their political affiliation. I think they were looking for someone else, and, incidentally, I went where they were waiting for this person. They looked at my ID. They called Evin Prison and gave my name, and Evin Prison had the list of former political prisoners from the time of the Shah, and they looked it up and said, "Arrest him."

13. They first took me to Karaj Beltway. At that time, they had set up checkpoints in the highways around Tehran; repenters or guards were posted at the checkpoints and were searching the cars. They blindfolded me and took me somewhere near the Karaj Beltway. I had heard that a leftist militant had repented and was identifying [newly] arrested members of the organization. The repenter in question knew me from my time at university; he was a member of Rah-e Kargar. I recognized him when I saw his hand through my blindfold, and later, when I heard his voice, I had no doubt about his identity. I said, "Why am I here? I am an ordinary person?" I had an unpublished communiqué of the FKO (Majority) about the blows the organization had suffered in 1983 [when the government started to dismantle it and arrest its members]. I was one of the members who was supposed to publish and disseminate

this communiqué. I had hidden it very well in my car, but they found it. It was in a Kleenex box on top of the dashboard. I denied that it was mine. I said, "I bought this just like that. I am a taxi driver. People to whom I give rides may have left it in the box." They beat me right there and said, "Tell us where this comes from." I denied knowing anything about it: "It is not mine, and I am not part of any faction." The repenter retorted, "Akbar Sadeqi, FKO (Majority) member, former student of the San'ati University. . . and you pretend to be a nobody!!!" I replied: "I was [all this] in the past, but now I am not part of any group."

Interrogation

14. I was transferred to Evin. Upon my arrival there they took me to the basement and started to beat me with a cable so that I would give out my appointments [time and locations] and the address of my residence. I gave my mother's home address. I wanted my family to find out that I was arrested and warn my wife in order for her to take the material related to the party out of our house, which in fact she did. Hence, she went into hiding and avoided arrest.

15. When flogged 50 or 60 lashes on the soles of the feet, many people faint or they get sick. Seventy lashes takes 15 minutes. Then they would take you for a walk for ten minutes, and then they would start flogging again. I don't remember how many lashes I received; I was focused on what to say so that I wouldn't give out any information. Between two lashes there is a second or two, which are the most beautiful moments, because the brain is working so fast

to help you avoid giving away any information. It is very beautiful. Under the Shah, they used to put you on your back and flog you. The Islamic Republic interrogators put you on your stomach, because it is easier to beat the sole of the foot. They would tie up your hands and feet and fasten your mouth and start flogging. If you wanted to talk, you should raise your finger. As soon as you did so, the flogging would stop and the interrogator would say, "Talk!" But if you played with them and talked nonsense, the flogging would start immediately. It is so much easier to be told that you will be punished and you are going to get 100 lashes, than to be told you are going to be flogged until you give up the locations of your appointments. When you know how many lashes you are going to take, you count or you scream and so on, but when you don't know how many lashes there will be, it becomes really hard. Some people have become repenters only because of the unbearable pain of such torture. When you give out what you know, the lashes stop for a while. Even many prisoners give information about imaginary appointments to stop the flogging for a while. I called the seconds between the two lashes "happiness." I read somewhere: "According to the interrogators, as well as the prisoners, the worst method of torture is flogging with a cable wire." It is interesting to know that people who are being flogged to give out information make noises such as no wild animal can make. But those who are being flogged for punishment make no noise. They remain stoically silent, because they know how many lashes they have to endure, 20 or 30, and then it will be over.

Three letters and two receipts from Shahram Shahbakhshi, who was arrested in 1981 and executed in the summer of 1988. The two documents in the foreground are receipts his mother received when she sent money to him in prison. Behind the receipts are three letters from him. The middle one, dated June 20, 1988, is the last letter he wrote from prison.

16. I was in ward 209 of Evin Prison for two and a half months. During the first month and a half, sometimes they would take me to the basement to be flogged and then bring me back up into the hallway and handcuff me to the radiator. After a month and a half in the hallway, I was taken to a cell that I shared with two others. I had no visitations. I was intensely interrogated every day, but I didn't divulge any secret information. I even managed not to reveal my wife's real name. My wife's last name had a suffix, and I gave her name without a suffix so that she couldn't be identified; she had also been a political prisoner under the Shah. Had I divulged her complete surname they would have identified and arrested her.

17. From Evin I was transferred to Gohardasht Prison. But I was still under interrogation. They put me in a solitary cell for eight months. I thought they would continue to interrogate me, but apparently I was put in the cell just in case new arrests would reveal new information about me, based on which they could start interrogating me again. I thought I had done well up until then, and for now they were leaving me alone. When you divulge very little information so that they could not figure you

out, or when you give out all your information, they leave you alone. But when you are in the middle and you divulge slowly and bit by bit what you know and they learn progressively about you from other detainees, you remain for a long time and constantly under interrogation.

18. In Gohardasht Prison, we were more harassed and humiliated. It was easier to bear prison hardship and humiliation under the Shah, because I was single and had no wife and child. The interrogators under the Shah were very vulgar and would insult your mother and your sister, but we had learned not to show any sensitivity about that, or else they would discover our weak spot. The interrogators in the Shah's prisons were trained in the U.S. or Israel. They were all older than we were. Therefore, when they tortured or insulted us we were less offended. But in the IRI prisons, we were blindfolded, but we still could tell from the voices if the interrogators were our age or younger. We were revolutionaries ourselves, while most of them had not even participated in the Revolution. They mostly had little education. So, when they insulted us, we used to get really offended. For instance, once one of the interrogators talked about my wife in a disrespectful way. I responded, "Watch your tongue! Or else I will reciprocate." So he began to beat me up.

19. I had my first visitation ten months after my arrest. I was spending my last month in Gohardasht Prison when I was allowed a visitation, and my mother came to see me. My mother had told me that if I were arrested again she would kill herself. And I feared she might have killed herself [upon my arrest]. She came with my sister. The visitation was through a glass partition and over the phone.

20. After eight months in Gohardasht, they transferred me to Evin Prison, to a room with 30 inmates in ward 3 of the Amuzeshgah section. Upon my arrival, they asked me if I was praying, and I said I was not. So they put me in a room where people were not praying. It felt good psychologically, though we were 30 people in the room. There were 14 rooms in each ward. We were in a very small space, 15 square meters [161 square feet]. Each person had 30 centimeters [less than 12 inches] for sleeping, so we had to sleep on our sides, like books. Three times a day we could use the restrooms; 30 inmates had 20 minutes to use the restrooms. The time for the first round would change every day. For instance if today the first round was at 8 a.m. [for our room], the following day it would be noon and this would create a situation for some of our cellmates who were forced to use plastic bowls or plastic milk bottles and urinate in the presence of their cellmates. And sometimes I would say, jokingly, I aspire neither to socialism, nor to freedom, but only to have a restroom.

Trial

21. I believe it was early 1985 when they took me to the court. The whole trial lasted between 10 and 15 minutes—I was given no notice and no lawyer. In court, they mentioned something that had not come up in my interrogations, but I knew it had been divulged by another prisoner. They told me that I had been in charge of collecting the weapons [taken from military

barracks, by our members, during the insurrectional days of February 1979] and handing them over to the Islamic Republic's authorities. I denied the fact and said I had no such responsibility. Had I answered yes to this question they would have wanted to know how many arms had I collected from where and from whom? The charges brought against me were being responsible for the FKO (Majority) in a small district of Tehran, as well as being in charge of a commission that spearheaded democratic activities, similar to present-day NGOs (women, unemployed, teachers, etc). As I tried to deny the charge [of collecting and returning arms], the judge said, "You know what happens if we discover that you were, in fact, in charge of collecting arms? Beating to death [he used the Arabic expression]. He threatened me and I was really scared.

22. There was a religious judge and two non-religious individuals. I was taken to court blindfolded, but once in the courtroom, they took off my blindfold. A cleric was sitting in front of me and two individuals were behind me, and I couldn't see them. [The judge] asked me if I was Marxist or a Muslim. I said, "I am a political person. I am supporting the FKO (Majority)." He said, "Respond to my question." I replied, "I am political and not interested in ideology [meaning that I supported FKO for political reasons and not for ideological reasons].

23. Two or three weeks later, I received my sentence. They came to my room and they called my name. The Revolutionary Guard showed me the sentence and said, "Sign it." It said seven years. I signed it. At the time they did not count the interrogation period. So I had to stay in prison for seven more years in addition to the two years that I had already served. After my trial I was transferred back to the ward 7 or 8 of Gohardasht Prison. But the names of the wards were changed later on.

Prison Conditions

24. At that time, every two weeks we had visitations. And every two weeks we were allowed to write a letter. [We did not have any] paper or pens; only when we wanted to write our letters did they give us pen and paper, and you had to write the letter immediately and then give the pen back. You could write only four lines. Officially I wrote the letters to my sister, but real addressee was my wife. But we didn't have a regular schedule for writing letters. Sometimes the gap was more than two weeks, and we had such an opportunity every three weeks or only every month.

25. In early 1986 or so, Montazeri's delegations came to the prison, and things improved. This was in Gohardasht Prison. As a result, the insults and humiliation decreased. There were fewer clashes between us and the guards. Novels and educational books were provided. This period lasted less than a year.

26. At some point, in early 1987, they [the prison officials] put us along with the MKO sympathizers and members of other groups in the same ward. This was a strange move. The MKO sympathizers were always together [avoiding contact with people from other groups]. But we were constantly in contact with other groups.

27. In early 1987, prisoners in Gohardasht
    Prison, in particular the MKO sympathiz-
    ers, became more outspoken and started to
    protest against the prison's bad conditions.
    Before, leftist prisoners were more vocal
    than the MKO affiliates. But usually we
    [the leftists] would be just two or three to
    protest and express our demands, whereas
    the MKO prisoners would protest collec-
    tively [all of them together]. They would
    demand the right to "exercise collectively"
    and would start exercising together. The
    Guards would deny them the right to
    exercise collectively and would beat them,
    but somehow the beating was not as bad
    as before. Or, for instance, when there was
    not enough food or if he had found worms
    in the food, we would raise our concern
    with the head of the prison, telling him,
    "We will go on a hunger strike if the food's
    quality is not improved." At that time our
    spirit was stronger, we were less fearful of
    them. There was less pressure [from them].
    This was also the time MKOs prisoners
    were receiving uplifting news from outside,
    telling them that the MKO situation was
    good and that victory was within reach.
    The stronger spirit of the leftists was due
    to the fact that they sensed an increase of
    popular discontent vis-a-vis Khomeini's
    regime and the regime's difficult position
    in the war with Iraq. During the Shah's
    regime, prisoners' protests were strongly
    repressed. My understanding was that
    [sooner or later] the ongoing protests would
    be also suppressed. Prisoners had grown
    bolder and their movement was changing
    from defensive to offensive.

28. In March 1988, we were still all together
    with the MKO. Later, in the spring of 1987,

for no apparent reason, the MKOs were
separated from us. One morning, they
took them somewhere where there were
no prisoners from other groups. After this,
the tension within the prison increased.
Every month, prison wardens would come
to check the ward. If they found a piece
of writing [by a prisoner] or handicrafts
[made by prisoners] they would tear it
down, or break it or confiscate it. This
had become a major issue with the prison
wardens. To which was added the fact that
they deprived us of newspapers or would
give very few newspapers. Recreation had
become another cause of problems, for the
wardens started first to reduce and then to
suspend our time of recreation. Shortage of
food was another issue. All these problems
would make prisoners go on strike. They
would first protest verbally and then show
their discontent through their acts. For
example they would put the food outside
the ward and not eat it.

29. To know how much bolder the prisoners
    had grown, suffice it to remember that
    during the time Lajevardi was producing
    repenters in great numbers, the MKO af-
    filiates, no matter how steadfast they were,
    never dared to say the name "Mojahedin"
    when they were talking about their group.
    If asked about their charges, they would
    say they were sympathizers of *monafeqin*
    [i.e., hypocrites]. If they used "Mojahe-
    din," they would be beaten so much that
    they would end up saying *monafeqin*.
    But at this time—in 1987—when asked
    about their affiliation, the MKOs would
    say "the organization," instead of using
    "hypocrites." It was a subtle but important

change, and it showed that their spirits were higher. They were beaten but they were not beaten so badly, so they would not give in. Rarely would they use [the term] "hypocrites" when alluding to their affiliation. Among the leftists, we would not fight for the name. But we had grievances [and would express them]. But the [prison authorities'] pressure started to increase progressively. So, for example, the guards would first take the prisoner to *zir hasht* and give him a warning. [In case the prisoner resisted] they would give him a few slaps. A few days in solitary confinement were the next punishment. But all this didn't deter the prisoners who grew more resilient instead.

30. Eight or nine months prior to the killings in Gohrdasht [fall 1987 or winter 1988], during the parliamentary elections, they blindfolded all the prisoners and took them out. They told us, "People who want to vote, come and stand on this side." I think ninety percent did not go. They threatened us all—"You don't want to vote; so what is your name?"—just to scare us and make us vote. There was one fellow organization member who had militated under my supervision years earlier. He asked me, "What should we do?" I said, "It is your own choice, but I won't vote."

31. They also had questionnaires. It used to be called "the exam." It very politely asked us the usual questions: "What organization were you active in? Do you still believe in your organization? If not, why? What do you think about the war? What do you suggest for improving the conditions in the prison?" This was in 1987. We each had a questionnaire; we were allowed to sit next to each other while filling it out but were not allowed to talk. For each question there was one space to write the answer. Some of the *sar-e moze'i* prisoners would respond earnestly: "The war is a bad idea for such and such reasons" or "the prison is a bad place; we should not even be here." They would even give their opinions about the regime. But I thought that we should not give accurate responses to these questions, because this was not a real discussion or a fair public debate. From my point of view, the whole process resembled more of an interrogation, because they wanted to know what we thought. These questions were given to us by the Ministry of Intelligence to collect information. So, some prisoners had somehow been informed about their organizations' official positions, publicized in a congress outside the country. And when given the form, they had inadvertently given, as their opinions, the official positions of their organizations. When one of the prisoners told us that he had done so, we asked him, "Why did you do that? Didn't your interrogator ask you how you know these things [the official positions of your organization]?" This prisoner was called in again and told, "Well! your opinions match your party's positions defined in their recent congress." I had heard before that, in Qezel Hesar, seven or eight sympathizers of the MKO had been executed in 1983 and 1984 for having given as their own opinions the MKO's official positions. [This was considered by the authorities to be the proof of the existence of an organized MKO network within the prison that was connected to the MKO outside the prison.]

Events Surrounding 1988

32. There was one point of view that held that prisoners' demands and actions in prison left the regime with no other option than to violently repress them. The other view held that the decision made to eliminate the MKOs and the leftists came from above and had nothing to do with the prisoners' attitude in the prisons. I am not sure which point of view was the correct one. But surely a mass killing of such magnitude couldn't have been an ordinary prison disciplinary measure.

33. The televisions in the wards were controlled remotely. They would turn them on and off whenever they wanted to. On 29 July 1988, newspapers and televisions were taken away. The visitations were cancelled as well. When they took the televisions, and prisoners asked why, the guards refused to respond. They would also not let us out for recreation. It was not unusual for them to be late for the recreation. We started knocking and said, "Sir, it appears you forgot! It is 8 o'clock. You should have opened the doors at 7." The guards said, "Ok, later." We kept knocking for one hour, but then they said that the recreation has been suspended. We said, "What do you mean it is suspended? Why has it been suspended?" but they ignored us. So there were different views about what to do about this—some suggested that we should keep knocking and refuse lunch and dinner until they explain why they have suspended our recreation time. Others said, "No, we first have to find out what is going on, and we should wait and

get in touch with other wards [to see if they know something]." There was a ward on the other side of the courtyard in front of our ward. The distance between the two wards was about 20 or 30 meters [66 or 99 feet]. Morse is usually useful when you are wall-to-wall neighbors. We would do Morse code with lights. We called this one "light Morse." The other ward responded that "their situation was the same, no television and no recreation." This ward was in a two-story building. It had two large corridors and its wards were separated from each other on the both sides. The public ward was on the upper floor, and on the lower floor was the solitary ward. Every one of these wards could hold up to 120 people. Our ward and their ward took turns to go get fresh air. We realized that everyone was in the same situation, and they wanted to go on strike.

34. From 29 July to 27 August 1988, we had neither family visits nor any news [from the outside world]. They would not even take anyone to the infirmary. One of the inmates was really sick. I think they took him to the infirmary, but they never returned him to the ward to update us. Basically, no one left the ward for that period of time. They made sure we were not informed of anything, and we were kept in complete ignorance of what was going on. Two or three months before these events, they had separated the prisoners according to their sentence and took the prisoners who had sentences of more than ten years to another ward. The prisoners had reacted by going on strike; they wanted to know why their situation

had changed. The ward in front of our ward was for the *mellikesh*. They also suggested going on strike. One of those whose story always saddens me was Mr. Sirus Adibi, who worked at the Water Organization. He was a low-ranking member of our organization. He was arrested in 1982. There was nothing incriminatory in his dossier. He refused to give a televised confession, so he remained in prison, as a *mellikesh*, until 1988 and was executed in the summer. There were a lot of these examples.

35. In one of the secondary wards there were approximately 30 sympathizers of the MKO. On 9 or 11 August, the MKO prisoners informed us via Morse codes that a cleric along with two others had come to their ward the previous night and had taken out the prisoners one by one and had asked them, "What is your charge?" meaning what was your political affiliation. They had taken with them whoever had responded, "affiliation with the Mojahedin" and left the ones who had said "affiliation with the *monafeqin*" in the ward. They also added that 27 of their cellmates, who had been taken away, were either transferred somewhere else or executed. But, because the MKO were notorious for exaggerating the news, we did not take their execution stories seriously. We figured that the absentees must have been transferred but we didn't know why the transfer had taken place at night.

36. During this same month something strange happened. They brought in a big truck. Our ward looked over the courtyard, and we had managed to make a hole in the blind so that we could see outside.

At about 1 or 2 a.m. one of these nights—I used to read at night, I slept late—I heard [the sound of] a truck engine. So I went to the room where the blind was pierced—the doors of the cells within the ward were open. I saw a big truck negotiating its way into the yard with difficulty. I wondered what this was; we had become very sensitive about everything. I had never seen a vehicle like this coming into the prison at 2 a.m. My friend and I woke up a prisoner who was a sympathizer of the Ranjbaran Party and a truck driver by profession. We asked him about the truck and he told us, "You came and woke me up for this? This is a truck for frozen meat!" We asked him what such a truck was doing here. He laughed and said, "What do I know what they are doing with it? They [the prison authorities] are crazy; maybe they are bringing us frozen meat." At the time it didn't occur to us what it was used for. But later we realized that it was there to move out dead bodies.

37. That day or a couple of days later, I cannot remember clearly, there was a huge commotion downstairs. Naserian and Lashkari were there. Lashkari was the head of prison security. Naserian was the former interrogator of the MKO. We saw Lashkari with a military gas mask. We knew Lashkari. We used to see him every day, and we could recognize him from his demeanor and his height. He was giving directions at the same place where we had seen the truck. They were spraying the space where the truck had been. It was like the process they used every year to get rid of scorpions, grasshoppers, and other bugs. Gohardasht was in the middle of a wilderness. So it was

not necessarily unusual. But that yearly sanitizing had become a cause of laughter, because it was this old guard who was supposedly spraying and, since he was confused, he did more spraying of us than of anything else. The fact that Lashkari was doing this himself was unusual, and it was doubly strange that it was being done in the garden. All the indications pointed to something strange: this unusual spraying, the frozen meat truck in the prison's yard, and the transfer of the 27 MKO affiliates who had not used the appellation *monafeq*. But we still couldn't imagine that something like this [mass killing] was happening.

38. On 27 August, the ward's doors opened. They said those whose names were called should put their blindfolds on and come out. It was precisely lunchtime. My name was among the ones called. There were 25 of us. We put on our blindfolds and went out, and though we were anxious, we were also excited, because we were finally going to go out to see what was happening. We thought they would ask us the same specific questions: "Do you say your prayers? Do you still believe in your organization? Are you ready to give a televised confession?" Before, all of us, *sar-e moze'i,* would say that we did not pray, we were still believing in our organization, and we would not give a televised interview [public confession]. But it had been three or four months since we came to the conclusion that these answers increased the number of *mellikesh*. The prisoner should say: "I do not have an opinion. I do not know. I am not out, [so I do not] know if I still believe

or not. But I will not give a televised interview." We should not answer very strongly. My closest friend had the same opinion, and he knew that, from the bottom of my heart, I did not like to answer this way. He warned me before I went out, "Don't lose it, boy!"

39. We were on the third floor. We were taken to the first floor, and what we saw there were many people sitting and waiting there. It was the same hallway but on the floor below. Lashkari arrived with a piece of paper in his hand. He just asked, "What is your charge?" and then he asked, "Do you still believe in your organization?" I said, "Well, I am in prison, what do I know?" "Are you going to give us an interview?" "No." He did not ask us about prayers, because he knew we did not say our prayers. The 25 of us gave similar answers.

40. We were all blindfolded, and we could not talk to each other. The guards were walking past, all the time, making sure we wouldn't talk to each other. I [discreetly] asked the fellow sitting next to me, "What was their question for you?" He said, "If I still believed in my organization." I said, "What do you think they mean by asking this question?" He said, "Nothing, it is the usual exam question." I replied, "I think it is much more serious than that." My understanding was that, since they had accepted [UN]Resolution 598 and Khomeini had drunk the cup of poison, meaning that they had been forced to accept peace, now they would have to reconstruct the country and free the prisoners. But since they don't want to release the prisoners before break-

ing them, they want to put pressure on us so that we agree to make televised confessions and attend the Friday Prayer. And only then would they release a great number of prisoners. They then led us toward a room, at the door of which a number of people were waiting.

41. I went in the room. They told me, "Take off your blindfold." So I thought that this was a good sign. I thought it meant that there would be a real questioning and that some high-ranking officials were present. But it also could be scary, because they let the people who were going to be executed remove their blindfolds, because they no longer cared if they saw their faces. But that also was just a thought—it was not what I focused on at the time. I saw three people sitting. There was a big table and everything looked very official. There was Lashkari at a table without a clerical robe, Nayyeri, and Eshraqi. There was another one—I am still not sure about his name—but he was the prosecutor of Karaj at the time, and currently [2009] he is the Minister of Interior, but at the time he was young and dressed normally, not like a member of the clergy. Nayyeri had a piece of paper. Before interrogating me, he said, "We are a delegation to review the situation of prisoners, so respond to our questions."

42. He asked my name and profession, and then my charge. I said, "FKO Majority sympathizer." He said, "Are you still a sympathizer?" I said, "Now I am in prison." He asked, "Do you pray?" I said, "No, Haj Aqa" [i.e. one who has gone on a Hajj pilgrimage]. He said, "We will beat you so much that you will start praying." He

then asked, "Will you give an interview?" I said, "No." "Are you Muslim?" "I am like my parents, yes I am a Muslim." "Are you a Marxist?" We knew that the mere fact of saying we were a Marxist was enough to get us executed. So when asked this question, we used to equivocate and avoid saying, "Yes, I am a Marxist," and rather say, "I am a political activist." But [that day] I responded, "I am Muslim." The one that did not have on a clerical robe said, in a very hooligan kind of way, "This does not work. You are Majority, you won't give us an interview, and you are Muslim, but you don't say your prayers. . . it doesn't work like that. . . ." I said, "Haj Aqa, if it is possible that I have been in prison for five years, then anything can happen." Up until now, Eshraqi had not said anything. Nayyeri said to the guy questioning me, "Let it be. . . . He is an apostate." Eshraqi said, "But, Haj Aqa, he said he is a Muslim." At that moment, two ideas crossed my mind: first, the issue here goes beyond flogging and interview, and second, that Islam is important here. Eshraqi said, "Mister, you have a wife and kids, just sign this," and he showed me a paper. I looked at the paper and saw that the foundations of Islam were summarized in three principles. "1. Believe in the transcendent God; 2. Believe in Mohammad the Seal of the prophets; 3. Believe in the resurrection and the Judgment Day." There was another line that was not to my liking: "don't believe in socialism and Marxism and Leninism." Before each line there was printed "I," and a space for one's name.

43. Now I only wanted to get out of there so I could think about what was going on and

how I could avoid giving them all they wanted from me. I said, "Haj Aqa, these are all too complicated for me. You are a clergyman yourself. I told you something very clear, 'I am a Muslim, and the rest is up to you.'" Naserian was behind me, he hit me on the head with a pen and said, "Get up, get up, Haj Aqa didn't I tell you he is *khabith* [evil]?" But he did not put me on the right or the left [in the hallway]; rather he put me near the door because there was no clear decision made about me. So, also there was one of my friends, Dr. .... , from the Tudeh Party, whom I had not seen for five or six months, because he had been taken to another ward —a person who was very strong, very tough, and I could see that he was signing the paper. So, I was surprised, because he was a symbol of resistance—why was he sign-ing it? And since I had not seen him in six or seven months, I did not know if there was something these guys knew that I did not. Quietly, I said, "I haven't signed this; why are you signing it?" I do not know if he did not hear me or if he was scared to say anything, but he did not reply. I said to another prisoner, "Why are you signing this?" and I got no response.

44. Then Naserian came, and he told those who had signed to stand up and follow him—I was still at the door in the middle. I had my blindfold on, of course. But I said almost automatically to Naserian, "Haj Aqa, I said I am a Muslim too," and

he said, "Well, come along"—as simple as that. I went with these guys; they took us in a line to a ward. The door was opened and there were three or four Revolution-ary Guards there. They asked our names and wrote them down. And then they said, "Are you the guys who don't pray?" But before we could say yes or no, they began beating us up. It was unusually violent. They beat us with stuff that we had not seen in prison before—like clubs, iron rods, lumber, and even chains. I had never seen beating with a chain, because it can blind or maim the prisoner. After the beat-ing, they threw us in a room—about 20 people. When we removed our blindfolds we hugged each other emotionally as if we had not seen each other for months.

45. One of my friends, whom I had not seen for a couple of months, was very upset. He was crying. I said, "Don't be upset, it is nothing; they just want to pressure us!" He said, "This is not about fear. I am worried for Alireza." Alireza Daliri was his brother and a member of the Tudeh Party. He said, "That was a trial we were at. In our ward we had received information about what was going on. I am very worried about my brother. He is very stubborn, and I am worried that they are going to execute him. During the whole month of August they were executing MKO sympathizers. And now it is the leftists' turn." We found out later that Alireza had been in fact executed on one of those days.

Cologne, June 2009

OFFICIAL STATEMENT • 4

انقلاب اسلامی

پنجشنبه ۲۰ فروردین ماه ۱۳۶۰ ـ شماره ۵۰۹

Subject:	Ten-point statement on freedom of the press and association
The official:	Prosecutor General of the Islamic Revolution, Ali Qoddusi
The occasion:	Publication of the new government decrees on political parties
Date:	8 April 1981
Source:	*Enqelab Eslami,* 9 April 1981

In the name of the Almighty

All parties and groups are hereby advised that from the date of this announcement, 8 April 1981, they should abide by the following:

1. Publication of daily newspapers and weekly, monthly, or yearly publications and the like are conditioned upon permission from the Ministry of Islamic Guidance.

2. Given the country's state of war, holding meetings and demonstrations requires approval from the Interior Ministry.

3. Opening offices for political parties and groups is conditioned on informing the Ministry of Interior, so that oversight, as envisioned in Article 26 of the Constitution, is possible.

Article 26 [Freedom of Association]:

The formation of parties, societies, political or professional associations, as well as religious societies, whether Islamic or pertaining to one of the recognized religious minorities, is permit-

ted provided they do not violate the principles of independence, freedom, national unity, the criteria of Islam, or the basis of the Islamic Republic. No one may be prevented from participating in the aforementioned groups or be compelled to participate in them.

4. No party or group has the right to arm its members or to otherwise use arms. Violators are subject to legal prosecution.

5. After the date of the issuance of this announcement, all armed parties and groups are required to give up their arms to the Revolutionary Guards, or the security forces, and obtain a receipt.

6. All parties and groups that have declared an armed struggle against the Islamic Republic of Iran may conduct political activity within the legal framework if they renounce their past position, give up their arms to the Revolutionary Guards or the security forces, and announce their new position publicly. Otherwise, they

will be prosecuted in the Revolutionary Court, according to the law, and they will be treated as enemies of God.

7. All political parties and groups are free to express their views and opinions, provided that they do not include lies, false accusations, or instigations.

8. Political parties and groups are not permitted to encourage or instigate strikes, indolence, sit-ins or any disruption in the country's institutions. Violators are subject to legal prosecution.

9. All political parties and groups are permitted to hold debates and political discussions in mass media, unless they have declared armed resistance against the Islamic Republic and have not changed their position.

10. All citizens and security forces are required to guarantee and observe the freedom of legal activities of the groups whose activities are not declared illegal by government officials.

Judicial and security officials are required to carry out this order, and political parties and groups will be prosecuted accordingly. This announcement serves as written guidelines for Revolutionary Courts across the country.

Prosecutor General of the Islamic Republic of Iran, Ali Qoddusi

Jahangir Esma'ilpur

ARRESTED: Spring 1982
DETAINED IN: Adelabad Prison and Shiraz Revolutionary Guards Detention Center
RELEASED: February 1989

1. My name is Jahangir Esma'ilpur.* I was arrested in 1982, in Shiraz, in the south of Tehran. I was in prison for seven years. In 1996, I came to the Netherlands.

2. I make this statement in support of an investigation into the mass execution of political prisoners in 1988 in Iran.

3. This statement is true to the best of my knowledge and belief. Except where I indicate to the contrary, I make this statement on the basis of facts and matters within my own knowledge. Where the facts and matters in this statement are within my own knowledge, they are true. Where the facts and matters are not within my own knowledge, I have identified the source or sources of my information, and I believe such facts to be true.

Pre-arrest Activities, Arrest, and Detention

4. I was a student in my first year at the university when the universities were closed during the Cultural Revolution.

5. In 1982, when I was 22 years old, I was arrested just outside of my home, in the city of Shiraz. My arrest was related to my affiliation with a Marxist organization. Officially, I was charged with being active in an anti-revolutionary group, the Fadai-yan Khalq (Minority).

6. During interrogation, I was tortured. They beat me on the back with a cable and on my feet with a cable. I was forced to stand on my feet for long periods of time, 24 hours to 32 hours. In the beginning, they wanted information from me. After that, they wanted me to adopt their ideas.

Trial

7. My trial lasted five minutes. The name of the judge was Hojjat ol-eslam Qanbari. I was sentenced to ten years' imprisonment. They showed me the sentence and I signed it.

Prison Conditions

8. My life in prison can be divided into two distinct periods. The first period started at the time of my arrest [spring 1982] and ended in the fall of 1982, when I was detained in Adelabad Prison in Shiraz. This was a time [spring–fall 1982] when supporters of various political groups held firmly

*The name of the witness and some details in his testimony have been changed to protect his identity.

to their positions, because their organizations were still politically and socially active in the country. There were a lot of executions during this period.

9. The second period was a very dark period in Adelabad Prison. It commenced in 1982 and lasted nearly four years [until 1986]. During this period, prison officials believed that, once tried and convicted to a prison term, the prisoner needed to reconstruct himself into a new being and become a repenter. Prison officials felt that just saying that you were a repenter was not enough; you had to prove you had truly repented by acting accordingly. For example, one would have to force one's brother onto the [torture] bed and flog him, or one would have to torture an old friend and fellow party member, or else go out on vigils with the Revolutionary Guards and try to recognize or identify others [fellow political activists]. Sadly, a number of those who had repented and were collaborating with the prison officials helped to implement this process of repenter-making. During this period there were 700 to 750 male political prisoners in the political ward [Adelabad Prison]. The vast majority of them faked repentance or collaborated with prison guards. There were only a hundred of them [who did not repent], and they were left at the mercy of this crowd.

10. Those who did repent and collaborate [with the guards] were released after two or three years in detention. We had someone who had a life sentence; he repented and was released 11 months later. There was another prisoner, Mohammad Bijanzadeh,

who was charged with supporting the MKO, but since he did not have enough money to pay the bail, he was kept in prison for seven years and ended up being executed in 1988.

11. In 1987, a representative of Ayatollah Montazeri, Hojjat ol-eslam Samadi, came to the prison in Shiraz. Prison conditions changed a lot as a result [of his taking charge of the prison's administration]. Collective prayers were no longer mandatory nor was praying individually. Reporting on other inmates or denouncing them was no longer considered a valid criteria for releasing a prisoner. This resulted in a crisis within the prison administration, and some of the Revolutionary Guards left the prison in protest. After three or four months he [Samadi] was removed from his position. For several months after his removal, prison conditions did not return to the tough and dark state that had existed before he took charge.

Events Surrounding 1988

12. There are some indications that the prison killings were planned. Yet there are other signs pointing to the fact that the killings were the result of a sudden and insane decision. My understanding is that the prison killings had to do with what happened after the war.

13. In late June/early July [before the MKO attack on Iran], the first group of prisoners was taken out of the ward; there were 40 or 45 MKO members. We [leftists and MKO members] were all held in the same ward. The prison's main office was near the *hashti* [the prison's main hallway]. In the *hashti*

they were each given a form to fill out. On this form they were asked questions such as, "If you were released what would you do? Are you still loyal to the MKO? Do you believe in the Islamic Republic? Have you already been pardoned?" These inmates filled out the forms and were taken back to the ward. They told their trusted friends about what had happened in the *hashti*. They had concluded from the questions that they might be released. They thought that since the war was over, they [authorities] had decided to release them.

14. After a few weeks, the same group that had filled out the forms was transferred to the Shiraz Revolutionary Guards detention center [Sepah Detention Center], which was an interrogation center on Sepah Avenue in Shiraz. Twenty-two to twenty-five days later, in mid- or late-August, one of the 45 prisoners, Abas Mira'ian, was returned to Adelabad Prison. That year Abas had been my cellmate. For five days after he returned, he would not talk to anyone. Another cellmate and I insisted on getting him to talk, and he only said, "They hanged all the kids [fellow prisoners, people the speaker feels close to]." He had been warned not to talk about what he had seen. But it was obvious that they had sent one person back on purpose to see what would be the reaction of the inmates upon hearing the news.

15. He had been taken into a basement where people were questioned and executed. In his two-minute trial he had been asked, "Do you believe in the Islamic Republic?" He had given an affirmative response. Then he was asked, "Do you believe in the

MKO?" He had said no. And then they had asked him, "If we tell you that right now some MKO member has come to Iran from Iraq and we want to execute him, would you be willing to hang him?" Abas had said he would do so. Then the guards gave him a cord while he had his blindfold on. Abas had started to cry and said, "I cannot kill anyone." He was then transferred to Adelabad. Two weeks later Abas was taken away with another group and was executed.

16. The first groups of people were tried in a few minutes and, not knowing what it was all about, they all responded frankly to the questions, without thinking. This was what the Death Committee members wanted, so that they could issue death sentences without hesitating. These prisoners did not know that they were in fact gambling with their lives. The succeeding groups of prisoners knew they were in a dangerous situation; they tried to avoid execution by giving clever and equivocal responses.

17. Some of the MKO sympathizers were taken to the Sepah Detention Center and brought back. Some never did come back, while still others came back twice and were executed the third time they were taken there. And some of them were spared. Maybe two-thirds of the MKO sympathizers were taken away like that. About 200 to 250 of the MKO people were executed.

18. At that point, we had heard that leftists in other prisons in Tehran, Rasht, and Ahvaz had been executed. But it was not until late September to early October (the Iranian month of Mehr) that they

called for me and two of my fellow leftist militants. It was the first time that leftists were transferred to the Sepah Detention Center, where inmates were interrogated and executed. We were taken there in an ambulance.

19. I was blindfolded, seated facing the wall, and the interrogator, identified by a pseudonym as "brother Hossein," stood over my shoulder and interrogated me. He asked me, "Have they come?" And I thought he was talking about the Mojahedin coming from Iraq, but I told him, "I don't understand what you are talking about." Once the interrogator explained that he was talking about the MKO, I said, "The charges brought against me are not related to the MKO and I don't agree with their political ideas, and so I don't understand what you're asking." He then asked, "Who is running the prison?" I responded, "Your agents." After this [interrogation] I was sent to a cell and kept in solitary confinement without anyone talking to me. For one week, no one came to see me; the detention center was rather quiet.

20. I was interrogated several times in Sepah's detention center. I was beaten the first time but not the second time. The interrogator told me, "You have created an organization within the prison, and I have brought you here to execute you. I will ask you three questions. If you are truthful, I will help you. Are you Muslim? Do you believe in Marxism? Do you believe in the Islamic Republic?"

21. I was convinced I was going to be executed and I preferred to say what I believed was true. So my responses were kind of truthful, but evasive. I would say, "If for you 'being Muslim' is understood in the narrow sense of praying, then I am not a Muslim. Socialism is a philosophical doctrine and I am not knowledgeable about it, but I do believe in justice and happiness for all human beings. Regarding the Islamic Republic, I believe in its foreign policy and support of the Palestinian people, but I am critical of its policies inside the country, just as Ayatollah Montazeri is critical of its internal politics. There are some issues I disapprove of." That is how I responded to his questions.

22. The authorities were always on the lookout to find excuses for executing political prisoners. The majority of the people who were executed that year had already been sentenced, and some of them had completed their sentences three or four years previously, but they were kept in prison. During the first months [following the killings], they [prison authorities] denied the crime, but later, when the killings became known to all, they declared they had executed them because they had been planning an uprising within the prison, and they had been in touch with the Mojahedin. In Shiraz, no leftists were executed.

23. I was released five months later, in February 1989.

Amsterdam, June 2009

Manuchehr Esshaqi

ARRESTED: July 1981
DETAINED IN: Qolhak Committee, Moshtarak Committee, Evin and Gohardasht Prisons
RELEASED: August 1991

1. My name is Manuchehr Esshaqi and I am 41 years old. I was a political prisoner in Iran for ten years, between 1981 and 1991. I was detained at the local revolutionary committee, Evin Prison, and Gohardasht Prison.

2. I make this statement in support of an investigation into the mass execution of political prisoners in 1988 in Iran.

3. This statement is true to the best of my knowledge and belief. Except where I indicate to the contrary, I make this statement on the basis of facts and matters within my own knowledge. Where the facts and matters in this statement are within my own knowledge, they are true. Where the facts and matters are not within my own knowledge, I have identified the source or sources of my information, and I believe such facts to be true.

Activities Before His Arrest

4. I became active with the Mojahedin about eight months before my arrest. Before that I was just a supporter. In those days, kids started early in school. My uncle was a political activist and the environment in our house was political. We read newspapers of leftist groups and the Mojahedin, and we discussed and argued. The Revolution had created an atmosphere that affected everyone. We engaged in publicity-related activities. We put posters on the walls, distributed leaflets, and sold newspapers.

5. Maybe if the environment in school and society had not been so oppressive, I would never have been motivated enough to get involved in all of this. About eight or nine months before, in political meetings, I saw [people] being beaten with sticks and clubs or stabbed. For example, my younger uncle, who was not even a supporter or active, had come to see one of the meetings in front of the university—just to watch. The regime's club-wielders attacked the meeting participants. They did so with clubs, knives, and chains. At the time, we ran away. We did not stay to get injured. They

stabbed my uncle in the back and tore his lung. I was in the hospital [with him] for three days because he was in a coma.

6. I went to the 30 Khordad [20 June 1981] demonstration with friends who were all high school or university students. I was the youngest. The others were between 16 and 20 years old. It was a shock for me. For the first time, they [the regime's security forces] were openly shooting at us. In Ferdowsi Square, when they started, bullets were coming straight at us. They were kneeling down as they would in a firing squad and were shooting at us. We were not armed at the time. The demonstrations were meant as a protest but no one intended to use arms. We could not even imagine that, two years after the Revolution, they would shoot at people who had been part of the Revolution.

7. After that, the arrests became massive and I did not go home anymore. All of us who were activists, including my brother, were well known [in our neighborhood]. In those eight months [before my arrest], we were called the Militia [by our organization]. We had not received any military training, but the name suggested that we were ready to put our lives on the line. It was more a physical and psychological preparation for activism, but not really for military activities. In fact, there were no such confrontations at the time—even after the June demonstration.

Arrest and Detention

8. I was arrested on 17 July 1981 in the Qolhak area of Tehran. It was precisely twenty days

before I turned 14. They [security forces] arrested people randomly. My friend and I were arrested together; we always met in this neighborhood. They put hoods over our heads and pushed us below the car's back seats and sat with their feet on us. We were taken to Qolhak revolutionary committee.

Manuchehr Esshaqi is on the far right, in a snapshot taken in northern Iran before his arrest.

9. The interrogation started at the Qolhak revolutionary committee. They asked us our names, details about ourselves. They accused us of having set fire to a tent belonging to Hezbollahi. This lasted from 2 p.m. to 6 p.m. We gave them false information about ourselves, and of course they suspected that they did not have the right information.

10. They then took us to the Moshtarak Committee, where the Revolutionary Guards interrogated us until around 11 p.m. The Revolutionary Guards and the prosecutor's office were acting independently of each other. We were then transferred to ward 209 in Evin Prison. Ward 209 was under the control of the Revolutionary Guards.

11. 209 is really the most terrifying part of the prison. Not many people survived to tell what happened to them in there. And most of those who have survived their stay in this ward have an image of it that is not accurate. I was able to see it in 1989, when its second floor had been made into an infirmary. I went there without a blindfold and realized how it was and how it differed from what I had in mind. From the moment you are arrested until the very last moments of your interrogation, you are blindfolded, so there is very little that you actually see. To make the place seem scarier, [the guards] would tell you, "Bend, otherwise you are going to hit the ceiling," or they would hit you on the head and say, "Your head hit the ceiling. Bring your head down so that it doesn't hit the ceiling!"

12. Upon my arrival at Evin [ward 209] they took me to the basement where prisoners were tortured. They made me walk down the corridor. People were sitting on the ground by the wall waiting. Some were going into the room and some were coming out of it. They took me to one of the people sitting on the ground. The agent kicked him and told me, "See? This is what will happen to you if you don't talk." He then told the guy, "Tell him to say whatever he knows." The prisoner, who was half dead, said, "Tell them what they want to hear." He had been beaten so much that all his body was infected and full of blood. He was in such a state they could not beat him anymore.

13. They took me to the place where they tortured people; it was like a bathroom. There were four different cables hanging from a hanger. They asked me to pick one [of the cables to be used for flogging me], and I picked the thickest one. I would always choose the thickest because it would not hurt quite as much. The pain from the thin ones would go all the way to my head. From behind my blindfold I could see the torturers. Their shirts were unbuttoned down their chests, and they wore their shoes and walked like thugs.

14. They sat me on a bench, like a wooden bench in a park. I was on my stomach, my hands were tied under the bench, and someone sat on my back and shoved a dirty, bloody piece of cloth in my mouth. There were two people on each side and each would hit me once with the cable. "Any time you have something to say, hold your head up," they said. Because I was still a kid, my head would automatically jump up each time they hit me, so they would stop to say, "What?" I would say, "What do you want me to say?" They would flog me for a while on the soles of my feet and then they would order me to put my feet in a bucket of cold water to stop the swelling.

15. I still did not identify myself so they did not know anything about me, just the name I had picked. While they were flogging me they would ask, "Where is your

gun? Where were you supposed to meet other people?" In our organization, the understanding was that if someone was arrested and if there was no news of that person, within 24 hours all the planned meetings were cancelled. So it was important to hold out for 24 hours [to protect our comrades from being arrested]. The prison authorities also knew about this rule. And that is why the torture and harsh treatment was so bad immediately after they arrested a person, and it lasted for one or two days. The interrogations and torture that followed aimed at obtaining militants' addresses, weapons caches, and safe houses.

16. I was beaten from 11 in the morning until 2 or 3 a.m [the following day]. Then they took me out of the room and made me sit in the hallway. Then they took me back in and beat me until dawn. When the call for morning prayer came, they locked me in the room and left. That is when I could see the torture room resembled a bathroom; the walls and the floor were tiled. You could see the sewer lines on top of it. I know that some people were hung from those pipes. I heard this from others. One of my cellmates was hung like this using the *qapani* method, so that as a result of this treatment one of his arms was completely paralyzed. He was hung like that for 24 hours.

17. They would tell me, "We beat you in a way that we could continue beating you. They tortured me two times. They gave me 70 to 80 lashes on the soles of my feet. I didn't count the lashes. They told me, "Why are you making such a fuss, we didn't give you more than 70 or 80 lashes?" Then they

flogged me on my back. When you are at the mercy of such people you don't humiliate yourself by begging them [to stop]. I would just tell them, "What do you want from me? I don't know anything?"

18. They did not hit more because that night they brought in someone who knew me and knew everything about me. And he told them all they wanted to know about me. So they knew that I had nothing more to tell them.

19. When I was in ward 209, I had heard one girl crying and asking the interrogator, "Mohsen has already raped me, what do you want from me?"

Trial

20. Three days after I was arrested my friend and I were taken to the religious judge. There were nine of us, to be tried together. They sat the nine of us down. Because we had been tortured we were barefoot. We sat on chairs. Then they put a table that was covered with a tablecloth in front of us to hide our swollen and bloody feet. There were cameras and they wanted to film the proceedings, so they made sure our wounds could not be filmed. During the proceedings some of [the relatives of] the Revolutionary Guards were present in the courtroom. It was a staged trial.

21. [Asadollah] Lajevardi was the prosecutor and [Mohammadi] Guilani was the religious judge. We did not face the judge. He read [out loud] to each of us the same [basic] indictment. There were some components common to all of the indictments, but each one also had additional elements.

We all were charged with "acting against the regime," "waging war against God and the Imam," and "corruption on earth." For me, he said only that I had participated in the 30 Khordad demonstration [20 June 1981] and that I was a sympathizer of the MKO, but they had nothing else on me. It took one minute to read the indictment for each person. Lajevardi requested the most severe penalty [the death penalty] for all of us.

22. The process did not go as well as they were hoping. They did not expect us to dare to defend ourselves after the torture we had been subjected to. But we did defend ourselves. The first person who got up to defend himself was from Lahijan, in the north of Iran. He stood up and said that his father was a peasant and that after the Revolution he thought that the era of feudalism had ended, but he saw that the Hezbollahis replaced local notables and nothing changed for the peasants. The judge did not allow anyone to speak for more than two or three minutes. The others [used this time] to defend themselves as well.

23. One of the [defendants] was my friend Parviz Ebrahimzadeh. He was 19 at the time and a chemistry student at Mashhad University. He explained the fact that there were no individual freedoms or any other freedom, and the space that had existed after the Revolution had been closed, that universities had been closed. The other defendants explained their motivation for joining the group they had joined or doing what they had done.

24. The person who was accused of having set fire to a tent belonging to Hezbollahis and allegedly causing the death of two people said, "When I set this place on fire I saw no one there. If such a thing has really happened, I am truly sorry. This was not my intention." But they were lying about the death of two people there. There was no evidence [against him], and the names of the two people who were allegedly killed were not provided and there were no witnesses. I think this was meant to move the television viewers. Otherwise, the charges of participating in the demonstration and waging war against God were enough to sentence someone to death.

25. I was 13 at the time, and no one asked me how old I was. I was accused of participating in the demonstration and being a sympathizer of the MKO. They had nothing else against me. The trial of nine defendants lasted one hour.

26. Then they took us out of the trial room and sat us down. Fifteen minutes later they came with the sentences and said, "Let's go." We were blindfolded and had our hands on each other's shoulder. Parviz was behind me and knew we were going to be executed. He told me, "Don't worry. I will be with you until the end."

27. Lajevardi came and kicked me in the leg. He just wanted me to talk to him. He asked me if I had erections during my sleep. [The age of maturity in Islam is when girls start having menstrual periods, and when boys begin having erections.] I did not know what that meant. [I thought this was an insult and] I returned the

insult to him: "erection yourself." At this point Lajevardi understood I had not yet reached the age of puberty. So he took me by the shirt and told me to go and stand at the end of the line. He also said something to the guards and left.

28. They put us all in a minibus with dark windows. I could see from under my blindfold. They took us up into the Evin hills and lined prisoners up four by four, and they stood me on the side. They executed them four at a time. Our hands were tied behind our backs. I was behind, and I could see from under my blindfold. There was one person in front of each prisoner, [each one] holding a J3 gun. Each prisoner would be shot three times in the chest. When they fell, someone went up and shot them one more time. I felt terrible, so I fell on my knees and cried. I heard someone say, "Take him back to 209." I realized that I had been put at the end of the row because I was going to go back to the cell.

29. For the next six months I did not know whether I was sentenced or what was going to happen to me. My family did not know whether I was dead or alive.

30. I was put back in the same small cell. It was a cell covered with soundproof materials. I could always hear sounds from the torture rooms because the sound would echo in the hallway. The soundproofing was not perfect. There was a light bulb, but it was protected by a metallic mesh, something so you could not break it. They turned it on and off when they wanted, so I never knew whether it was day or night. I was kept there for two or three weeks.

31. Ward 209 was a three-story building. The rooms where they tortured people were located on the lower level. The cells of the people like me who were under interrogation or awaiting execution were above the torture rooms. The third floor was for the prisoners who would leave ward 209; they were kept there until they recovered [from torture].

32. We were treated badly. There we were not considered as living human beings. Sometimes they would not feed us and if you asked, "What about food?" They would say, "What do you need food for? You are a corruptor on earth and are going to be executed." They did not give us water; they would not let us use the bathroom. They told me every day, "Tonight you are going to be executed."

33. After three weeks they put me in an open-air cell, with barred roof, on the third level. They did not tell me why I was being moved. They did not say, and I could not ask. We would not ask any questions. They would always tell us, "You are not here to ask questions." From there they took me to the public ward, or rather it was a public cell where prisoners were held together.

34. About six months [after my arrest], they took me back to ward 209 again, and the interrogator talked to me. His behavior was very different [compared to] the first time. They put the sentence in front of me and asked me to sign it. It was a small piece of paper bearing the Islamic Revolutionary Court seal, saying I was sentenced to ten years for "sympathizing with the *monafeqin*" and "acting against the Islamic

Republic of Iran's regime." They pulled the blindfold up a little so I could sign but I did not have time to read the details.

35. I was relieved after knowing my sentence. My brother had the same sentence and he was able to bring his sentence sheet out. A few years later they came and handed us our sentences, but then, later, they came in and told us to leave the ward, searched everywhere and took them [the sentence sheets] back. They could not find my brother's [sentence sheet]. He had sewed it to his underwear, and when he was released he brought it out.

36. Four or five years later I saw my interrogator, because he had become the head of Qezel Hesar Prison. He saw me first, but he was not sure I had recognized him. He came forward and asked, "How is it going?" After talking to me for a little while he asked me, "Did you recognize me?" I said, "Yes." I had never seen his face, but I could recognize his voice and it made me feel very odd—it gave me shivers.

Events Surrounding 1988

37. In January–February 1988, I was in ward 4 of Gohardasht Prison. One day they came to our ward and they called all the prisoners whose sentences varied between 15 and 20 years imprisonment. My uncle (my mom's brother), Ja'far Hushmand, was among them. He had been arrested at age 17 (he was three years older than me), in 1981, and sentenced to 17 years. They transferred all of them to Evin. I think they took a great number of prisoners from several wards in Gohardasht Prison. We could

hear them hitting and kicking the prisoners while they were transferring them. They took 37 prisoners from our ward. We felt that something was going on, something dangerous.

38. I think at that point they had already planned the killings of the prisoners. For there was no precedent for picking and transferring so many prisoners to another prison after six years and without any reason! All the prisoners who were transferred were MKO sympathizers. Generally, if there were transfers, it would be one or two prisoners. I don't remember the exact date of this transfer, but it was in the winter, because at the time they also moved us from ward 4 to ward 1. They took all our belongings. They sent us to ward 1. I remember that for three days I was very, very cold because we did not have any blankets or warm clothes. On the third day we got our belongings back.

39. On the third day I fell sick. My kidneys were infected so I had a very high fever. There was a doctor in our group, and he made a huge pot of tea and forced me to drink all of it and said, "If you do not drink this, you will not survive." Finally, because I still had a high fever, they took me to the infirmary and I had penicillin shot.

40. After this transfer, the situation changed in prison [in] that the [prison authorities] were more lenient with us and the prisoners had become more demanding. For example if the food was not enough we would refuse to take it in. Most of our demands concerned prison conditions. The prison guards were not reacting violently. They

would say to us, "Eat or don't eat. Do as you wish." Sometimes they would reduce our food ration. Sometimes we would refuse to eat because they had reduced our recreation time. Instead of allowing us to get six hours of fresh air they would give us only two hours or simply suspend our recreation and keep the door closed.

41. At that time, they kept giving us questionnaires. Any time a prisoner was moved from one place to another, they would ask us to give our name and information, charges, or our sentence. During the first years when the environment was really terrifying, we would write on the forms that the charge was *monafeqin*. Nobody dared say anything else. But now we were bolder and so prisoners would write "sympathizer," and then they would kick the prisoners and say, "Sympathizer of whom?" The reply was, "You know better." They wanted to break us and make us insult our own group.

42. The Revolutionary Guards and Naserian would use any opportunity to make us fill out these questionnaires. In the middle of the 1988 winter, they started to distribute the questionnaires. If we asked them, "What is it for?" they would say, "It is to organize the visitations," or they would make another pretext. They wanted to know what our [ideological] position was. During the first years they often asked us if we believed in armed struggle. But now they asked us only what our charge was.

43. All this was done before the mass killings of prisoners started. They also brought a newly arrested MKO sympathizer to our ward. This had never happened before. [Before] they had never put the new prisoners and old ones together. Talking to the newly arrested prisoner lifted our spirits [because he would update us on the regime's problems].

44. Shortly before the killings, after they announced that the war was over, they removed the television and newspapers from the rooms.

45. In our ward, ward 1, everyone was sentenced to ten years or less. A couple of nights before we were moved from ward 1 to the jihad ward, I and a few others saw from the window that far away Lashkari, the head of the prison, and some Revolutionary Guards were bundling something in white sheets that they were closing like a bag and tossing into the back of a truck. It looked bizarre, but we had no idea what it was. It was only later that we realized that these must have been bodies that had been removed from the Gohardasht Hosseinyeh (the multipurpose room).

46. Around the time they started the killing, they took us to the jihad ward, which was located in a separate one-story building. Usually ordinary prisoners were kept there, not political prisoners.

47. One or two days after we were moved, Naserian came there to check on us. Naserian was the head interrogator of ward 3 of Evin Prison. That was not his real name. When he entered the jihad ward, one prisoner, Shir-Mohammadi, asked him, "Why are we here? We do not want to work." It was a very bad exchange and Naserian said, "Anyone who does not want

to stay here—come out!" There were maybe 200 [of us] and maybe about 80 went out. Everything happened very fast. There was not enough time to confer or to react in an organized way. I did not leave but my brother [Mohsen] left. The doors were shut immediately. I had two brothers in prison with me. A few hours later they called my older brother, Mehdi. What I know about the killings is what my brother Mehdi told me.

48. Mehdi said that on 5 August 1988, he was taken to a hallway where he had to sit. In a room in this hallway the committee was officiating. When he went to the hallway, he saw [from below his blindfold] that there were broken watches and rings; private objects [personal belongings] were lying on the ground. A number of blindfolded prisoners who had been just sentenced to death were sitting on one side of the hallway and a number of prisoners on the other side. The death row prisoners were those who would start breaking their watches, their rings and other personal belongings so that no one could take them once they were executed.

49. While Mehdi was waiting his turn, one of the prisoners who was sitting opposite him in the hallway had told him that they were taking people to be executed. Mehdi knew that the situation was very serious. He never trusted these people [authorities]. Naserian took Mehdi into the room and said, "This is the eldest brother. I haven't brought in the younger." One of the members of the committee asked him, "Would you ask for a pardon from the Imam and

the people?" Mehdi signed the paper [asking for a pardon].

50. When they brought Mehdi out of the room, instead of taking him back to where people were waiting to be taken to their cells, they threw him somewhere with some of the people who had not yet been tried. It was chaos. There were about 30 people in there, including my other brother Mohsen. Mehdi was able to tell him, "Accept whatever you are told to accept. They are executing people." At first his cellmates didn't believe him. But Mehdi had insisted and told them he had seen it himself. Most of these prisoners [followed Mehdi's advice] and came back [were not executed].

51. They took them [Mehdi and the prisoners who had not been tried] to the committee. Mehdi told the guards that he had already been to the committee, but he was ignored by them. Naserian saw him behind the door of the courtroom and sent him back to the cell. Mohsen went to the court and agreed to sign the paper asking for a pardon and came back. Maybe out of the 80 people who left [the jihad ward]—when the tension with Naserian broke out—only about 30 returned. These are only approximate numbers.

52. Some of the people very close to me were killed. Mohammad Zamiri was arrested in 1981; he was coming back from work on the day of the big demonstration [20 June 1981]. They arrested him by mistake and kept him as a suspect. He was not even a serious sympathizer, but in prison he became a sympathizer. He always said, "I do this for the kids." ["Kids" is a familiar way

of referring to a group of people that the speaker feels close to. Here, it may mean "I do this for our friends."] Even when they were taking him to that room, he would say, "I give my life for the kids [my prisoner friends]."

53. We never thought that Mehdi Fereiduni would be executed. We used to call him Mehdi the brain, because he was always teasing everyone. Mehdi and his friends all belonged to a soccer team. They had been arrested along with their coach. Mehdi had been first sentenced to 15 years' imprisonment. His sentence had been later reduced to 8 years. He had nearly finished serving his sentence. [In the summer of 1988] when he realized that many of his fellow soccer players, who were his best friends, were being executed, he got mad and refused to sign a letter demanding to be forgiven by the murderers of his friends. No one thought Mehdi would refuse to sign the letter; he was not confrontational and never argued. He just liked to play soccer. But in a few [fateful] moments he decided not to sign.

54. Another friend of mine, Ali Akbar Bak'ali, had three days left to complete his seven-year sentence. When he came out of the [Death Committee] room, he said [to a cellmate]: "I won't be able to cope yet again with the unbearable prison conditions and pressure we were submitted to during the 1980s. We were in such a humiliating position." He never returned. My friend Shir-Mohammadi was my grandmother's neighbor; he also was executed. He was born in 1964; he was the same age as my uncle, three years older than me.

55. My uncle Ja'far (my mother's brother) was executed at Evin Prison. Ja'far was 17 when he was arrested. He had gone through terrible torture. The first time I saw him after my arrest, I saw him from the window. He had washed his clothes and he wanted to hang them in the courtyard to dry; so he had only his pants on without a top. His whole back was completely black from bruises. The backs of his feet were also all black and blue. His pants were rolled up so I could see his calf up to his knee, and when he turned around to go back into the ward I saw his face and realized that it was my uncle. It was only then that I realized that my uncle had been arrested. He was only as active as I was: participating in demonstrations, selling newspapers, putting posters up, distributing leaflets.

56. My uncle and I spent six years together in prison. He was also arrested accidentally in a trap they set for people. Whenever something happened somewhere, they [state agents] would arrest anyone who could have potentially been involved. They knew, for example, that people like us wore sneakers and jeans and looked like casual, sporty people. The Hezbollahis never wore jeans or sneakers. Everyone in our ward really liked Ja'far. He was always smiling and everyone could confide in him and he would boost their spirits, and everyone called him "uncle" because my brothers and I called him "uncle." He was very patient. The pressure on people who were older and had kids and family outside was much greater. My uncle would sit and listen to their complaints for hours and hours.

57. My brother Mehdi told me about Majid Moshref whose father was a clergyman from Qom. When Majid came out of the committee room and sat on the side reserved for death row inmates, he told my brother, facing him on the other side, "I agreed and signed the demand for pardon. But Naserian took it and tore it up, telling me to sign it again." At this point Majid refused to sign again. "I chose death over obeying Naserian," he told my brother and he added, "Naserian wanted to break me, but I broke him." Had he signed again, Naserian would have asked him for more, to attend the Friday Prayer. Naserian was particularly harsh to prisoners who were popular among their fellow inmates. He would suspend their visitation rights and throw them in a solitary cell on any meaningless pretext.

58. For several days after we realized what had happened we were all very upset. No one talked in our ward; there was complete silence. They had liquidated all the wards' prisoners; no one was left alive from the wards on the upper floors. All the prisoners of wards 1–8 had been executed. Our ward, the jihad ward, was separate from those wards. They had picked the most popular and the most resilient prisoners and had executed them. There were a few prisoners with long-term prison sentences left alive, but this was because they were not that active and headstrong.

59. A few days after all these executions happened, they came to us. It was our turn, but they did not take us to the committee; [instead] they brought the forms to us— [the forms that were given] to the people in that committee room. It was the same form, asking for pardon from the Imam, the Leader, and the people and this kind of nonsense that we were required to sign. If anyone showed any reluctance, he would be taken to the committee.

60. The international pressure about the killings helped stop the committee's work; otherwise we would have been executed as well.

61. In late September we finally had our first visitation. The three-member committee had left the prison. My mother came and she was wearing black. That was when I found out for sure that my uncle had been executed. After that, I became unsettled and was being more forward with the guards, so they put me in solitary confinement.

62. One of our concerns was how to explain the reason for the executions to family and friends of the executed prisoners. What could we tell them? Why were they executed? What could we say to their relatives? Also, we did not know if we were going to stay alive and leave the prison or not. We were in a state of uncertainty as to whether it was really over. Until the day we were released, we were not sure if we would ever be released. Naserian would say, "You think you would go out of here? Who knows if you would ever get out of here."

63. A few months after the killings, in early March 1989, we could have group visitations with our families in the same amphitheatre [the Hosseinyeh] where our friends had been executed. From below their

blindfolds some of the prisoners had seen people being hanged. There were people, in the chaos, who were taken to that amphitheatre [where the executions took place], but later the mistake was realized and they were brought back. So these prisoners saw the room and told us what had happened with details and showed us where people had been hanged.

64. There was a stage in the Hosseinyeh where they [the authorities] would stand to give speeches. Above the stage there were iron bars across the ceiling. The bars were old and rusty so you could still see where the rope was tied. The rope left marks in the rust. There were marks from four ropes. They would put a bench there, put the rope around the neck, and then push the bench.

65. Before the visitation began, Naserian made a speech. He said, "We were wrong to give you such long prison sentences; we, in fact, nurtured our own enemies. Your families are going to come and visit you here, so don't be too arrogant, don't talk too much, and just visit with your family whom you haven't seen."

66. When I was released I did not feel free. I could not go anywhere alone. It was very strange for me to be free. Whatever I did [after I was released from prison], I could hear only what the other prisoners were saying to me, "When we get out, let's go and have ice cream here," or if I was in a suburb or place in Iran that someone had described [I thought only of my fellow prisoners].

67. Inside prison we were not alive nor were we dead. When we came out, it was the same thing, as if we were still in prison. I had difficulty walking in the street, I had no balance; I had to walk along [the side of] the street, walking by the wall, touching the wall. My mother's sister was in prison for five years, and she knew how I felt. She had been through it so she accompanied me wherever I went because she understood. I am still not really living. There is nothing that makes me really happy. Sometimes my child makes me feel happy. Whenever I go out to have fun, I am always trying to have fun, but I find it very difficult.

Paris, June 2009

OFFICIAL STATEMENT • 5

Subject: Hashemi Rafsanjani's opinion about the MKO and its leaders
The official: Islamic Consultative Assembly (Majles) Speaker, Ali Akbar Hashemi Rafsanjani
The occasion: Interview with the *Jomhuri Eslami*
Date: 24 April 1981
Source: Hashemi Rafsanjani, *Interviews, 1981–82*, ed. Mohsen Hashemi, 1378 (1999–2000) Tehran, Daftar
                e Nashr e Ma'aref e Enghelab, p. 30–32

. . . I objected to part of their work [the MKO], that is, their ideology. They are still beholden to that ideology. In reality, the Mojahedin Organization has been the original source of this deviation. Their main books are, in their entirety, an amalgam of Marxist ideology and Islam.

. . . In my opinion, the portion of your question in which you stated that the distinctions between various revolutionary groups were blurred during the early days of the Revolution is incorrect. In fact, distinctions had appeared two to three years before the Revolution, even when we were imprisoned. Even there [in prison], differences between various movements, Islamists, eclectics, [and] nationalists—who at that juncture were either influenced by or combined with Islam—were conspicuous, and the prominent individuals of each camp were already known. Hezbollahi activists were also identifiable after the Revolution, when they were promulgating Hezbollahi ideals and were fighting misguided groups. Most of the individuals you named had a record of activism. During those days, the late Ayatollah Motahari* was hated for his insistence on pure Islamic ideology and his opposition to groups with deviant ideologies. We were boycotted by these groups in the prison. The late Ayatollah Mofatteh† was repeatedly threatened and was subjected to [so-called] denunciation. The late Mr. Araqi‡ confronted these groups in prison... However, from early on, I objected to their ideology—an ideology that they are still clinging to. Their misguided approach is rooted in the founding of the organization. Their main books, which they

---

*Ayatollah Morteza Motahari (1920–1979). A cleric and former student of Ayatollah Khomeini, Morteza Motahari promoted the political role of the clergy and was opposed to the amalgamation of Marxism and Islam. Before the Revolution he served in Tehran University as the Head of the Department of Theology and Islamic Studies. At the time of his assassination (1 May 1979) by anti-clerical revolutionary Muslim militants (Forqan), he was the president of the Constitutional Council of the Islamic Republic of Iran and a member of the Revolutionary Council.

†Mohammad Mofatteh (1928–1979) was a cleric, former student, and follower of Ayatollah Khomeini. He was assassinated on 18 December 1979 by Forqan militants.

‡Mehdi Araqi (1930–1979) was a pro-Khomeini Islamist militant. After the victory of the Islamic Revolution he was designated as the head of Qasr prison. He was assassinated on 13 August 1979 by Forqan militants.

themselves are no longer promoting, were written for the purpose of creating an amalgam of Islam and Marxism. I did not meet them personally, but some who knew them better said that they, in full sincerity, had chosen this path for the purpose of creating a bridge [in their opinion] between Marxism—which fights imperialism—and the Muslim masses of Iranian people—which comprise our society. One of their clear mistakes was choosing Marxism as the banner for their struggle. They spoke continually of injecting Islam into Marxism or injecting Marxist formulas into Islamic concepts. They wanted to create something new. Therefore, with much jubilation, they trumpeted this as their biggest achievement. They claimed that the People's Mojahedin of Iran Organization was the only Muslim group that had succeeded in building a bridge between Marxism and Islam. This mistake forced them to shove a number of ideas down the throats of the youth as Islamic concepts. Through

misleading words and grand Marxist slogans, which were full of claims of love for humanity and fighting tyranny, the youth were deceived in their first encounter with them. Leftist writers from all over the world had worked on these slogans. Even we, who had studied Islam for 10 or 20 years, were affected by these words. However, we had enough analytical capability to recognize the mistakes and realize that the essence of their argument is in conflict with Islam. . . . A small number of them joined true Islam, which showed that this movement cannot be beneficial now or in the future. I wish that the rest would take counsel and correct their path. Unfortunately, however, they still insist on following their path. . . . It is best if nefarious political organizations are annihilated. Righteous political organizations, however, are those [in our opinion] that are founded upon Islamic jurisprudence, as is the Islamic Revolution itself.

Ebrahim Fatemi

DETAINED IN: Evin Prison, Moshtarak Committee Detention Center, Tehran

1. My name is Ebrahim Fatemi.* I was born in Tehran in 1969. I was a political prisoner in Iran during the 1988 prison killings, and I now live in a European country.

2. I make this statement in support of an investigation into the mass execution of political prisoners in 1988 in Iran.

3. This statement is true to the best of my knowledge and belief. Except where I indicate to the contrary, I make this statement on the basis of facts and matters within my own knowledge. Where the facts and matters in this statement are within my own knowledge they are true. Where the facts and matters are not within my own knowledge, I have identified the source or sources of my information, and I believe such facts to be true.

Arrest and Detention

4. I was arrested in Tehran. I was charged with sympathizing with the Mojahedin Khalq Organization. I was active in a resistance cell that was discovered. All the members had been identified, and we were arrested. I knew that this work was dangerous. I had joined the MKO five months earlier. Initially, as a high school student, I was active in the organization's propaganda efforts, but I advanced [within the organization] and joined a resistance cell. In the cell, besides me, there were two main members, one of whom managed to flee the country. There were two other people who helped. They were arrested and received various prison sentences.

5. I was linked to the MKO through my brother. My brother, who had left Iran, returned and was killed in a clash [with security forces]. We never got his body back but we know that authorities had shown his body to prisoners in order to identify him. They had buried him along with a great number of executed prisoners. We paid the cemetery employees and managed to open the grave to make sure that it was really his body that was buried there. We took a picture of his body.

6. I was taken to a section in Evin Prison called the Elteqat [hybrid] Section. [The interrogators believed that the ideology of the Mojahedin was *elteqati*, a mixture of Islam and Marxism. The section was under the control of the Ministry of Information. At the time the prosecution had its own detention center in Evin Prison, as did the Ministry of Information.

7. For the first two months, I was in solitary confinement. The pressure was mostly on the person responsible for our cell, because he was the main person and had also returned to Iran after having left. We were

*The name of the witness and some details in his testimony have been changed to protect his identity.

not tortured as much. They wanted to know about what I did before joining the resistance cell and what I did after I joined. The interrogators wanted to know who my contacts were and, since I didn't live at home anymore and was in the resistance cell, what other houses I was supposed to go to in case I was in trouble. I was blindfolded the entire time except during my trial.

8. During the interrogation, they beat you on the soles of your feet but when they want to punish you they beat you with a thick cable that has a metallic end so that the cable lands fully on you. It is an electrical cable—it is plastic and inside it there are wires. They didn't ask for specific information.

9. The main interrogator's name was Tavana and his deputy's name was Ahmadi. After we went into the Moshtarak Committee, their identities became numbers, for example, Ahmadi was number 77 and Tavana was called 34. I know that Tavana is his real name because one of his relatives was arrested and brought to our cell. I heard from other prisoners that Ahmadi was the deputy's real name. I know they used these numbers because prisoners always talked to each other.

10. My interrogation lasted approximately three weeks, during which time I was under the jurisdiction of the prosecutor. Then I was taken to ward 3. Our cells were closed; we did not see anyone. It was a transit area. They brought people there from solitary confinement before taking them to the wards, so the number of people kept changing. There were 20 to 40 people.

When there were 40 people, they would move them out fast. The average number of people was 25 or so.

Trial

11. A couple of months after being arrested, I was taken before the Revolutionary Court. I was not blindfolded. The prosecutor, the judge, and myself were present during my trial. I do not know who the prosecutor was but later I learned that the judge's name was Mobasheri and that he was the head of the Revolutionary Court. His photos are everywhere.

12. The trial lasted five minutes maximum. I was sentenced to prison for sympathizing with the MKO and membership in a resistance cell. We had no right to defend ourselves in the light of the circumstances of our arrest. I spent five and a half years in prison.

Prison Conditions

13. After a month in ward 3, I was taken to ward 5 and three months later I was moved to ward 6. I was kept there for approximately a year and a half. We had visitations every two weeks and then once a week. Each ward had a visitation day.

14. In 1987, we protested the prison food. The prison environment had changed and was more open because of Meysam [head of Evin Prison, appointed in the fall of 1986]. For some of those who took part in the protest, they issued sentences that included flogging, solitary confinement, or being deprived of visitations. My punishment was six months in solitary confinement, 50

lashes, and deprivation of visitation rights. Protests continued occasionally. Sometimes prisoners refused to go to visitations. Once they brought some repenters to our ward whom we didn't want to have there. Prisoners tried to push for improving their detention conditions.

15. In January–February 1987 [end of the Iranian year 1365], they conducted a full assessment of our ideas. They were from the Ministry [of Information] and they established themselves in one of the wards of Evin Prison, where they took all the prisoners. But you had the option of refusing to go to talk to them. They gave us a form containing many questions, ranging from your place and date of birth, to your family situation, as well as questions such as "Do you pray? Who prays in your family and who doesn't? What is your favorite color?" Their goal in asking these questions was to determine who we really were and what we thought. It was really comprehensive. For example, "What does your sister think? What are her beliefs?" The questions were extensive and in depth. I filled it out but some didn't. The wards had different views. In some wards, everyone refused to fill it out. Some prisoners gave ridiculous or wrong answers. For example, instead of black, they wrote yellow. They didn't tell us why we were being asked to do it.

16. The forms were very long. It took me two hours to fill it out. It took around six months for everyone to fill out these forms (sometime between January–February 1987 and the summer of 1987 approximately).

Events Surrounding 1988

17. The reclassification of prisoners started after the episode of the forms, in January–February 1988. Prisoners who were sentenced from one to ten years were held together. Those whose sentences were more than ten years, those sentenced for life or to execution, those who had been arrested for the second time, and the youngsters who were younger than 21 or 22 years of age (they were called *saghariha*—the minors) were constantly moved around.

18. There were newly arrested political prisoners but they were not mixed with the others. The recently arrested were in the cell above us. This was all after the restructuring and re-classification of the prisoners. [Among the newly arrested,] some of them had attempted to leave the country, others had come back as messengers [for the MKO], and [there were also] ordinary people, arrested on the border or caught through the telephone.

19. Our ward was among the ones that had a television because it was a repenters' ward. We also had some recently arrested prisoners and those who were punished, and some who had not repented. The television was always on and we followed the news regarding the war. Wards 2 and 4 had the most repenters in them. Ward 2 was the *kargari* [workshop], and ward 4 was called "jahadi" because most of the prisoners there were repenters. Their communicating doors were open. Ward 2 did carpentry or sewing. Ward 4 prisoners were doing more sophisticated or easier work, such as translations, cooking, or gardening. Prisoners from other wards were not mixed with these prisoners.

We didn't work. Our placement there was a punitive measure. Around May 1988, they divided ward 4 in two. We were in one half, and repenters, in the other.

20. During the parliamentary elections [mid-May 1988], they brought a ballot box into the courtyard. Whoever wanted to vote could go out and do so. It was not mandatory but they wrote down the names of people who voted. What was important was whether prisoners voted or not; they did not worry about who they were voting for. I didn't go. We could see the courtyard from the window. We had a little opening in the blinds and we saw that they were taking down the names of those who were voting. At the time, the prison environment was more open and we were not under pressure.

21. Throughout the time I was in prison, the [prison wardens] questioned us every now and then. They asked us, "What's your name? Which group do you belong to"? They would beat anyone who dared say Mojahedin. If we said "the organization," they would ask," what organization? The one distributing electricity, or meat. . . . ?" They forced us to say Mojahedin and then there was always lashing and beating. They would take the prisoners to court, where they were sentenced to flogging or solitary confinement or being denied visitations. But at the time of the executions, they did not react. They just said "all right, he is from the Mojahedin."

22. We had in-person visitations up to the beginning of the executions. Our ward's last visitation day was on Monday, 25 July, and it was Eid Qorban [a religious celebration].

On 27 July, a group of prisoners from another room had their visitation. Upon their return, they said that they had seen a notice stating that there would be no more visits for two months. This was 27 July. It was two days after the MKO attack.

23. Ali Mobaraki was the first person to be executed. He was born in 1960. On 27 July, they called him out of our ward and he never came back. A few hours later, they came and asked for his belongings. Now he is buried in Behesht Zahra cemetery in Lot 93. I visited his graveside very often. Until around mid-August, people did not know that executions were occurring. After Ali Mobaraki was taken, they started taking one or two people at a time, during the first two or three days. They took those who had not been sentenced. And then they started to take the prisoners who had been sentenced but about whom the guards were sensitive. When we asked, "Where are you taking these people?" we were told, "to a different ward." The Revolutionary Guards said, "the war is over. There is a court for pardoning prisoners. It is to release prisoners."

24. This process lasted for a month, until 25 August. On that day they took 15 of us together, including me. They took us to ward 209. It was maybe at 8:30 in the morning. We began to understand that this court is not about granting pardons. We saw that people left and did not come back and that the [guards] collected their belongings. When we were on our way to ward 209, the guards started teasing us saying, "You are all goners. This is a no-return hallway." I knew that this was very serious but some of us refused to

believe it until the very end. One person asked them, "What do you want from us?" I told him, "All they want is your life."

25. Then they took us to the solitary cells in ward 209 and kept us there until about 4 or 5 p.m. Even the solitary cells were divided. Those taken to court did not return to their cells but were taken to different solitary cells. Out of the 15 who were taken that day, three didn't come back. Twelve of us returned. I and some others were taken one more time, but they didn't have time to take all of us to court, so we came back without having been tried.

26. A week later, I was called again, for the third time, alone this time. But they didn't take me to 209, I was questioned right there in the ward. In the office of the ward they kept me there for eight or nine hours. They also called some of the people who had been called before, but no one was executed.

27. I think that they didn't want to execute several people from the same family. For example, I had two friends, Majid and Amir. After they executed Amir, they tried to convince Majid to give in. They kept him for a month but Majid would not renounce his beliefs. Eventually they executed him too. He was 23 or 24 years old. The Revolutionary Guards told us about this case themselves. There was another person, Davud Zargar, who was the nephew of a judge in the anti-narcotics court. They kept him for two months so that he would not be executed, but he too was executed, in September.

28. We learned about the executions because the ordinary [non-political] prisoners had seen barrels of slippers being taken out. These prisoners were held somewhere else but in the workshops prisoners were mixed and they talked [to us]. They said this is not about moving people to another location; they were bringing out barrel after barrel of slippers. We heard the news from them three or four months later. The ordinary prisoners had been charged with making the hanging nooses. In the beginning, executions were carried out behind the office of the prosecutor, with cranes. It was hastily put together and it was too visible there. After a while, the court and the hanging place were moved to the basement of ward 209. They tried the prisoners upstairs and then took them downstairs to be executed.

29. They had put a big refrigerated container at the door of ward 209, and then, a month after the executions, they removed it. When they took us to ward 209 by minibus, we could see from underneath our blindfolds. The container was as big as a room, maybe eight or ten meters [30 feet] high. We never saw it taken away but there is no way it could have contained all the people killed, so perhaps they put the bodies in there to keep them cool so that it wouldn't smell, and then moved them with trucks at night.

30. Also, some Revolutionary Guards inadvertently let slip some information. There was a guy called Javad—he had been arrested for an ordinary crime in 1979 and had been there ever since. Lajevardi offered to hire him as a guard. He remained there until 1991. He was a simple-minded person. He would come and tell prisoners about the execution scenes or, for example, the story

of Majid and Amir and the fact that they had tried not to kill the second brother.

31. We also heard through the families that they were returning the belongings of those executed to their families at various [district] committees. Also our own cellmates who had relatives in prison and went to visit them told us that they were no longer there. After the executions, when a person called Zamani became head of the prison, he told us frankly, "We do not want to have political prisoners. If [prisoners'] sentences are heavy, we will execute them, and if they are light, we will release them. We don't want to have a prison issue anymore." This was in the winter of 1989, before the general amnesty was granted. Their general policy was to avoid having too many political prisoners.

32. [After the summer killings] there were fewer executions. They executed only those who had heavier sentences and who had not repented. For example, at the time they had arrested two people because they had tried to leave the country; they had done absolutely nothing. Had they been arrested six months earlier or two years later, they would have received six months maximum, but because they were arrested at a time when the authorities did not want political prisoners, they were executed. One of them was 30 and had a wife and child. The other was 25. The authorities thought that anyone who wanted to leave the country intended to join the Mojahedin, but such was not the case. Many people just wanted to leave the country.

33. After my release, I met with the families of those who were executed and went with

them to the cemetery. Those who were executed in 1988, in particular those who were Muslims, are mostly in the Behesht Zahra Cemetery. But [unlike 1981] they are spread out. My brother was buried with 20 other executed people in one area, and the person responsible for my [resistance] cell [who was executed in 1981] was buried together with eight individuals in another section. For example, section 41 is filled with people who were executed in 1981 and it does attract attention. But those killed in 1988 are buried separately and mostly in the older sections of the cemetery. They deliberately didn't bury them collectively in order not to attract attention. You don't see two buried next to each other. On their tombstones, the date of death is not correct. They mostly say October or November even though they were killed two months earlier.

34. After my release, I was happy to be free but I also knew that, though I was not in their claws anymore, as long as I was in Iran they had a grip on me. In prison, they can swallow you directly. Outside, they can arrest you. It just takes longer. I had to go and report to an office of the Ministry of Information called Daftar Peygiri [the office in charge of controlling former prisoners] for a year and a half. In the beginning I had to go once a month and after that I went every three months. With the Daftar Peygiri and the controls, being in Iran or being in a prison is not much different. It was only when I came out of Iran that I felt free.

June 2009

Mersedeh Ghaedi

ARRESTED: June 1982
DETAINED IN: Ward 3000 (Tehran), and Evin and Qezel Hesar Prisons
RELEASED: May 1990

1. My name is Mersedeh Ghaedi and I am 54 years old. I was a political prisoner in Iran for eight years, between 19 June 1982 and 1 May 1990. I was detained in Ward 3000 in Tehran and in Evin and Qezel Hesar Prisons. I now live in the United Kingdom.

2. I make this statement in support of an investigation into the mass execution of political prisoners in 1988 in Iran.

3. This statement is true to the best of my knowledge and belief. Except where I indicate to the contrary, I make this statement on the basis of facts and matters within my own knowledge. Where the facts and matters in this statement are within my own knowledge, they are true. Where the facts and matters are not within my own knowledge, I have identified the source or sources of my information, and I believe such facts to be true.

Arrest and Torture

4. I was arrested on 9 June 1982 (19 Khordad). I was arrested with my two brothers and my sister-in-law. My brother Sadeq and I were both affiliated with the Peykar Organization (the Organization of Combat for the Emancipation of the Working Class). I am now active with the Worker-Communist Party of Iran. My other brother and sister-in-law were affiliated with a different Communist party. We all opposed the Islamic Republic and our activities involved going to meetings, publishing and distributing political materials, and reading books on Communist theory and practice—all peaceful, non-violent political activities. None of us supported armed struggle.

5. At the time of my arrest I was living in our family home. My brother and his wife had their own apartment, and my other brother, Reza, was visiting from the city of Ahvaz in the south of Iran. We were eating lunch together when the guards broke into our home. They attacked me from behind and hit my head. They dragged all of us

outside and into a car and began beating us. They took us all to Ward 3000. The guards kept saying to us, "You are a Communist, you are counter-revolutionary; we will kill you all because you don't accept the Islamic Republic of Iran."

6. After inspecting us, they immediately separated us and took us to rooms that the prisoners called the "torture chambers."

Prison Conditions and Torture

7. We were taken down some stairs to a place where there were small rooms. The doors leading into these rooms were so low that I had to bend down to enter. Inside there were beds. They made me lie down and they tied me to the bed. My hands were handcuffed behind my back and my feet were tied with my ankles bound at the end of the bed. My feet were tied in a way so that they were raised a little higher than my hands. When I was tied in this position they would flog the soles of my feet. The cables they used had different diameters depending on the intensity of torture they wanted to inflict. These different cables would be used in stages: if you refused to give information they would begin using the thicker cables.

8. The first time I was taken for this torture they beat me for two or three hours. I kept saying "I have no information. I am a nobody." Finally they stopped and they took me back upstairs, telling me that they would give me an opportunity to think about it. I was held in solitary confinement for many months.

9. Throughout this time, while being tortured or being held waiting for interrogation, I could hear screaming from girls and boys from the other rooms. On the wall and floor of the room there were blood stains, and there were empty syringes all over the floor from the injections they were using on the prisoners. I believe they were using the injections to wake prisoners up when they passed out. I never received an injection, but there were syringes all over the floor.

10. During my first year in Ward 3000 I was not allowed any visits. They allowed me to use the telephone only three or four times and I was not allowed to tell my parents where I was. The guards listened to my telephone calls.

11. After about a year I was moved to Evin Prison. In Evin we had visits from family every two weeks. But there was a glass partition and we talked over the phone. The visits were dependent on what was going on inside the prison. If the prisoners went on strike or were sent to solitary confinement, they would lose their visitation rights.

12. After the first few months I did not suffer torture in the same way as I had in the first few months of my imprisonment. But there were other forms of mistreatment. For example, for the first few years we were refused food during the day during the fasting month of Ramadan. Even though we were not Muslim, the guards would force us to observe the fasting ritual. If we did not get up before dawn we were given only one meal a day, after sunset.

13. At the time I was arrested I had thyroid problems and had to be medicated. As a form of torture, the prison officials refused to allow me to take my medication. For six years while I was in prison, I was not given my medicine. As a result of being denied my medication, I had many health problems and I lost approximately 20 kilograms [44 lbs]. I weighed only 47 kilograms [104 lbs] and my heartbeat was 150 beats per minute. I was so weak I could not walk and I was trembling constantly. But the prison officials refused to give me the medication I needed. I believe this was another form of torture.

Trial

14. They took me to court around June 1983, a year after my arrest, when I was transferred to Evin Prison from Ward 3000. I was taken to court wearing a blindfold. Once I was inside the courtroom, they removed my blindfold. There was the judge of the Revolutionary Court, the cleric Mobasheri, and one other man, who was acting as scribe. During the Shah's regime, political prisoners were at least provided with legal representation. I was not provided with a lawyer. I was not even given advance warning or time to prepare psychologically for the hearing. This was standard in Iran at that time. My hearing lasted six or seven minutes, at most.

15. The judge started the hearing by saying, "I am the one who judged your brothers and your sister-in-law. I already executed one of your brothers and if your other brother does not repent, if he does not renounce his beliefs and does not become a good person, then I will execute him as well." He explained that my brother would not renounce his beliefs and acknowledge the legitimacy of the regime by publicly apologizing on television. Until he agreed to do that, he risked execution.

16. The judge then read my indictment. I was accused of membership in a Communist party and taking part in certain activities of a Communist organization, such as attending meetings, distributing leaflets, and hiking in the mountains. Mountain-climbing was a common activity labeled as political because we would climb mountains together around Tehran and discuss political issues, often holding a meeting or conference at the top of the mountain. I was also charged with not believing in God. The judge told me that I should try to become a good person. Then he said to me, "Think of your family. How many members should they lose?"

17. I responded to him by saying, "I don't have anything to say. I reject all the charges. I do not have a lawyer." I did not accept the Islamic leadership. I did not accept the legitimacy of their government or the judicial system. On this basis, I refused to accept the charges.

18. About two weeks later I was taken to a room called the "verdict implementation room." As usual, I was blindfolded. My blindfold was removed when I entered the room. I do not remember who was there, but there were several bureaucrats sitting behind a table. I did not recognize any of them. They gave me a piece of paper on which it said I had been sentenced to eight

years in prison. They told me to sign the sentence, but I refused. They told me to "get lost." We were often insulted like this.

Events in 1988

19. I had terrible thyroid problems, but the prison authorities did not allow me to be treated. But this time, it was different. They had decided to allow me to leave the prison in order to have surgery. My appointment was one day after Khomeini publicly announced that he accepted the UN resolution on the Iraq war and "drank the poison cup." My appointment had long been planned. I was taken out of my cell to be transported to the hospital, but they refused to let me leave the prison, saying that no prisoners were being allowed out of the prison. The Revolutionary Guards said that no one would leave until further notice. At that stage we still had newspapers in the prison.

20. The next thing I remember happening at that time was that the men had their last visits with their families. [On 20 July 1988], two days after Iran accepted the UN resolution, their families were told that they should not come back until the prison authorities told them otherwise, because there would be no more visitations. One of the men had told his visitors, "I think something is going on, and I might not see you again. There is a hurricane coming." I learned this later because his sister was my cellmate. Once the visitations had begun again, her family told her what her brother had said at their last visitation. He had been executed in 1988.

21. Then around the time of the acceptance of the UN resolution, the televisions were removed from our ward. I was in the "education ward of Evin Prison" [the Amuzeshgah]. The Mojahedin women seemed really nervous. It seemed to us they knew something was about to happen and they even packed their bags as if they were waiting for it. But for those affiliated with the Communists, we had no idea what was happening. We did not know anything.

22. Around this time, all of our recreation time was stopped. We were no longer allowed to go out into the courtyard to exercise. The newspapers stopped altogether. No one was allowed to go to the infirmary, and no medication was provided to prisoners. We were given nothing except our three meals a day.

23. I cannot remember the exact date, but it was at 10 p.m. on a Wednesday evening when the guards began calling the female Mojahedin prisoners out of the cells, ten at a time. The women were taken away, but they did not take their belongings with them. Everyone, including the MKO prisoners taken from the cell, thought and assumed that they would be back. Some time after taking them out, the guards came back and took their belongings.

24. Almost every evening after that, at around the same time, the guards would come to the cells and call a list of the Mojahedin. Normally it was ten people at a time. From my ward they took 40 people in the space of a week or so. It all happened very quickly. Suddenly the rooms were empty. Of the 47 people taken from our ward,

only three women survived. They were not brought back to the ward, but we heard from prisoners in other cells, through communication by Morse code, that three women had survived. We also learned from the women in the jihad ward (the repenters' section), which was below our section in Evin, that Mojahedin women in their ward were also taken away. Again, only the Mojahedin were taken.

25. By mid- to late-August, all of the Mojahedin were gone from the cells. It was then that the guards began to call the leftists. As before, they took ten women at a time. The leftist women were also taken for a brief hearing to be questioned about their beliefs. But unlike what we had heard about the Mojahedin, the leftist women were asked mainly whether they believed in God and whether they would pray. After the questioning, most of the women were taken to ward 209 of Evin. There they would be flogged every day, at each call to prayer, until they agreed to pray. Because we had been moved to a newer part of the prison where the corridors were larger, we could hear the flogging and screaming. Some of the women received over 1,000 lashes during that period. Many of the women attempted suicide because they could no longer bear the pain and the psychological distress. Two women did kill themselves. For all of us who had been in

prison so long, it was unthinkable to give up on our beliefs and to begin to pray. Death was the preferred option.

26. From my ward only one leftist was executed. But many were taken for questioning and then to ward 209 to be flogged until they prayed. Fortunately for me, by early September, the committees had stopped. I was never taken before a committee.

27. In October the visitations started again, but I was not allowed any visits until December 1988. It was then we realized the full magnitude of the killings. As more of us had visits from relatives, we learned how many people had been killed.

28. I was finally released in 1990. I had been very ill, losing a lot of blood because of my thyroid problems. In those final two years I had to be hospitalized several times. I am sure that their refusal to give me my medication and treat my thyroid condition was another, intentional, way of inflicting pain and putting pressure on me. When I was finally released I looked like an old woman, much older than I do now. This was because of my illness and because of the prison conditions. After leaving prison I had to have a significant amount of medical treatment, both in Iran and subsequently in Norway, where I first resided [after leaving Iran].

London, June 2009

OFFICIAL STATEMENT • 6

كیهان

Subject: Government's position vis-à-vis political groups and parties
The official: Government spokesperson Behzad Nabavi
The occasion: Speech at a meeting with representatives of the Union of Factory-based Islamic Associations
                at the headquarters of the Revolutionary Guards Corps in Tabriz
Date: 1 May 1981
Source: *Kayhan*, 2 May 1981

The first category comprises groups that clearly defend the Revolution and sacrifice their lives for the Revolution. The Government of the Islamic Republic has made its position clear about these groups. It will strongly support them, and it will provide them all that they need. The second category comprises the ones that are in agreement with the government and do not cause any trouble. They are free to operate within the legally acceptable framework of the country. The government's position on them is clear. The third category comprises the ones that oppose the government but do not harm the government. Yet, they pose as protectors of people's rights. As long as these groups do not take up arms, they are free. But if they go beyond what is permitted in the legal framework we will strongly confront them. These groups may have offices and newspapers, but only with the government's permission. The fourth category comprises the ones who are directly fighting against the government of the Islamic Republic. They are at war with us, and we will fight with them. Komala, the Democratic Party of Iranian Kurdistan (DPIK), the Fadaiyan Khalq Organization (Minority) and the People's Mojahedin of Iran Organization are included in this group. The Government will confront these organizations. They [the Mojahedin] are, with a hundred percent certainty, a seditious group. Hypocrisy and sedition are fully visible in their actions. We have to prepare ourselves for confronting them. They really don't have anything, and they cannot make any political analysis. On one hand they unite with Ghasemlou [leader of DPIK] and Ezzeddin [religious Iranian Kurdish leader who opposed the IRI] to spread their decadent Marxist ideology among the people, and on the other they make deals with American groups. We have to be alert so that we can disarm them, because they have lost everything and now they have reached a state of nihilism.

Rahmat Gholami

ARRESTED: May 1983
DETAINED IN: Sepah Detention Center, Zanjan, and Zanjan (formerly Martyr Ruzbeh School) and Abhar Prisons
RELEASED: February 1989

1. My name is Rahmat Gholami. I was born on 21 March 1959, in Bandar Anzali. I was affiliated with the Fadaiyan (Minority) and was imprisoned in Zanjan Prison during the prison killings of 1988.

2. This statement is based on an interview conducted with me in Frankfurt on 30 June 2009. I make this statement in support of an investigation into the mass execution of political prisoners in 1988 in Iran.

3. This statement is true to the best of my knowledge and belief. Except where I indicate to the contrary, I make this statement on the basis of facts and matters within my own knowledge. Where the facts and matters in this statement are within my own knowledge, they are true. Where the facts and matters are not within my own knowledge, I have identified the source or sources of my information, and I believe such facts to be true.

Arrest and Torture

4. I was working at the Ministry of Energy in Zanjan. I was also politically active before the Revolution but I became more involved during the Revolution. I was in charge of the organization's propaganda section in Zanjan. Along with other FKO (Minority) sympathizers, we would organize meetings, write communiqués, and we wrote slogans on the walls. At that time our organization deemed all the regime's factions equally counter-revolutionary and against the interests of the people and the working class. That is why the release of all political prisoners and the fall of the Islamic Republic were the slogans of our organization.

5. I was arrested at work on 1 May 1983 in Zanjan by plainclothes agents. They did not show me a warrant. They said they wanted to talk to me for only two minutes. Then they took me to their car, put a hat and blindfold on me, and took me to the Islamic Revolutionary Guards' Detention Center in Azadi Square in Zanjan. The interrogation took place in the basement where there were some very small solitary cells about 70 x 180 centimeters [2.3 x 5.9 feet]. They were so small that tall prisoners could barely fit in.

6. My interrogator was someone called by the name of Mustafa or Behruz Qorbani. I think his real first name was Mostafa but I am not sure. Usually, in order to obtain a confession, through *ta'zir* and flogging, prisoners were taken blindfolded to a

special room dedicated to this purpose and located on the upper floor. When they took us for punishment we were blindfolded, but, during the interrogation, sometimes we could take the blindfold off. My arrest and interrogation took place at the time when the regime decided to arrest a large number of Tudeh Party sympathizers and members; it was also concomitant with the re-interrogation of MKO prisoners accused of reorganizing within the prison. All these people were put in solitary cells in the Revolutionary Guards' Detention Center. I was in solitary confinement for 12 days and in a general ward for a month. During this time I had only one visitation, which was a month after I was arrested.

7. Usually the interrogations took place at midnight or very early in the morning, when prisoners were not able to focus. The interrogator wanted me to write about the organization and my fellow militants. The interrogator would give me a pen and paper and say, "Write." They wanted to find other members and sympathizers of the FKO (Minority) through me. But I kept saying that I did not have any information and didn't know anyone. But I actually did know them—for example Mr. Mas'ud Mafan, my organizational friend and roommate who had fled from Zanjan but was still politicaly active in Tehran. I also knew Mr. Ali Hassanlu and some other activists. These people's names had been revealed to the interrogator by someone arrested before me. Since I didn't give them any information about their whereabouts, my interrogator told me, "if you don't give me the information, based on the religious judge's

fatwa, you shall be subjected to *ta'zir* (punishment). By *ta'zir* he meant torture with a strap or a cable or. . . .

8. During my 12-day detention in the Sepah center I was tortured three times. Twice I was taken to the *ta'zir* room, where they tried to extract information and a confession from me. First they would blindfold me, and then they would cover my head with a hood, so that I could not see the torturers. Obviously, I had seen my interrogator before. The first torture was flogging with a cable. The second time they used a kind of filled hose. They would lay me on the floor and one person would sit on my chest, while the other would keep my feet up. The interrogator and his colleagues would flog me on the soles of my feet. They would stop every now and then to see if the excruciating pain would make me talk. But I passed out both times after a few lashes. And both times they woke me up, made me stand on my feet and ordered me to walk on the spot so that my injured feet wouldn't get infected. According to Shari'a law, the flogging sentence should consist of 74 lashes. But in practice they [the interrogator and his colleagues] would never abide by the sentence. They would flog more in order to break the prisoners and coerce them to confess. My feet were injured and infected.

9. The third time, the warden rushed in and called me out, but because of the injury to my feet I couldn't walk properly; he dragged me, without blindfold, to the wardens' room and menacingly ordered me to lie on the bed. He then tied my injured feet to the bed frame with an electric cable and

started to beat me with a hose. The pain was unbearable; I started to cry while asking him why he was beating me. He said, "Don't talk." While my eyes were open, he flogged my wounded feet 30 to 40 times.

10. There were a lot of members and followers of the Tudeh Party recently arrested and many of the MKO's followers were being re-interrogated because of their activities inside the prison. Owing to the congestion in the prison and the lack of solitary confinement cells, they transferred me to a public ward. There was a toilet inside and only one triple-decker bunk bed. Most of the prisoners would sleep on the floor, and, as I was the newcomer, I would sleep next to the door.

11. A month later, I, along with all of my cellmates, was taken to the main prison for political prisoners on the Khayamshahr beltway in Zanjan. Built before the Revolution for scout activities, the building had been used after the Revolution as a school for a while [Martyr Ruzbeh School] and later it was turned into a non-standard prison building. The building had three floors:

A) The basement: there were mainly *sar-e moze'i* prisoners and it had two sections: the general ward and the section containing wards 2, 3, 4, and 5.

B) The ground floor: there were the office of the prison chief, the office of the guards, the infirmary, several solitary confinement cells, and a prisoners' ward.

C) The upper floor: Here were mainly repenters. There was also a mosque, public hall, library, and wards 6, 7, and 8.

12. They had put iron bars over the windows, and they had completely covered the windows with some yellowish plastic, so that prisoners could not benefit from sunlight. The prison population was more than its intended capacity and the wards were rather small. They took us to the upper floor in a rather big ward that was formerly the mosque. On that floor, in all the wards, we were about 80 inmates. The number of people in the prison varied at times; that year, the prison's total population was around 170 or 180 people. In some wards, you could barely see the outside through the broken edges of the windows.

13. In the spring of 1983, the food for the prisoners came in very small portions. It was mainly a little yogurt with bread, or bread, cheese, and little grapes. Later on, the quality of food got better. For quite some time, however, the rice they were giving us had black heads and tails. Some of our cellmates refused to eat it. They would take us out to the courtyard for one or two hours a day, but they would take inmates from each floor separately, so that they could not communicate with the other wards.

Trial

14. I was taken to court three months after my arrest. In the early summer of 1983 I was taken to the Islamic Revolutionary Tribunal located in the IRGC's building in Azadi (Freedom) Square. On the morning of my trial, they [prison wardens] told me to get dressed and be ready, but they didn't tell me where they were taking me or why. My trial session was very short; I can say that it lasted five minutes. The religious

judge was Hojjat ol-eslam Naseri. I was not blindfolded. The judge and I were alone in the courtroom. He was the son-in-law of the Friday Prayer Imam of Zanjan. He posed many questions.

15. It was more like an interrogation than a trial. Naseri wanted to know the hiding place and the activities of the people they were looking for. He wanted to know if they had fled from Iran or not. I would respond, "I don't know" or "I don't know them." He sarcastically told me, "You wanted to sink the Islamic Republic boat. I will keep you in prison so long that your hair will be the color of your teeth." I kept rejecting all the charges brought against me, charges such as: "collaboration with the FKO in order to topple the Islamic Republic," or reading and distributing books (the list of which was recorded in my file as evidence). As he finished reading these charges, Naseri asked me if I had anything to say in my defense. I insisted on the fact that, at the time of my arrest, I had stopped being politically active. [At this point] he said, the trial session is over, and, "if you have anything to say, send it to me in writing." That meant that if I wanted to collaborate, I should say so in writing.

16. Six month later, in September 1983, I was verbally notified of my sentence, by Panahali, one of my interrogators. I was given a jail term of 14 years and six months. I had been under arrest for six months, so the total of my jail term was 15 years. At the time they did not give the sentences in writing, whereas before, prisoners received written sentences. This is an important point: the reason they were no longer giv-

ing written sentences was that prisoners who had finished serving their sentences, but who had not been released, were using their written sentence as evidence for filing a petition.

Prison

17. In the spring of 1987 the situation in prison became terrible. In my opinion, it was the time when elements from the Ministry of Information progressively took control of the prisons, through the State Prisons Organization, and transformed Zanjan Prison into a horrific place. Before that, and because the prison had not originally been built as a prison (but as a scout building), it was easy for the inmates, from different wards, to communicate with each other and exchange information. The newly designated prison director, Kheradmand, was very tough and violent. He blocked all passageways [between the wards] and cut off all means of communication. He imposed a morbid and frightening silence upon the prison.

18. They gave us, the political prisoners, gray uniforms to wear. The uniforms were similar to the uniforms ordinary convicts had to wear. To me and to some of my fellow inmates who were *sar-e moze'i*, [it seemed that] they wanted to humiliate and break the political prisoners by forcing them to wear a uniform. Most of us, the *sar-e moze'is*, refused to wear them.

19. According to the new regulations, the lights would go off at 10 p.m. On 27 June 1987, when the lights went off, they started to take, one by one, the prisoners who were held in the basement wards, for question-

Wood carvings made by Rahmat Gholami
when he was a prisoner in Zanjan Prison

ing in the prison's office. There they were asked if they would agree to wear the prison uniform. Those who refused to wear the uniform were conducted to a small cell on the ground floor. Eighteen people, including myself, refused to wear the prison uniform. The room we were sent to was tiny, 2 by 3 meters [6.5 x 10 feet], without a window and without sink or toilet. It was hot and we had no space; we couldn't sleep that night. The following morning they took the soap away just to see who would protest.

20. In the summer, on 28 June 1987, six of the prisoners who had protested, including me, were selected and exiled to other prisons for sedition. One can say that they had picked two prisoners from each political organiza-

tion or doctrinal affiliation. One prisoner was exiled to the police prison in Abhar. Some others were exiled to the police prison in Zanjan.

21. I was the only one to be transferred to the Revolutionary Guards Detention Center [formerly the administration building of the prefecture, then expropriated by the IRGC and turned into their offices, solitary cells, and women's prison]. There I was kept in solitary confinement for one month. During this period, I was mentally and physically pressured by the wardens. One day, two wardens came into my cell and told me that I was arrogant in prison, and they said, "You dare to challenge us? We will break you." For instance, during the first few days of my being held in

solitary confinement, my toothbrush broke and I asked the warden to buy a new one for me from the prison store. But he denied me the right to buy a toothbrush from the store.

22. Prisoners were given a very short time to use the toilets. Once I had to wait seven hours before being allowed to use the bathroom. They also were given a very short time to get their food ratio. But since I was being punished they made it even more difficult for me. After I had served my solitary confinement term [29 July 1987], I was sent back to Zanjan's Martyr Ruzbeh Prison, but this time I was kept in the repenters' ward, on the upper floor, where I was under the surveillance of one of the repenters by the name of Hassan. He was constantly watching me. Every one of my moves was controlled, even when I went to the bathroom. Hassan was an MKO member who had been sentenced to death, but he had been spared because he had repented. I was in this ward until the 1988 killings. At that point the *tavvab* and *sare moze'i* wards were no longer separate.

23. The new director made sure there was no more communication between the wards. Prisoners were not allowed to talk to the guards or demand anything. Before, the prisoners of each ward would elect a representative among themselves, who would represent them and communicate their demands and needs to the prison authorities. But at this point, the prison authorities declared: "We will appoint someone as your representative who will be the only one communicating with the prison authorities." They changed the organiza-

tion of the wards. Some of the hard-line repenters were sent to the basement where most of the *sar-e moze'i* people were detained. [As a result] the atmosphere in the wards became horrible, literally horrible. As soon as two prisoners would start talking to each other, the appointed representative would call the wardens and tell them, these two are talking, or they are doing political analysis together. This meant that we didn't even have the right to speak to each other. This situation continued until the summer of 1988.

24. The pressure was increasing every day. The management of the prison was really tough and would not give us any explanation for the harsh treatment. They did not allow anyone to talk. There was a very young prisoner who, in spite of his young age, was smart and sharp. He assessed the atmosphere and the situation of the prison very well. He gave me useful information, such as who was a repenter and who was not. When they transferred me from solitary confinement to the ward upstairs, he was happy to see his friend and former cellmate and got close to me. This friendship became an issue for the wardens; they took me to the office of the prison and punished me for it. They hit my head on the wall two or three times while I was blindfolded.

25. There was no regular system for visitations. As my family had to travel from Tehran to visit me, I had very irregular visits.

Events Surrounding 1988

26. In the spring of 1988 the [country's] situation was very complex. We understood from the news about the [Iran-Iraq] war

that the Islamic Republic was in a bad situation. We knew that on 18 July 1988 Khomeini had accepted UN Resolution 598, an acceptance that had been for him as bitter as drinking a cup of poison. We still had a television until 27 July and were aware of the MKO attack.

27. On 27 or 28 July 1988, we were in the courtyard when the warden came and read the names of 25 or 26 of the MKO people. He said they should pack up their stuff and be ready. No one knew what was happening. We were thinking that maybe they had built a new prison up to the [regular] prison standards, and maybe they were moving these prisoners to the new prison and the remaining prisoners would be transferred there later. Among those who were called was one of the zealous repenters, who, unaware that they were going to kill him, was enthusiastically packing and kept calling the wardens to let them know he was ready. The wardens kept silent and didn't tell us anything. The visitations were suspended. The television was taken away. Newspapers were no longer provided. Even the radio, which had always been on the loudspeakers, was turned off. We had no more contact with the outside world.

28. A couple of days later, another group of MKO affiliates were taken out of their cells. The corner window of the room where the toilet was in the ward on the upper floor was broken—from there we could see the courtyard where prisoners from other wards were taken for recreation. We could see who was missing. In my prison in 1988, only MKO members and sympathizers were taken away. As far as I know,

no non-MKO prisoners were taken from our prison to be executed in the summer of 1988. Some of these [MKO] prisoners came back after two or three months; those who came back did not say where they had been or what had happened. The prison atmosphere was so bad and terrifying that no survivor dared to talk about the tragedy. Even describing this environment is difficult for me. The MKO people would not share information with us, the leftists. And we preferred not to know anything, because we were worried that, if we knew something, we might reveal it under torture.

29. There was an MKO prisoner, Nasser Hassanpur, who had been released from Tabriz Prison in 1986 because of a heart ailment. After his release he had gone to get his exemption from military service, but since they needed soldiers [without considering his heart condition], they drafted him, put him on a bus, and made him wear a military uniform and sent him to the frontline. In the front, once they realized that he had been a political prisoner, they arrested him and sent him to our prison in Zanjan. One night, after 10 p.m., while the guard was checking on the prisoners with a flashlight, to see if all of them were in bed and sleeping [and not talking to each other], he dragged Nasser out of bed, on the pretext that his eyes were open. Nasser retorted, "I am in my bed; I cannot sleep." This response was enough for the guard to take Nasser downstairs, where we could hear him being badly beaten, and at some point we no longer heard his voice. They took him and we never saw him again.

One courageous cellmate, braving the danger, wrote a complaint letter to the prison director, and protested the ill treatment of the prisoners.

30. We could not evaluate precisely how many people went missing in 1988 [after the killings]. From our own ward, in two days, they took around 30 prisoners. There were two brothers in our prison; the older one was in our ward and the younger one in the ward downstairs. The guards came into our ward and told the older brother, "Take your belongings and come." But then they said, "No, you go back [to your ward]," and they took the younger brother [and executed him].

31. The prison's tough rules were strictly enforced until late October 1988. In mid-November visitations started again, and this was when we became aware of the tragedy that had befallen us. Up to then we had been guessing that the situation was horrendous, but we couldn't imagine that they would take away a whole group of people and kill them. [For instance] Bijan Eslami Eshpela, who was born in 1960 in the port of Anzali, was affiliated with FKG. He was in Gohardasht Prison, serving a three-year prison sentence. They also killed him in 1988. I could sense the depth of the tragedy through the sorrow of those who came to visit me. [Before the killings] I had tried to demand my transfer from Zanjan to Tehran Prison. Through his visitors, Bijan had warned me, "Do not come to Tehran, it is terrible here."

32. One of my cellmates, Mas'ud Mas'udi, and his brother Sa'id were also among the victims of the summer of 1988 killings. Mas'ud was a 30-year-old teacher and Sa'id, his younger brother, was only 25 or 26 years old at the time of his execution. They were both MKO sympathizers.

33. I was released on 18 February 1989. I was the last political prisoner to be released. The rest had all been released. There were only a few kept in the solitary wards whom I did not know. My parents left the deed to their home as bail for my release. I also had to fill out a form. It was written on the form that I could not engage in any political activity or I would be arrested and would receive the harshest possible punishment. It was a print-out and all we had to do was sign it.

34. I was also interrogated after I was released. I had to report to the Revolutionary Guards' intelligence office in Zanjan for a year after that. In the beginning I had to sign in every week, and then gradually it changed to once a month. The last time that I went there, they told me that I could go to Tehran and sign in there, which I wish I had not done. Once I went to Tehran, it was like I had just been arrested and the interrogations had started up again. Once, I asked about all those interrogations and questions and answers, but the person in charge threatened me badly.

Frankfurt, June 2009

OFFICIAL STATEMENT • 7

اطّلاعات

Subject: On the dangerous nature of the MKO and the necessity for the whole people to be [members of] the intelligence organization

The official: Founder and Supreme Leader of the Islamic Republic of Iran, Ayatollah Ruhollah Khomeini

The occasion: Speech delivered at a meeting with relatives of the victims of the bombing of the headquarters of the Islamic Republic Party and with the [surviving] members

Date: 2 July 1981

Source: *Ettela'at*, 4 July 1981

Today it is everyone's duty, all citizens of Iran, to open their eyes and ears and monitor the movements of these people [members of the Mojahedin Khalq Organization (MKO)]. It is an act of negligence for the people to simply sit by and expect only the members of the Revolutionary Guards, the committees, and the government to perform these duties. Today everyone is duty-bound to remain vigilant regarding this issue. These saboteurs are sleazily performing their subversive work and are, unfortunately, engaged in misleading our unsuspecting young daughters and sons. It is the responsibility of the parents to be more attentive to the fact that their children are the targets of these subversive elements who, in order to muddy the waters, try to corrupt and thus take advantage of our youth for their evil purposes. Every parent and every relative has the duty to guide and advise these misled youths, these boys and girls, and prevent them from embarking on a path that is contrary to that of the people and Islam. They should not sit idly by while their children go among the people and commit acts of sabotage and then get caught and suffer the consequences of their deeds, here in this world [as opposed to the day of reckoning]; they should not let that happen. These children have been deceived and they need advice and guidance. . . . Today is the day when you, all of you together, must be ready to wrest this country from the hands of corrupt forces and lead it to prosperity. Today, all of you should be the Intelligence Organization, be its members. If we come across any one of these saboteurs, we are duty-bound to point them out to the security agents so that they can arrest them and hand them over to the courts to be put on trial. The trials must be fair and according to Islamic tenets. We should not sit still and allow the saboteurs to continue to expand their subversive activities. These people are mercenaries whose task is to expand their work and incite riots anywhere they can. They are bent on destruction in the hope of gradually scaring people into abandoning their rightful path. Once the nation retreats, the saboteurs will creep onto the stage to destroy a nation and parliament and [replace it with] a political order that looks Islamic on the surface but is in fact what they, and the Americans, want it to be. We must not sit by as mere spectators. We must be active and involved. Those who have sacrificed, [whose loved ones have become] martyrs, must become more active, because they have lost valuable individuals. They must, therefore, track down those who have perpetrated and continue to perpetrate these crimes. . . .

Advice for Those Affiliated with the Hypocrites [MKO]
Once again, I call upon those who have not yet become truly deviant to make a clean break with the hypocrites who have taken up arms against Islam. I do not mean for you to advise them to forgo violence and, at the same time, ask me not to have recourse to violence either. For that we mean that they and we are alike [and we are not alike]. You must have known them, and their views and goals, by now. You must have seen and read their manifestos. How could you not separate them from us, since we are, at least, Muslims! We are bad Muslims!*

I often told Mr. Banisadr to distance himself from them. God knows I repeatedly told him that they [Mojahedin] would be his undoing, that these wolves who don't have any principles, would eventually destroy him. He did not listen. He kept reiterating that those who have surrounded him were truly loyal and such. But I knew that this was not the case. I had told him that the capital-

ist people could not be of any use to him either, that he was being used as a pawn. The Monafeqin would not be of any use to you either. The moment they come to power they will cut you off. For you believe in the verity that there is no God but Allah whereas they don't. They describe monotheism as class-based. They believe that there is no day of resurrection and that there is nothing beyond the material world. But you don't. The day they prevail, God forbid, you shall be their sacrificial lamb. They will have made you their bridge to victory, which will be burned once they cross it.

Improvement and Betterment [of oneself] in the Month of Ramadan
. . . It is not you who have forsaken Islam, it is the nonbelievers, [those] who have taken up arms against Islam, who have taken to the streets and killed innocent people. You surely know the punishment in Islamic law for that. Islam has ordained the fate of he who goes out in the street, armed, and frightens [and terrorizes] people; he does not even have to kill anyone. God has specified the punishment of the corruptors who take to the streets and intimidate believers, and you surely know what it is. It is enough for you to explain the problem, state that the answer is in God's Holy Book and such is the punishment of the transgressors. You should explain this Islamic legal issue and have it endorsed by your group. Why are you floundering? What are you expecting them to do for you?

. . .

Our War with America and Its Refuse
We should not forget that we are at war with

*An expression commonly used by the clergy, traditionally as a reminder of the human fallibility that is responsible for faults and not the essence of the creed.

America. We are at war with America and its refuse. These groups of refuse disguised themselves while we were oblivious. They are still there. You should identify each and every one of them and introduce them to the courts. Don't wait until they set fire to some place. They want chaos to take place, or an explosion to happen in order for people to get disengaged. But they saw that the opposite happened. This [philosophy of and desire for] martyrdom united everybody. . . . The goal was that the issue of America be forgotten. A group would discuss the Soviet Union so that America would be forgotten. On the very day of Ashura [day commemorating the martyrdom of Hossein, the third Imam of the Shi'ites, the Prophet's grandson], one group would abandon the cry of Allaho Akbar and would whistle and clap instead. The goal was to make the people forget about the slogan "Death to America." . . .

Advice to People Who Are Associated with
Monafeqin [hypocrites: reference to MKO]
I repeat my advice to those who have not completely deviated. I advise you to separate yourselves from these monafeqin, who have revolted against Islam. You should not ask them to stop the violence and then turn around and ask me to stop the violence. [Here Khomeini refers to moderate oppositionists who blame both the Mojahedins and the government for resorting to arbitrary violence; basically he is alluding to his former Prime Minister Mehdi Bazargan.] This means that they are the same as us. I believe they [who think this way] have seen their [the Mojahedin's] Methodology [the Mojahedin's book on their ideology]. They [the Mojahedin] have published their ideological texts, and these gentlemen [liberals like Bazargan] have probably seen them. They equate them with us, while they know that at least we are Muslims, even if bad Muslims! No, they are not separating themselves from them. . . . These monafeqin will be of no good to you [Khomeini is addressing Banisadr in this paragraph]. Whenever they get power, they will remove you as well. Because you say, "There is no god but God," and they are opposed to this. They consider monotheism to be about social classes. They consider the afterlife to be right here, in this world. They do not care about anything except this world. But you do. God forbid, on the day that they reach victory, you will be sacrificed. For them, you are only a bridge towards victory. When they pass this bridge they will destroy it. They do not want anyone to bother them. You have not left Islam, but for those who do not believe in Islam, have revolted against Islam, have taken to the streets, and have committed murder—you know what the Islamic punishment is. And you also know that the armed person who takes to the streets—he does not necessarily have to kill people—when he intimidates people, Islam is clear about his fate, and you know this concept. [Khomeini is here equating demonstrators with corruptors on earth whose punishment, according to the Holy Book, is death.]. . . You at least should talk about this one issue. Issue a statement saying, "The concept is in God's Book. These people, who are corruptors, have taken to the streets and are intimidating the people. According to God's decree, this [death] is their punishment." Make a written statement and acknowledge this Shari'a rule, and put your group's signature under it. [Khomeini is asking Mehdi Bazargan's organization to approve of his policy of terror]. . . .

Mehrdad Kavousi

ARRESTED: June 1982
DETAINED IN: Evin, Qezel Hesar, and Gohardasht Prisons
RELEASED: May 1992

1. My name is Mehrdad Kavousi. I was a political prisoner in Evin Prison during the 1988 killings of political prisoners.

2. I make this statement in support of an investigation into the mass execution of political prisoners in 1988 in Iran.

3. This statement is true to the best of my knowledge and belief. Except where I indicate to the contrary, I make this statement on the basis of facts and matters within my own knowledge. Where the facts and matters in this statement are within my own knowledge, they are true. Where the facts and matters are not within my own knowledge, I have identified the source or sources of my information, and I believe such facts to be true.

Arrest and Torture

4. I was born in 1960 in Tehran. I graduated from high school in Tehran in 1978 and entered the university in Shiraz the same year. I started studying physics at the University of Shiraz.

5. I became politically active during the Revolution and continued through the early 1980s. I joined the Mojahedin Khalq Organization (MKO) around 1981. I was active with them on the side; I was not a cadre or a member, but I supported them. When I was in Shiraz in the 1970s and the early 1980s, the universities were still open. I was politically active, and when the MKO opened offices in Shiraz I attended their meetings. From 1981 on, I became more active and I worked in the MKO office. After the armed uprising, I remained active, but our activities were underground.

6. I was arrested in the summer of 1982 in Tehran. I had returned to Tehran when the university was shut down. I was detained for three days at the local committee and then I was transferred to Evin Prison.

7. I was interrogated for almost nine months before my trial. In the beginning [when I was first detained], I was interrogated at least once a week. Then in the final weeks

of my detention period, the [frequency] of the interrogations increased and I was interrogated every day. The way the Mojahedin functioned was that every day I had to get in touch with my contact and inform him that I was fine. We knew that if someone had not established contact one day, then he or she was assumed to have been arrested. The government interrogators knew that this was the MKO protocol.

8. They designated an interrogator for me starting on the first day. I was interrogated, beaten, and tortured so that I would give them information about my contacts before they [my contacts] realized that I had been arrested. When the interrogators learned that I had been held for two days in a local committee before being transferred to Evin, they stopped putting pressure on me to get the names of my contacts. They knew that whoever was supposed to meet me was not going to show up because [it was known that] I had disappeared.

9. There were different methods of torture. They were flogging me with a cable on the soles of my feet, and also on my body. I was tied to the bed and beaten. To this day, I have no feeling in my right foot as a result of the torture that I was subjected to in prison. [Another method of torture they used] was strangling. They would suffocate me to the point that I thought I might die. They also used a method called the "moving bed." I was tied to the frame of a bed. The base of the bed was removed, so there was nothing beneath me. This was a sort of horizontal *qapani* torture; they would tie your arms together, one from below and one from your shoulder. They would tie my wrists together—one hand over my shoulder and one from my waist— and hang me. They also hit me on the neck with a heavy object, like a nightstick. It was like being electrically shocked; it was so painful.

10. The building we were taken to for interrogation was next to the prosecutor's office. I only found out about my charges when the trial began. During the first two months of my detention, I had no visitations. After that, I had a visitation once a month. Only my father or mother could visit. My parents were panicked and very frightened when they came to visit for the first time because they did not know where I was and what had happened to me. They found me accidentally, and they knew that there were going to be beatings and torture—the [political] atmosphere had led them to believe that people were treated badly in prison.

Trial

11. Nine months after my arrest, in late February or early March 1983, I was taken to court for the first time. I was not given any notice. Blindfolded, I was taken before the judge; they never took off my blindfold. It seemed as if the judge, the person who took me to court, and I, were the only ones present in the room.

12. The judge enumerated nine charges against me, all of which related to my activities with the MKO: "sympathizing with the MKO," "providing financial and other resources for the MKO," and "acting against the Islamic Republic." His only question was, "Do you have any defense?"

I told him that all the nine charges that he was bringing up were all actually the same one [charge], that is, "being active for the MKO, and for freedom and democracy." The judge told me to leave the room. The Revolutionary Guard standing outside the courtroom appeared and asked me, "Would you agree to do an interview or not?" I said, "No."

13. I received my sentence two weeks after the trial. [My sentence was] ten years' imprisonment.

Prison Conditions

14. From the time I was taken to Evin Prison to the day of my trial, I was kept in a 4 x 5 meter [13 x 16 ft.] cell that housed about 80 people. The number changed because people came and went based on recent arrests or transfers, but, on average, there were around 80 of us. When I was arrested, only ward 209 of Evin had cells for solitary confinement. There were 80 [solitary] cells there in total, but all of them were full.

15. We had only about ten minutes of fresh air per day, when the guards would take us to the little courtyard. We had a total of 15 minutes to use the restroom and the shower, and to wash our dishes. We had one television that had only one channel, and was only on during the news or when [they showed] interviews of political prisoners in the Hosseinyeh at the prison.

16. These interviews had a very negative impact on the prisoners' morale. They were broadcast only in Evin, and directly for the prisoners. Usually, they would bring a group of people in the afternoon to the Hosseinyeh and interview them. These were, in fact, confessions but the authorities preferred to call them "interviews."

17. There was very little food and the quality was extremely bad. For example, if we had vegetables we would say, "They have cut the grass in Evin and brought it for us." If they had something with chicken, we would say that "the chicken has passed by the pot today," because there was no chicken in the pot except a little piece of skin or something. They would also give us bread and dates. But generally, there was not enough food, so we were always hungry.

18. The prisoners' psychological state was even worse than the food. They would, at any time, day or night, take a few prisoners out for interrogation.

18. The prisoners were generally very young. There were many 18-year-olds. There were also 16-year-olds and even younger people. Younger prisoners were held in other cells.

20. We were not separated into different political groups. In addition to Mojahedin, there were people from different groups: the Fadaiyan (Minority), Arman Mustaz'afin, the Forqan Group. There were also royalists and some supporters of the Shah (including the Shah's brother, Hamid Reza). In subsequent years, we also had Tudeh members and Bahá'ís. The prison population included sympathizers of all the political groups that were active in Iran before the events of 1981.

21. The interrogators' assumption was that prisoners still held firm to their beliefs. If

any [prisoners] changed their views in favor of [the regime], [the prison authorities/ guards] would ease the situation for them. At the same time, they would ask them to report on their cellmates.

22. Two weeks after I received my sentence, that is, in March or April 1983, I was transferred from Evin to Qezel Hesar Prison. I was in Qezel Hesar for three and a half years, until the summer of 1986, when I was transferred to Gohardasht Prison and then back to Evin. I was sent to the same ward [in Evin] that I was in before being taken to Qezel Hesar. The living conditions in Evin had improved because the number of prisoners had decreased.

23. Around the fall of 1987, they started to separate [the prisoners] based on [the severity] of their sentences. Ward 4, the *mellikesh* ward, was for people who were about to be released, those who had finished serving their sentences, and those whose sentences were about to end. Before 1988, the condition for release was to repent, agree to be interviewed, or affirm your hatred [of your group]. I was in ward 1 (upstairs) with people who had sentences ranging from 10 to 15 years. There were about 135 prisoners in my ward. People who were sentenced to 15 years and more were in ward 1 (downstairs). Ward 3 held people who were sentenced to between 5 and 10 years' imprisonment.

24. After separating the prisoners [by length of sentence], they closed the wards' doors for about ten days. This was before Bahman 1366 (January 1988). They did not give explanations to the prisoners [about why

they were being separated]. There was no communication possible with other wards. So there was no possibility of exchanging any information. In Esfand 1366 (February–March 1988), they closed the ward's doors again for a week or two. We did not understand why they did that.

25. Starting in Bahman 1366 (January–February 1988), every now and then, the more experienced guards would raid the ward. They were looking for evidence to prove that there was a political organization in the ward. They did that more than ten times. Prisoners had carved knives out of spoons so that they could share food, for example, to cut up apples. A prisoner had made paste from old newspapers, and then turned it into weights, so that he could lift weights. The guards confiscated the knives and the weights. Normally they searched us as we were being transferred between cells and wards. They would search the prisoners completely and go through their belongings. But this was unusual. They [the guards] would not normally come into the cells and raid the cells in this way.

26. At the time, we could choose our own cells in the ward. After 1987, [prison authorities] no longer interfered in these choices. For example, the Mojahedin prisoners were in one ward, the leftists in another, and so each group's members would be in cells with like-minded people. The cell doors were open so we could communicate with each other [inside the ward].

Events Surrounding 1988

27. We occasionally went on hunger strikes to protest the inhuman conditions of the

prison. In January 1988, we were on strike again. About 20 people from our ward were taken to be interrogated. They were beaten and tortured and even threatened with execution. Maybe 10 [prisoners] among the 20 [taken] were returned to the ward before the killings started. They told us that the interrogators were insisting that there were political activities going on in prison, that there was an organization within the prison, and that they had to confess to it. They were under a lot to pressure to say that, but we did not really know why.

28. Around April–May 1988, one of my cellmates, who was responsible for the ward, was taken to the Moshtarak Committee for interrogation. My cellmate was told that they were going to execute us all if we continued to protest and go on strike. He was told to tell the other prisoners that, from 1987 on, the Ministry of Intelligence had been created and had taken over Evin. They were based in ward 209.

29. Around June 1988, Naseri, Montazeri's son-in-law, came to Evin. He had come to Qezel Hesar Prison before and introduced himself in that way. He used to come to the prison and talk to the prisoners and get their views on the prison. This time around, he asked to see those who were in charge of each ward. I was one of those people. I was in charge of the prison store. He wanted to talk to us separately. He [Naseri] took us together outside the ward, not outside of the building, where there were no Revolutionary Guards around; it was only us with Naseri.

30. The conversation started as usual, [with his asking,] "How is the situation in Evin?"

But then he told us that every item (such as knives and other instruments) that had been taken away from us during the raids had been taken to the Hosseinyeh and exhibited there. The families of the martyrs were brought in to see the kinds of instruments that were being used by the prisoners to threaten the guards. We were very surprised. Naseri said, "I don't know why they are doing this, but the situation seems unusual to me." He said, "It seems that they are gathering evidence against you." And he ended by saying, "Be very careful."

31. Months before the 1988 executions, the families of prisoners had established a special relationship with Montazeri. They [the families] kept going to the city of Qom to meet with Montazeri. These meetings led Montazeri to use his influence to get some of the prisoners pardoned. Many of the prisoners had their sentences reduced— even in our ward. In June 1988 about 20 prisoners from all political groups were called and were told that they had been pardoned and that they would be released in September. All—except for one—were executed in the killings. This one person had been removed from the ward and taken to a solitary cell to wait to be released, but he wasn't.

32. We received one more bit of news before the killings. One or two weeks before the killings, a prisoner from ward 3 was taken to the Moshtarak Committee, then called Ward 3000. There, he was told that prisoners had been divided into three separate color categories. White meant that the prisoner would be released. Yellow meant that the prisoner would be kept in prison.

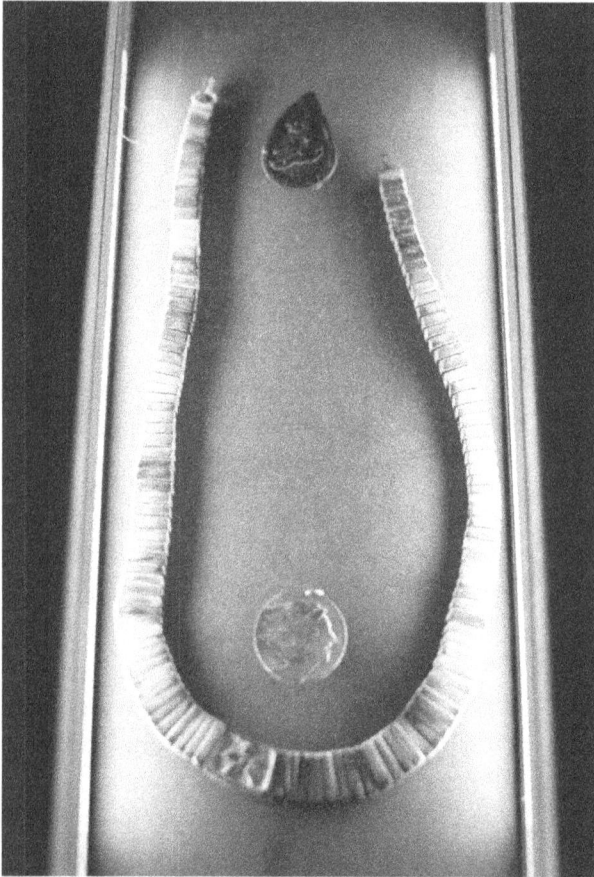

A necklace made out of date pits, with the date March 21 (the Persian New Year) carved on it. It was made by Alireza (Shapur) Eskandari, who was executed in 1988, as a New Year's gift to his wife, Efat Mahbaz, who was also in prison at the time. The pendant at the bottom is a woman's profile that he carved on a coin, offered to his wife on the occasion of 8 March, International Women's Day.

Red meant that the prisoner was going to be executed. They had not specified who would be in which category, but they had asked him to inform other prisoners. The prisoner from ward 3 had seen one of our cellmates in the prison infirmary and told him.

33. In Tir 1367 [June–July 1988], they took away our televisions. I remember that, after they took the television, we were able to hear the news a couple of times from a radio that was on somewhere in the prison building and could be heard in the ward.

That is how we realized that an unusual situation was occurring. The radio kept playing military marches. The guards put tremendous pressure on the prisoners in all the wards.

34. We had no news from the outside world, but later we heard from other wards that an operation had been launched and there was an attack (Forugh Javidan [Operation Eternal Light]). Later, once the doors were open, we heard about the MKO operation on the border from a prisoner in ward 4 (the *mellikesh* ward). He had learned about

the Forugh Javidan attack and, while in line for the infirmary, he had passed on the information to one of the cellmates in ward 1. He was beaten up by the guards for trying to talk, but he managed to convey the information.

35. We had a feeling that the situation was not normal, but we could not determine why. We knew that Iraq's bombardments of Iran had increased. My ward was the last ward to have visitations, on 23 July. This was one day before the MKO attack. After that, there was no visitation. The executions started on 28 July, at 10 a.m.

The Executions

36. On Thursday, 28 July 1988, the prison guards came to ward 1 (upstairs), where I was held, and told the prisoners to put their blindfolds on and come out in a line. They were unusually hurried and were asking us questions individually: "What ward are you in? What is your charge? What have you been sentenced to?" What was unusual was that everything was being done in a very hasty manner. Eventually everyone was questioned. I was in the first group to be taken from the cells. There were about 80 of us prisoners, and we were taken to ward 209. We filled up the solitary cells since there were more than 80 people, [and 80] was the capacity of ward 209. There were only solitary cells in ward 209. Some of us were also kept in the hallway.

37. The next day, around 10 a.m., I was taken in for interrogation. The voice of the interrogator was not familiar. He asked the same questions as before, including about

our charges. I told him that I "belong to the Mojahedin." From almost a year before, this had been our response. Instead of saying *monafeqin*, we said "Mojahedin." Then the interrogator took me back to my cell and, an hour later, I was put in a minibus with nine or ten people and driven to the building where the prosecutor's office was located. We all were blindfolded.

38. The court was located outside this building. When we entered, I could see from underneath the blindfold that there were other prisoners there with blindfolds on. After half an hour, they took me to court. Someone told me to remove my blindfold. The religious judge was [Hossein'ali] Nayyeri. There were four or five other people, but they were behind me. I could see only Nayyeri. Someone behind me [said], "Respond to the questions that Haj Aqa asks of you." I turned my head to see whom [this person] was talking to, and I was told, "Just look ahead of you. Don't look back."

39. Nayyeri asked the same questions: name, charge, the sentence, and if I was willing to ask for a pardon. [I said,] "Why should I ask for a pardon—what is happening?" Nayyeri asked, "Don't you know what has happened outside?" [I said,] "No, we are prisoners, how can we know what is happening outside?" Nayyeri said, "Are you rejecting the *monafeqin* or not?" [I said,] "Why should I do so?" Nayyeri said, "Don't you know that they have been spying for Iraq for years?" [I said,] "Well, I condemn spying. But this is none of my business." People who were behind me were also talking. They did not say that the

Mojahedin had attacked, but they were saying, "[The] Mojahedin are terrorists, they have killed people." They and the judge were trying to encourage me to reject the Mojahedin and do an interview. [I said,] "No, no, I am not going to do anything." Nayyeri said, "Take him out." I put on my blindfold and after a while they took me and a number of other people back to the solitary cells in Evin by minibus.

40. I was in solitary for about ten days. There was a hot water pipe passing through my cell. In the winter, they used it as heating for the cells. It was a big pipe, about 1.5 meters [5 ft.] above the ground, and I could climb on it and, with difficulty, look outside through a small window. From my cell I could see a number of people being taken away every afternoon in a minibus. I knew some of the prisoners.

41. One time, I asked a Revolutionary Guard what was happening and why I had been brought there. He said, "We are going to execute all of you and then you do not have to worry anymore." I realized then that executions were taking place.

42. On 6 August, I was taken outside into the hallway. I saw that some new people had been brought in and I recognized the uniforms of the Jamshidabad Prison. Those prisoners were charged with military violations. They had identification signs on their chests. They were replacing us in the solitary cells. They did not call them by name, only by number. A former cellmate, who had been detained there, had told me about the uniforms and identification signs of Jamshidabad Prison.

43. I was taken to a cell in the entrance area. The building I was in had four floors and 100 cells on each floor. I was taken to one of the cells in the first row. I was on the third floor. Because the cell number started with the floor number, mine was 314 or 315. I tried to get in touch with other cellmates using Morse code. In those cells, communication was possible. The person in the cell next to me had no idea what was happening and thought that all this was about pardons. The person on the other side did not respond. The person in the cell below me was clearly not political and had been arrested only six months before. But that person gave me some news about the Iran-Iraq War. I was held there for ten days.

44. One day I could hear someone opening the cell doors and asking questions of the prisoners. The cells were close to each other, so we could hear people talking in the hallway. Evin's deputy director for security, Mojtaba Halvai, came to my cell. I had not seen him before, but other prisoners knew him. He told me to put my blindfold on and come out. Three or four other people were waiting outside their cells. They lined us up and took us on foot to the buildings of ward 325. Halvai was leading us.

45. We walked 500 or 600 meters [approx. 0.3 mile]. When we got close to the building, the guard stopped us. Halvai introduced himself and we went in. There was no exchange between us. We entered ward 4 and they put us all in one public cell. There were other prisoners there, including two repenters. It was a really bad situation. You could see fear in everybody's eyes. We

were wondering what had happened to the other prisoners, and we were constantly thinking, "What are they going to do to us?" A few days later, when we were out to get some fresh air, a Revolutionary Guard who lived in my neighborhood recognized me. He told me that I should be very careful and not talk to anyone. He said, "Every day, they are taking a number of people and they do not come back." During this period some people were taken from the cells, and they never came back. I was there for nearly two weeks.

46. After about two weeks, I was taken to court again. Outside the courtroom I sat next to other prisoners. A guard asked me, "Are you Merhdad Kamali?" I said, "No," and he told me to sit down. Fifteen minutes later, the court members left for lunch. The court closed and they took us back to our cell.

47. In late August, we were in cells with closed doors. Then in September, they brought in prisoners who had survived in Gohardasht. After the executions, they were asking prisoners who survived to confess, agree to be interviewed, or write rejections of their groups. I refused these options. In late January–early February 1989, they took some prisoners away to talk to them and pardon them. They did not pardon the Mojahedin prisoners. They separated the leftists and released some of them.

48. I think that, of the 135 people in our ward, only five or six survived. I was the only one who was able to get out [of the country]. I have a precise list of the 135 people who were with me in ward 4. While in prison, I wrote down the names of those who were killed and those who survived, and I have it. With the help of other prisoners who survived, we prepared a list of 850 to 900 individuals in prison.

49. I think it was accidental that I survived. I was taken to be executed but, for whatever reason, I was not. I think that 90 percent of those who were not executed survived accidentally or for specific reasons. For example, if there were several siblings, the regime would let one live. There were people who had fallen asleep outside the courtroom and had not heard their names being called. Some stayed alive because Montazeri tried hard to stop the executions. The demonstrations in Europe had also some effect. Most importantly, they had killed 90 percent of the prisoners and no longer felt they were in any danger.

50. I stayed in prison until I served my sentence. I had been sentenced to ten years. I was released in 1992, four years after the killings.

Sweden, September 2009

OFFICIAL STATEMENT • 8

جمهوری اسلامی

Subject:	Those municipal public prosecutors who are lenient toward corruptors [on earth] will be punished themselves
The official:	Prosecutor General of the Islamic Revolution, Hojjat ol-eslam Hossein Musavi Tabrizi
The occasion:	Interview with the Islamic Republic's state television about the opposition groups
Date:	18 September 1981
Source:	*Jomhuri Eslami*, 21 September 1981

Those Municipal Public Prosecutors Who Are Lenient Toward Corruptors [on Earth] Will Be Punished Themselves.

. . . The Government must be the government of Allaho Akbar [God is greatest]. This is what the people want from us. We are not seeking titles [and positions]. We cannot sit still and not react to those whose purpose is to carry out acts of sabotage through armed [attacks] and explosions by Molotov cocktail, and to those who aid and abet them. . . . If they are arrested, we will not [put them in jail so that they can] eat and sleep and feed off of the public treasury. They will be prosecuted on the streets. Whoever picks up a Molotov cocktail and confronts the Islamic Republic [on the street] will be prosecuted right then and there. When they've been arrested and taken to the Prosecutor's Office, they have been tried, and their sentence is execution. These people are outlaws and they terrorize and frighten the population; they attack the Islamic Republic; they trample upon the memory of thousands of martyrs; they waste the people's treasury. Killing them is not just

permitted, it is a religious imperative. Whoever is involved in armed conflict on the streets, as well as those who hide behind such armed insurgents, strengthen and guide them, and supply them with motorcycles and cars, will be executed upon arrest and without delay, on that same night, upon the testimony of two Revolutionary Guards or other people [witnesses] who testify that they were indeed involved in the armed conflict or had supported those who were involved in the armed conflict against the Islamic Republic. The parents of these hypocrites [reference to members of the Mojahedin Khalq Organization] should not expect us to grant a pardon, because we cannot turn a blind eye [to such events] and forgive when [the Iranian] people are watching. I also direct and order all municipal public prosecutors to adopt this same approach, or they will be punished themselves. We cannot sit idly by while a few youngsters who know nothing about Islam, and are surely guided by

142

American mercenaries, play with Islam's reputation and [disrespect] the blood of thousands of our martyrs. . . . When America lost all hope of winning the war from the outside and realized that Saddam could not possibly break our Islamic state, it began waging a war from within [Iran] through supporting a movement that was begun by [former President] Banisadr and the [always] ready-to-collude liberals, and was spearheaded by the hypocrites [the Mojahedin]. . . . [He added:] We seek an Islamic Republic; but such a regime is not only about praying and fasting. One of the main directives of the Islamic Republic is that it is a religious imperative to kill whoever stands against it and the just Imam of the Muslims [Ayatollah Khomeini]. A prisoner taken from among these people must be killed, and greater injury must be inflicted upon their wounded to ensure their death. Look up Sheikh [e Toosi's] book "al-Nahayeh [fi mojarrad al-fiqh wal fatawi"] written a thousand years ago, Allameh's book "Mo'tabar" of 600 years ago, etc; the orders are the same. [Our] dear clerics and preachers are duty bound to bring this religious jurisprudence issue into the open, [which was] written about by old religious authorities. These verdicts are not new issues raised by us, but old directives that have remained the same [through time]: Anyone who disobeys the just Imam and stands opposed to the regime will receive a death sentence. It is very important that parents take their children by the hand, [guide them,] and save them from falling into the abyss. If the children refuse to follow, they should disown them; [in the meantime] they should not be angry with [or hold any grudges against] the regime [for the punishment it imposes], nor should they expect clemency. The Imam has said all that needs to be said about showing these people clemency. He has worked to bring them onto the righteous path, and has [even] allowed them time before their arrest. Let them come forward and turn themselves in. Those who are afraid [should know], we have discussed the issues and will guarantee their safety. [These individuals] should direct us to their weapon depots, their people, and their dens of treason so that the mini-group opponents of the regime can be destroyed. If those who have been misled [into opposing the regime] reflect a little and come to their senses, they will leave such organizations that are made up of people with peculiar ideologies. . . .

Hossein Maleki

ARRESTED: September 1980
DETAINED IN: Evin, Qezel Hesar, and Gohardasht Prisons
RELEASED: May 1991

1. My name is Hossein Maleki. I was a sympathizer of the Forqan Group and I was a political prisoner from 1980 to 1991. I left Iran in 1995.

2. I make this statement in support of an investigation into the mass execution of political prisoners in 1988 in Iran.

3. This statement is true to the best of my knowledge and belief. Except where I indicate to the contrary, I make this statement on the basis of facts and matters within my own knowledge. Where the facts and matters in this statement are within my own knowledge, they are true. Where the facts and matters are not within my own knowledge, I have identified the source(s) of my information, and I believe such facts to be true.

Pre-Arrest Activities

4. I was 15 when I became interested in politics. When I was 17 years old I met a group of the followers of Shari'ati, by the name of Forqan, and of Akbar Goudarzi, who was the main theoretician behind the Forqan organization. I got to know them through my cousin. I was not a member but rather a sympathizer of the Forqan Group, which held positions critical of Khomeini and the Iranian clergy. Their interpretation of Islam was different from the clergy's interpretation. And Forqan's militants thought that through their actions they had to draw a line differentiating their revolutionary Islam from the reactionary Islam of the clergy. I was not in hiding; my activism consisted in openly distributing Forqan's books and publications. In Dey 1358 [late December 1979–early January 1980], Forqan was dealt a blow—the leaders of Forqan, including Akbar Goudarzi, were arrested. Nevertheless, two or three high-level members survived the arrests and escaped. Rasoul Giahi and Mohammad Motahedi were among the escapees. After three to four months, they were able to regroup and start publishing the magazines again. At that time, I was not directly connected to the organization, due to the fact that all connections were cut off. How-

ever, I acted indirectly—I would get the magazines through my cousin, and I would distribute the publications where needed.

5. In 1979, after the arrest of my cousin, agents of the committee [a district-based revolutionary committee] came to our house and arrested two of my brothers who were not involved in politics at all. They released them within 24 hours. In the same year, one day when I was at my aunt's house, I was arrested along with my two cousins and Ali Hatami (a Forqan member who was executed on 24 May 1980). We were identified through the connections we had before the Revolution. Some members of our circle before the Revolution had subsequently turned into Hezbollahis. They detained us for 48 hours at the committee; they briefly interrogated me and my younger cousin, who was my age, and then they released us. But they kept my older cousin and imprisoned him for about six to seven months. Upon his release, he went into hiding, but in 1981 he was arrested again, and was subsequently executed.

Arrest

6. I was arrested on 27 September 1980, by two plainclothes agents, on Revolution [Enqelab] Avenue. I was carrying a bag containing Forqan commentaries on the Qur'an. They opened my bag, saw the books, and arrested me. They took me to a committee station near the university next to Vesal Avenue. Twenty-four hours later they took me to another committee station, which was in the vicinity of Bagh-e Shah. The next day, 29 September, they transferred me to Evin Prison. Between 6

and 27 September, my cousin and younger, 16-year-old, sister were arrested as well. My sister was three years younger than me. In the first committee, a cleric came to interrogate me. He said, "These are Forqan books. Who are you?" I gave him a false name. He said, "This is a false name. Your address is probably false, too. If you don't tell us the truth we will send you somewhere where you will learn how to behave."

Detention

7. They immediately took me to ward 209. Lajevardi walked into my room. He said, "Well, you know that we have arrested all of you [Forqan members], and you still don't give up. Why are you doing this?. . ." I responded, "I have a headache. Could you please give me a pill?" He left. That evening, they took me to be interrogated. I did not receive any food. Before my interrogation, they brought in a man whom I knew from before. I realized that he had been arrested earlier. He had given in, and he was cooperating with them. He said that we were mistaken. He told me that it would be better if I told them the truth, because "they know everything." When my interrogation started, they first gave me a pen and a piece of paper, and they instructed me to give them my personal information. My interrogator's name was Sadeq, he called me by my first name and said, I know you so you had better write down the truth. I wrote it down. He then said, "Write about your activities." I told him that I was not involved in any activities. At that point, they took me, blindfolded, to another room. They laid me down on a bed, and

started to whip me with a cable. After about thirty or forty lashes, they made me stand up and asked me who had given me the books. I think it was about 7:30 or 8 p.m. when they took me back to my cell. My feet were in pain. They brought me dinner, but I did not eat it. I slept until morning. For the next week, I think I was interrogated for about an hour every day. They beat me only in my first interrogation session. There was one instance in which we got into an argument, and I said something derisive about Motahari. The interrogator slapped me. But I was whipped only on the first night.

8.   Something interesting happened at that point. Before 20 June 1981, the interrogators would cover their faces; their eyes were the only part of their faces that was visible. But our eyes were open both during interrogations and beatings. After June 1981, this was reversed. From that point on the interrogators wore nothing on their faces, but we, the accused, were blindfolded for the entire process.

9.   A while later something happened that made me realize their information about me was rather complete. In 1979, our neighbor's children had brought home three rifles from a military base [vacated by the army and invaded by the populace during the insurrections of the week of 11 February 1979]. I myself did not really know what I was buying the arms for. The reason we gave for buying those weapons was that we wanted to send them to Afghan guerrillas or others. We bought the weapons at a very low price. It was the very beginning of the war in Afghanistan, and Afghan groups were fighting against the government. I later found out that my older cousin had gone to Afghanistan in 1978 and 1979. He had even met and spoken with the famous military leader Ahmad Shah Mas'ud. Afghanistan was the pretext we used to justify purchasing the weapons, but in reality we had no contacts with any Afghan citizens. So I purchased the weapons and, through my cousin, I sent the weapons to my aunt's grandson.

10.   After about three weeks of interrogation in prison, my interrogator called me downstairs and told me that I could make a phone call home to talk to my mother. I called home and talked to my mother. I was about to end the conversation when my interrogator turned to me and said, "Don't hang up, I have a message." Once I finished talking to my mother, he said, "Tell your brother to get back the money you paid for the weapons from your neighbor. Tell him to bring the money over here." I was very shocked. I asked, "What's the story of the weapons?" He said, "You know that story better [than I do]. We're counting this among the lies you have told us." I was astonished that he did not hit me because of this. He took me back to my cell. Two days later, they took me to the infirmary of ward 209. My brother was there with a Revolutionary Guard. He told me that he had retrieved my money from our neighbors.

11.   Except for the encounter I had with my brother in the infirmary, my first real visit came about three months after my arrest. I could have a visitation once every two

weeks. A guard from ward 209 would accompany me when I had visitors. I was in solitary confinement from the day I was transferred to Evin, which was 29 September 1980, until 4 April 1981.

12. I remember that in February or March 1981, a commission to investigate reports of torture in prisons came to meet me in solitary confinement. They were astonished to see that I was still in solitary confinement although my interrogations were concluded. I told them that even though I was insisting on having a trial, they repudiated me, stating that I had to wait until those with whom I was connected were arrested. It was, in fact, necessary to complete my file before the trial. I told them that these were just excuses. What if my contacts are never arrested? Do I have to remain in prison forever? There was only one of my contacts who had not been arrested. In fact, he was never arrested. I heard that he was unfortunately killed in a firefight later on.

13. On 4 April I came out of solitary confinement. They took me to the same ward as the other Forqan supporters. I was there for about two to three weeks. Afterwards, they sent me and another person to another section because we were deemed to be "undesirable elements." They sent us to ward 5. Those involved in the Nojeh Coup [a foiled 1980 pro-democracy insurrection by a group composed of army officers and political activists] were kept in that ward. There were no more than 42 or 43 people in that ward. Once it got more crowded, they transferred us and the Nojeh prisoners

from ward 5 to one of the four main wards. We were there for about two weeks. Upon our return to ward 5, the number of prisoners in the ward had suddenly increased from 42 or 43 to about 70 or 80. In September–October 1981, they transferred all of us to ward 6, the adjoining ward. A few days later, they separated us from regular [non-political] prisoners and the Nojeh Coup prisoners, and they moved us to a building in the upper section of the prison referred to as the "Amuzeshgah." I was kept in solitary confinement until October–November 1981.

Trial

14. They tried me in October–November 1981, about a year and a month after my arrest. They took me back to ward 209. One of the interrogators told me to lift up my blindfold. I did. There was a table behind me and a bookcase right in front of me. He asked, "What did you do with these weapons?" Someone who was sitting next to him said, "Haj Aqa, these weapons belong to someone else." He asked me, "Will you interview?" I responded, "No. I am not important enough in any way to give an interview." He said, "In our opinion, Yazid's soldier is no different from Yazid himself." I told him that I was a nobody. He asked, "Will you cooperate?" I told him that I would not, because I had not done anything wrong. He said, "Get out." That was my trial.

15. There was a table behind me, and Haj Aqa was sitting on the other side of it. Later, I learned that the presiding judge in my trial was Nayyeri. He had a young voice. From

the descriptions that we had heard, I realized that he was Nayyeri. Nayyeri, a younger cleric, had recently come to Evin. There were three Shari'a judges at that time. Besides Gilani, who was well known, the other two were Mobasheri and Nayyeri. Some Forqan members were tried by Mobasheri, and some were tried by Nayyeri. Mobasheri was middle-aged, perhaps in his 50's. Nayyeri was not older than 30. His voice was that of a young man, which showed that he was Nayyeri. It could not have been Mobasheri.

16. After my trial they took me back to solitary confinement. The day after my trial, the interrogator called me in and told me that I had to do an interview. I said, "I was a nobody. Why should I do an interview?" He said, "Look, you have to do the interview. If you don't agree to, they will execute you." He then took me to a room where two former Forqan members, including my aunt's grandson, were being held. They both were cooperating with the authorities. They said that I had to agree to the interview, otherwise I would be executed. They said, "Just tell them you agree." I agreed. After two days, they handed me my sentence. It was a page filled with explanatory notes. It talked about me being an enemy of God and spreading corruption on earth, and so on and so forth. I saw that the word "execution" had been crossed out and "life in prison" written down instead. I wrote, "I have read this," and then I signed the document and gave it to them. There was really nothing serious in my file. Even my interrogator did not believe that I should get the death sentence. Nevertheless, at

that time, agreeing to do the interview was an important factor for them. If you accepted the interview, it meant—at the minimum—that you no longer supported the movement that you had belonged to in the past. As far as I know, my cousin Hassan Malekipur did not accept the interview, and he was executed [in 1981].

Prison Conditions

17. After I received my sentence, they sent me to a place called ward 6, a solitary ward. [Inmates' ages] varied from 10 to a maximum of 31 years of age. I think there were about 14 or 15 cells. I think on average there were about 20 or 25 people in each cell [there was no communication between this ward and other wards]. There were no beds in the rooms. We [the prisoners] were jam-packed next to each other. There was a guard named Mohammad-Reza Naghdeh. Once every few days he would come at night and he would call a number of the youngest kids [and he would take them outside]. They would give some of them weapons, and then they would tell them to open fire. Then they would tell them to gather the bodies of the executed prisoners and put them in a car. These kids' psychological state was very bad. In the middle of the night they would have panic attacks and scream. Upon my arrival in this hall, I had seen a pile covered with a blanket next to the door. Before the door was opened, I saw Mohammad-Reza Naghdeh kicking the pile. I saw that something moved under the blanket. Naghdeh said, "Have you learned how to behave or not?" I asked another prisoner if he knew what was going on outside, because it appeared that there

were a number of prisoners under the blanket. He said, "Apparently they were taken to help with the executions. They were told to shoot and carry the bodies of those who were executed. The blanketed men had refused the orders. For three days, they were made to sit there with a blanket over their heads as punishment."

18. There was a Revolutionary Guard named Seyed-Javad Hosseini. He was a pervert. I can say that he tried to abuse younger prisoners at night. There was also a guard named Abdollah. He had abused young prisoners once or twice. A number of the Forqan prisoners had learned about this and reported it to Lajevardi. Abdollah had been removed from his post. I myself didn't witness this [Abdollah abusing child prisoners]. But later, when we mixed with non-political prisoners, I heard them talking about it. They referred to him as a "face love-maker." They said that he was a sexual pervert, but that he did not intend to actually do anything. They said he just liked to look at good-looking men.

19. I was in the children's ward from October 1981 until June 1982. They transferred eight of us to Qezel Hesar Prison—unit 3, ward 1—in mid-June 1982. Haj Davud Rahmani was the prison chief there. In the first three to four months, our problems were the same as other people's in that prison. Every once in a while, the guards would find an excuse to pull someone out of his cell and beat him. I think this was their way of maintaining prison discipline. They did not want the prisoners to feel that they were free to do what they wanted; they kept an atmosphere of fear over us

all the time. When Haj Davud went to Mecca the prison atmosphere changed. For example, the number of people attending mass prayers dwindled, and, at the end, the *tavvabs* (those who had repented) were the only ones who showed up for prayers. When Haj Davud returned and saw what was going on, he started beating people. In our ward, for example, he came in and took about 30 or 40 people out of the ward. He beat them up and, for further punishment, he transferred 22 of them to Gohardasht Prison. They would make our breaks shorter, or they would force us to listen to the coerced interviews that they had obtained from others and make us attend ideological lectures.

20. I was punished twice and sent to the *zir hasht*, where we were kept standing the whole night. The second time I was punished was because I had bought lemon juice for one of my fellow prisoners. The other prisoners [who had not given an interview] were not allowed to purchase anything from the prison store. [At some point when] a delegation came to visit the prison, one of its members asked, why are these people standing still? And a little while later the head of the prison came and told us, "Get lost," and sent us back to our ward. I was in Qezel Hesar from June 1982 to 1986.

21. One day in 1983, Haj Davud came to the ward. I do not know what the person in charge of the ward had told him, which resulted in Haj Davud's summoning a number of the prisoners. My name was on the list. There were seven or eight of us all together. Haj Davud and a guard,

who always accompanied him, started to beat us. Then, Haj Davud told the ward chief to bring anyone he knew out of the ward. In our rough estimate, they took about 90 people to the beating room [*zir hasht*]. First, they beat us as a group, and then they beat each of us individually. We had to say we were sorry in order to be sent back to our cells. With the exception of two prisoners, all of us said we were sorry. Two days later they called me and 15 others. From the punishment ward, they transferred us to unit 1 of ward 1. This was where the Marxist prisoners were kept. Wards 2, 3, and 4 were used for Mojahedin members. While in that ward, we saw horrible things. Some of the inmates were repenters who had collaborated in the punishment of women prisoners who were put into "coffins." Some gave in and started to do interviews. The prison atmosphere had changed completely. We had to watch confession interviews from morning to night. It was a lot of pressure; for me, this was much worse than being beaten. If I am not mistaken, this tense atmosphere started in December 1983 and continued until June 1984, when there was a rumor that Haj Davud was about to leave the prison.

22. Then, all of the political prisoners were transferred out of Qezel Hesar Prison. They took a large number of political prisoners to Gohardasht Prison. They transferred others, including me, back to Evin, where we remained until early February 1988. During that period the atmosphere improved somewhat, owing to the departure of Haj Davud Rahmani and Lajevardi from Evin. A number of factors contributed to our [the prisoners'] new situation:

the prisoners' efforts, and international and UN pressure on the regime regarding human rights. We no longer caved under their pressure. We would go on hunger strikes for various causes or boycott the food. We would elect a representative to be in charge of the ward, and we succeeded in convincing prison authorities to separate the *tavvabs* from the other prisoners; they were taken to other wards. This was a result of our own efforts. The quality of food had been bad since 1982. There were many nights when we could not eat the food at all.

23. In February 1988 I was taken to Gohardasht Prison. We were divided into different sections. The prisoners were mainly those who had almost completed their sentences and were not willing to take radical political stands [against the regime]. They had put us in a ward referred to as the one for people who were not troublemakers. They took us to vote in the parliamentary elections, but we did not actually vote. We simply dropped a blank ballot into the box.

24. Three things happened to me, which, when put together, point to the 1988 mass executions. I believe that the 1988 mass executions were planned in advance, perhaps [as long as] one or two years before the Mojahedin operation.

25. One of the three issues pertains to Shari'atmadari. Shari'atmadari and his group established themselves in Qezel Hesar Prison in early 1985. They would bring with them the publications of different political groups. This created a whole new situation for us, and gave us access to the

viewpoints of all political groups [that were banned in the society]. They did this within the framework of their so-called "political propaganda work," which aimed, as they put it, to enlighten us about political parties. But their approach was different. They did not force the prisoners to watch videos or listen to their lectures. I do not know which government entity they were representing, whether they were from the revolutionary prosecutor's office or the Ministry of Information.

26. One day in the summer of 1985, Ma'ssumi came to our ward. (I later heard that his real name was Hassan Shayanfar, and that he was still working alongside Shari'at-madari at the *Kayhan* newspaper, a Tehran daily). He was collaborating in "political propaganda work" with Shari'atmadari. It may have been the end of July or early August. It was warm. He came into our ward and sat at the back of the ward. I do not recall how or why, but about seven or eight of us, including me, sat next to him. He started talking.

27. He started to talk to us. He said, "We try to find out about the situation of the political prisoners. We have concluded that there are three types of prisoners. One type consists of the ones who have abandoned their political movements and are cooperating with us. Those are the ones that you refer to as repenters. Another type consists of the ones who are no longer tied to their political movements, but they are not with us either. They want to move on and go back to their lives. The last type consists of the ones who have not only not broken ties with their political movements but are

now against us. We want to identify these three groups and treat them accordingly. The repenters will of course be released. Those who want to move on and live their lives and are willing to not be involved in politics, but are not with us, I believe they should be released and allowed to go on with their lives. As for the third type, we want to deal with them in a way that is appropriate to them." These were his exact words.

28. What Ma'ssumi said in this conversation proves that they aimed at evaluating the inmates' [opinions] and finding out what was going on inside the prisons. He tried to engage us in a political discussion. He wanted to talk about political movements in general. For example, he wanted to talk about the positions that political groups took vis-à-vis the government, or about the Mojahedin's move to Iraq and their alliance with Saddam. Another topic was the positions that leftist groups were taking. These were the issues that he wanted to discuss, but he saw that we were not interested and that our questions were about our problems within the prison. MKO affiliates would avoid any political discussion and bring up prisoners' problems. Ma'ssumi wanted to talk about politics but could see that the prisoners were not interested.

29. The second incident happened in February 1988. At that time, we were in ward 3 on the lower level of Evin Prison. On or about 11 February they suddenly came to the ward and pushed the prisoners into their rooms and locked the doors—this continued for three days. On the first day that the doors were closed, we saw armed guards

standing on the roofs, there were many of them. This was unprecedented. I had been in prison for seven years at that point, and I had never seen the guards holding arms while standing guard. The Revolutionary Guards would stand guard on rooftops, but were never armed. One of the prisoners had asked one of the guards about what was going on. The guard had told him that it was an exercise and that it was over. The prisoners in this ward (ward 3) were mostly Mojahedin members and leftists. We were usually in conflict with the prison officials, and several hunger strikes took place in our ward. After this incident, they transferred all of the prisoners in our ward [including me] to Gohardasht Prison.

30. The third incident I wanted to mention involves a Mojahedin supporter, named Massoud Moqbeli, who was among those executed in 1988. He was in our ward but was not transferred to Gohardasht, but instead he was taken to the joint committee for interrogations [Moshtarak Committee] in the spring of 1988. I do not recall the issues about which he was interrogated. One of his interrogators, known as Tavana, had turned to Moqbeli and said, "Tell your friends that we are coming after you. This time will be different."

31. In 1986–87, for about a year, every now and then we were taken to the office of the Ministry of Information in Evin, and they would ask us political and ideological questions. During that year, I was taken there once. I remember that they called us and we went out. We put on blindfolds, and a guard took us to that building. We sat there, and they called our names, one by one. We would go in, and they would put questionnaire forms in front of us. Whoever wanted to answer would answer, and whoever did not want to, would not. The forms asked about our political views. For example, "What do you think about the Islamic Republic? What do you think about America?" Or they would ask what we thought about a particular policy of the Islamic Republic—these were their questions. Or they would ask, "What do you think about Islam?" or, for example, what we thought about the Islamic Republic's policy regarding the war with Iraq and whether Iran should continue the war. There were a number of questions like that.

32. I think there were about three pages of questions. There were a few centimeters of empty space between questions for us to write our answers. I responded that I was not going to answer because of the inquisition-like nature of the questions. Most of us did the same thing. What actually surprised us was the fact that they did not react harshly. We thought that maybe the Islamic Republic had become democratic and compassionate. After all, we were telling them that what they were doing was an inquisition, and they would listen without reacting harshly. At the same time, however, things were very different at the revolutionary prosecutor's office. A Mojahedin supporter would be beaten there if he introduced himself as a "supporter of the organization" instead of as a *monafeq*. [Obviously, the fact that they were not reacting to our responses meant that] they were evaluating the prisoners.

33. When I consider the three incidents together, it becomes clear to me that the 1988 executions were decided upon and planned in advance. They had evaluated the prisoners. Even in their later interactions [with us], they pointed to these evaluations. In 1986, the commission appointed by Montazeri had commuted my life sentence to eight years of imprisonment. My sentence was to end in August–September 1988. At that time, they called for me and another prisoner. It was in the midst of the trials. When we went there, the person in charge of our files asked me if I would do an interview. I said yes. Then he started cursing: "Damn you! Last year when we asked you, you said that it was like an inquisition and that you wouldn't participate. Now that you see that the situation has changed, you are ready to do an interview." It was clear that they were referring to the forms that we had filled out previously. The courts relied on those forms as well.

Events Surrounding 1988

34. Before the executions started, we did not notice any unusual incidents; we found out only that several prisoners were transferred from Kermanshah Prison. The Mojahedin used Morse code to communicate, and they learned that the new prisoners were also Mojahedin supporters.

35. In July 1988, we were told that there was a problem with the septic tank that they had to fix and that we were being transferred to the jihad ward downstairs, where those who were willing to work were held. There were mostly non-political prisoners along with some *tavvabs*. Our ward did not want

to be with the jihadis; one or two people protested and were beaten up. We finally went there but did not unpack. They took us to a warehouse that was separate from the jihadis. There was no television for two days, but there was a loudspeaker in the yard, and it continuously played revolutionary and patriotic songs. I even remember that they played "Oh Iran, Oh Bejeweled Land" two or three times. From then on all visitations were suspended. I think our last visits were one or two days before they accepted the ceasefire. We did not have visitors after that, until October–November 1988.

36. There was a guard who had a calm demeanor and did not beat the prisoners. He came to our ward two or three days after the executions had begun (but we did not know about them yet). We told him that we did not want to stay in that warehouse building. He turned to us and said, "Just lie low and live your lives. Unpack your belongings and go on with your lives. This is not a normal situation." We were still in a state of uncertainty, when one day, about a week after the executions had begun, Naserian came to the jihad ward. One of the prisoners asked, "Why don't you address our situation? Naserian replied, "You don't want to stay here? Go get your things and come." At the same time another guard, whom we called "Mammad the Hassle," said, "Whoever does not want to stay here should come here and stand in line."

37. We all stood in the line. Naserian went into an office room and sat down. We went

into that room one at a time. Mammad the Hassle and two other guards stood next to the line in order to ensure that the prisoners who came out of that room did not talk to the ones on the line. We could see, for instance, that out of five people who went into that room, four would return to the ward and one would stay on the other side of the hallway. When my turn came, Naserian asked, "What is your charge?" I said, "Forqan." He said, "Get lost. Go to your ward." I said, "Mr. Naserian, we don't want to stay here." He said, "Get the hell out of here. Go back to your ward." The Mojahedins who had replied *monafeq* [when asked about their charges] had also been told to go back to the ward. Overall they separated about 35 or 36 people out of the 110 or 120 [who had been in that line], and took them upstairs.

38. The next day, we saw that about 14 or 15 prisoners who had been taken upstairs were returned to the ward. They were in a terrible [psychological] state. They could not speak at all. One of them finally said, "They are killing upstairs. They are trying everybody. When they took me in, Eshraqi, Ra'isi, Nayyeri, and another one were there." He continued, "They take you in there and ask you some questions. Then you come out. They make some sit on the right side and some on the left side."

39. We asked him what had happened to him. He said that before he went in, another guy who had realized that he would be executed had given his watch to him and then he had said, "I am leaving now, farewell." He had then realized that they were really executing the prisoners. When he went

in, Nayyeri had asked him what he was charged with. He had replied, *monafeqin.* At that point Naserian had said, "Haj Aqa, this guy was among the group who didn't want to be part of the jihad ward. He was among the group who didn't want to work." Nayyeri had asked, "Is that true?" He then responded, "No, I didn't want to go there because there were a number of sexual perverts at that place." There was a defrocked cleric in that ward who was a pervert. It had occurred to him to use the cleric as his excuse. At that point Eshraqi and Nayyeri wanted to end the proceedings and sentence him to death. Ra'isi, however, had told him that if he could show them the defrocked cleric, they would accept his story. That was why he was brought downstairs accompanied by two guards. They had sent him to the warehouse to identify the defrocked cleric. Anyway, that was how he survived. A few others who had said *monafeqin* when asked about their crime and who did not have a bad reputation in prison survived as well. Out of the 36 or 37 prisoners who were tried, 14 or 15 returned. They executed the others. And this is from a ward that Naserian himself had praised as peaceful.

40. One of the prisoners who was executed was named Reza Abbasi. He was a quiet guy who kept to himself. He spent his time studying English. We were surprised that he was executed. He was not articulate. A couple of other prisoners and I spoke with the guard whom I talked about earlier. We asked him to bring that guy back. We told him that this guy was not articulate, and that he could not answer their ques-

tions properly. We explained that he might say something inappropriate and be sentenced to death. The guard went upstairs to talk with Naserian. But when he returned he said that he did not know where that guy was. He told us that they were not allowed to go upstairs that much. He said that when Haj Aqa is upstairs, they are not permitted to be there.

41. We thought that after they were done executing the people upstairs we were next. As far as I can recall, they did not take anyone from our section to be tried. Inmates were less confrontational and more compliant in our ward.

42. About a month or two after the executions, we suddenly had a wake-up call. We would wonder: "What has happened? Why has this happened? Where are the rest of the prisoners?" We used to buy figs from the prison shop. When we bought figs, we would clean them and wash them first, and we would keep them. This way, we always had some figs ready to eat. After the mass executions, we asked the prison store for some figs. The figs they sold us were already washed and cleaned. I later found out that those figs had belonged to prisoners who had been executed. They had taken the figs from their cells after they were executed, and they had resold them to us.

43. We stayed downstairs until October–November 1988. At that time they told us to give them the phone numbers of our family members, so that they could tell them to come visit us. When on 11 February 1989 Khomeini granted amnesty, they transferred all of us to Evin. The first

time we started to ask questions was a few months after the killings, after we had been transferred to Evin. We started counting to see how many of us had survived, and how many had been executed. After a while, some prisoners were released and about 300 to 400 of us remained, or even fewer, I don't remember exactly. The prison situation had fundamentally changed. We had surrendered. We no longer caused any trouble. We had accepted their terms. For example, when they told us to wear prison uniforms when we had visitors, we agreed to. We no longer went on hunger strikes or celebrated political events. Before the executions we did not accept things like that.

44. I believe they [the authorities] were the ones who lost. Had they succeeded earlier with their policies, there would have been no reason to commit such a crime [the mass executions] and cause such a catastrophe. Yes, it broke our spirits, but let me tell you [the reader] something. It is true that they broke our spirits, but there was a line, a sort of unwritten rule that all prisoners understood. That line, which we did not want to cross, was the line of collaboration with the regime. Those who were executed observed this rule. The rest, whether released before the executions or after, tried not to cross this line. So in retrospect, even though our spirits broke after the executions, our achievement was great. At least we are at ease with our own consciences. We did not betray anyone [in order to get released].

45. For a while, they wanted us to cooperate with them. Then, they wanted us to observe prison regulations. They succeeded with regard to the latter. The prison

atmosphere had become non-political. They knew that most of us, from a religious point of view, did not believe in them at all. [We didn't consider them to be true Muslims.] It might be true that we would not do anything against them inside Iran, but we did not believe in them either. But they had no significant issues with us. We did not agree to cooperate with them, and they were no longer asking for it. There was a guy named Zamani. He was the chief intelligence officer for Tehran. Once in a while, he would call a few prisoners to talk to them individually. They would quote him as saying, "In our opinion, the era of political prisoners is over. We don't need anything else from you. We're looking for an opportunity to let you go. But you should know that if you're caught again, you will not be returning to prison. You will be dealt with right away." And that was what they did.

46. They never called me in for any administrative matter in the period before my release. I only went to see Naserian once, and that was because my family had requested a furlough for me. Naserian asked me, "How long have you been here?" and a few other questions in the same vein. I was wondering why they were so sensitive about me, since they didn't even put me on trial during the prison killings. But when my family tried very hard to get a furlough for me, Naserian did not agree. When Naserian left, they replaced him with another interrogator. His name was Sheykhpur. He agreed to my furlough the first time my family put in a request. It was my first

furlough—after ten years and one month of imprisonment. It was in October–November 1990.

47. The first time was very interesting—seeing people outside of prison was very interesting. I am not exaggerating; I did not sleep more than six or seven hours during those three days. I was up all the time. People would come to visit me. I went for walks with my brother. My family requested another furlough after a month or two. After my second furlough, I asked my family not to request any more furloughs. It was hard for me. I did not like to go out. Seeing the world outside of prison made me uncomfortable and sad. I actually preferred to stay in prison.

48. One day Lajevardi came to talk to us. I asked him, "You have released so many prisoners. Why are you still keeping us in here?" He laughingly said, "Every shop owner keeps some change in his cash register. You guys are that change in our cash register." They would say that even if there was only one day remaining in our sentence, they would designate our release as a pardon. In 1991, many of our sentences were ending. They started releasing the remaining Forqan supporters. We all had at least ten-year sentences, but they released all of us in 1991.

49. What they required from the prisoners was to condemn all groups that opposed the Islamic Republic. We were also required to agree to do an interview any time we were asked to. Most of the prisoners acquiesced to these demands, but there were some who would not agree to do the interview. But in

fact they didn't make us give the interview; what mattered to them was that we agreed to it. Their policy had changed.

50. After I was released, I took the university entrance examination in 1995. My rank was good, too. Out of 400,000 or 500,000 exam-takers, I was ranked in the top 1,000. But I was not admitted. Everybody was surprised that I was not accepted, considering my rank. Maybe the Ministry of Intelligence had something to do with it. Maybe it was because I had selected only universities in Tehran, and my rank was not good enough to get me into a Tehran university. Anyway, I tried. There were some former prisoners who were able to go to university. But I think they would not let them go any further than a bachelor's degree.

51. In my case, I worked with my brother at a printing office. He had an advertising office, and that was where I worked until 1996. After 1996, I did the same work independently. And then I left Iran. I did not feel safe there. We would hear about things that happened to former prisoners. For example, I heard about a guy named Hushang Mohammad-Rahimi (an MKO supporter), and also about Asghar Bidy and Mehrzad Hajian. Mehrzad used to work in a translation agency in Revolution Square, and I used to visit him once a week. One time I went there and his colleague said, he has not come and he has not called either. I went there several times again, and each time he was still missing. After a while I heard that Mehrzad had been arrested along with Hushang and Asghar, and no one had heard from them since. And later we learned that they had been killed in the security forces' detention facilities.

Switzerland, October 2009

OFFICIAL STATEMENT • 9

جمهوری اسلامی

Subject: Killing rebellious hypocrites is justice par excellence
The official: Chairman of the Islamic Republic Assembly of Experts, Ayatollah Ali Meshkini
The occasion: Tabriz Friday Prayer sermon
Date: 25 September 1981
Source: *Jomhuri Eslami*, 27 September 1981

... [I]f a number of *monafeqin* rise up against the Revolution, the Imam [Khomeini], and the Islamic government, they must be punished, and killing them and chaining them up is justice par excellence. Islam's survival in this country depends upon the Islamic government and whoever rebels against the Islamic government rebels against the Qur'an. *Monafeqin* neither accept Islamic laws, nor are they beholden to universal norms. The world has never seen such treason and criminality as these self-proclaimed believers in true Islam have committed. Therefore, in every street and alley and anywhere else they revolt against the Islamic government, the Islamic punishment, which is execution, should be carried out against them on the spot. Imam Ali's justice should be carried out in the world. ...

[He then told the students,] In the same manner that our troops are fighting, devotedly, at the war front, you have to study, devotedly, at your bastion, which is the school. Islam and this nation will not allow some who have false ideas, such as Communist thoughts, to corrupt the minds of our youth. And our sisters should abide by the Islamic *hijab* at all places and under all circumstances. If they don't, it will have adverse consequences. The people who live without Islamic *hijab* are effectively insulting Islam, and therefore Muslims will not allow them to do this.

Seifollah Mani'eh

ARRESTED: September 1981
DETAINED IN: Eshratabad Committee, Tehran; and Evin, Gohardasht, and Qezel Hesar Prisons
RELEASED: October 1989

1. My name is Seifollah Mani'eh.* I was born in Tehran, in 1963. I was arrested on 29 September 1981 in Tehran. I left Iran 11 years ago and live currently in Denmark.

2. I make this statement in support of an investigation into the mass execution of political prisoners in Iran in 1988.

3. This statement is true to the best of my knowledge and belief. Except where I indicate to the contrary, I make this statement on the basis of facts and matters within my own knowledge. Where the facts and matters in this statement are within my own knowledge, they are true. Where the facts and matters are not within my own knowledge, I have identified the source or sources of my information, and I believe such facts to be true.

Pre-arrest Activities, Arrest, and Detention

4. I became politicized as a teenager during the Revolution. I first took part in political activities, against the wishes of my parents, with a politically unaffiliated neighborhood group that was against the Shah. I was only 16 years old at the time. I went to "Iran Technic" High School near Enqelab Square. I was young, but I joined in the protest when the population took over the army barracks [11 February 1979]. I even took a gun from the barracks, a gun that was probably taller than me at the time and had a bayonet! Later, I learned it was a G3.

5. In those days, in our school neighborhood, in Enqelab Square, a politicized crowd used to gather and debate. This is where I became familiar with the MKO. My father had a cousin in the MKO, so it was

*The witness used the name Seifollah Moni'eh in the companion volume by Geoffrey Robertson.

through him that I became affiliated with the MKO. I began selling publications for them. I joined their reading groups, and their mountain-climbing activities. The main purpose of going mountain climbing was to strengthen our character and to learn to confront difficulties. We did not think that things would lead to violence.

6. I used to attend gatherings and protests organized by the MKO while we were still in the political phase [using peaceful political means to protest against the regime's policies]. When Banisadr was the president, we used to encourage him to speak out against the regime, and I used to attend meetings held by Mas'ud Rajavi, the leader of the MKO. I also attended smaller local protests against the regime's occupation of the headquarters of the smaller MKO-affiliated associations. Khomeini's henchmen, who were also called the Phalange, would obstruct these groups' activities, such as their selling publications and books. They would raid the meetings of other political parties and disrupt them. As far as I remember, hardly six months had passed since the beginning of the Revolution when they began to restrict freedoms and start their purges, which [later] included closing the universities.

7. To sell our publications, for instance, we had a team of three. Selling MKO publications was in fact a form of political activity. When someone was selling a publication at that time, we were quite sure some [pro-Khomeini] people would come by, confiscate the publications, and beat up the seller. I also remember that we used to be given only three publications to sell per individual so as not to lose them all. The rest were with another person called the storekeeper, who used to stay about 100 meters [300 feet] away from the seller and hide them in a bag. Once the three publications were sold, the storekeeper would give him another three. They [the regime] did not want us to sell these publications —they would accuse us of being anti-revolutionary. . . .

8. I was not at an age to predict the future. My main issue was freedom—why we were not allowed to be politically active. My political activities were limited to some protests and talks about politics and beliefs. . . . I never thought we were engaging in such a violent path. We occasionally heard the news of a person being killed in Shiraz or another city, but I never thought thousands of people would soon die. I never thought things would change that fast, and that the MKO would enter a military phase. I think neither the organization, the sympathizers, or the affiliate organizations were completely ready for that.

9. I quit high school and worked for the organization full-time in different districts. I had to leave my parents' house because my mother was upset about my political activities. . . .

10. On 20 June 1981, I attended a demonstration near Ferdowsi Square. In fact the demonstration had been disrupted and people were scattered and split into groups of 300 or 400. It was not concentrated in one place. The pro-Khomeini militia attacked the gatherings but there were no direct clashes with demonstrators. They only forced the demonstrators to disperse and the demonstration was suppressed.

11. I do not remember that the organization [MKO] had planned for or was prepared to engage in violent confrontation with the regime's thugs or security forces. What happened during the demonstration resulted in violence. I do not recollect if I heard gunshots or not. I didn't see anything related to any shooting. I didn't see anyone injured with bullets. We knew that the Revolutionary Guards were there, and we saw them arrest scores of demonstrators and put them into the Revolutionary Committees' cars. . . .

Arrest

12. I was going to an appointment on 29 September at around 10 in the morning. At the crossroads of Keshavarz and Kargar Avenues, two armed individuals suddenly put their weapons to my head and told me to hold my arms up and get close to the wall. When I held my arms up, I saw there were two Colts [pistols] against my neck, and two people started searching me. I had nothing with me. They handcuffed me, and they took me with them. They were wearing formal clothes but no specific uniforms. They took me to a government building. They walked me there. I saw someone running away; I recognized him. He was in my group during the political phase, when we were distributing publications together. He was trying to hide from me. I understood that he must have been arrested by the Revolutionary Guards and was collaborating with them by identifying the people he knew. They [the Revolutionary Guards] saw me by chance in the street. His name was Esma'il; he was known as Esi. I heard [later] that he

helped to identify a lot of people who were subsequently executed. I heard that he took refuge in Germany.

13. . . . The two who arrested me looked worried and anxious—they were not actually Revolutionary Guards. At the time I did not notice that they were security guards of a government building. When Esma'il recognized me, he went to them and asked them to arrest me. They kept me in that building until the guards [Revolutionary Guards] came and took me to the Eshratabad Committee.

14. Once we entered, they blindfolded me and started the interrogations. I had been handcuffed in the back—they opened the cuffs and handcuffed me again in the front. We were in a room of about 25 square meters [270 square feet]. They started flogging me with a cable. They first started flogging while I was standing blindfolded. They were saying that I was at an appointment. They wanted me to say who I had an appointment with so they could take me back to the place and arrest the other person as well. However, the friend who was supposed to go to that appointment never went to it, and I never saw him.

15. So, I was flogged for about two hours while standing. Then the method of flogging and torture changed. They tied my feet with a (wire) cable and laid me down on my stomach. Esma'il sat on my back and pulled so that my feet came up. Then, they flogged me on my soles. This person [Esma'il] came in the same car in which they had taken me to the Eshratabad Committee. He never spoke, so I could not recognize

his voice. I was blindfolded but could recognize him through the blindfold. He did not notice that I had seen him. He was directly cooperating in flogging me. . . .

16. The interrogators said that I was connected to the organization and had an appointment. But they did not know me. I denied everything and told them I was not affiliated with any organization, and that I did not know what they wanted from me. But they continued torturing me. They handcuffed me with reverse hanging [qapani], and the flogging continued as well. They continued until dark. They took me to a ward which was not very big. Once I entered, I noticed there were five or six other people in it. I stayed the night there. They told me that we were in the Eshratabad Committee.

17. I stayed in the Eshratabad Committee until morning. My feet were less inflamed [then]. They told me to jump to decrease the inflammation. They took me to Evin at 8 in the morning. . . .

18. They [Evin's interrogators] did not know anything about my activities, but I knew how much the person who had reported me knew about me. First, I tried to say nothing, to explore how much he had told them about me. The interrogator would beat me and say whatever he [Esma'il] had reported. This way, I was able to find out how much of my past activities they knew so that I could resist effectively. . . . I found out that he knew nothing about me. He only knew that I was active during the political phase. . . . I left the room to go to the restroom, and I noticed on the way that everyone was sitting with swollen, tied feet.

My feet were swollen [as a result of the flogging at the Eshratabad Committee] and I could not wear shoes.

19. It [the interrogation] continued until the night. I finally told them that I was a sympathizer during the political phase and had attended a couple of meetings, but I no longer had any connection [to the MKO]. Once I wrote this, it was enough of an excuse for them to keep me in prison. It was late. They sent me back to the ward—they would continue the beatings and interrogations in the morning. They took me to ward 4 of Evin. Once the door was opened, I noticed there were about 80 people in the room. The room was about 30 square meters [300 square feet]. . . .

20. I do not remember if it was the same night or the next—we heard a huge sound like a load of iron bars falling off a trailer. I did not know what the sound was. They [my cellmates] said they were executing [prisoners].

21. Some nights, according to what we counted, there were about 80 coups de grâce ("mercy" shots). Some nights, there were 60 or 30. We could only estimate the executions by the number of mercy shots. . . . I expected to be executed any day.

22. One night the warden came to our cell and called several of the prisoners' names. They returned after two to three hours with their hands covered in blood. They were mentally broken. They had been taken to collect the bodies of the executed prisoners and put them in a car. They were given weapons to shoot them and when they said they would not, they were told, "So we

will kill you instead." They were told that the next day was their turn. It happened about 10 to 15 days after my arrest. I was in ward 325, room 4, for 10 to 15 days. Then they took me to the Amuzeshgah.

23. During the Shah's time, the Amuzeshgah was one of the office buildings in Evin Prison that was converted to prison wards after the Revolution. There, the doors were all closed and the windows had metal blinds. The number of arrests was too high; the ward was so crowded, and there was no empty space. So the arrestees were taken to the Amuzeshgah and from there would be taken to interrogations. The Amuzeshgah had two wings, one with even numbers and the other with odd. I was in ward 5, room 8. There were 14 to 15 persons in that room. It was a small room, maybe 12 square meters [130 square feet]. There was no bed. We used to sleep on the floor. . . .

24. In Evin, I went for an interrogation one day and after that . . . they never called me again. After a while—I was among the group whose interrogations were not finished—they took us to Gohardasht. . . . I was in solitary confinement in Gohardasht for two months. They interrogated me there. . . .

25. Almost each time [during the interrogation session], the interrogator . . . would flog me for two hours, stand above me, and say, "Write." Then he would leave me in the room and go to the next person. The same thing would happen the next day. They took me for interrogations 15 times in two months.

Trial

26. I was tried by Nayyeri in Gohardasht. The interrogator took me blindfolded to the court. There was no lawyer. They asked if I had participated in a demonstration, if I was in Amjadieh Stadium, if I sold Mojahedin publications, and if I participated in the 27 September demonstration. I said that when I got there, the demonstration was already over. I did not realize that my interrogation was not finished. They did not ask any ideological questions. The entire court session lasted about five minutes. I was sentenced to 12 years in prison: eight years to be served in prison and four years of a suspended sentence. That meant that if anything happened or if I were involved in any activities after the eight years, I would be brought back to prison. I still have my court order. After that I was in a solitary cell for two to three days.

Prison Conditions

Gohardasht and Qezel Hesar (from fall 1982 to summer 1986)

27. Once I got my sentence, I went to ward 19 of Gohardasht. After a year, ward 19 of Gohardasht Prison was closed and we were transferred to Qezel Hesar Prison during the time of Haj Davud's directorship. We were all blindfolded. . . .

28. I could see through my blindfold. Haj Davud was sitting in a chair. He asked my name. I said my name. . . . Then he said, "Do you know a *monafeq*?" I said no. He said, "Are you a *sar-e moze'i*?" And I said I did not know what that meant. They started beating me. They kept slapping,

kicking, and beating me with a cable for about ten minutes. They said, "We will give you a hard time here, Qezel Hesar is not a hotel." This was the reception and registration method there.

29. Once everyone was beaten up, we lined up facing the wall. They said they would take us somewhere so that we would renounce our positions and stop dissenting. We did not know what they were talking about. They took us somewhere called "quarantine" in ward 6, unit 3. It was a very small room, 1 x 1.5 meters [3 x 5 feet]; we had to stand and take turns to sit down. There was a double bunk bed; there was no space to sleep. The ward had a bathroom and restroom. We were allowed to leave our room to use them three times a day. We could not talk to each other. We had to eat alone. They were using the repenters to monitor us. They [the repenters] used to beat us. They had authority to do so. They were converted into wardens. . . .

30. I was there for a year and a half. There were prisoners from different groups. We were not allowed to talk. If someone talked, Haj Davud would come with five to six guards, would take him [the prisoner] out, and would start beating [him] in front of all of us. They would beat him on the face. They told us that we were like wax that they wanted to reshape (re-educate us), and we did not want to be reshaped (re-educated). . . .

31. [In Qezel Hesar] we often picked fights with the repenters. They would allow themselves to treat us as if they were our wardens. We sometimes confronted them. Once, they tried to force us to clean the outside area, and we refused to do it. This caused the five of us to be taken to the *zir hasht* for torture. . . .

32. They took the five us there [the *zir hasht*]. There we were beaten by the guards. They played soccer, using us as balls. The next day Haj Davud came and told them to take us to "the famous cemetery, where they will learn to become human beings." They took us to the barn, where they had made some cardboard "graves" and would lay the prisoners down in these places on their sides. . . . I was sleeping on my side for a week. A repenter with a beard was also sitting above my head reading the Qur'an. There was no sound there; if you talked the punishment would get worse. I had pain on one side of my body and my shoulder. I was tired and worn out. We thought we would stay there longer, but they sent us back to the ward without asking anything from us—and without a single one of us having repented. . . .

Evin (from summer 1986 to fall 1989)

33. I was in quarantine for one year and seven months. Then, in 1986, Qezel Hesar was closed. . . . I was transferred to ward 5 of the Amuzeshgah in Evin. . . .

34. From the absolute oppression of Qezel Hesar Prison, ruled by Haj Davud, we were transferred to a place where the rules were more relaxed due to international pressures. We thought that we had successfully claimed our rights. And thus we should be more outspoken about our beliefs. We started a hunger strike. It was a time when the prisoners wanted to get closer to each other, to discuss and exchange ideas.

All these [activities] had been considered crimes in Qezel Hesar. They would torture prisoners for these reasons to the point that they would get unstable and repent. Now, in Evin, we thought we could express ourselves, and we no longer called ourselves *monafeq* but instead used "Mojahed." Later [in retrospect], I realized that the Ministry of Information had allowed us to have those illusions [so that perhaps we would become bold, and not dissimulate as much as we had previously, and thus could be easily identified as steadfast].

Events Surrounding 1988

35. About seven months before the killings, we were asked to fill out a form. The form included questions about our charges, sentences, and details about us and our political affiliations. The questions were typed. They asked us to sign them. The leftists did not have the problems that we had; they just wrote the name of their organization—the Minority Left, for example. But as far as we were concerned we had to choose between the "*monafeqin*," the "organization," or the "MKO"; the word we chose would immediately reveal our political position. I did not fill out the entire section because I was worried. I put my name and bio there. The space for what I had been charged with, which had four to five lines on which to write, was left blank. I do not remember if I signed it or not, but I certainly did not put anything in the political affiliation section. . .

36. It was February 1988, and they came and called me to go to the infirmary. It was around 10 a.m. They called me, but I had not signed up to go to the infirmary. I put the blindfold on to go to the infirmary, but they took me to the Asayeshgah. The Asayeshgah was actually a building full of solitary cells. . . . He took me somewhere else for interrogations.

37. He was the only person there, and his name was Zamani. At the time I did not know who he was, but he later introduced himself. In fact, Zamani was the representative of the Ministry of Information in Evin Prison. . . .

38. Zamani made me come to his office. In that room I had a blindfold on, but, from what I could see, it did not look like a normal interrogation room; there was no space to lay the prisoner down and beat him. It looked like an office; there was a desk. I sat on a chair and he also sat down. He started to discuss politics with me. He tried to make me talk with him. He said the Mojahedin are finished, they don't exist anymore. I even remember his telling me that people are against the Mojahedin and swear at them. I kept totally silent. At the end of his conversation he said, "Well, now you have an organization within the prison, and you are issued directives to follow. We know that there is an organization in your ward; tell me how it is structured and what kind of relationship you have with it."

39. He realized I was not responding. I thought he had unstated goals. The bottom line was that he wanted to know what was going on in our ward and what the MKO positions were in there. He wanted to know what the prisoners in ward 5 were thinking. These topics were over the red line for me. I didn't want to enter into such

a conversation. He wanted me to report on others. This was an evil discussion. So I kept telling him, "I don't know about an organization within the prison, and I don't know what the prisoners' political views are." I was just silent and didn't let the conversation go further. Then he asked, very openly, "What is going on in the prison, in ward 5 of the Amuzeshgah, where you are? Tell me about the organization within the ward." And then he would charge me with being part of the organization. This was just an allegation; he had no document or evidence to substantiate his allegations. First he asked me, "What is your rank in this organization?" And at the end he accused me, "You are part of the organization and you are linked to outside the prison through this organization."

40. This was how it went for hours. After it ended, they took me to a solitary cell. At this point I realized that I was not allowed to go back to the ward and I was under interrogation. I had not brought my belongings with me. The guards brought my things that my cellmates had put in a plastic bag for me.

41. They called me again the next day. That day, he [Zamani] started threatening me. He ended the political discussions, and the first thing he did was to take out a cable from his drawer. He had different kinds. He started beating me with the cable. He said, "You can be beaten or not. You have to tell me what is happening in the ward you were in. What do the others think? What are the connections?" I kept saying that I had no information, and he continued beating me. He beat me from head

to toe while I was standing. I sometimes sat due to the blows. Then he would stop hitting and start talking. After a couple of days, I heard a noise from some equipment. I realized then that he was recording my voice during the interrogation.

42. He could never prove that he knew anything about the ward. I could not connect what he told me with what I knew about the ward. He spoke very generally and kept beating me. They took me to Zamani's office every other day, sometimes every day.

43. The way they treated us—that is, the interrogations and the torture—was a drawn-out process. If you are beaten quickly, you are completely destroyed in ten hours. But when they beat you every day for two months, a small but regular dose of beatings would open your wounds but not deepen them. This method is a kind of torture. . . . I was being interrogated and flogged every day. I was subjected to psychological distress, anxiety, and stress. I kept asking myself, "Am I being taken in today or tomorrow? Will they beat me today more than yesterday? This anxiety destroys one's mental health.

44. While I was in solitary confinement, those prisoners who had been brought there before me were taken for their last interrogation sessions or their interrogation had already been completed. Zamani played their recorded voices for me—for example, the voice of Ali Ansariyun whom he had interrogated himself. I was one of the last prisoners taken to be interrogated. One or two days after my interrogation started, one of my friends from the same ward was

called for interrogation. On the days that I was not interrogated, it was his turn.

45. He [Zamani] also showed me videos of Ansariyun, for example, and of another one of our people (who is still in Iran). The films showed that they had confessed, and the interrogators told me I too had to confess. I did not know what I had to confess to. They wanted me to say that there was an organization within the prison. I was confused. Did he want me to say that there is an organization there? Was organizing in prison a crime? I was beaten with a cable and I had to agree that there was an organization there and to say that there was an organization there.

46. Really there was no organization. There was no hierarchy or pecking order. I had no organizational relationship with anyone. . . . We had solidarity to defend our interests. These were issues related to our living together and to our common problems in prison. . . . This solidarity was interpreted as our having an organization and being politically organized. If together we refused to repent, to betray ourselves, this refusal would be interpreted as being organized. [If we protested that] we were hungry, that there was not enough food, the quality of the food was poor; if we got up and cleaned the room together, [for all this] the guards would accuse us of organizing.

47. I was interrogated and flogged regularly with a cable for two months. After two months, they asked me to confess in front of a camera. I said, "No." For a whole week I was beaten with cables, every day. I

had to give in. He [the interrogator] wrote down what I had to say on a piece of paper, and he put it in front of me. [The paper said] that I was part of an organization in the prison, that I had organizational contact with the outside, and that I was in charge of the prisoners' contact with the outside. They had made up the whole story, and claimed that [my organizational contacts] were established through visitations. Whereas my only visitor was my mother, who was opposed to the MKO and always had been (she threw me out of the house because of my political activities), but the interrogator did not care. He insisted that I had contact with the outside, which was a pure lie.

48. On one of the last days of my interrogation, I thought it was going to be the same old story. He [the interrogator] took me to the room, and he beat me with a cable without even talking to me. I did not know why he was beating me without talking to me. Before, he would talk to me first, and then he would beat me. But this time, he just started beating me. I was very tired, and his beatings made me scream. He stopped after about two hours. Then he took me to another room. I sat on a chair, and he told me to take my blindfold off. I took the blindfold off, and there was a big, professional television camera. There were three cameramen there. There were two spotlights. They showed me a part of Ali Ansariyun's and two others' confessions to convince me that I had to confess. Zamani told me, "Say it." I sat there and the camera started to roll, and Zamani said, "Say, say what you have to say."

49. I was in a very bad psychological condition. I had lost my mental balance. I felt as if my time had come. I was forced to confess to things in which I didn't believe, that did not exist, and by doing so I was putting at risk my fellow detainees in ward 5. If I confessed [to the existence of an organization], that meant everyone in my cell had an organizational contact with the outside and were part of the organization inside the prison. I was in such nervous disarray that I had forgotten how to write. I couldn't write. I couldn't even write my own name. He [Zamani] wrote [the confession text] and gave it to me [to read]. I was psychologically devastated. I could no longer bear the daily interrogation sessions. Several months of beatings had affected me. My soul and body had become very weak. I felt I shouldn't do what they wanted me to do, yet doing it was the only way I had to survive. I had no choice, this [daily torture] had to end. I knew that confessing to having contacts with the outside was gravely incriminating, but I had to surrender.

50. I looked at what he had written for me. I said my name and my personal information, and I got to the place where I had to say, "I am a *monafeq*." But I could not say it. Instead, I said, "I am part of the organization." Suddenly the camera stopped and the lights went off. Zamani grabbed me and took me out of the room and flogged me, nonstop, for nearly half an hour. He took me back inside the room and told me to say it again. Then I read it again. I do not remember much. I did confess that I was linked to the organization and that I was getting directives from them and bringing them [the directives] into the prison. The cameras stopped once I said that.

51. He then took me to my cell. My interrogations ended about 15 days before the [Persian] New Year [March 21]. I spent the New Year of 1988 in a solitary cell on floor 3 in the Asayeshgah. Since they had called me for the infirmary, I had been interrogated for two months. I was in a very bad mental state. I felt all my prison time [during which, paying a very high cost, I had refused to submit] was wasted. I thought that confession was a big sin. I blamed myself a lot. I felt very bad, even though I had been coerced to do it by the prison warden. But it hurt me a lot. One day they told me to take my belongings and they took me back to the Amuzeshgah. But they took me to ward 4 instead of ward 5. . . .

52. For a long time we did not know what was happening. I never knew when the killings began. I still do not want to talk about those days. But one day we noticed that they called a prisoner. When the prisoner came back he said, "They are killing." We did not understand why they were killing or whom they were killing. The visitations had stopped. At first we did not believe the prisoner who said that people were being killed because we could not figure out why [they should start killing], although we could feel the heavy atmosphere within the prison.

53. I remember a Revolutionary Guard whose name was Hasani brought a desk into ward 4 and sat behind it. From then on, every morning he sat at that desk until nightfall. There was no precedent for a

Revolutionary Guard being inside the ward just sitting and looking at us. Perhaps when the executions started, they wanted to keep an eye on people. Others said perhaps he was there to watch and identify people who were to be taken to be executed, for by then we believed the killings were actually occurring.

54. One night, late at night—maybe 9 or 10 p.m.—they came into the cell. They read a number of names, including mine. We knew, at the time, that the executions had started. We knew that wards 3 and 5 had been emptied. We knew that these prisoners had been taken away, but we did not know to where. We knew that no one knew where they were. We asked ourselves, "Where are these guys? Why should they execute so many people? Executing one, two, ten people, could perhaps make sense, but mass executions didn't make any sense. All prisoners were not charged with the same crime, to be executed en masse at the same time. Unbelievable as it appeared to us, the change in the prison atmosphere was so obvious, that we all felt we were on death row, and whoever's name was called might not come back. So when our names were called, we said goodbye to the other prisoners. They took us blindfolded to another ward, ward 209, by minivan. That ward belonged to the Ministry of Information. We were put in a room.

55. I remember that we sat facing the wall, and we knew that there were other prisoners there. It was crowded. There were a lot of Revolutionary Guards. There was a hastiness in the way they moved around—they were in a hurry. The Revolutionary Guards were not uttering a word as they paced among us. They would not let us talk or move. It was a very strange atmosphere. They would go around the room calling names, yet they were not calling in a loud voice, so the prisoners would not know who was in the room. They would whisper in our ears, are you that person? And if he said yes they would take him. If not, they would ask another person. Slowly the room was emptied. People were being taken away and not coming back. No one returned to tell us what was going on. We knew nothing except that they go into a room but do not come back. We kept waiting. It was about midnight, or 12:30 a.m., when they came and said, "The court is in recess, get up, everyone." They took us out and took us to the minibus to go back to the Amuzeshgah. Of our group, only one cellmate, whose name was Seifodin, did not go back with us.

56. Most of the Evin prisoners had been executed. I think prisoners in wards 3 and 5 had already been killed and now they had come to the wards where prisoners were less uncompromising and less confrontational with the wardens. In there they would pick individuals they knew from before. Anyhow, we went back to the ward and were not executed.

57. All their efforts consisted in keeping the prisoners uninformed about what was happening. For that reason the kitchen staffs were not informed about the killings and the fact that there were fewer people to feed. Because of this, that night there was much more food for us than we were used to.

58. One day, soon afterwards, I and some of the others were taken out again. They took us again blindfolded on a minibus to the same 209—we sat there. But again, I was held all evening and it got too late, so the court was in recess. I was taken there twice but they didn't call me and I returned to the Amuzeshgah.

59. About a week later, it was in August, I was taken again, along with 10 or 15 other blindfolded cellmates, on the minibus to ward 209, where we sat facing the wall. We waited for our names to be called, but again they did not call my name, and I went back to the Amuzeshgah.

60. Then one day, they came and took all those in the Amuzeshgah to the old ward 325. Some remaining prisoners from Gohardasht were also taken there. We were all drowning in sorrow. We had all been together in prison for almost seven years. We had endured torture and beatings together. But suddenly all of our friends had disappeared and we were left with a group of people we didn't know.

61. We tried to boost each other's morale to avoid collapsing. In fact the prison wardens had decided to massacre us, but we didn't know what our crime was. We couldn't even be charged with the crime of opinion, because we did not express any opinions [in prison]. The point is that I never said that I am an MKO affiliate and I approve of the MKO armed rebellion against the regime. When did I say that I wanted to topple the Islamic regime of Iran with the help of an organization or an ideology?

62. A few days passed, and they came and called my name. They called Reza Shemirani, Mohammad Raktam, Mostafa (whose last name I have forgotten), and then Mostafa Naderi and some others. They called about eight of us. We thought the killings had started again. It seemed that the killings were stopped for two weeks. Then we said goodbye to the others. We left the room with all our stuff— a plastic bag with a couple of pairs of underwear. We went, blindfolded, to 209. Zamani was there. He said, "Well, leave your belongings there." Then they separated us and took our belts and searched our pockets. They put us in solitary cells—three people in each. Well, there were three of us in one cell, and I assume other [cells] were like ours as well. I was with Reza Shemirani and another person, who had tuberculosis. When we went there, we thought the executions had been started again. This was the third time I was taken to be executed. We sat there, waiting. One day passed. We were listening to the outside noises to see when they would come. We were trying to figure out what was happening outside. We were waiting for death every second. We were there for three days, but we were returned to the ward. Everybody was happy to see us back. The killings had been stopped.

63. One day Zamani called me again. I did not know where I was going. They took me blindfolded to 209. Once I arrived he said, "How come you are here? Did they forget to execute you?" He bore a grudge against me, because after all of my confessions, he could not use them [because I had not been executed]. He pushed me towards the

wall and put his hands on my throat. I was stuck, pinned to the wall, and could not breathe. He asked, "Do you know that we can kill you? Do you know that your life is in my hands?" I said, "Yes." And he said, "So now you have to collaborate. What is going on in the prison?" I said, "which prison? You have killed them all? Have you left anyone alive so that you could ask me what he is doing?" No one was left who could be associated with my past. Most of the survivors didn't know each other. I said, "Nothing is happening in prison, what are you looking for? [I was amazed by] his obsession with the organization [within the prison], this obsession with contacts and solidarity [among prisoners]. I said, "I don't have any information! I know nothing! I don't speak to anyone. You have killed everybody, and nothing is happening in the cells."

64. They transferred us to the Amuzeshgah. They gave us newspapers and brought back the television. Then, they resumed the visitations. My mother came to visit, and she looked panicked. She said she had come several times to visit me, but they did not allow it. Then she said that people who had come for visitations were given luggage or plastic bags and were told, "These are your child's belongings. Go now." To some [parents who came to the prison] they did not give any information, they were just told, "[your child] is not here; he has been transferred [somewhere else]." They were lying. My mother was very anxious. She said, "I can't believe you are alive, they have killed so many people. So many people are missing."

65. I was arrested on 29 September 1981. Based on the court order, I was supposed to be in prison for eight years, and I was released in 1989 with a bit of delay. The reason for the delay—which I think was about 20 days—was that there was a problem with the deed to the house that we had to provide to secure my release. It was mandatory for whoever wanted to be released to give an interview. This [confession], for a period of time, was in written form, and, at other times, was to be given in the presence of other prisoners. We [the prisoners] had collectively decided to give the interview.

66. After I was released, I endured some social deprivation because of my imprisonment. I did not continue my studies—I was too old to start studying. During the time I was being interrogated and the month that I was directly tortured by Zamani, I had totally lost my mental and physical abilities. I had lost the ability to write. Even now, when I get stressed, I cannot write. I totally forget how to write, and then I have to give it some time until I am able to write again. My handwriting is totally different when I am normal than when I am stressed. I forget words and how to write them. This happened to me because Zamani was interrogating me and was forcing me to confess and write.

67. I always expected them to come for me. I had this bitter experience—even after the 1988 killings, they re-arrested some of those who had been released and killed them. I never trusted this regime.

Denmark, September 2009

کیهان

Subject:	Who is an apostate and what is his sentence in Islam?
The official:	Shari'a Judge for Tehran's Islamic Revolutionary Tribunal, Ayatollah Mohammad Mohammadi Gilani
The occasion:	Interview with the *Kayhan*
Date:	October 1981
Source:	*Kayhan*, 19 October 1981

Ayatollah Mohammadi Gilani, the Shari'a Judge for Tehran's Islamic Revolutionary Tribunal, responded to the following questions put by *Kayhan*: "Who is an apostate and what is his sentence in Islam?":

"Apostasy" in the Arabic language means "defection" and, in the parlance of Islamic scholars, means to defect from religion, to blaspheme, after [having been enlightened by] Islam. The proof of apostasy may be a direct quote expressing a clear blasphemy, such as if someone says: "I left Islam," or "I doubt God [exists]," or by saying something necessitating blasphemy, such as if someone says: "God—God forbid—is an inorganic being," or "God is the same as the law of creation." We have seen these in some of the writings. Or the proof may be in an act, such as: someone performs an act which clearly is a proof of ridiculing and demeaning Islam, e.g., contaminating the holy Qur'an—God forbid—with dirt or stepping or spitting on it with the intention to insult. The same goes for performing the aforesaid insulting acts against the

Honorable Mecca, the holy shrines, or the books of Islamic precedence and jurisprudence. Apostasy is also committed by denying one of the principles of Islam. The principles of Islam are those that are clear and obvious to those familiar with Islam, such as the principles of Resurrection, Prayer, and Fasting. There is no doubt that denying the principles of Islam is blasphemous, but the problem and the argument lie in deciding if just denying the principles of Islam is as blasphemous as "denying monotheism and the Prophets." In other words, is the denial of the principles of Islam, by itself, sufficient to constitute apostasy, the same as denial of monotheism and the Prophets? Or is it because the denial of the principles of Islam—such as denial of the requirement for prayer—is based on the denial of the Prophet, and the denial of the Prophet is apostasy, then by extension it is said that the denial of the principles of Islam is apostasy? Some religious scholars have recognized the denial of the principles of Islam as apostasy, and some have said that it is not apostasy by itself, but it is blasphemous if it is accompanied by denial of the prophecy

of our dear Prophet of Islam. Our lofty Sheik...
(Khomeini), leader of the Muslim community—may
I be sacrificed for him—in the writings of Al-Vasileh
has accepted this conservative approach and has
ruled that if someone, because of developing
doubts, denies one of the principles of Islam, such
as doubting the requirement of prayer or the visit
to Mecca, and thinks that the prayer and the Mecca
visit were required for Muslims during the first
period of Islam and are no longer required in our
times, then this person is not sentenced to blasphemy, in contrast to the aforesaid quote, by which
[he] is sentenced to apostasy. There are two kinds
of apostates, voluntary and innate. A voluntary
apostate is one who was born into Islam, meaning that his parents, or one of his parents, were
Muslims at the time of his birth. An innate apostate
is someone whose birth was otherwise (who was

born to a non-Muslim family). The sentence for the
voluntary apostate is death, and his repentance will
not be accepted. His wife will be forbidden to him;
she must observe a widow's waiting period [prior
to marrying someone else]; and his belongings
will be distributed between his inheritors, even if
he is alive. But there is no requirement that the
innate apostate and the female apostate, innate
or voluntary, be sentenced to death for apostasy,
and their repentance will be accepted. The Muslim
children who have become associated with and
related to various Marxist groups are sentenced to
apostasy, except for some of them who, according
to the order of the Imam—may his shadow cover
all—regarding the denial of the principles of Islam,
may be outside of the apostasy ruling, which distinction and ruling is up to the experts in the field.

A photograph from 1980. The banner reads: "The university is the
stronghold of liberty and we will protect it at the cost of our lives."

Mohammad Reza Matin

ARRESTED: April/May 1983

DETAINED IN: Sepah Detention Center, Orumieh Police Detention Center, and Orumieh and Tabriz Prisons

RELEASED: June 1990

1. My name is Mohammad Reza Matin. I was born on 11 June 1949 in Salmas. I was detained in Tabriz Prison during the 1988 prison massacres.

2. I make this statement in support of an investigation into the mass execution of political prisoners in 1988 in Iran.

3. This statement is true to the best of my knowledge and belief. Except where I indicate to the contrary, I make this statement on the basis of facts and matters within my own knowledge. Where the facts and matters in this statement are within my own knowledge, they are true. Where the facts and matters are not within my own knowledge, I have identified the source or sources of my information, and I believe such facts to be true.

Arrest and Torture

4. I lived in Tabriz in Azerbaijan Province where I had been a Tudeh sympathizer since 1976. I was a high school teacher at the time I was arrested. I taught economics in different high schools. I was a member of the teachers' association, but my main activities were party politics. I was 35 years old at the time of my arrest.

5. I was arrested on 29 April 1983 in the city of Orumieh. It was a Friday, and I had been invited to my sister's house. It was around 6 p.m. when I went back home to meet someone, [a fellow party sympathizer] who had, apparently, been denounced. Security forces came to my house to arrest me. Two were wearing Revolutionary Guard uniforms but the rest of them were plainclothes agents. They searched the whole house, turning it upside down. I had a photocopy machine and printing equipment in my house. [Because all newspapers, except the pro-regime ones, were banned, and our party could not openly publish its views], the party would send its analysis, and we used the photocopier to distribute the party's views and analysis.

I was lucky that my wife and 18-month-old son were not home.

6. I was taken to the Orumieh Sepah Center on Daneshkadeh (College) Avenue. They started torturing me as soon as they arrested me. It was so bad that my feet still bear the scars of the torture I endured then. They beat me with a cable. They laid me on my back on a military bed. Someone sat on my knees and someone else sat on my chest. They put a blanket over my head so that I couldn't be heard outside. For a second the blanket moved and I could see who was flogging me. He was my interrogator, a native of Orumieh, by the name of Ahmad Ghaffari. I knew him from before I was arrested. This guy was a student in the school where I taught. He might have been 21 or 22. When I first was brought into the Sepah Center, I took my blindfold off for a second, and he was the first person I saw. When one gets flogged on the foot, the cable turns and flips and the unprotected wires would injure the foot. [The cable] hits the top of one's foot too; that is why my feet are still damaged. They would flog me from both sides of the bed. Flogging the swollen feet would result in breaking the skin on the soles of the feet. The first day I was tortured from 8 p.m. to 2 a.m. They wanted me to give them my contacts' names. They also were asking where I had hidden arms. [At the end of the interrogation session] they took me from the interrogation room to a cell on a rolling cart because I could not walk. I was almost unconscious. My feet were severely swollen. I was alone in the cell.

7. On 30 April [the day after], at 8 a.m., they took me back for more interrogation. I was blindfolded. After the interrogation they returned me to the cell. I was not a known person in Orumieh. Other Tudeh members did not know me. I had only one contact there. That same day, in the afternoon, my contact and our party's underground cell were denounced. In the evening, at about 7 or 8 p.m., when it was already dark outside, they took me out of my cell and confiscated my watch. The prosecutor's representative, Morteza, took off my blindfold. I saw that my contact (Heidar), who had been arrested, was there as well as the person who had denounced both of us. [You could see that] he had been badly tortured. They forced him to slap me. When I protested they started to hit me. This time the beating was more severe than before. I think they beat me until midnight. But I don't remember because I fainted. The beating was accompanied with swearing and insults, very humiliating insults. They wanted to break the prisoners [with the combination of beating and humiliation]. A broken prisoner is more prone to give out information. They had also arrested other members of the Orumieh branch of the Tudeh Party. They were all detained in the same room. So they dragged me by my hair and shirt and threw me in front of them. They then took me to my cell, but I could not hear and I could not move. I think they brought a doctor. It seemed like I was bleeding from head to toe. Ever since that day, my hands shake. I have never recovered from that.

8. They took me in again on the third day because they thought I had some more

information that I had not given. They wanted to know whom I knew from other organizations in other places, such as other political groups—like the MKO, or from my high school, where teachers were politically active. I had some resources from the party, such as money, a camera, and the party checkbook. I had told my wife that, if I ever got arrested, she should throw these things away, but they thought we had arms and they were looking for arms. And when I said that I did not have arms, they put more pressure on me.

9. The skin on my foot broke, and the sole of my foot was bleeding. I lost consciousness very, very quickly. So they stopped beating me. They kept screaming at me, "Tell us, tell us." They were slapping me and punching me in the face, so I lost consciousness again. They threw cold water on me to get me to wake up so they could continue the interrogation. They put me up against a wall. Someone came in, but I still had a blindfold on. They told me that if I did not confess, they would execute me that night. After a few minutes, I felt like something was held to my head, and the guy told me to pull my blindfold up a little bit, and I saw that he was holding a gun to my head. I was low to the ground, so I could not see the person's face. He told me, "If you don't tell us, I will shoot you." But I thought they were bluffing because if they wanted to kill me they would have to take me outside, and I did not think that they would do it there. I knew that they were not really going to kill me. After a few minutes, the guy with the gun said, "This guy is never going to change, so we should get a conviction from the judge and execute him." And

they took me to my cell. My feet and my legs up to my knees were completely swollen. I had to drag myself to the bathroom because I could not walk. I had a very high fever for a few days, which may have been because I had a very bad ear infection.

10. On the sixth day after my arrest, a guy named Mostafa, the person responsible for the [Revolutionary] Guards detention center, took me to Taleqani Hospital in Orumieh. They took me barefoot because I could not walk or put shoes on my feet. The doctor said, "We have to hospitalize him." Mustafa said, "We cannot leave him." I had an infection and the doctor said, "If we do not hospitalize and treat him, he will lose hearing in his left ear." Mostafa still said, "We cannot leave him." The doctor gave me a lot of antibiotics, and they took me back to prison. I have lost 60 percent of my hearing in my left ear. After that, I was in solitary confinement for nine months.

11. They wanted me to give an interview. I never agreed to give an interview. They wanted me to condemn the Tudeh Party and introduce myself as a Muslim.

12. I was alone in cell 9 in the Orumieh Detention Center. The size of the cell was only 1.2 x 2 meters [3.9 x 6.6 feet]. I was not allowed to go out and get fresh air. The light in the room was on day and night. Once, the lamp burned out, and it took about a month to replace it—I was in absolute darkness. I used to sit by the door to be able to use the light coming in through the door slots to see to eat. I could not control my hands; I would normally

lie on my stomach to be able to eat. During those nine months, there was only an empty milk can in which I could urinate. I would empty it at each turn that I had to go to the toilet.

13. During those nine months I tried to exercise and sing songs to keep up my spirits. The medical practitioner of the Sepah [Detention Center] would come every two days to change the bandages on my feet. He would drain the infection from my feet and give me antibiotics. It was a month before I could walk again. But the wounds on my feet remained for another six to seven months.

14. My wife was pregnant. My second son was born on 7 May. My family knew that I had been arrested. Orumieh was a small city, and they knew that the detainees would be taken to the Sepah Detention Center. At my mother's insistence, the prosecutor allowed me to have a visitation after six months. They kept me seated at a table so that my family (my mother, my wife, and my two sons) could not see my feet. I saw my newborn son for the first time. I did not see my sons for another seven months after that.

15. Seven to eight months after my arrest, the religious judge of Orumieh, Hojjat ol-eslam Yusef Imani, called for me, as I was the only one who had not repented. They took me blindfolded. I saw from below my blindfold that there were some people sitting around the room. The religious judge told me to introduce myself. He said, "As far as we know, you do not believe in Islam, so we think you are waging war against God." He added, "You can only

go to the toilet twice a day from now on." He ordered the guards, "Take him to the toilet after everyone else has gone and wash the toilet after he finishes because he is unclean."

16. I witnessed a lot of bad scenes during those nine months. Once there was a group arrested from Mahabad [a city in Iranian Kurdistan]. There was a guy who was tortured severely. I saw him in the cell; he was lying down and was hardly breathing. His feet were in a pool of blood. I saw that he could not breathe anymore. His head fell. He died in front of me. I knocked on the door with my fist, then shouted and slammed on the door. The guard opened the door. I told him that the man had died. He slapped me on the face and said, "One less person to feed." I later heard that his name was Mahmud Khezri, and he was from Saqez and was also a teacher, like me. He was between 55 and 60 years old. He was from the Kurdistan Democratic Party.

Trial

17. After nine months, on 3 February 1984, they took me to the Orumieh police prison. It was really interesting to see the sunlight after such a long time. It was a temporary detention ward; I was there for a month before I was transferred to ward 12 of Orumieh Prison. There were 116 of us from different opposition groups—the Bahá'í, the Mojahedins, and the leftists—but none of us was allowed to get fresh air. There was a big hall with triple-decker beds next to each other. I slept on the floor for the first 40 days as there was no bed for me.

18. Before getting the definite verdict, I was under psychological pressure because I was afraid of being executed. I used to sleep on the third bunk and I always had nightmares—I would tie myself to the bed with the bed sheet to avoid falling off while having nightmares. They usually took the prisoners for execution at around four or five in the morning. Every day when they brought us bread, I thought they were coming for me. I used to have a visitation once a week. My mother and my wife used to go to the court frequently. My mother wanted me to repent so as not to be executed. I was under emotional pressure. I was also under pressure from the prison officials.

19. In February 1985 they took me to the Orumieh Revolutionary Court for the first time to pursue the investigations. The examining judge wrote the indictment of me and asked me several questions to which I replied. They tried me in March. I was not blindfolded in court. I defended my positions. The religious judge threatened to sentence me to death and told me that, if he had the power, he would execute me. Then, they took me back to the prison. My family had been informed that I had been sentenced to death, and it seems the religious judge had [unsuccessfully] asked for my execution three times. The religious judge told me that I was a Mohareb infidel [an infidel who wages war against God] because I had not accepted Islam and because I had not given up my positions. The third time the judge requested my execution the Supreme Judicial Council said it was illegal and incompatible with my crime.

20. The second year [I was] in prison, there was a delegation representing Montazeri, led by Hojjat ol-eslam Bahari. They took me to a room called the "video room." Mr. Bahari asked me, "Why are you insisting upon your positions?" I said, "I have committed no crime, and you yourself have said that people are free to have opinions and that everyone is entitled to his own opinion." He informed me that they had annulled my death sentence and reduced my sentence to life in prison. A year later, they reduced the sentences of those with life sentences—in particular for groups like us that were not armed. I received a sentence of five years' imprisonment.

Prison Conditions

21. I was in prison about six and a half years, two of which I spent in solitary confinement. I was in the Revolutionary Guards detention center in Orumieh for nine months. I had been in solitary confinement for seven months when I was taken to Tabriz Prison and then, in 1988, I was put in solitary confinement for another six to seven months. It was two years in total.

22. When I was in ward 12 there was just one small bathroom, so we could wash once a week for six to seven minutes. After 14 months in ward 12, those of us who were holding onto our ideas (the *sar-e moze'i*) were taken to rooms that were around a small courtyard. Then, our situation was better. This was in 1985. They gave us a small stove to warm up our food. The food was not bad—it was almost good. Breakfast was a piece of cheese and bread. Usually, we got some rice once a day. I

had an ulcer, so I had trouble with food—I could not really eat it. But the quality of the food was not bad. We were not left hungry—we had enough food. Families also gave money. Twice a week, those responsible for the prison supermarket would come and ask if we needed to buy anything.

23. During this period we were still under pressure. They called us into the "video room" and told us, "If you accept what we are asking of you, we will let you see your family in person (not behind the screen) and we will release you." During my three years in Orumieh Prison only once was I allowed to meet my family in person, thanks to a student whom I had taught at night [before my arrest] and who was an officer in the prison.

24. On 7 February 1986 they came and took all of the prisoners to a building called the "workshops." It was a very long building, all the way at the end of the prison. At the end, on each side, there was a big room. There was a young Bahá'í guy there—Mehrdad Maqsudi—he was very depressed. On the anniversary of the Revolution, 11 February, he put oil on himself and set himself on fire. He was around 21 years old. He died right there.

25. We felt they were going to transfer us but we did not know to where. We had not had visitations for two weeks. One day, very early in the morning, the doors of the "workshops section" opened, and they started calling names, and those who left did not come back. Then, it was my turn. I had on sweat pants and a shirt. They

emptied my pockets, and all my stuff remained in the prison. They put us on a bus. They had put mud on the outside of the bus so we could not see out of the windows. They had even put a panel between the driver and us so that we could not see anything. We got to Tabriz Prison around sunset. Before we got there, they had discovered an MKO organization inside the prison, and some of them [the MKOs] had repented. We were put in a ward under the supervision of these MKO repenters.

26. There were ten or eleven of us in the room. There were also a few other prisoners from Tabriz Prison who had not repented. We had one hour to get fresh air each day. One repenter would sit on the last bed and monitor what we said and take notes so, we could not really talk much. We only talked about normal things like family, weather—nothing in particular.

27. After four or five months, towards the end of 1986, they took us to ward 4 of Tabriz Prison. It was a really terrible ward. The ward was known as the "closed door." There was a curtain over the door so that we could not see the hall or the corridor. You could not speak one word to one another. [If you did] they would make you sit on the bed and they would throw a military blanket over your head, and you had to stay there for six hours under the blanket, just sitting. Sitting on the bunk bed was difficult for tall people, but they wouldn't allow them to lie on the bed [while their head was covered by the blanket]. Then after six hours and on the condition that you did not talk any more a

repenter would come and take the blanket off. We could not even exchange meaningful glances to communicate. One time, because I had looked beyond the curtain when they brought the food, they took me to the courtyard out in the snow. They left me in the cold for four hours just looking at the wall.

28. And then they took me to solitary confinement for about four months. The solitary cell was very dirty. Generally, the blankets were stained with human excrement and had not been washed. That section was managed by the Revolutionary Court.

Events Surrounding 1988

29. Since a few months before the executions started, we had been under a lot of pressure. In early June 1988, they took us to be interrogated. When we were taken to the prosecutors and judges we were not blindfolded. [Whereas this time] we were blindfolded and could not see them, from the type of questions they asked it was obvious that these interrogators were from the Ministry of Information. They had three or four questions. The questions were not the usual ones. The questions were: "Do you believe in Islam? Are you still holding onto your positions? Are you ready to do an interview?" We did not know why they were asking these questions. I told them that I would not do an interview, but that I was no longer holding onto my positions. I thought they would execute me if I told them that I still held onto my positions. But I did not say I was a Muslim.

30. After this initial interrogation in June 1988, they took me back into those filthy soli-

tary cells for another two to three months. There were a lot of lice. I was wearing nothing but my underwear because of the heat and the fact that the lice would lay their eggs in your clothes. They had treated everything with DDT, but there was still a huge lice problem. I had the same bowl to eat in and to pee in. I tried to walk all day; I did exercises and would sing the songs I knew.

31. While I was in solitary confinement, the Iran-Iraq War ended and the MKO attacked Iran's borders. On our way to the bathrooms, we could hear a television in the hallway, so we had heard about the end of the war. From that day on, we stopped having visitations—maybe until the end of September. There was no news from the family. We felt during this period that something was happening in the prison. We noticed that some of the MKO repenters who used to take the prisoners to the clinic had disappeared. We felt they were going to do something with us, and we did not know what had happened to those prisoners.

32. We would ask the person who brought food for us, "What date is it today?" and would then draw a line on the wall. One evening in September a Revolutionary Guard appeared and told me, "Put your clothes on," and he took me to take a bath because I had not taken a bath in two and a half months. My clothes were very dirty. He gave me soap to wash myself and my clothes. I had about half an hour. A repenter came and the Revolutionary Guards gave me to the repenter, and he took me to have a visitation. Later on I was informed

that my mother and the mother of another cellmate had poured oil on themselves in front of the prison and threatened to set themselves on fire if they did not show them their children. When I saw my mother, she said, "Son, all of your friends have been executed." I had had no idea until then. They took me back to solitary confinement after this.

33. After two days, a couple of people who seemed, from the way they looked, to be representatives of the Ministry of Information (we knew they were not normal guards—they did not look like guards) asked me what the conditions were here. They asked, "Why are you in your underwear?" I said because of the lice. They asked me if I had a toothbrush. I said, "We have nothing here." That evening, they brought me back to ward 4. But the situation had changed. Now there was not as much pressure. Ward 4 was empty. Prisoners said that some had been taken to [join] the Mersad Operation to identify people who had been arrested or wounded. Some who had come back were tanned, which showed that they had been kept out in the sun. Some were executed. About 18 MKOs who had come from Orumieh Prison were returned to that prison and executed. In the provinces, they had started executing the MKOs first. It was the case in Tehran as well, but there they executed the leftists too. Of the leftists, no one was executed in Tabriz except for one person, Motale' Sarabi, who was from the FKO (Majority). I do not know why he was executed. Then they released some others. The prisons were nearly empty. They kept only the *sar-e moze'i*.

34. My prison term was ending in 1989. But they had not counted the time I was in the Revolutionary Guards detention center, so all together it was six years and two months. Therefore, I was a *mellikesh*. When my family and my wife would go to the prison authorities, they would ask, "Why don't you let go of him? His sentence is served." The Orumieh prosecutor would say, "We are not happy with his behavior or his morality." We were in fact [under the jurisdiction] of Orumieh but being held in Tabriz Prison. In June 1990, I was let out, eleven months after my sentence was finished. The son I had barely seen was in second grade and the other was in third.

35. I had a car, and I worked as a cab driver. I had lost my job. I had a piece of land I had bought from the Ministry of Education cooperative, but they had confiscated that too. I missed teaching. For six years I could not leave Iran. I went to apply for a passport regularly, but they would tell me that I was not allowed to leave the country. Every week for six years I had to report to the local office of the Information Ministry in the same detention center where I had been imprisoned. Even when you went to say you were still there, they would put your face against the wall. They would ask me, "Who have you seen this week? Where have you been? What have you done?" After six years I got my passport.

36. I came to Germany in 1998. I am an asylee here.

Cologne, June 2009

OFFICIAL STATEMENT • 11

Subject: What to do about the political groups who confront the Islamic Republic
The official: Speaker of the Islamic Consultative Assembly, Ali Akbar Hashemi Rafsanjani
The occasion: Interview with the magazine *Ayandesazan*
Date: 29 November 1981
Source: The interview was republished in Hashemi Rafsanjani, *Interviews, 1981-82*, ed. Mohsen
                Hashemi, 1378 (1999–2000) Tehran, Daftar e Nashr e Ma'aref e Enghelab, p. 158-162

Question: We would like students to know what to do about the political groups who are now confronting the Islamic Republic. Explain the political nature of these groups, their goals, their contradictory positions, and tell us the responsibility of the Students Islamic Associations in the schools regarding the influence of these groups?

Answer: . . . [The] nature of the [Tudeh Party] is extremely clear. They have never had a shining record. They fought the previous regime as part of the anti-government movement and their own particular slogans [and tenets.] Even if their struggle has been beneficial in the past, the nature of this party is not good at all. They are against religion. The only thing that we fight for, and will continue to fight for, is Islam, whereas their texts and their thoughts are atheistic and misleading. Young people who have joined them with their youthful zeal, solely for the purpose of [joining] the struggle, [have been misled] and are misguided. The Tudeh Party made poor decisions during Dr. Mossadeq's government. After Dr. Mossadeq, many of them went back and made a deal with the regime. The regime infiltrated them, and took away their oppositional character. Therefore, they betrayed the struggle. [Of course] one cannot expect anything other than that from a group with atheistic and Communist roots. In my opinion, they can never respect spiritual concepts. [And as far as we are concerned] we do not even accept [and recognize] them. At our most optimistic, we consider them a bunch of misled persons. And if we want to be pessimistic, they do not have a favorable situation, politically.

Iraj Mesdaghi

ARRESTED: September 1981
DETAINED IN: Anti-narcotics Prosecution Office Detention Center, Tehran
RELEASED: October 1981
RE-ARRESTED: January 1982
DETAINED IN: Evin, Qezel Hesar, and Gohardasht Prisons
RELEASED: June 1991

1. My name is Iraj Mesdaghi. I was a political prisoner in Iran for ten years. I was held in Evin, Gohardasht, and Qezel Hesar Prisons. I was a supporter of the Mojahedin. I left Iran in 1994. I am now a political refugee in Sweden.

2. I make this statement in support of an investigation into the mass execution of political prisoners in 1988 in Iran.

3. This statement is true to the best of my knowledge and belief. Except where I indicate to the contrary, I make this statement on the basis of facts and matters within my own knowledge. Where the facts and matters in this statement are within my own knowledge, they are true. Where the facts and matters are not within my own knowledge, I have identified the source or sources of my information, and I believe such facts to be true.

Arrest and Torture

4. I was first arrested in 1981 after the 20 June demonstration. The situation was very bad then. I was arrested in the street because one of my relatives showed me to the Revolutionary Guards, saying that I had connections with the Mojahedin. They came to the store, and they took me to a detention center in the north of Tehran. This center was the prosecution office building for narcotics. At the time, this [narcotics] center had a section for political prisoners.

5. I was tortured for six hours. They hit me and tortured me with an electric cable. They lashed me on the soles of my feet. I was tortured there three times. The authorities realized that they did not have any information about me. All they had was what my cousin had told them: "He

is a Mojahedin sympathizer." When the head of that center came to our cell, he asked, "Why were you arrested?" I said, "They accused me of supporting Banisadr's coordination office." [This was an office put in place by the beleaguered president Abolhassan Banisadr to muster popular support for him in 1980–81.] He looked at me and said, "They were right." At this point I realized they did not know much about my political activities; my cousin knew that I was supporting the Mojahedin, but she did not know anything about what I was doing. So they released me because they did not have any information about me. Also, some of my friends knew someone who was powerful in that center and he was in charge of my case. They used this man's influence to get me released. The guards searched my house and the whole neighborhood. They talked with neighbors, but nobody said anything about me. When I was released, the head of the center said, "If you come back here, I will kill you with my own hands." I said, "Ok." I was held there for about one and a half months—about 40 days.

6. After I was released, I was out of prison for about two months. I did not work. I pretended that I was working at a company at the time to show that I was working, but I was not actually doing anything. Some friends and I ran this company, which was in a building that also belonged to the prosecution office. I was not involved in any political activities at the time because my last connection [with the MKO] was cut; therefore I did not have any political ties. At the time, it was very hard to get

a [political] connection and to have relations with friends. Two or three months later, in January 1982, I was arrested at that company. I was 21 years old. They did not tell me why I was being arrested. They just called my name, blindfolded me, put me in a car, and took me to what I believe was a base in the south of Tehran, where they whipped me and hit me on the soles of my feet with a cable.

7. Then they interrogated me and asked me questions about various people. They would give me the names of individuals and ask me to give information about them. I said, "I do not know anybody. I do not know what you're talking about." Then, during the beating, they asked, "Who is this person? Who is that person?" I knew some people they mentioned—they were my close friends—but they were not politically active. At that time, I did not know why I had been arrested, so I was confused about why they were mentioning my closest friends who were working with me but were not politically active. I did not know what to say. After two or three days at the base, they took me to Evin Prison. At the time, they did not tell me where I was being moved. They moved everybody to Evin Prison after two or three days. I found out when I got to Evin Prison that a guy who knew me and was tortured very savagely had said something about me.

First Trial

8. At Evin Prison, I was taken alone to a courtroom nine months after I was arrested. There was just a judge; no secretary or anyone to assist him. The judge came to

the corridor, took me, and we went to the courtroom together. I took off my blindfold and I saw a judge in the room, but I did not recognize him. I was sentenced to ten years on charges of supporting the Mojahedin, taking part in demonstrations, and being active in support of the Mojahedin.

Prison Conditions

9. In Evin Prison, in 1981 and 1982, many prisoners were in very bad, critically bad, health—including one of my friends who was in critical condition in the prison infirmary. A common problem for prisoners was kidney malfunction, and they needed dialysis. Some prisoners could not walk because of the torture; they could not move because they had been beaten on the soles of their feet. Thus, prisoners could not be taken to court because of their injuries, so they would bring the "court" to the prisoner's room—meaning the guards and the interrogators would come to prisoner's cell. [When the "court" would enter the cell,] prisoners who were lying on their beds would be ordered to cover their faces with blankets. They would then call a name, which meant that the court would hear the case of the person whose name was called. In short, the court would hold a session in the presence of other prisoners.

10. In 1982, a lot of people were severely tortured and pressured to confess in televised interviews. People who were tortured were told they had two options: either give a televised interview and stop being tortured, or the torture would continue. The intensity and severity of the torture inflicted upon prisoners were unthinkable. The offer to give a televised interview did not mean that they would be released or that their prison sentence would be reduced. It only meant that the torture would stop, and they would be executed sooner and would not have to bear more torture. The pressure of torture was such that the prisoner would rather be executed than be continually tortured. I know a lot of people who made a televised confession and were executed afterward. Some of these people were Abbas Sahra'i, Kuroush Khavarian, Mehran Asdaqi, Mohammad Reza Jamali, etc. . . . They all made televised confessions and were executed afterward.

11. When they want you to do a televised interview, there is no end to your torment. Today, tomorrow, next week, next month—for how long [would the torture continue]? As time passes, certain information is going to be useless [to the authorities, so there is no more need for torture and the prisoner knows this]. Whereas the same is not true when the prisoner is under pressure to make a televised confession [a public confession is always a victory for the authorities—whenever the prisoner gives in]. There is a lot of pressure on the prisoner when they want him to come to do a televised interview, or when they want him to do something else.

12. In 1983, they took me to solitary confinement and tortured me many times because they said that I was part of a network of prisoners who were active in the ward. I was in solitary confinement for nine months and was tortured weekly in the cell. Several people would beat me and lash

me with an electric cable. They asked me about the prisoners' organization within the prison and about detainees who were kept in the same ward I was in. Sometimes the guards would not even ask a question. They would just tell me to talk. I would say, "What should I say?" At first they would say I should write the names and all that I knew about almost 130 people. I did not know what to write. They would say, "You must write. You remember."

13. One day, Asadollah Lajevardi came to my cell when I was in solitary confinement. He said, "You will talk." I said, "I do not know anything." Then he ordered the guards to torture me. At that time, I was very weak.

14. We were moved to Qezel Hesar Prison in January 1984. There were 20 to 22 people with me in a cell that was four square meters [about 40 square feet]. We did not even have enough space to stand up. We used every space in the cell. It was not easy.

15. In March 1984, I was taken to Evin Prison for more interrogation, questioning, and torture. They asked me the same questions as before. They asked me about everything: what I was doing outside the prison, how I was related to the Mojahedin, and about my activities. I was tortured more this time than I had been when I was [initially] arrested. I was tortured 13 times.

16. Later they took me back to Qezel Hesar Prison when a group of prisoners was moved there from Evin Prison. My face was swollen. I did not want them to see my face or my feet because I knew that if they saw that I had been tortured, they would wonder why I had been tortured in Evin Prison and would become suspicious of me.

They called my name, "Iraj Mesdaghi. Are you here? We were looking for you."

17. Then they took me to another section, which they called "judgment day." They also called this section the "grave," because, they said, "This is a grave, and we want you to feel the pressure of the grave." They made me sit in a small space, a little bit bigger than a coffin. I was blindfolded the entire time. You could not stand in this space; you had to sit on your knees. The space had two wooden dividers on the left and right sides, a wall on the front side, and was open on the back side. It was like a box with an open side. You could hear the loudspeaker all the time playing readings from the Qur'an and mourning songs.

18. We were under their control all the time. They would send repenters to check on us all the time—each hour, each day, even in the toilet where there was no door, just a blanket [where the door should be] which had a hole in it. They did not even let us cough or chew loudly, because when we made noises they said that we were giving some sort of signal to other prisoners or boosting the morale of the prisoners. The guards would beat us when we made sounds.

19. When I was in this section [the grave], a guy came and took me to a special section where they started interrogating me again. They said, "You escaped from Evin." I said, "I did not. I'm here, I'm a prisoner. How could I escape? How could I go somewhere? Am I free to go anywhere? Evin's authorities called my name and transferred me here [Qezel Hesar]. If you want to kill me, then kill me." They did not believe me.

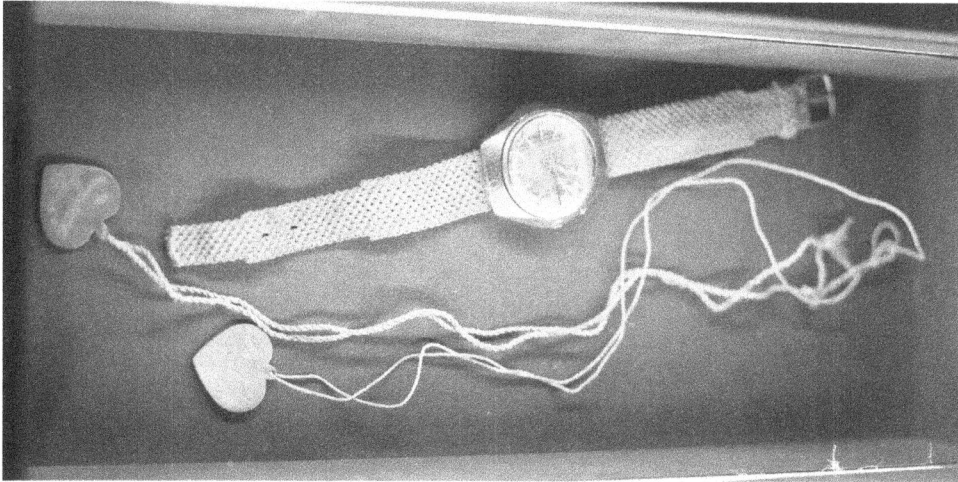

A watch that belonged to Majid Simyari, which was returned to his family after his execution in 1988. He made the watchband from threads he took from rubber socks. The two hearts were made of coins. On each one he carved the names of his wife, Esmat, and his son, Sahand, and he had them smuggled out of the prison as gifts for them.

They said, "You know that you escaped here." They forced me to talk again about my activities and what I did before I was arrested. They did not ask me if I prayed and did not question me about religious issues because, at the time, they knew that I prayed more than they did. They did not talk about the ideology of the Mojahedin either. I may have been in the "judgment day" section [the grave] for about one and a half months. Other people were in that cell for eight, nine months. [During the interrogation], they made me stand up for a very long time—maybe two or three days. I was hallucinating. I could not sleep. I do not remember a lot of things from that period of time.

Second Trial

20. In 1985, I was taken to Evin Prison to be re-tried. They interrogated and tortured me again. They asked me the same questions. When I was re-tried, the judge was with someone who was trying to trap me with his questions. I believe the judge was Ali Mobasheri. I could see him because I did not have a blindfold on. It was only judge Mobasheri and a secretary in the courtroom, no one else; no prosecutor.

21. I was re-tried on new charges. They accused me of being involved in a network created within the prison. I told them that if this were true they should name my superior within this hypothetical network, and I asked who would be the [supposed]

person that I was in charge of within this network. But they did not have anything to say, as they did not know anyone. They accused everyone of being part of a network in prison. The leftists and the Mojahedin were together. We [the prisoners] were doing things together, but it did not mean that we had our own organization. We were eating together, or organizing classes—for example, French, English, mathematics, physics, and Persian literature. We had organized activities, and the guards knew that. This was in Gohardasht Prison [where it was more relaxed and we did activities together]. In Qezel Hesar Prison, it was prohibited to do anything, even to talk or have classes.

22. I was accused of having contact with prisoners. I said, "It's not against the law. Where is the law [that says this is illegal]?" The situation in those days was not like the situation in 1981, 1982—it was a little bit better, [meaning] I could be bolder. In this second trial, I was asked the same questions about my political affiliation and was given the same indictment. The questions were about what I did. I said, "Why am I being tried for the same charges that I was tried for before?" The religious judge said, "Let me see." Then he checked. He said, "Yes. I do not know why you are being tried again for these things that you were tried for before." He asked me if I was ready to do a televised interview in prison in the presence of other prisoners. He asked me if I was ready to condemn the Mojahedin. I said,

"I'm neutral. I do not want to talk about political things." I was trying to equivocate and avoid talking about my political affiliation. They did not say exactly what they wanted me to say in the television interview. They just wanted me to talk.

23. At that time [of my second trial], I was still an inmate of Qezel Hesar Prison. I had been transferred to Evin for this second trial and, after a few days, I was returned to Qezel Hesar. They did not give me a new sentence after my second trial in the autumn of 1985. Perhaps they thought that my first sentence of ten years in prison was enough.

Prison Conditions (continued)

24. One year later, in 1986, we were all transferred to Gohardasht Prison because they evacuated all the political prisoners from Qezel Hesar Prison. They moved us in buses. The treatment at Gohardasht Prison was similar to what was implemented in Qezel Hesar Prison. I was kept with other prisoners. There were 100 to 200 people in a ward. There were about 190 people in our ward; we had enough space.

25. I was not tortured, so to speak, but I was beaten, and they also sent me to solitary confinement three or four times as punishment for celebrating the religious festival Eid [Qorban]. I was in solitary confinement for a month. The longest time I spent in solitary confinement was two and a half months, in Gohardasht Prison.*

*Prisoners were sometimes punished for their religious observances, owing to the fact that they had taken the initiative together and were acting outside of the prison authorities' control. Also, celebrating a religious festival would confirm their Muslimhood, something that the regime denied by branding them as *monafeq*, or hypocrites.

26. One time, they took me and 24 other people, blindfolded, somewhere. When we arrived at the meeting hall, we were allowed to take off our blindfolds. I saw a guy who had been tortured and forced to do a televised confession to recant his beliefs. I saw a camera and the guy—who at the time I did not realize was one of my own friends. We were all taken there to watch him while he was recanting before the camera, so that he would be under even greater pressure. I said, "I do not want to stay here." There were eight of us who protested against being brought to attend our fellow prisoner's confession. The guards were standing on both sides and made a tunnel with electric cables. They started to beat us with cables [because we wanted to leave the room]; it was very painful. No torture is as painful as being beaten with these cables. All of us were unconscious in the hallway while the prisoner was reading his confession in the meeting hall. After the televised confession was over, they brought the prisoner into the hallway and forced him to read his confession to us there. At that time, Arab was the assistant prosecutor. He ordered the guards to beat us and told us, "Do you think all this is over? Wait and see, when the imam issues the fatwa, we will show you then." We were beaten so much that we fainted. Then the eight of us [those who had protested] were punished and sent to solitary confinement. I was in solitary confinement for almost two months. This was before the mass execution.

27. When we were in solitary confinement, [usually] our cell was checked many times a day [by the guard]—maybe ten, twenty times. The guards checked on us all the time in our ward. The small window on the door was opened and closed all the time and you could not feel secure there even when you wanted to use the toilet because you felt that someone was watching you. But in those days [during the two months before the prison massacre], nobody came to check on you, and all of the prisoners felt secure. It was not like before.

Events Surrounding 1988

28. There were changes in prison leading up to 1988. A lot of prisoners were chosen and transferred from Gohardasht Prison to Evin Prison. I was in ward 2 at the time. They changed the numbers of the wards to confuse people and to make it difficult for the prisoners to exchange information about what was going on in different wards. In those days, people who were arrested and came from outside the prison brought information to the prison about what was happening in society and about the opposition's activities. The buildings in Evin Prison were very close to each other. A great number of prisoners were detained in Evin's sections, and they communicated with each other. When they transferred prisoners from Evin Prison to Gohardasht Prison, the newcomers would update Gohardasht prisoners on what was happening in Evin.

29. It was spring [1988] when they started bringing prisoners who had been disciplined from Evin Prison to Gohardasht to the ward below our ward, without exerting

any control over them. The guards knew that we were communicating with them. Because when you put two prisoners [in two adjacent cells] close to each other, [it is inevitable that] they will make a connection with one another. I sensed that they wanted to mix us together and share information because they could have taken them [prisoners from Evin] to another ward where the solitary cells were vacant. Or they could have put them on upper floors so that they would mix with leftist prisoners [as opposed to MKO prisoners]. For example, I knew that the solitary cells on the first floor were empty. Yet there was no reason for the Mojahedin or the leftists to exchange views in those days; they had parallel lives. It was better to put the Mojahedin near the leftists because we were on second floor, and they were on first floor.

30. The newcomers would tell us about their time at Evin Prison, such as when prisoners went on hunger strikes. We would talk about what was happening outside of the prisons; we would exchange information about the opposition and about society. We would talk about the regime's defeats on the war front, and about the prisoners' mothers' protest gathering in front of the revolutionary prosecutor's office in the city of Qom. We would exchange our analyses of the Mojahedins' strength. We would also elaborate on what was happening in Iraq.

31. When the NLA [National Liberation Army of Iran, established in Iraq by the MKO] was established in 1987, everything changed in prison. I heard about the establishment of the NLA during a meeting with my family. Before that, we had received some information about the NLA because some people who had recently been arrested were connected with the NLA. They had come from Iraq or Pakistan. Some of our friends in the prison had a small television that they converted to use as a radio so that they could hear the Mojahedin's radio broadcast in prison. They did this for almost two years. The guards did not know. The prison was under heavy security [but] prisoners were listening to this radio and spreading information. We knew that if there was armed conflict between the NLA and the IRGC, at the last stage [of the conflict] they [the guards] would kill us [MKO prisoners]. They told us this from the beginning, from 1981 and 1982, and they even reiterated it in April 1988. They would warn us saying, "Do not think that if something happens, we will let you out. At that time, we will kill you. We're going to throw hand grenades into your cells. You are *moharebs*; therefore you're not going to leave the prison." Lajevardi also said that the *monafeqin* should not feel secure, and this guideline was written in the newspaper. They also said this to the leftist prisoners.

32. The Mojahedin had an army, and they [Iranian authorities] knew that any released MKO prisoners could join the MKO again. And that is what happened in some cases; after their release some of the MKO prisoners had in fact tried to connect with the MKO and had become active again — some of them even fought against the regime.

33. One day in 1987, after the NLA was established, they took me and two other prisoners to Lashkari [whose real name is Taqi Adeli], who was the deputy director of the prison in charge of prison security. He knew me very well, and he turned to us and he said, "The authorities have given us a free hand to deal with you and even to kill you." Then Lashkari said, "You [have] established [an] army. Now fight and we will fight." He was mocking us. Then he said that it was prohibited to eat lunch together from now on. They did not like us eating together because they thought we were organizing among ourselves. [As such,] starting in the summer of 1987, we were not allowed to eat together or do any exercising together.

34. It was autumn of 1987 when they approached all of the prisoners one by one at Gohardasht Prison. They asked us about our affiliation, the name [of the organization], what we had done, our education, if we were ready to have a so-called interview, and if we would condemn our organization. I believe it was late November or early December 1987 [the Persian month of Azar (21 November–21 December)]. Lashkari was accompanied by all the guards of our ward—[the guards from] different shifts. They were behind the door of our ward. We were summoned behind the door, we were blindfolded. The point of the blindfold was to cause psychological pressure. The questions were not asked in the presence of other prisoners. They had put a desk behind the door. The questions were asked there; we were not asked to sign anything. We would sit there, and then they would ask the questions. The whole sequence didn't last more than five minutes.

35. Lashkari knew me very well. He did not ask me any questions. He said, "Iraj Mesdaghi, father's name Rahmatollah, ten years in prison?" I said, "Yes." He just wanted to tell me that he knew everything. Then he said, "Are you going to do an interview?" I said, "You know me." He said, "Go. Dog. Monafeq." And then he did not ask me anything more. This questioning lasted maybe one minute, no more than that.

36. I think they did the same thing with the leftists. In January when they split us up, they did not just separate the leftists from the Mojahedin. The Mojahedin were separated [among themselves] and the leftists were separated [among themselves]. They were subdivided into red, yellow, and white: *mo'aned* [red/enemy]; *monfa'el* [white/passive]; *tavvab* [yellow/repenter]. *Mo'aned* meant that the prisoner was an active enemy. *Tavvab* meant the prisoner was collaborating with the regime, and *monfa'el* meant that he was passive and represented no danger if he were with the *tavvabs*; however he could become dangerous if left alone with the *mo'aneds*. Lashkari said, "We want to separate the rotten, corrupted eggs from the good eggs." He did not say why.

37. Masud Moqbeli was one of my friends. He had been taken to the Moshtarak Committee and the interrogators told him, "We know that you are a *monafeq*, and an active one. We know you have your own organization inside the prison. There will be a big purge within the prisons." They

then gave him [Masud Moqbeli] a short-wave radio and they told him, "You can listen to Radio Mojahed [in your cell]. But it's useless because we are going to kill you." He was in solitary confinement in the Moshtarak Committee in March–April 1988. He came back from the Moshtarak Committee in April and told other prisoners about this. I heard about Moqbeli's incident from other prisoners after the massacre. He had a chance to tell other prisoners before the massacre, but no one thought anything of it because we had heard the same thing—that they were going to kill us—for seven years.

38. I thought that maybe they wanted to punish some prisoners, or wanted to give new sentences to some prisoners, or wanted to put pressure on certain prisoners to break them. I could not have guessed that they were going to kill us.

39. After the prison killings took place and we were transferred to Evin Prison, the Evin survivors told us that, in May 1988, a representative of Ayatollah Montazeri, Hojjat ol-eslam Naseri, had come to Evin Prison. He had asked to talk with the representatives from section 1 of Evin. He spoke with five detainees in that ward. One of them, for example, was responsible for the ward, another guy was responsible for cleaning, and the other was responsible for the store. Out of the five of them, four of them were killed, and one of them lives in Stockholm. He is a close friend of mine, Mehrdad. Hojjat ol-eslam Naseri had told them [the five prisoners of ward 1], "There is a plot." He had said that he did not know exactly what the plot was, but he

knew that something was happening. Hojjat ol-eslam Naseri had told them that they [prison authorities] were going to make an exhibition in the Hosseinyeh of Evin Prison of all the things they found in the prison from the prisoners. [Each ward has a Hosseinyeh. It is the amphitheatre. It is a public space used for praying, but also used for entertainment.] For example, we had a knife which we made from a spoon. They knew that we did not use these things to kill or do harm. We were living [in the prison] for seven or eight years, so we used the knife to cut watermelon, cucumber, onion. They knew we needed something to cut [the things we ate]. We made a lot of things in prison, even weightlifting equipment. They wanted to show the judiciary that the prisoners were conspiring in prison. Hojjat ol-eslam Naseri had warned, "Be careful. Do not give them any excuse to do something, maybe you do not believe me. I do not have anything at stake here. I just want to warn you that there is something happening. I do not know what they want to do. But I don't have a good feeling about it." At that time Naseri represented Ayatollah Montazeri, who was still Khomeini's designated successor.

40. It was the end of June (29 or 30 June) when we heard a little bit of information about the Mojahedin operation in Mehran, Ilam province, called Chelcheragh [Operation Forty Lights, the name of one of the attacks of the Mojahedin, which happened on 20 June]. But we did not get all the information [about this operation] until 30 July (8 Mordad), after the Forugh Javidan attack took place. Five days after

the Forugh Javidan attack we got more specific information about Chelcheragh and Forugh Javidan through the loud-speaker and from the prisoners who had been transferred to our ward from the very section in Gohardasht Prison where the MKO prisoners had turned their television into a radio. The news came from Radio Mojahed. I did not know at the time that they had started the killings.

41. On 30 July (8 Mordad), we were taken to the courtroom. I was the first one. I did not know why we were taken there, or where they were taking us. They opened the door to my cell. I was so afraid. I thought maybe they heard what we were talking about. We were all talking. It was nine o'clock in the morning. I was the only person who had a watch in the ward. I thought that I should give a signal to the others that the guards were in the ward and that my fellow prisoners should stop talking. We had agreed that while we were talking nobody would flush the toilet, because the flush was known to be the signal to stop the conversation. I flushed the toilet and everybody stopped. After one minute the door opened. I was afraid they were going to punish us [for communicating]. When I realized that it was not about that, I relaxed—more than I should have. I did not know they wanted to kill us. I could not sense the danger.

42. They took us to the courtroom on the first floor. I was the first one. There were about 30 to 35 of us in that ward. We were blind-folded. They did not speak to us when they took us; they just said, "Come out. Let's go." We did not take our belongings. We

were taken to the door of the ward and we stood there. When you stood leaning your head on the wall, you could see what was happening in front of you. I saw Lashkari and he asked the guards, "Who brought them?" The guards said, "Seyed ordered us to bring them." Seyed was one of the Revolutionary Guard officers in the prison. Lashkari said, "No. Take them back to their ward. Bring anyone that I call." There was a rivalry between Lashkari and Seyed, each claiming authority over the other. Lashkari wanted to show that he was mak-ing the decisions. Lashkari was the one responsible for the security of the prison.

43. We were sent back to our cells because of the rivalry between them. When I came back to my cell, I went to the little hole in the mesh that was in front of our window. We could not see outside, but I had made a hole and I tried to see what was happening. I saw a mustard-colored Mercedes-Benz that I had not seen before. I got in touch with my friend, Faramarz, who was in another cell. We were speaking through the ventilation units. He asked, "What is happening?" I said, "I do not know. What do you think?" I told him that I could see a Mercedes-Benz.

44. It was in the afternoon when they came and took us [from solitary confinement] to our old ward. They did not say why; they did not say anything. We realized later that they needed the building because it was the only one that was isolated; on [one] side was the prison yard and on the other side was the clinic. You could not get in touch with anybody in the prison in this build-ing. We were taken to the ward; all our

friends were there. We talked to our friends. They did not know anything; they asked us about a person who was taken out of the ward that same morning. We did not know why they took eight people that morning. That night, a guard came to us and said, "What [was] Mansur Qahremani's father's name?" He did not say, what *is* his father's name. He said *was*. People were asking themselves, "Why didn't they go and ask Mansur? Why don't they ask him his father's name?"

45. That night we went to the Hosseinyeh of our ward. From there, we could see that something was happening in the *suleh*, the storage place. A lot of *pasdars* [guards] were there. The guards were excited and trying to see something there. We thought that maybe something interesting was happening. We were talking and guessing. It was 9 p.m. on 31 July. One of our friends saw Lashkari with a wheelbarrow carrying ropes. The courtyard was lit. Gohardasht had a lot of lights everywhere. We did not see prisoners.

46. The next morning, they called some of my friends. We did not know where they were taken. They did not take their belongings. One of them was Hossein Bahri; his sentence was going to be finished in a couple of days or weeks. Then Mehrdad Ardebili was taken out—his brother was an Iranian diplomat—and Ahmad Nuramin. Different people with different situations were called; therefore, we could not reach any conclusions about what was happening.

47. At this time, we were living in a public ward on the third floor. They took three

people on 1 August [10 Mordad] when Lashkari came to our ward with the guards, the *pasdars*. When he came to our cell, he said, "Everybody sentenced to 10 years, or more, sit next to Iraj." There were about 50 of us. Lashkari asked the guard, the *pasdar*, to write down the names. I was the last person, because they started on the other end and then Lashkari said, "Let's go." He took everybody except for me. I said, "I am sentenced to ten years." Lashkari said, "Shut up." Then he kicked me and said, "That's enough." We were confused. Before [this incident], Lashkari always took me whether I had or had not done anything.

48. After that, I realized that they were giving us more food. It was Friday night, 5 August [14 Mordad], when I realized [what was happening] because dinner was boiled eggs. We were supposed to have two eggs per prisoner, but there were more than four or five eggs for each of us. [The quantity of the] other food we received was not [easy to gauge], but eggs are very specific and we could count them. I was thinking, "Maybe my friends are not alive, and they do not need any food." I had a hunch and I lost my appetite and I could not eat.

49. Then [on 6 August], I was again taken out of the ward. There was a desk in the corridor. The conversation outside the ward took about five minutes. Lashkari wanted me to declare my hatred of the Mojahedin. I said "No. I'm not going to." Lashkari said, "Why don't you want to denounce the Mojahedin? Why don't you want to leave prison?" I said, "I want to leave prison. If you let me go, I will go." He said, "You

should [do a] television [interview before the prisoners].” I refused. He said, “. . . will you at least write something?” I said, “No, it's meaningless. Why should I do that? I do not want to talk about politics.” Eventually he gave up and said, “Get lost.”

50. I was then transferred to a new ward. Eight of us were transferred after we were questioned by Lashkari. We were taken to the building that was like a terminal before people were sent to court. I spent about two hours in the vicinity of the court before being summoned inside the court-room. We were taken one by one. I was taken to court after lunch. They told me to take off my blindfold. I recognized some of the [people in the room]: Nayyeri, Eshraqi, Shushtari, Ra'isi, and Naserian. I recognized them because I had seen them in the courtroom, in prison, in our unit, [and also because] their pictures were in the newspaper. We knew Judge Nayyeri from our previous trial. Eshraqi was a prosecutor. Shushtari was the head of the prison organization. Ra'isi was Eshraqi's deputy in charge of the *goruhak* (political groups). There were more than ten people in the room. I do not know how many Revolutionary Guards there were. At least five people were sitting around the table. Nayyeri was the only person writing something. I believe he was drafting the sentence.

51. First they asked me my name, family name, father's name, my sentence, the group I was affiliated with. I said, “I was a sympathizer of the organization.” He said, “What organization? Which one?” I said, “The organization, you know.” They said, “No, say the name of the organization.” I said, “Massoud Rajavi's organization.” At that stage we did not want to say the word *monafeqin*. For two years we had not said *monafeqin*. Nayyeri said, “Are you going to ask for amnesty?” I said “No.” He said, “Why?” I said, “Because I was sentenced to ten years in prison. Seven years [have] passed. If I wanted to do so, I would have done it two or three years [after my arrest], but not after having served two-thirds of my prison sentence.” Then Eshraqi asked me, “Did you know that the *monafeqin* attacked the frontier?” I said, “I heard something.” He said, “Ok, what is your opinion?” I said, “I'm not responsible for that. I do not have any view about it.” He said, “You do not have anything to say about that? Are you not a Muslim? You are seeing these crimes and you have nothing to say?” I said, “It's none of my business. I do not care about these things. I have nothing to do with it and I'm not interested. I'm not responsible.” Nayyeri told me to “Go and write: ‘The organization has attacked the frontier’; write that you are not involved with the *monafeqin* and condemn them [*e'lam bera'at* from the *monafeqin*].”* I said, “I'm not going to do this.” Nayyeri then said, “You must write, be it two words, two sentences.” I told him, “This is not my issue. I do not want to be involved

---

Bera'at means that in the religious sense one is condemning the group and at the same time making oneself innocent. In other words, *bera'at* means that not only is the person *not* a Mojahed, but also that he actively condemns them. It was not sufficient for a prisoner to say that he did not care.

in this polemic." He said, "You must write something." I thought that maybe they were not going to kill everyone, because if they wanted to kill everybody, why would they insist that I write something? I said, "If you release me, I would pledge in writing that I renounce any political affiliation and will not engage in politics anymore." Then a guard told me, "Hey, listen to Haj Aqa." I was very nervous. Then I said, "I'm not going to do that." Then Nayyeri said, "Ok, let him go out. Give him a paper to write down whatever he wants to write." My trial lasted 15 or 20 minutes.

52. I was sitting with my pen and paper outside the courtroom, by the door. When I came out of the room, four or five people were sitting there and they were writing something. Then Naserian gave me a paper and he said, "You must write your hatred of the *monafeqin*." I said, "No. Haj Aqa told me something else." He said, "No, you should write this thing." I said, "Let me go and talk to Haji [Nayyeri] himself." Naserian did not want Haji to know what was happening. He said, "No, no, sit here and write down what you want." I sat down and wrote the pledge they wanted from me. On the paper I wrote, "I, Iraj Mesdaghi, was arrested in connection with the People's Mojahedin Organization. I

had no connection with this organization before my arrest, I did not have any relationship with this organization during my detention, and I pledge that if I am released I shall not engage in any political activity." That night, because of what I wrote I was not executed.

53. One of my friends was killed because of this. His name was Mahmud Zaki. When I went to the court, I saw that Mahmud came out when Naserian and I went in. When Nayyeri was talking to me, Naserian came back in. Nayyeri told him, "He accepted here." He [Naserian] said, "No, he changed his opinion outside." Nayyeri said, "Take him to his ward" [not to be executed]. I did not know what they were talking about and that they were going to kill Mahmud that night. Then Naserian took me outside the court to the prison corridor.

54. In the following days I was summoned to court three more times and, in the end, I agreed to declare in writing my "hatred" of all political organizations [opposing the IRI], with an emphasis on the Mojahedin. And thus I survived the massacre. I was still waiting to be summoned to court one more time, when the commission suddenly stopped its work with the Mojahedin.

Paris, June 2009

OFFICIAL STATEMENT • 12

جمهوری اسلامی

Subject:	On dispensing justice in Islam and the spiritual guidance of prisoners
The official:	Prosecutor General of the Islamic Revolution, Hojjat ol-eslam Sayed Hossein Musavi Tabrizi
The occasion:	Press conference
Date:	14 December 1981
Source:	*Jomhuri Eslami,* 15 December 1981

"We have been providing prisoners with audio-visual programs, which are being carried out in many small towns and contain lessons on the interpretation of the Qur'an and the Nahjolbalagheh [writings of the first Shi'a imam, Ali], and answer questions about ideology. They [prisoners] are given tape recorders to listen to speeches, and are visually exposed to books, of which a million have been purchased. These [undertakings] have been well received by the prisoners. They read ideological newspapers and pamphlets, and receive lessons through audio and video tapes. A television channel is [also] set up for them for the purpose of spiritual guidance. It operates in Evin Prison and has a range of six to eight kilometers [4–5 miles]. These television and radio channels, which allow us to broadcast programs 24 hours a day [nonstop], began operating on Sunday, which is an excellent accomplishment. Televisions are installed in all prison sections and rooms, and nationwide television programs are aired at their usual times; guidance and ideology lessons are broadcast on the spiritual guidance channel. Other than these spiritual guidance and ideology lessons, God willing, we have asked devout teachers and religious folk to give them on-site audio-visual lessons, and have also sent them preachers. These [actions] have been so positive that [officials] report prisoners are now enthusiastically accepting the programs, have been spiritually guided, and that a friendly [if not] brotherly relationship has developed between the prisoners and the judge, assistant judge, and prosecutor. . . ." When asked about the difference in the punishment of political prisoners and regular prisoners, Mr. Musavi replied: "We have no political prisoners in our courts. Can those who play with the country's dignity [and prestige] martyr 72 of our best people [allusion to the bombing of the Islamic Republic Party's headquarters], martyr Ayatollah Madani by placing a bomb in his pulpit and prayer room, and kill the disinherited masses by placing a bomb at the train station, be referred to as political convicts? We do not have political convicts; these are terrorists, conspirators, traitors, and savages who will be prosecuted in an Islamic court, just like other convicts. They will be dealt with by Islamic laws, and punished accordingly."

Rezvan Moghaddam

ARRESTED: May 1983
DETAINED IN: Moshtarak Committee Detention Center, Tehran, and Evin Prison
RELEASED: November 1985

1. My name is Rezvan Moghadam and I am an Iranian refugee living in Berlin, Germany. I was born in Khoramabad, Iran. I was a political prisoner in Evin Prison and the Joint Anti-Sabotage Committee in 1983 and 1984. My husband, Ali Asghar Manuchehrabadi, was a political prisoner in Iran between 1983 and 1988. My husband was executed during the 1988 killings.

2. I make this statement in support of an investigation into the mass execution of political prisoners in 1988 in Iran.

3. This statement is true to the best of my knowledge and belief. Except where I indicate to the contrary, I make this statement on the basis of facts and matters within my own knowledge. Where the facts and matters in this statement are within my own knowledge, they are true. Where the facts and matters are not within my own knowledge, I have identified the source or sources of my information, and I believe such facts to be true.

Arrest and Torture (Pre-arrest and Political Activities)

4. My husband, Ali Asghar (Asghar) Manuchehrabadi, was, like me, born in Khoramabad, in 1951. He lived there and finished high school in Borujerd. He was very talented; he obtained his high school diploma in mathematics. He was admitted to the University of Tehran to study mathematics. He studied mathematics for three years but then went back and passed the university entrance exam and was admitted to the Polytechnic School to study mechanical engineering. He graduated in 1976 from Polytechnic University (today's Amir Kabir University).

5. There were seven siblings in my husband's family. At the age of 11 he had lost his father. His mother was a very able woman and managed to raise all seven of her children on her own; and they all studied at the university level and received master's degrees in engineering and became engi-

neers. My husband was also very sensitive about social justice and inequality because of the hardship his mother had been through in raising her children.

6. I met my husband after the Revolution, through his sister, who was a friend of mine, and we were married in 1980. We have two children: a daughter who is 26 and a son who is 28. They were both born in Tehran, but now they live in Germany.

7. [Before the Revolution] Asghar was a member of Navid [the Tudeh Party's underground group, active before the Revolution]. My husband's activities with the group were mostly cultural; he translated articles from Farsi to English and English to Farsi. I was also a member of Navid. I would do press reviews for the organization and would summarize the speeches of the party officials.

8. Asghar was a very trustworthy person. During the three years that we lived together, I never saw him lie. He was very orderly, thorough, rational, and, at the same time, very sensitive.

9. During the Revolution, many factories had been nationalized or confiscated [by the state] from their owners or had closed down, and, as a result, many engineers were jobless. The Jahan Chit textile factory in Karaj was one of those factories [that had been closed]. My husband became the technical director [in order to reopen it], and oversaw and fixed all their machines. He brought the factory back into operation. He worked there for about six months, until May 1983. By then the factory's production level had reached a good level.

Arrest

10. In May 1983, the Islamic Republic started arresting members and supporters of the Tudeh Party of Iran. One day, Asghar came home from the factory at 4:30 p.m. or 5 p.m. My daughter was three months old at the time. I left my daughter with my husband at home and went out shopping with my son and my sister.

11. When I left the house I noticed that there were people following me. Two young people, maybe 11 or 12 years old, a man in a military uniform, and an unshaven man with a checked shirt were following me. At first I thought I was imagining things. But then I realized they were really following me. I did not want to go home because I did not know whether they wanted to arrest me or harass me. Finally, I decided that I had to go home to determine what was happening. When I went back, I went in the house, and I heard some very loud knocking at the door. This was the external gate. When I went up the stairs, I could see that the apartment door was open. What I saw was that Asghar was sitting there and six armed individuals were around him, holding machine guns, and our daughter was lying on the floor. They ordered me to go with them [along with my husband], saying, "We only need you for less than two hours. We will ask you a few questions and bring you back."

12. I left my son with my sister, who was staying with us at the time. But I took my daughter, whom I was breastfeeding. We were shuffled into a car and blindfolded. Some of the men were really well dressed—they did not look like Hezbollahis. We

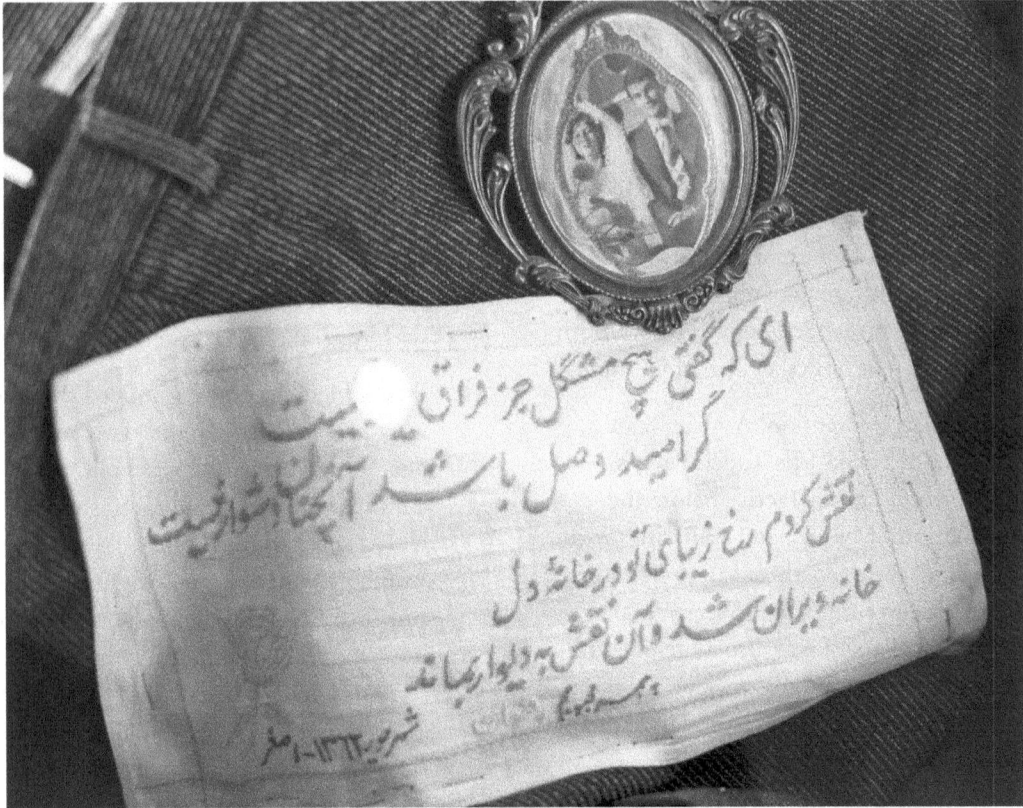

A wedding photo of Rezvan Moghaddam and Ali Asghar. In the background is the pair of corduroy slacks he wore for the wedding. The embroidery, made by Asghar while he was imprisoned, is a love poem for Rezvan, dated September 1984.

went some distance from the house. They drove for a while, and then they started to beat my husband in the car, and they beat his head in particular. They took us to the detention center of the Joint Anti-Sabotage Committee. They were insulting my husband, saying: "You are anti-revolutionary! You are against the Imam! You are one of those people who want to overthrow the Islamic Republic! You are an apostate! You are bastards! You should be killed!" It was a long time ago, so I do not remember

exactly what their insults were. They were laughing hysterically and insulting us. They took us somewhere called Moshtarak Committee on Sepah Avenue. Obviously I didn't know where we were, but that night they had arrested many people and there, someone whispered, "I know this place, it is Komiteh Moshtarak." Once we were inside, I did not know where they took my husband.

13. I was put in a solitary cell. The first time we had a visitation was three months or

more after being arrested. I was allowed to see my husband for five minutes in the presence of the interrogator in the Moshtarak Committee Detention Center.

Prison Conditions

14. I spent at least 16 months in the Moshtarak Committee Detention Center, of which 14 months were spent in solitary confinement. Sometimes there were two or three of us in the [no longer solitary] cell. There were no windows to the outside world, with no sunlight and no fresh air. The room was maybe 1.2 x 1.8 meters [smaller than 4 x 6 feet]. My daughter was with me in the cell, but there was no outdoor recreation time, and my daughter's health deteriorated badly. There was no hygiene. Only three times a day, they would open the door and allow me to go blindfolded to the bathroom. We were also given a smelly blanket. I was in cell 8 and there were people being tortured just below my cell, so I could hear screams day and night. When I tried to lie down and sleep, I could hear people screaming even louder. I had a nervous breakdown as a result of constantly hearing people scream under torture. I lost my appetite altogether. The smell of food made me nauseated. I lost 28 kilograms [62 lbs.] during my stay there. What they did to people was unimaginable. Wolves would not treat their prey in this way.

15. I could no longer breastfeed my daughter, Nassim; she became ill and had diarrhea. She had a very high fever. But I had nothing to treat her fever with. I told them, "If you don't let my child out of prison, I will go on a hunger strike." So I stopped eating.

After 24 hours, they came and collected all of the children in that ward and gave them back to their families. I had not had a visitation since my arrest. For 11 months we had no visitations. Nassim might have been six months old when she was taken out of the prison; it may have been late June, I don't remember the exact date.

16. It was around 18 March [a couple of days before the Persian New Year], when my mother-in-law came for a visitation with my children. We were allowed to meet in the same room [no glass partition]. My son, Navid, was about three. He did not want to leave me, but the guards pulled him from my arms by force.

17. From May 1983 to May 1987, they moved my husband several times from prison to prison—I know he was in the Joint Anti-Sabotage Committee, and then he was moved to Evin, then to Qezel Hesar, then back to Evin—but I do not remember the exact dates of these transfers. I know he was tortured a lot, and he lost many of his teeth. He lost 80 percent of the vision in his left eye because of being hit on his head so much. The medications that were sent to prison for his eye never reached him. [After my release,] I paid a lot of money for purchasing these medicines. At that time I had been fired from my job and, in my difficult financial situation, it was very difficult to acquire these medicines. Each time I would ask the prison authorities, "Why don't you give my husband his medicines?" But I never got a straight answer. I tried three different times to get his medicines and injections to him, all to no avail.

Trial

18. After I was released, I was informed that Asghar had been sentenced to two years in prison. The reality is that they had nothing against us, so they fabricated a case against both of us.

19. My trial was a joke. It was in a room and the interrogator was behind me so I could not see him. Two clerics were sitting there and they talked about my charges and talked about things that were not true. They accused me of spying for foreign powers, infiltrating government bodies, acting against national security. It was all lies. At the time of my arrest I was teaching in a high school. I was teaching math to senior high school students when I was arrested. Before that, I taught math education in the Teacher Training Center.

20. I rejected the charges. My trial lasted ten minutes, maybe less. They adduced no evidence of the charges they had made against me. I did not have a lawyer—no one was given a lawyer. I rejected all the charges. During the period we were held in the Moshtarak Committee, we were never informed of our charges.

21. I was released in 1985. I had been held in prison for two years.

22. My husband was arrested in 1983, so according to his sentence he should have been released in 1985. But he was not released. They told me that "he is not educated yet and he does not accept our conditions." No matter how often we objected to Naserian [about the illegal detention of my husband], who had been one of Evin's butchers, he paid no attention. He was also the prosecutors' representative in Qezel Hesar Prison. Several times he said to me and to Asghar's mother, "I will not let him leave the prison alive."

23. Naserian was someone who wanted to break people and crush them. Asghar was not someone who would have submitted or given in. I think Naserian was a pseudonym.

Events Surrounding 1988

24. My husband was a *mellikesh*, from sometime after 1985 until the time they executed him.

25. After Qezel Hesar, they transferred a lot of the prisoners back to Evin. Asghar was there. In April 1988, when we went to visit Asghar, young children could go to their fathers and be held. When our child was in his father's arms, suddenly the prison guard came and said, "The visitations are over and children must go." But Navid [our son] put his hands around his father's neck. The guard came, took Navid's hands, and removed him forcibly. Asghar objected and said, "The way you are treating us is not right." The guards started to beat my husband in front of the children. They hit him in the face and his eyeglasses broke on his face. I still have those broken glasses in Iran.

26. In May 1988, some of the prisoners were transferred from Evin to Gohardasht Prison. During the transfer prisoners had been badly beaten. Some had been beaten and thrown down the stairs so forcefully that one of them suffered an internal

hemorrhage as a result. Another one had been hit in his testicle. They used prisoners as punching bags. They had beaten them really badly. Many had been gravely injured during the transfer and were not allowed any visitations for a month and a half, the time it took for the traces of the beatings to disappear. From then on, it was clear that they had plans for the *sar-e moze'i* prisoners, and my husband was a *sar-e moze'i.*

27. Several times they called us and said, "Bring deeds, so that we can release him on bail." And each time we took the deeds [to the prison authorities], they would refuse them and say, "He is not repenting yet."

28. When we were allowed to visit again [after the transfer to Gohardasht], the prisoners told their families what had happened to them [during the transfer]. So the families tried to do something for the prisoners. For example, we went to Qom several times to meet with Ayatollah Montazeri. We kept getting promises that they would try to obtain their [the prisoners'] release. But nothing ever came of it.

29. Around late June or early July 1988, he [Asghar] was transferred again to Evin. They put him in solitary confinement. After he was transferred there I had only one visitation with him. And the entire visitation took place behind glass. This, my last visitation with Asghar, was on 19 July 1988.

30. Two weeks later when we went for the next visitation, we were told that there were no more visitations. When we asked why, we were told, "We are reviewing their files for their release."

31. My husband was kept in the "release ward," the *mellikesh* ward. Most of the families who went there for visitations got the same response: they were reviewing their files for their release. But we got suspicious because we did not understand why, if they were reviewing them for release, we could not have a visitation. Each time we went to Evin, we couldn't get a straight answer from the staff. We went to the prosecutor's office. We tried any relevant institution or official. We contacted Mr. Montazeri. We went to the Prison Organization's office on Mo'allem Avenue. And we kept going to Evin Prison, and didn't get an answer, nor was there any information printed and posted on the wall. In Evin I would say to the guard, "Why suspend the visitations if they are to be released?" We were treated harshly. There was a man, in the visitation section, named Haj Karbala'i—he was really brutal. Each time I went there, he would say, "Oh, here you come again. Don't show up here until we call you."

32. It was around November when some families were allowed visitations. They came back and told us that some people had been killed. Those were terrible days for us. On 26 November 1988, I received a call. A man who did not introduce himself said to me, "Tomorrow around 3 p.m., come to the big door of Luna Park [an entertainment park near Evin] accompanied by a man." We used to go there, to get our visitation card, go through the body search, and then get on a minibus that would take us for the visitation to Evin. But this time, when we went there we saw there were some other families. They gave us a bag. They

said, "Your husband has been executed." That day, when Haj Karbala'i spoke to me, he looked very happy—as if he was celebrating.

33. The person who gave me the bag was 27 or 28 years old; he was one of those who used to read the names of the prisoners due for a visitation. In the bag, there were his [Asghar's] broken eyeglasses, his broken watch, and some clothes. His wedding ring was not included in the bag. There was no money. There was no will. That is it. He had a two-year sentence, but he was executed.

34. We learned later that they had had some sort of trial again, and they had been asked three questions: Do you believe in Islam or not? Do you pray? Are you still approving [of] your organization or not? Some people who survived told us this. If they did not pray, they would have been flogged five times a day until they prayed.

35. I believe these killings were planned and [had] nothing to do with the Mersad Operation. The guards' behavior had become more violent. The transfer of prisoners to Gohardasht Prison had started in May. They had prepared it in their plans. All this happened before the Mersad Operation, and had nothing to do with Mersad.

36. I remember Montazeri and Rayshahri's memoirs, and the trial of the brother of Montazeri's son-in-law—when Montazeri had asked Khomeini for these prisoners to be released and Khomeini had refused. The leadership had this plan in mind. Realizing that Khomeini was about to die, they got

written authorization from him to carry out the massacre. This happened before the Mersad Operation. In my opinion, it was a premeditated and precise plan to rid them of a great number of prisoners with whom they did not know what to do.

37. My last visit with Asghar lasted five minutes, as usual, and we were separated by a glass partition. He told me that he had been transferred to solitary confinement. Asghar's mother wrote a letter to Montazeri, saying, "My son served his sentence three and a half years ago, and he has still not been released. His vision is deteriorating, and he needs medical assistance." Two people from Montazeri's office went to visit him in Gohardasht in June 1988. One of these gentlemen—who was also a cleric—told Asghar that, "You are part of the wealth (assets) of this country," and they ordered his transfer to Evin [for him] to be released. At that time people did not know that there were actually two factions [within the national leadership]— Montazeri supporters and Khomeini supporters. Obviously the report of those two individuals was ignored.

38. There were changes after February 1988. They released a bunch of people in January or February 1988—after that there were some obvious changes in the staff and personnel. Naserian was still there, but they [prisoners] could feel that there were changes in the prison administration. The behavior of the staff toward the prisoners grew worse.

39. In June 1988 when I was following up on the promise of my husband's release, the

prosecutor's office was on Mo'allem Avenue. I used to go to the second floor. I do not remember names, but there was a cleric who was our interlocutor. One day he told me, "Lady, I am telling you this, just pray for him to be alive. Don't worry so much about his eye and medicine and such things." I got upset and said, "Why? What has he done?" He said, "Well, what can I tell you?" It was clear [that] he knew something that he could not tell me.

40. Someone by the name of Mahbubeh, whose husband was a Tudeh affiliate, had a relative who was a Revolutionary Guard who worked in the prison. That guard had told Mahbubeh, "When you see your husband in visitation, tell him to comply with whatever prison authorities demand." Mahbubeh's husband was executed too.

41. [As previously mentioned], when I was told about Asghar's execution, I asked [the prison staff], "Why did you kill him?" The response was: "he was an apostate." When I asked for his will, I was told, "Apostates don't have wills, wills are for Muslims." I asked, "Where is he buried?" I was told, "You will be informed later." No matter how many times we inquired [about the burial place], they never gave us a straight response. Twenty-one years have passed since then, but we searched for ourselves and guessed where [our loved ones were buried]. At the time, the mass graves were so shallow that you could see part of their clothing.

42. We could see blankets thrown on the side of the cemetery that were bloody. There were some grayish colored blankets.

When I was in the Joint Anti-Sabotage Committee, I had had that kind of blanket. I saw one blanket scrunched up that was covered in dried blood. I called several people to see it there, but they could not bring themselves to touch it; we all felt sick.

43. As victims' relatives, we became one big family. We used to go together to Khavaran Cemetery. We became very close emotionally—we always commemorated the anniversary together.

44. I have been arrested twice for celebrating these commemorations. The first time was two days after my husband's execution was announced to me. I was in Golha Square with two other ladies, [and we] were going to visit another lady whose husband had been executed. Several armed men surrounded us and put blindfolds on us and took us to a detention center—I do not know where. Two of the people were released before me. I was arrested on a Tuesday and was kept until Thursday. They threatened to kill me. I had two bangles that they took forcefully from me, and they said they wanted to execute me. [They said,] "You have to commit and give us a guarantee that you will not have any ceremony for your husband." I told them that I would have a commemoration, and I would do whatever I could for my husband.

45. One time they said, "Why is it that you make so much fuss about this?" I said, "You killed my husband who had only a two-year sentence!" One of the interrogators said, "Can I apologize to you? Even

in a move, a bunch of belongings break. There has been a Revolution here. Some people die." [I said,] "Are you comparing human beings to washing machines?" He responded, "At the time, I was on the war front. If I were here I wouldn't have let them kill Asghar." Of course they are all liars.

More Recent Events

46. With my sister and brother-in-law, we were in a car on Takht-e Jamshid Avenue. A car with three passengers stopped our car. It was about 7:45 a.m. on a Friday. They asked for our IDs. And I said to them, "You are stopping us, you should show us your IDs!" He said, "You shut up!" He took out a letter and showed my brother-in-law, and said to my brother-in-law, "We have a warrant to arrest this lady and take her to court." I said, "Well on Fridays, there is no court and you have to tell me why—you cannot just take me, what is my charge?" The men opened the car door on my side and said be quiet and come out.

47. Asghar's picture was in my bag, and I wanted to give it to his sister to take to Khavaran. They would not let me do this. They made me sit in a Peugeot. There was a driver and someone next to the driver and someone with me in the back. They were all armed. They drove very fast and took me to the south of Tehran. I had to keep my head down, and each time I tried to sit up to see where I was, they would yell at me to keep my head down. He grabbed my neck and pushed me down. I said, "If you are a Muslim you shouldn't touch a woman." I was told to shut up again. They took me to a building that had no signs indicating what it was. I told them that what they were doing was illegal and inhuman. [I said], "You have no right to do these kinds of things to people." This happened on 29 August 2007. Many other people were arrested that day for the same reason [trying to commemorate in Khavaran Cemetery]. They held me for a day—from 8 a.m. to 3 p.m.

Berlin, July 2009

اطلاعات

Subject:	Open discussion on issues raised by Evin prisoners
The official:	Islamic Revolutionary Prosecutor of Tehran, Assadollah Lajevardi
The occasion:	Questions and answers with Evin prisoners in Evin Prison
Date:	The second week of January 1982
Source:	*Ettela'at*, 19 and 20 January 1982

Last week, Assadollah Lajevardi, the Islamic Revolutionary Prosecutor of Tehran, participated in an open discussion with Evin prisoners and answered their questions regarding prison issues and daily concerns. One of the detainees asked Mr. Lajevardi:

"[Prosecutor General] Mr. Musavi Tabrizi has said in an interview: any person arrested by us is apprised of the charge(s) brought against him within 24 to 48 hours. But [how is it that] there are individuals here who [since their arrest], one to six months ago, have not even been called for questioning, and do not even know what they are accused of?" . . .

[*Response by Lajevardi:*] "Our duty is to question you shortly after [your arrest]. But you all know that for this regime, we had built no prisons, nor prepared any interrogators or prosecutors. We did not expect to see such a day [of such opposition]. As I brought to your attention earlier, we left the responsibility of questioning, interrogating, fact-finding, pursuing, prosecuting, and looking after [the accused] to our brothers who are few in number. [And] we have no plans for increasing their numbers because we are hopeful that a red line will soon be drawn on such misguided actions [as yours], and that they will cease to exist forever, thus stopping us from [having to] waste our resources on such matters. . . .

". . . On the other hand, you yourselves are to blame because prior to [the month of June] the charges were stated and brought in an hour against any individual who was arrested. Now, you have participated in armed, unauthorized demonstrations and have been arrested by Hezbollah; this doesn't require us to inform you of any charges, since you yourselves know better the reason for which you have been arrested, as do we. . . . There's no need [for us] to inform you of the charges against you."

One of those [prisoners] who had repented asked the following question of Mr. Lajevardi: "As you are aware, the conditions that were set by the judiciary for releasing prisoners were that they should express remorse and repent. [So] when prisoners are not released, does it not create an issue in people's minds that it is because they have not repented? Yet, Mr. Musavi Tabrizi said in an interview that 90% of the prisoners have repented [but still remain in custody]. How do you explain this?"

. . . [*Lajevardi responded:*] "God may have accepted your repentance, but proving this is important to us. When this is proven to us, rest assured that you will not be kept here for even a moment. However, proving this issue is somewhat difficult. Put yourself in our place and also consider the issue of the *nefaq* [hypocrisy—pejorative term used as reference to the Mojahedin Khalq Organization]. You will see that those who, in our presence, repeatedly claim to be Hezbollahis, and say they have repented, once [they are alone], seated next to each other back in a room, embark on a different type of discussion.

". . . There have been individuals who have repented. As I told you before, we released the ones about whom we became certain. In your case, too, if we become certain and convinced that you have repented, you will be freed."

. . . In response to a prisoner's question as to why they were not allowed visitations, Mr. Lajevardi stated:

". . . We do not trust you. That's why we're not going to allow you to visit with your brothers and comrades of the Organization in some garden so you can exchange information. . . . No, we will not do that."

Ebrahim Mohammad Rahimi

ARRESTED: November 1979
DETAINED IN: Evin Prison
RELEASED: September 1980
RE-ARRESTED: June 1981
DETAINED IN: Gohardasht Prison
RELEASED: August 1991

1. My name is Ebrahim Mohammad Rahimi and I am 55 years old. I came to the United Kingdom on 1 September 2008. I was granted political asylum in August 2009. The first time I was a political prisoner in Iran was for one year, from 1979 to 1980. I was re-arrested in June 1981, [and that time I was in prison] for ten years, before being released in 1991. I was mainly in Gohardasht Prison.

2. I make this statement in support of an investigation into the mass execution of political prisoners in 1988 in Iran.

3. This statement is true to the best of my knowledge and belief. Except where I indicate to the contrary, I make this statement on the basis of facts and matters within my own knowledge. Where the facts and matters in this statement are within my own knowledge, they are true. Where the facts and matters are not within my own knowledge, I have identified the source or sources of my information, and I believe such facts to be true.

Arrest and Torture

4. I was first arrested just after the Revolution in 1979, but I was released in 1980. At the time of my arrest I was a shopkeeper. I remember that one day one of the men in our neighborhood, an older man with a family, had been caught drinking alcohol. The Revolutionary Guards decreed the punishment of a public flogging, and they brought him to the square in our neighborhood to carry out his punishment. I told them, "You have no right to do this." The guards replied to me, "This is an Islamic country and no one has the right to drink alcohol." The whole neighborhood gath-

ered together and tried to stop the guards from flogging the man. The guards began clashing with the people, shooting their guns in the air, trying to scare us. Because of the commotion caused, the guards could not flog the man.

5. The next day the revolutionary prosecutor implemented a directive that anyone who opposed the Islamic orders of God was to be arrested. I was listed as one of those people who had interfered with the Islamic orders of God, and so I was arrested. When they came to arrest me I tried to resist them, but they shot me in the leg. I was in prison only a short time.

6. I was arrested again later, in 1981, for being a member of the Mojahedin Khalq Organization (MKO). I was taken to court and sentenced to ten years in prison for my political membership. I served the full ten-year term. I still have the scars on my feet from the torture I received in prison.

Events Surrounding 1988

7. I was held in Gohardasht Prison in ward 3—the upstairs ward. There were 200 people in my ward. Some people were leftists and some were Mojahedin. I would estimate that there were about 120 Mojahedin and 80 leftists. I believe 190 of those prisoners were executed during the mass killings.

8. We heard the news that the MKO had attacked Iran over the radio—we had no television. But then they stopped allowing us to listen to the radio. Once the Mojahedin attack was crushed, the executions began.

9. We were taken out of the ward, 20 people at a time. The guards took us out into a large corridor. We were all blindfolded. The guards would ask our names and then we waited for our turn to be called.

10. Lashkari came to speak to us in the hallway. He did not like me. As he passed me he said to me, "Your trousers look like they are from America. You are a sissy!" I got very angry with him, and we had a confrontation. He grabbed me and attacked me, and then all the guards started to beat me. My blindfold fell off during the beating, so I was able to look around the corridor. At the end of the corridor, on the left, one room was serving as a courtroom; there were Nayyeri, Eshraqi, and Naserian. I had heard from the other prisoners that the commission these people were involved with had been ordering the executions of the prisoners. I did not know of them personally, but I had seen photos of all of them before in the newspapers. I recognized Nayyeri because I had seen him during my interrogations in 1981, and other prisoners had subsequently told me that was his name.

11. They left the other 19 people in the hallway, but because of the confrontation I had had with Lashkari, they said, "Put him back in his cell." The guards took me back to the ward and told me, "Shave your moustache! [The guards considered having a moustache a sign of dissent characteristic of leftist or MKO members.] In the morning we are going to execute you." The next day they came to my cell, they tied my hands, and they shaved off my moustache.

Two carvings by Majid Simyari. Simyari, who was from Iranian Azarbaijan, carved his son's name, Sahand (which is also the name of a mountain in Azarbaijan), on a piece of asphaltum that he probably found in the prison courtyard (top), and he sculpted the map of Iran on a coin that he found (shown below).

12. But I was never again taken to court. They never came back for me to take me to be executed, though I lived in fear that they were going to. I discovered later that I had been saved because one of the prison officers, Ezzat Shahi, had recognized me. We had been in prison together under the Shah, before the Revolution, and I had helped him back then, in 1977, by sending information from him to his friends on the outside. When I had the confrontation with Lashkari in the hallway and my blindfold fell off, this man, Ezzat Shahi, recog-

nized me. I believe that Shahi had been on the panel that had advised the judges on the prisoners' behavior and character while in prison. Shahi was a high-ranking security official. He had also served as head of the Central Revolutionary Committee. He has written his memoirs about that time. Several years after I left prison I found out that he had saved me by taking my name off the list. But others were not so lucky. I believe the other 19 people that had been in my ward were all killed. We heard later that my sisters had been executed in Evin on 5 August 1988, two days before we were brought before the commission. My brother had been with another group of people. When Nayyeri heard my brother's name he told him to go out, and that they would call him. They never did call him, and from there they sent him to solitary confinement. Later we heard that since Nayyeri had killed our sisters two days earlier, he had spared my brother. I saw my brother again two months after the killings were over, when we became cellmates.

13. In the ward where I was returned there was a window from which we could see out into the courtyard adjacent to the Hosseinyeh. The windows were barred, but we had twisted one of the bars so that there was a small space through which we could take turns watching what was happening outside. We could see the guards dragging corpses and putting them into large black trash bags or body bags. The black plastic looked much stronger than a normal trash bag. There was a large truck parked nearby. The guards were throwing the bodies inside these big bags, into the back of the truck. I could not estimate how many bodies there were. I do not know where they took the bodies.

14. The guards soon realized that we were watching what was going on, and so they came into the ward, beat us, and then moved us to a different ward where we could not see outside.

15. My brother and I were finally released in 1991. When we were released the assistant prosecutor told us, "This time you were lucky, but next time you are not going to be lucky again."

16. Of the five siblings who were arrested, only my brother and I survived. After our release in 1991, my brother, who was working and living a normal life as an engineer, disappeared in 1993. He was abducted and we do not know what happened to him, but I suspect that he was executed without a trial. One of the political prisoners who had seen my brother in prison told me that he had been executed. He told me this after he was released on bail. But no formal public announcement was ever made about my brother's death. The authorities still hold the deed to the property that our family was forced to turn over as bond for him when he was initially released [in 1991], and they will not return it, saying it is because my brother is an "MKO in Iraq." But we believe he was murdered by the authorities.

17. I left Iran in 1997 because I felt threatened. Guards often came past my door and harassed me in very subtle ways. After my brother was abducted people kept coming and would park cars outside of my home.

London, June 2009

OFFICIAL STATEMENT • 14

جمهوری اسلامی

Subject: Whoever disobeys the government is disobeying the command of God and His messenger
The official: Speaker of the Islamic Consultative Assembly and Temporary Friday Prayer Leader, Ali Akbar
                Hashemi Rafsanjani
The occasion: Tehran Friday Prayer ceremony at the University of Tehran
Date: 7 January 1983
Source: *Jomhuri Eslami*, 8 January 1983

Hashemi Rafsanjani, the Temporary Friday Prayer Leader: "One Who Disobeys the Government Is Disobeying the Command of God and His Messenger. This means that whoever disobeys an Islamic government order has committed the most serious deviation. . . . The laws of the Islamic Republic create duties for the people, and they are necessary. If you want to disobey, you are infringing on both the people's right and God's right. You will owe both the people and God. . . . The government of the Islamic Republic issues certain orders. Whoever does not obey is unjust and a traitor. Those obeying, however, are performing an act of worship and will be rewarded by God. The Islamic Republic will, also, provide benefits to you. When you act in this way, your children will be good Muslim kids. They will be accepted at schools and universities and they will get good jobs. They will be respected, and they will be elevated in society. Those who pay neither Khums [one fifth of their income] nor taxes will have children like themselves who will be despised by society. An immoral person cannot enter a university, as you can see.

He will not be able to take part in important projects, and he will be rejected by society. Now we are in the fourth year of our Revolution. After 10 or 15 years, the lines will be drawn and [disobedient] individuals will be known. Today, a person who disobeys the government is the same as a person who disobeys God and his Messenger. . . .

"Naturally and of necessity, selective hiring was introduced for this purpose [of ridding the system of liberals and anti-revolutionaries]. As on many other occasions, the Imam continued to provide us with his [invaluable] advice on this matter. We told the selective hiring committees and other institutions that they should avoid excesses. However, the strong resentment against liberalism that had developed within revolutionary forces, in addition to the fear of infiltration of leftist and anti-Islamic forces, led the revolutionary forces to commit some excesses. The Imam, as a perceptive leader, saw what was going on in the country. However, an appropriate time was needed for a swift corrective action. You have seen the Imam say on numerous occasions that we should not be strict. There are persons who were corrupt in the past but now they are fine. Let them stay. We said the same thing and gave advice from this stage. Unfortunately our fine forces, who are occasionally infiltrated by malevolent persons and occasionally make mistakes themselves, led these institutions to extreme actions. This was done by either our ignorant friends or our smart enemies who had infiltrated our institutions."

A newspaper photograph of a demonstration at the entrance to Tehran University, 6 December 1978—*Pars News Agency*

Ahmad Najarha

ARRESTED: August 1982
DETAINED IN: Evin, Qezel Hesar, and Gohardasht Prisons
RELEASED: March 1989

1. My name is Ahmad Najarha. I was born on 16 January 1960. I was a sympathizer of the Fadaiyan Aqaliat (Minority) Organization. I was a political prisoner during the prison killings of 1988.

2. I make this statement in support of an investigation into the mass execution of political prisoners in 1988 in Iran.

3. This statement is true to the best of my knowledge and belief. Except where I indicate to the contrary, I make this statement on the basis of facts and matters within my own knowledge. Where the facts and matters in this statement are within my own knowledge, they are true. Where the facts and matters are not within my own knowledge, I have identified the source or sources of my information, and I believe such facts to be true.

Political Activity

4. In the year 1982, the Aqaliat newspaper published an article entitled "Organizing Military Units." The article explained the fact that, since 20 June 1981 (30 Khordad 1360), the situation had changed from the political phase to the military phase. The problem was one of survival. In fact, willingly or unwillingly, they had followed the Mojahedin Khalq Organization. The Aqaliat, while being political, was at the same time militant. This meant that they would expropriate [rob banks, for instance], and they were armed. For example, the person in charge of me was a person by the name of Ali Khayat. I think it was a pseudonym. He was armed. He had cyanide. I always pretended that I did not know that he was armed. We [the opposition organizations] had no choice other than to go underground. Owing to the circumstances and the events of 30 Khordad [20 June 1981: mass demonstration against the impeachment, by the parliament, of then-President Abolhassan Banisadr], all the Marxist groups had, willingly or unwillingly, to go underground to carry out their activities. The political phase had changed into a military one.

5. In those days I used to work as a laborer. In fact, before the organization went underground, I did not carry out many political activities. I was just an unimportant sympathizer. I used to read and buy books. I did not have any contacts with the organization and, even if I did have some contacts, they were not recurring ones. Being in contact was not easy. But after they shut down the universities, activities

started to take place locally and in groups. The coming together of groups—going to the mountains and similar activities—were taking place. Most of the talks were political, but we worked specifically with our own cell in the sense that there were no more theoretical discussions and we had entered into the practical phase. But the idea of armed action and military units remained on paper. Terror and fear had filled the atmosphere, and such actions [armed actions] were no longer possible. Later, I realized that the leader of the organization in Tehran had left the country. We were working without leadership—autonomously. In the hierarchy of the organization, we occupied a very low rank.

6. In reality, I belonged to a support group. Our work was to collect money, give out publications, and write slogans. When my contact, Ali Khayat, told me [for example] that by tomorrow we needed some money, I believed that he did and would go about finding money. I never found out how the money was used. For security reasons, it was not possible to ask Ali Khayat who he was in touch with and what kind of activities he was involved with.

7. They did not give us any military training, but as I was young and adventurous I liked these activities. Some members of our group would go from the University of Azarbaijan to Mahabad and then to the north of Azarbaijan [Province], and would buy arms such as Kalashnikovs from behind Qazi Mohammad Square. Then they would separate the parts and, one by one, they would bring them to Tehran. I

did not perform such actions, but I knew that some of the people who lived in the dorm in Azarbaijan brought arms from Mahabad, Maragheh, and Reza'ieh. At that time the task was to liberate. For example, they held up gas stations and took their money. We were mostly involved in defensive and purveyance activities, and providing facilities.

8. At that time, in eastern Tehran, the Aqaliat and Mojahedin collaborated. For example, we would obtain printing materials from the Mojahedin, as we could not use the public publishing places. Aqaliat's activities were underground. We would use rudimentary equipment—we had to Xerox for example. But the Mojahedin were better equipped than the Aqaliat. They were greater in number, and therefore had more means. More people would participate in their demonstrations, and their supporters paid more attention to security issues.

9. One of the interesting events that is worth mentioning is the fact that the public prosecutor's office had infiltrated the Mojahedin Organization. A person by the name of Piruz left our group and joined the Mojahedin. The public prosecutor's office had already infiltrated that [Mojahedin] cell and, by providing them publishing facilities, tried to obtain as much information as possible about the cell. Piruz had become a repenter and was participating in the public prosecutor's operation. My interrogator, who went by the name of Mehdi, was also an infiltrator into the Mojahedin group from the prosecutor's office.

10. One day Piruz came to my father's house. Our home had two doors. One door

opened into the garage in which my father and brother's cars were parked. There was a smaller door on the lower floor that I used to come in and go out of. That day I was reading Tarikh Tamadon [History of Civilization] by Morteza Motahhari [a cleric and close associate of Khomeini]. He [Piruz] wanted to come in, but since he was no longer in our cell, there was no reason for us to be friends. He wanted to come in out of curiosity. I shut the door but his head was in the way. He started asking, "Are you seeing Ali or not? How long has it been that you haven't seen Ali?" I did not give him any proper answers, as I thought he was no longer one of us. At that time I did not have any suspicions about him, but my answers [to his questions] turned to my advantage later because Piruz was gathering information for the intelligence agents.

11. I discovered [the truth] much later. In a meeting that Piruz had with one of the Aqaliat followers by the name of Ahmad Jalal al-Din, it was Mehdi—the same interrogator of branch three or four—who, with a group of Revolutionary Guards, attacked and arrested all of them. This was later told to me by Ahmad Jalal al-Din. They had beaten him severely.

Arrest and Detentions

12. Before my arrest, I heard from Ahmad's mother that his identity had been revealed. I then decided to be cautious in order not to get caught and I tried not to stay home. I just went there to shower and quickly left and spent the night at other places. The public prosecutor and my interrogator knew this and never went to my house.

They roamed the area in a Peykan [a type of car] with armed guards.

13. On 24 August 1982, as I was leaving my house, I heard a voice from a Peykan station wagon saying, "Ahmad, dear, come." I was surprised that that person knew my name. I went closer and saw that Piruz was sitting in the car. Hamid and Mehdi, who later became my interrogators, were also in the car. I was trying to figure out how to run away. I started walking towards my house with the excuse of saying goodbye to my mother. One of the guards in the car stepped out of the car and followed me with a Kalashnikov. At this moment I decided not to flee in order not to make things more difficult for my mother. So they arrested me and took me to Evin Prison.

14. We used to sleep in the *zir hasht* of Evin. My interrogator had short hair and a scruffy beard. He wore a white shirt with the shirttail out, over his pants; and he folded the backs of his shoes down and wore them like slippers. We had to wait behind the door to the ward. People who had already been interrogated sat on one side and those who had not sat on the other side. I always tried to delay my turn by asking to go to the toilet. Haj Aqa would give me a rope or stick as they considered us unclean and did not want to touch us. I would take one end and he would guide me, blindfolded, to the toilet. Once in the toilet, I could push the blindfold up. Once, I heard someone crying. It was the cry of Ahmad Jalal al-Din. They had broken him. Ahmad was one of the trusted and learned members of our group. It was very frightening and unbelievable for me. He

said, "Be cautious; Piruz has given every-one's name but I have not mentioned your name."

15. My interrogation took over two months. My interrogator was a university student by the name of Mehdi, which was not his real name, of course. They interrogated the Mojahedin in ward 3 and the leftists in ward 6. The person who had given my name had named me as a leftist. They took me to interrogation regularly and [tortured me]. In reality, I had nothing special to tell them as Piruz had told them everything about me.

Trial

16. The judge was a cleric. There were three of us [prisoners] present—Faramarz Zamanzadeh Shushtari from the Fadaiyan (Majority) who I think was killed in 1988, and Mansur Abbasi from Rah-e Kargar. My trial took no more than ten minutes. The cleric told me, "Take off your blind-fold, I will read your charges. Whatever you accept to be true, say, 'Yes,' and what-ever you don't, say, 'No.'" He read eight accusations—for example, collecting mon-ey, writing slogans, distributing publica-tions, and photocopying leaflets. I accepted some of the charges and rejected others. He said, "Come and sign here." This is where I saw the prosecutor's document about my interrogation. They had underlined with red ink what they considered to be a problem. [The judge] said, "Will you agree to do an interview, Mr. Najarha?" I said, "No." He asked, "Why?" I lied, saying that "if I were to do an interview, I would not feel safe. I could be in danger in the ward."

He asked, "How about a radio interview without images?" I said, "No." He said, "You don't speak with enthusiasm. What has become clear to us is that we do not know where you are in the organizational chart of your group. I will sentence you so that you sit here in prison until you start speaking and tell us where you were on the organizational chart."

Prison

17. They gave me my verdict about a week or ten days after the trial. I was condemned to seven years.

18. They took me to Qezel Hesar Prison on 24 or 25 November 1982. I was in unit 1 of ward 3. Later they exiled us to unit 1 of ward 4. Most of the people there were Mojahedin, and they were all taken there as punishment.

19. We were always worried that we would remain hungry—especially those who were stronger and exercised. When, after the prayer session, the repenters brought food, we would say that the caravan of happiness had arrived! Between 1982 and 1984, repen-ters were in charge of distributing food. They gave us the leftovers and took the best parts for themselves. In our food, there were some traces of chicken or protein. We would chew the bones in order not to lose anything. The repenters were in cells 1 and 3. As you went toward the end of the ward, which consisted of 23 cells, people were more steadfast in their beliefs. I was taken from cell 21 to cell 19. The last cells were near the toilet. When they turned on the fans to clear the air, we could not breathe in our cell. I do not know how we

made it. I had lost weight. I had turned yellow. My red blood cells had decreased a lot. Terrible food, stress, fear, and sleeplessness—all this because we said no to these gentlemen. But in that context, we were all together, and we did not know any better. People were idealistic and, because of their beliefs, they withstood all the hardships. I was single. I did not have the responsibility of a family, so it was easier for me.

20. When they closed Qezel Hesar Prison, around December 1985, we were transferred to Gohardasht. In the winter of 1987–88, they separated prisoners based on their steadfastness. The guards were not too sensitive about us. Our ward was called the academics' ward. The other leftists would say, "These people are academics and liberals." They gave us that name because we did not want to have a confrontational attitude with the regime.

21. The Tudeh members and the People's Fadaiyan (Majority) tried to disobey the prison rules. For example, prisoners were not allowed to exercise in groups, but they [Tudeh and FKO members] all insisted on working out together. I liked to exercise, and there was no problem when I did it on my own. But these groups were provoking the guards, who would then not allow us to get fresh air, would cut the hot water off, and would take those who had been unruly to *zir hasht*.

Events Surrounding 1988

22. Our ward had between 80 and 110 prisoners. The number varied. There were small individual cells—for example our cell consisted of three people: myself, Dariush

Abbaszadeh of the Ranjbaran Party, and Abdollah Reza'i. After Khomeini accepted the resolution ending the war, they showed us the interviews of Sa'id Shahsavandy, who had been captured in the Forugh Javidan operation, and another person, who was wounded and had an IV attached to him, on a bed. In these interviews, they said that the Mojahedin intended to capture Tehran from the south; that the Mojahedin had armed political prisoners and were planning to enter Tehran with tanks. These statements were lies that the regime wanted to spread. In this interview we were accused of having contacts with people outside the country and of being linked to the Mojahedin in this attack. Dariush Abbaszadeh belonged to the Students' Confederation outside the country. He was older than me. He warned us that they wanted to kill us and that we had to be careful. We were leftists, and we still are, but if they were to ask us if we were Muslims, we had to say that we were.

23. A few days after the interviews were aired, they took the television away. We used to say that we had a vegetative life. We could not go out for fresh air; we had no visitations, and no newspapers. There was an information vacuum. We knew nothing from outside the prison.

24. We were lucky that the regime was not too sensitive towards us. They had started from the *sar-e moze'i* ward. We were among the last wards. We learned through Morse code that they were executing [people]. We could hear some noise but my cellmates said that they were unloading steel rods: "Today they unloaded steel rods 23 times."

In reality it was not the sound of steel rods. They were killing prisoners, but we did not know it.

25. A person by the name of Behnam Karamy, who belonged to Peykar or the Rah-e Kargar Organization, knew how to interpret Morse code. And we would exchange information when we could, in the toilet or bathroom, through Morse code. During the same days, we found out through Morse code that more than 300 had been executed. At first we did not believe it, but soon a terrible fear overcame us. After that we understood that the government was settling accounts.

26. After removing the television, they gave us a form with a few questions to which we had to respond before returning it. At the time, the situation was already extraordinary. The form consisted of several questions that they wanted us to answer. "Are you a Muslim? Are you willing to do an interview? Do you pray?" In reality these were the same questions that Lashkari had asked of us earlier. He once asked me, "If you are not *sar-e moze'i* (steadfast), why don't you ask for a visitation in person or for leave to go out and see your parents?" By asking these favors, you implied that you had no hostility towards the regime. I was single; I had just a few more months to serve. Requesting anything of them was against my principles. So I never made such a request.

27. I owe my being alive to Dariush Abbaszadeh. After the interview with the Mojahedin was aired on television and we were given the forms to be filled out, he called me and closed the door behind me.

He said, "Be careful, the regime wants to kill all of us. Don't argue with them at all." My understanding was that the time was very sensitive. It was a time of military rule, and we should not stand up to a military regime or else they would execute us. We had been in prison for years, and our freedom was close. Thus, we decided to be much more cautious.

28. People in the group that got the forms after us were upset. They complained that we had set a bad precedent by filling out the form. But they themselves also filled out the form. Some of the Mojahedin called themselves *monafeqin* in the form, and we, who were Marxists, wrote that we were Shi'a Esna Ashari [the state religion of Iran] and similar absurdities. We thought that it would be enough to say that we were Muslims, and that they would not execute us for not praying.

29. After several hours they collected the forms, told us to put our blindfolds on, and they took us to the corridor which led to the *zir hasht*. I had a blindfold on and could not see. Several people were asking questions in front of us. A Kurdish man from Sanandaj by the name of Farzad Fakhrol'olamai, belonging to Komala, was ahead of me.

30. When Fakhrol'olamai went to the room, I placed my foot under the door so that I could hear what they were saying. I heard the voice of Haj Davud Lashkari, who asked, "Mr. Fakhrol'olamai, what is your offense?" With a Kurdish accent he said, "Komala." Lashkari asked, "How old are you? Are you Muslim?" "Yes, Haj Aqa,

I am a Muslim." As Lashkari was asking questions, he was hitting him on the back. He said, "You pray don't you?" "No sir, I don't," he answered. [Lashkari] said "Allaho a'lam [God knows better]." Then he told the guards, "So beat him." They were flogging people in the adjoining room. For every prayer they [missed], it was ten lashes. He was lashed and left there. I could hear the sound of the cable.

31. Reza Ghafari from the Rah-e Kargar was next. He is now in England. Dr. Ghafari said that he prayed, and they did not beat him. We had said [on the form] that we were Muslims but we did not pray. After Mohammad Najar, it was my turn.

32. I went in. Only Lashkari asked questions: "Where are you from?" I said, "The east of Tehran." He asked, "Are you a Muslim?" I said, "Yes sir. My mother is a Haji [has visited Mecca]." "Do you pray?" I said, "No Haj Aqa, I am little lazy. I cannot get up early in the morning." Then he told them, "Give him his round of beating for this time."

33. Two people took me to the punishment room. They took my socks off. They placed me on a bed in a fashion that my face was facing the mattress. They tied my legs down and someone sat on my back so that I could not move. Another person was pressing my face into the mattress so that my screams would not be heard. Then they started hitting the soles of my feet with a cable. After five or six beatings, the pain became so unbearable. I said, "Sir, I will pray." The prisoners were divided into two groups. For example Faramarz

Zamanzadeh, a student from Shushtar, went to the other group. He was executed. He was my age.

34. I was really dazed. They took me to another room. I partly removed my blindfold and saw the people who had been beaten before me. If someone did not pray, they would beat him five times a day for every call to prayer.

35. Those who were flogged could not resist for more than two or three days. After some time, they brought a group of blindfolded people to our ward. They were the "theoretical people," who were quite strong in their beliefs and had been political prisoners under the Shah. Then they told them to pray. They said, "Haj Aqa, allow us to go and make ablution." He said, "It is not necessary. You can do *tayamom* [waterless cleaning ritual] here." They did this in order to shatter their pride and show that even the "theoretical people" were broken here. When they bent down for supplication, the guards smiled and left.

36. The Mojahedin in our ward were not headstrong, and they came back. Two from the FKO (Majority) group also returned. Many of the prisoners were executed. From our ward, the Polytechnic University students Faramarz Zamanzadeh, Jalal Fattahi, and Mansur Najafi Shushtari—who belonged to Vahdat Komonist—were executed. Mansur was older than me and had previously gone to India and then Sweden. He had studied electronics and mechanics and had been active with the Students' Confederation outside the country. I heard that he was a Trotskyite. Jalal Fattahi had been sentenced to life under the Shah.

He was a poet, a Polytechnic University student, and was from Borujerd. They had found arms on him in 1981 in Tehran. He belonged to the group Ashraf Dehqani, a branch of the Fadaiyan. He was so tired of praying and prostrating to pray that he said he would prefer to be executed. "I will no longer bend," he told us. Mohammad Shahbazian, who was an assistant professor at the University of Tehran and a Tudeh member, gave me his shaving blade, and knowingly went to be executed.

37. After the massacre, on a winter day, Haj Davud came to the Gohardasht Hosseinyeh and said, "The Imam has said that we no longer want to have political prisoners. Anyone who wishes to stay can do so, but he will leave this place horizontally—you have come here vertically and will leave horizontally." This meant that if we did not obey them, we would not get out alive. We had to perform group prayer (*namaz jema'at*). At prayer time, they would make sure that everyone was present.

38. One day at the end of winter, a Revolutionary Guard came to our section to inform us that we would be transferred to Evin in order to be released. He said, "You were academics, you studied philosophy and languages, and wished to leave the country. Make sure that we do not catch you crossing the border."

39. I was freed in March 1989. I was 31 years old. For five years I was not allowed to leave the country. For the first four weeks, I had to present myself to the public prosecutor's office in Evin. Once, I went there with a colored shirt; they pointed at what I was wearing. They took my picture and fingerprinted me again so that they had a picture of what I looked like at the time.

40. Then, I had to present myself to the committee of the east of Tehran every two weeks. I was not allowed to leave Tehran without permission. Every time, the nightmare was revived. They made me wear a blindfold and face the wall, and they asked questions. For example: "Whom have you seen, what did you do, why don't you marry, or what do you think of some issue?" I would say, "I don't have any opinion." They would say, "How could you not have an opinion?"

41. When I was released, it was terrible. I was always worried about being re-arrested. I was having nightmares. When evening came, I was terrified. Even when my brother tried to get me out of the country, I just left my suitcases and ran away. The thought of being arrested again was too unbearable for me. For two and a half years, I had to present myself [to them]. Then they asked for someone to act as a guarantor for me. They required that person to be an office employee.

42. For me, sharing these memories is not pleasant. I feel as if I have climbed a mountain, and I no longer want to look back.

Cologne, June 2009

OFFICIAL STATEMENT • 15

كیهان

Subject: On university admission requirements
The official: Central Committee for Student Selection
The occasion: [Excerpts from] Published response to criticism by two Majles
               deputies regarding the criteria for student selection
Date: 3 January 1987
Source: *Kayhan*, 3 January 1987

Mr. Mohammad Mehdi Rahbari-Amlashi, the MP for Rudsar, and Mr. Qassem Me'mari, the MP for Ahar, had each made comments about the criteria for student selection in the pre-agenda session of the Majles. Their comments were published by *Kayhan*, on 11 and 18 November [1986]. The Central Committee for Student Selection has issued the following response [to the two MP's comments]:

"... In general, establishing the requirements for accepting students in previous years and this year has been the prerogative of the distinguished High Council for Cultural Revolution, which, in accordance with the good wishes of his Excellency Imam [Khomeini], are binding. ... The requirements for acceptance, which are dependent on the High Council, are as follows:

1. Belief in Islam or [one of] the other divine religions [Islam regards Christianity and Judaism as divine religions; i.e. revealed by God to a prophet].

   Note 1: The proof of the applicant's belief is the person's own declaration and no one has the right to arbitrarily question or investigate those beliefs.

   Note 2: When, upon entering college, a student claims to be a Muslim or a believer of another divine religion, his claim will be accepted unless the contrary is proven and established by a competent and official court, in which case, the right to education (or, if he is already accepted, his right to continue his education), will be taken away.

2. Clean record that indicates no opposition to the Islamic Republic of Iran.

   Note : Should a candidate have a record of opposing the regime, a retraction [or change of views] must be ascertained.

3. Ascertaining the absence of moral turpitude.

4. Clean record indicating that applicant was not a member of SAVAK; is not a Freemason; [and is not] a member of one of its affiliates.

"First, with regards to the principle of student selection and the philosophy behind it, it must be pointed out that given the current state of [our] universities, which according to the gracious Imam [Khomeini] may take another twenty years before they reach a point of excellence, it is clear that not everyone, with whatever level of education, may be allowed to enter an institution of higher learning. It is necessary to establish a minimum [standard for] education. On the other hand, given that the capacity of our universities is less than one-tenth of the number of applicants, it is only natural that under such conditions [a system] of prioritization [for acceptance] be established so that at least those who are enemies of or opposed to the regime do not take the places of those whose qualifications are compatible with the Revolution. . . ."

Mehrdad Neshati Malekians

ARRESTED: October 1982
DETAINED IN: Evin, Qezel Hesar, and Gohardasht Prisons
RELEASED: October 1988

1. My name is Mehrdad Neshati Malekians and I am an Iranian refugee living in Frankfurt, Germany. I was born in 1960 in Tehran, Iran. I was a political prisoner held in Evin, Qezel Hesar, and Gohardasht Prisons between 1982 and 1989. I was in Gohardasht Prison at the time of the 1988 executions.

2. I make this statement in support of an investigation into the mass execution of political prisoners in 1988 in Iran.

3. This statement is true to the best of my knowledge and belief. Except where I indicate to the contrary, I make this statement on the basis of facts and matters within my own knowledge. Where the facts and matters in this statement are within my own knowledge, they are true. Where the facts and matters are not within my own knowledge, I have identified the source or sources of my information, and I believe such facts to be true.

Life and Political Activities Before His Arrest

4. In 1982 I was living in Tehran with my wife and working as a tailor. We had just had a son, who was 15 days old when we were arrested.

5. I was politically involved with the FKO (Minority). I had mostly been involved in propaganda activities and in the distribution of FKO publications and leaflets with the FKO's committee for Tehran's southern wards. This was the only connection I had with the organization. I was not a full member or cadre. I was only a sympathizer of this organization. My wife was also active in the same organization.

Arrest and Detention

6. On 11 October 1982 I had two separate meetings with two different members of our cell arranged for that day. The first meeting did not take place because my colleague did not show up. Then the second meeting did not happen either. I knew something must have gone wrong. I found out later that both of these contacts had been arrested. Later that same night, I was told that the Revolutionary Guards were looking for me.

7. I did not go home to my own house [that evening] but instead went with my wife to my mother-in-law's home. Our son was only 15 days old and was ill. At 2 a.m., the security agents came and arrested us both. They did not have an arrest warrant. They did not identify themselves, but we later

discovered that they were from the prosecutor's office in Evin Prison. They took us along with our 15-day-old son to Evin. We were both taken to ward 209, but my wife was taken, with our son, to the women's ward.

Interrogation

8. I was taken for interrogation the next morning. The person who arrested me was also my interrogator. I was blindfolded but I recognized him by his voice. I was flogged and interrogated from 8 a.m. until noon. They did not seem to have much detailed information about me. They asked me questions that—based on information I had gathered from other political prisoners—were the "usual" questions. These included: "Whom have you been meeting with? Where do you meet? Which organization are you affiliated with?"

9. In fact, they had been looking for my wife. She was in charge of the women's committee of the FKO for southern Tehran. I refused to give them any information, and so I was flogged. During those four hours I was repeatedly questioned and beaten. I told them my name was Sa'id. Sa'id is my second surname and I used it as my pseudonym in our organization [the FKO (Minority)].

10. Around noon they brought in a young woman from the southern Tehran committee. The interrogator told me to listen. He asked the girl if she knew "Sa'id." Unfortunately, she knew me, she knew that was not my real name, and she told them so. In 1981, when one of the important members of the group [the poet Sa'id

Soltanpur] had been executed, we had held a memorial service in our home. This young woman had been there, and she [was the one who] identified me. The interrogator now knew that I had lied about my identity and that I had been in touch with the organization.

11. I admitted that I had been a sympathizer of the FKO (Minority) at one point, but I added that currently I was not active in the organization. The interrogator became very angry. He kicked me and beat me terribly. Since I did not know how much they knew, I refused to give any more information.

12. Later that day, at maybe 7 p.m. or 8 p.m., the interrogators brought in another former FKO sympathizer who had given them more information about me. Still, I admitted only that I was a sympathizer of the organization. They decided to punish me by flogging (*ta'zir*) because I had not collaborated. The interrogator told me that he had obtained the sentence of *ta'zir* from a cleric by the name of Ghafari. I doubt the interrogators had sought the cleric's approval, and in my view they were deciding on these punishments by themselves, whenever they felt like it.

13. My reaction to these beatings was to scream, to insult the guards, and to generally cause a great deal of chaos for them. The beatings were terrible. They would put a blanket over my head and two guards would sit on me—one on my chest and one on my legs. The pain was excruciating.

14. For the first four days, I was constantly interrogated for new information about

other people in the organization. They wanted information in order to arrest more people. These first few days were the most important because if they could break you, they could arrest everyone else connected with you in the organization. But if the detainee could resist for a few days, the organization would realize that the member had been arrested and would thus change the related schedules and planned operations. My wife and I were in the same cell of the organization and had the same person in charge of us, so we did not have much new information to give them.

15. In total, I spent a month in ward 209 of Evin Prison. Throughout this first month, I had no news of my wife. One time during the interrogation, when I was being flogged with a cable, the interrogator brought my baby son into the torture room and said, "Talk for the sake of your son." I refused. They beat me again. The interrogator said, "Well, at least kiss him." I reached up and took off my blindfold in order to kiss him. The interrogator beat me again and shouted, "I told you to kiss him, not to look! You cannot see him!" They put my blindfold back on, and I kissed my son. I did not see him or my wife again until three months later. My son was held in prison with my wife for about three months but was then released to our family.

16. After those first few days, and in the following weeks, the [goal of the] interrogation changed from seeking information on the organization (such as who else was involved and where we met) to seeking information about my personal political views. For example, they would ask me

what I thought of armed struggle, or what my take was on other political organizations, or they would inquire about my views on Marxism and such things.

17. I was trying to give answers that would keep me from getting into any more trouble. When they asked me whether I was a Marxist, I answered, "No." But the interrogator pushed me to write "Yes," telling me I was lying. The interrogator beat me and punished me severely until I wrote "Yes."

18. After a month of interrogations, which decreased in intensity as time went on, I was taken to room 2 of ward 2 [a public ward, a section of the prison that contained several cells, where a number of prisoners were held together, rather than in solitary confinement] of Evin Prison. On a Friday, ten days later, an interrogator appeared and took me from the ward. It was unusual because it was a Friday, and usually there were no interrogations on the holy day. The interrogator, whom I knew as Mehdi, beat me and kicked me as he forced me down the stairs to the interrogation rooms in ward 209. I did not understand what was happening because it was unusual to be hit so much. He yelled at me and said, "Now we know everything, and you did not tell us anything."

19. When we got downstairs, I could hear my wife's voice. We were blindfolded, but when I heard her voice I realized that they had left us together in the hallway at the same time. We were able to communicate for that short period of time. My wife told me about the women we knew who had been arrested. I asked her if the person in

charge of us had been arrested or not. She did not know. We only had a few minutes together before I was taken into the interrogation room. I told her I had not confessed anything. Inside the room I was not beaten with a cable. I was just kicked and slapped. They asked me, "Do you have a person in charge of you? Who is this person? Why didn't you tell us about this person?"

20. The interrogator put a lot of pressure on me to admit to being part of one of the organization's cells, an actual member, rather than simply saying I was a sympathizer. But, again, I refused. In the end, I confessed in writing that I had been active in the organization but only as a sympathizer, not as a member. I did not think that they knew how involved I was in the organization. And, more importantly, anyone who had admitted to having been an actual member or cadre of the organization was executed. From 1981–82 until the winter of 1984—while Lajevardi was in charge of Evin Prison—they executed every single person who had been a member of the organization, including repenters who had assisted the guards, put together organizational charts of opposition groups, and helped them identify other members. I knew that even if I gave information it would not prevent my execution. It was, therefore, better to stay quiet.

21. My wife was transferred again in 1984, from Qezel Hesar Prison to Evin, to be interrogated and put under pressure to help with clarifying the chart and the structure of our organization so that they could have a better understanding of it.

Trial and Sentencing

22. In September or October of 1983, one year after my arrest, I was put on trial. The president of the tribunal was a cleric whom I did not know. The entire process lasted maybe ten minutes. I had no legal representation, advance notice, or time to prepare. I had not been notified of the charges brought against me. I did not see the indictment dossier. There were two people in the room: a religious cleric and another person who was not a cleric. The cleric had my file, which had been prepared by my interrogator. As far as I remember, the questioning by the religious judge began as follows: "Are you a sympathizer?" "Yes, but just a sympathizer." Sympathizers were those who did not have any role in the main organizational cells. He then asked, "Are you a Marxist?" I said, "No, I am not a Marxist." The judge said, "But in your dossier you say you are a Marxist?" I responded, "During the interrogations I was forced to say I am a Marxist but I am not." He then said, "Your family name is Malekians; are you a Muslim?" I said, "I am Armenian." "How did you marry a Muslim girl then?" the judge asked. I said, "It is very simple, a cleric married us and did not ask me if I was a Muslim." The religious judge said, "You are not a Muslim and you have married a Muslim girl. Therefore, your child is a bastard and you must divorce your spouse." I said, "I will not divorce my wife, and I did not tell you that I am a Christian." And that was the end of our conversation. After my trial I realized that my wife had been there and had been tried at the same time.

200 rial bills that Mehrdad Neshati Malekians received as a gift in 1983 from a fellow prisoner. On the right of each bill he painted flowers and doves; the brush was made out of his own hair.

23. A week later, I was presented with a paper and I was told to sign it. But I was blindfolded, so I could not read it. I pulled my blindfold up enough to see the paper, but I could not read what it said. I asked the guard and he said that I was sentenced to five years in prison. I had been detained for one year so the total of the years spent in prison would be six years. I later heard my wife had also been sentenced to five years in prison.

24. In the fall of 1983, after my sentence was handed down, I was transferred, along with a group of political prisoners including my wife, from Evin Prison to Qezel Hesar Prison, where I was held until 1986. My wife was released in 1986 after she agreed to give an interview.

25. Qezel Hesar Prison was composed of three large wards, which were separated by tall walls. In each ward there were four large sections; in each section there were 24 cells

and four small sections known as secondary sections. Between 1983 and 1985, there were 700 inmates in ward 1, and we did not have any space in which to sleep. The hygienic conditions were inhuman and, in addition, we were harassed and beaten by the guards and the repenters, which made life unbearable.

26. [My time in] Qezel Hesar was the worst period of my life. I would have rather been in interrogation all day, every day, in Evin than detained in Qezel Hesar. It was terrible. We were under a lot of pressure. Had what we endured at that time lasted six more months, 90 percent of the inmates undoubtedly would have either committed suicide or gone crazy. This was during the time of Haj Davud's directorship [summer of 1981–July 1984]. He imposed his despotic rule on Qezel Hesar Prison. In Qezel Hesar, I was detained together with prisoners from different political groups and repenters in the same section (section 1, unit 3).

27. One day [after Haj Davud was no longer the head of Qezel Hesar], I was summoned to Naserian, the prosecutor's assistant in the prison. He told me that they were releasing my wife because she had agreed to give an interview. He said that if I also agreed to give an interview, to denounce my organization, and to sign a pledge that I would not be involved in any further political activities, then they would release me too. I said to Naserian, "I won't give an interview." As we were walking in the hallway I told Naserian: "If giving an interview is the condition of our release, how come the repenters are not released?" Because of

my refusal, I remained in prison after my wife was released in 1986.

28. It was around this time, in 1986, that the prison authorities kept asking the prisoners to give these interviews, so that they could be released, because they wanted to clear the prisons of political prisoners. When they realized that they could not persuade the remaining prisoners to give interviews, they opted for another solution. Five prisoners would be taken together into a room to give these interviews, and only one would be required to read the confession. The other four would not have to say anything; they would only have to sit, listen, and let themselves be filmed while they were listening. This was when Meysam was the prison's director. Even if it was a political concession on the part of the prison authorities, it was still difficult for us to give in. They knew it [accepting their conditions] would break us—to break us was what they wanted. So I could not agree to give an interview or to participate in the televised confessions.

Gohardasht Prison

29. In October or November of 1986, I was moved to Gohardasht Prison. I was first put into ward 14, which later became ward 8. All of us in Qezel Hesar were moved at the same time. They were removing all of the political prisoners. At that time, we were put in mixed cells with the MKOs. There were about 150 people in my ward, and the doors of the cells were mainly kept open. There were no repenters among us. The repenters had their own wards: the labor ward and the jihad ward, which were

located in a different building, so we had no contact or communication with them.

30. The wards were slowly filling up with prisoners who had come from Qezel Hesar or from Evin. These were all prisoners who had been in prison for some time. The newly arrested people [after 1984] were taken to Evin Prison instead; they were not mixed with us.

31. At some point the prison management's policy changed. For instance, as prisoners in Qezel Hesar [when Meysam was in charge], we had had some rights, such as exercising together and organizing, in matters related to food and hygiene. In Gohardasht Prison, we were not allowed to exercise in groups. The toilets there were in our cells, for the cells were originally designed for solitary confinement, and yet they had put three or four of us in each cell, which was a problem. Having so many people and the toilet in that space was difficult. While sleeping, one or two of us had to sleep in the corridor of the ward.

32. In Gohardasht, for the first time, we were allowed to elect someone to be in charge of our ward who could represent us in negotiations with the prison authorities regarding our problems and our demands. During that time we had issues with the guards regarding our demand to exercise together in the prison yard. Exercising together was very important for us. I was elected as the representative of our ward for two months, and during that time I had to fight with the prison authorities over the most basic of prisoners' rights.

33. Family visits were another subject of disagreement and tension between the prisoners and the prison authorities. The MKO prisoners wanted to be able to meet with their relatives in person and not from behind the glass [partition]. Then some of the MKO prisoners were moved from our ward, and, as far as I remember, it was after they had asked to visit with their relatives in a room [with no partition]. The guards told us that the MKO prisoners were transferred because they [the prison authorities] wanted to separate the religious from the non-Muslim prisoners. But this separation was never completed. We had MKO prisoners living in leftists' wards and leftists detained in MKO wards.

Situation in 1988

34. I was in Gohardasht Prison at the time of the executions. I remember changes in the spring of 1988. People on television were beginning to speak out against the war.

35. While I was in Gohardasht, a group of clerics and prison authorities came around and it was said that they were evaluating the prisoners' cases. I was not interviewed by any of them. No one came to talk to me about a pardon or being released.

36. From the ward's radio, which was broadcast over loudspeakers, we heard about the end of the war. In the summer [July–August]—I do not remember the exact date or day—the visitations stopped. During the last visit, we realized that some changes were ahead. It was in early Mordad [the week of 21 July], and behind us was a row of Revolutionary Guards. Usually, they

allowed children to come to our side of the glass, but this time they did not. I asked to get my son, but they would not let me. That night, after the visitation, the guards came into our ward and took all we had— for example, any televisions or newspapers or anything else in the ward. It was taken, and it was gone. We did not know what was going on. I was not responsible for the ward—our representative was an MKO prisoner. But we did not know why the guards were doing this.

37. We were cut off from the outside world. All recreation was suspended. The food was usually brought by Afghan prisoners who were common criminals and they were usually alone, but during that time, a Revolutionary Guard accompanied the prisoners bringing our food. Our only contact [with the outside world happened] when we tried to listen to the news from the door of the ward. The radio was on somewhere, and so we tried to hear something from outside. Morse code between the cells was another means of communication. In the evenings, we would communicate using a piece of paper on which we would write messages and send them from one floor to another with a thread. That was how we tried to communicate, exchange news, and inform each other about what we had decided. We could communicate between the cells, but there was great fear in the ward.

38. During that period, sick prisoners were not allowed to go to the infirmary. The infirmary was frequented by prisoners from different sections, and it was a good place to exchange information. The fact that no one was allowed to go to the infirmary deprived us of this source of information; we could not have any contact with the MKO prisoners who were held in the secondary sections.

39. By the third week of August, they took away the first group of prisoners from our section. These were prisoners who had been charged with being sympathizers of both the MKO and the FKO (with dual charges). We knew through our Morse code communications with other prisoners that of all the prisoners who had been taken away from the wards, only one had come back. On 27 August they came to our section and took four prisoners with dual charges. These prisoners had been arrested and indicted by the prosecutor's office of the city of Karaj, and they had been tried in Karaj. One of them was returned to our section after a few hours. When we asked him what was happening, he said, "They posed a few questions, such as: 'What is your charge?' or 'Do you accept the charges that were brought against you?' 'Will you agree to make a televised confession?' And they told us, 'We are here to separate the prisoners from each other.'" It is worth noting that these were the usual questions we were asked and we did not find them strange. The three others did not come back but we did not know what the problem was and why they did not come back.

40. We were still worried for the three prisoners who had not come back when, two days later, on the morning of 29 August, we heard noises from upstairs (in ward 7). We kept silent to figure out what was going on.

After an hour and a half, the noise stopped and there was no more noise upstairs. We tried to communicate [with ward 7] but no one responded, so we knew that there were no longer any prisoners there. Around lunchtime they came to our section. They had brought a lot of blindfolds. They blindfolded all of us. They took us [the leftists] to the corridor outside of our section. We sat facing the wall. They would take us one by one to a room. [In the room] I heard someone talking to me; I recognized Lashkari's voice. He asked me to identify myself and then asked me if I was still loyal to my group or if I was praying. After these questions, I was taken back to the corridor.

41. After one hour, they put us in a line and took us toward the infirmary and the visitation hall. On our way, we could hear other prisoners screaming; it was clear they were being beaten. They took us to the last section of the building and assaulted us with whips and cables. They then divided us into two large cells in the middle of the visitation hall. This was where the MKO prisoners were held previously. We quickly started to brainstorm, trying to figure out what was happening. We had never before been punished like this and with such violence.

42. The understanding of the FKO (Minority) prisoners was that the Islamic Republic had been vanquished in the war. Given these circumstances, we would expect harsh treatment in prison, with the objective of making us renounce our steadfast beliefs. They thought a return to Haj Davud's regime in prison was highly probable.

Some of them [the FKO (Minority) prisoners] had been political prisoners during the Shah's rule. They reminisced that in 1975 something similar had happened in the prisons. The alleged escape of some prisoners had triggered a violent repression: some prisoners had been tried again, some sent to solitary confinement, and some others had even been executed. The FKO prisoners believed that the end of this war would result in similar repression.

43. We had been in that cell for an hour and a half when we heard noises from outside. It was the sound of blows and the screams of the prisoner who was receiving them. We did not know what was going on. We heard another voice asking, "Will you say it [your prayer] or not?" We thought they were flogging the MKO prisoners who had been converted to Marxism [in prison] and were refusing to pray. We thought they were being tortured because they refused to pray.

44. As we were trying to understand what was going on, we noticed that there were messages written on the lower part of our cell's wall; one of them, for instance, was: "X number of our fellow prisoners have been taken to be executed and X number were taken to be tortured." We read, for instance: "Today, 30 people have been taken away." We could guess that many prisoners had been held in our cell, but we could not figure out when the messages were written on the wall. We could not make sense of some other messages, and, all in all, reading them did not help us make sense of our situation. All in all, we did not know anything.

45. Suddenly the door opened and Naserian, who was one of the prison directors at the time, came in and picked a number of people. I was one of them. We were blindfolded and taken into the hallway leading toward the infirmary and then the visitation hall, and from there they took us downstairs. We could hear noises but could not understand what was said. Then they made us stand in line by a door. I believe there were six or seven of us. The first one to be called in the room was Jahanbakhsh Sarkhosh, an FKO (Minority) sympathizer.

46. We did not know any of the guards there. They were not part of the prison's crew. [While Jahanbakhsh was being questioned,] a guard came out and asked me, "Do you know the guy who went in?" I said, "No." [I was blindfolded; I could not see who went in]. The guard said, "He is very brave," and then he went back in the room. I could hear Jahanbakhsh protesting and arguing inside the room. The guards came out and again asked me the same question and added, "He is really brave. He is really a man." After a few minutes Jahanbakhsh was taken out of the room, but they made him stand on the opposite side of the hall.

47. Then, I was led into the room and took my blindfold off. There was a cleric behind the desk and a non-cleric was sitting next to him—later I was told the cleric was Nayyeri and the person sitting next to him was Eshraqi. There was another person there whom I had not seen before. There were a lot of files and folders on the table and in the room. At that moment, Naserian entered the room. He knew me and during the time I was representing the ward I had had a lot of arguments with him. Naserian said to the judge, "Haj Aqa, this is one of the *sar-e moze'i* [steadfast]. He is a *mellikesh.* He is one of those who always makes trouble and organizes [the prisoners] within the prison." And so I said, "Haj Aqa, he is lying. I am not a *mellikesh.*" I had not yet served my sentence. Naserian did not say anything more. Nayyeri opened my file and asked, "What is your charge?" I said, "Aksariat ['Majority,' meaning FKO (Majority)]." He asked, "Do you still believe in it?' I said, "I don't know what has become of it and what it says today; I have been here for six years." He [Nayyeri] said, "Are you a Muslim?" I did not really respond. He looked at the file and said, "Are you Armenian?" I said, "My Father is Armenian but not my mother. My mother is Muslim and I was mostly raised in my mother's family." I thought it was best not to respond to these kinds of questions, but rather equivocate so that nothing could be ascertained. He said, "So you lived in a Muslim family; you grew up among the Muslims? You are therefore a Muslim."

48. At this point Eshraqi asked, "Are you married?" [I said,] "Yes." [He asked,] "Do you have any children?" [I said,] "Yes." Eshraqi added, "So you are a Muslim and you have to pray." I said, "No, I won't." He said, "You have to. You have to because we are trying to segregate prisoners." He insistently said, "You will pray." He then told Naserian, "Take him out." Naserian put a piece of paper before me and said, "Sign it." I tried to read what was written but he did not let me read it and told me to sign it. I signed it without knowing what I

had signed. They made me stand on a line opposite from where Jahanbakhsh was standing. Then Eshraqi came out of the room. Nayyeri asked him, "Haj Aqa, where are you going?" Eshraqi said "I am going to beat these people up and come back." I could not imagine that by beating he meant executing; I thought he meant they were going to torture them with cables.

49. Then we [a few prisoners] put our hands on each other's shoulders [in a line] and went upstairs. I recognized Jalil, who was in front of me. He had difficulty walking. I tried to talk to him but he did not respond; perhaps he did not recognize [me]. The next day, Jalil committed suicide. He cut his abdomen with a piece of glass. Jalil was one of the four prisoners who had been arrested in 1979 and had been sentenced to two years' imprisonment. In 1981, he had been tried again for the same charges and sentenced to five years' imprisonment. I was told that Nayyeri held a personal grudge against him. Of the group arrested in 1979, most had been released except for Jalil and another member. Later, one of Jalil's cellmates told me that Nayyeri had told Jalil, "I am going to make sure you are going to be walking on your knees and praying before you get out of here."

50. We were expecting to be taken back to our cells. But they did not [take me back to my cell]; they put me in an empty cell located in the middle of the hallway. I took off my blindfold and realized I was alone. I wondered why. The only thing I could do was to try to establish contact with the people next door who had been in the same section with me. I told them about my

trial. I was still not aware of the executions. I just reported through Morse code what had happened to me. They did not know anything about the executions either; they were as uninformed as I was.

51. I was left there all night with no food, no toilet—nothing until 8 a.m. Next door people were in a similar situation. Naserian came to collect me at 8 a.m. the next morning. He told me, "You must pray," and I said, "No, I won't. I am Armenian and I will not pray." They took me to another cell; four other prisoners were there. Akbar Shalguni was one of them. He was from the Workers' Party [Rah-e Kargar]. There was someone from ward 7 from the FKO (Minority). I did not know him. Two others were from the Tudeh Party. They came from the secondary section number 40 where Tudeh and FKO (Majority) prisoners were held.

52. Akbar Shalguni was from the ward where they kept people who had been sentenced to more than ten years' imprisonment. He had been taken out of his section along with two other prisoners on 28 August. In conversation, Akbar mentioned the executions [that were taking place in prison], but I did not believe him and asked him how he knew about it. Akbar said, "I ran into Mohammad Ali Behkish in the hallway leading to the tribunal, and he told me about the executions." When I heard the name of Mohammad Ali Behkish and realized that he had been the source of the information, I believed he [Shalguni] was telling the truth. I knew Behkish. He would never spread news without making sure it was true; he would never spread

rumors. He himself [Mohammad Ali Behkish] was executed by these criminals.

53. We started brainstorming about what we should do. The five of us decided to tell them that we would not pray. Our experience in prison had taught us that if we gave into one of their demands they would keep asking for more concessions, and who knows what they would require from us next. Naserian came to our cell and asked, "Who refuses to pray?" Among the five of us, two people said without hesitation, "We will pray." The rest of us found ourselves in a strange and unexpected situation. The response of these two people was strange and somehow funny. In retrospect it makes me laugh, but at the time it was unsettling.

54. They took the three of us who had refused to pray to the hallway. There, we understood where all the screams and moaning we had heard had come from and what triggered them. They had put a bed there. They first put Akbar on the bed, and then it was my turn. We were each given ten lashes. My blindfold was loose, and I could see around it. I did not recognize any of the guards. The guard who was flogging us said, "God, I am beating [them] for your contentment." These first ten lashes I got—I do not remember being beaten like this during my whole interrogation. The blows were so hard—as if the cable was made of iron. Either the cables were not made of the same material as those which were used to flog us during our interrogation, or the guard was better at flogging than the previous ones. The cable was directly hitting the broken flesh of my feet. The guards were beating us with zeal,

trying to break our resistance. The violence of the blows was shocking, as if they wanted to kill us. Never during my interrogation had I been beaten so ruthlessly. Now I could understand why the prisoners were screaming and moaning. They were not targeting our backs, but only the soles of the feet. [Once they were done with the lashes,] one of the prison wardens said, "Now stand up and run in the hallway." While running with me, our third fellow prisoner who had received his ten lashes told me, "I can't take it anymore." I told him, "Then tell them you will pray." After running, there were only the two of us [Akbar Shalguni and the witness]. They gave us ten more lashes each. Our feet were covered with open wounds.

55. Akbar and I were returned to our cell. After a short conversation, we both decided that when they came to beat us for the afternoon prayer, we would tell Naserian that we would pray. We thought that we would be taken to our own section and could inform the other prisoners of what was happening, and perhaps spreading the word could save the lives of some of them.

56. In the evening Naserian came to our cell and asked, "Are you praying?" We said, "Yes, we will pray." We were expecting to be taken back to the ward. But he left the two of us in the same cell where we spent the night. The following day, 30 August, we did not hear from Naserian or any other prison warden. We were still in the same cell. Later we heard that they may have been away attending the commemoration ceremony for the former prime minister [and president], Raja'i, who had been killed

in a bomb attack in 1981. Every year, on 30 August, there was an official commemoration ceremony.

57. On 31 August, they came to our cell and called me. I was blindfolded and taken to a room on the first floor of the prison. I noticed there was no noise—it was completely quiet. After a few minutes, I realized that I was taken along with four other prisoners whose sentences were going to be finished soon. An assistant prosecutor gave us a form to fill out. There were four or five questions such as: "Which group were you a member of? Are you steadfast in your opinions? Will you give an interview?" I just wrote, "I will not do the interview."

58. [After filling out the forms,] I was taken along with three other prisoners to the same cell. Two of them had been transferred from Evin. One of them was Azim; he was a member of the FKO (Majority). [In the past,] we had been together in ward 8. On the way back I told Azim about the killings and asked him to inform other prisoners about it. I do not know why this happened, but in the afternoon around 6 p.m. in the section where we were held, all the cells' doors were opened, and all the prisoners came out into the section's hallway. It was an important event—we could speak to each other and figure out who had been executed. At this point a number of guards came to the hallway and forced us to go to the Hosseinyeh to pray. We all pretended to pray and then returned to our cells.

59. That night we realized that two prisoners who had come from Karaj, Jahanbakhsh

Sarkhosh and Mahmud Qazi, had been executed. From the FKO (Minority), Majid Vali, and from the Tudeh, Ali Na'imi and those who had been tried in Karaj's prosecutor's office and were serving their prison sentences, had [also] been executed. I knew 13 or 14 prisoners from section 7 or our own section, section 8, who had been executed.

60. That night they took a number of the prisoners, including myself, away to another section. In that section there were about 40 prisoners from different sections [separated from our cellmates and put in one section]. It seemed that everyone knew what had happened, and everyone pretended to pray. A group of us who knew each other from before was trying to figure out how to inform other prisoners, who were still kept in the other sections and did not know about the killings, about what had happened. We kept searching for a way to let them know. Our section was completely silent. It was a difficult situation. We could not trust anyone. Making contact, particularly through Morse code, could result in punishment.

61. In the end, a few of us decided to try to establish Morse code communications with other prisoners at any cost. One of our cellmates, an FKO (Minority) prisoner by the name of Behnam Karami, volunteered to do so. I told him, "Do you know that if you are caught in these circumstances you may be executed?" We made sure he understood the risk he was taking on. He said he was willing to take this risk. We planned together so that other prisoners could be informed. [After we communicated the news to them,] they refused to believe it at

first. But after more exchanges of information they started to grasp the extent of the crime that was being committed in the prisons, and they started to inform other prisoners. We wanted all the prisoners to know what was happening so that [once before the court] they could make an informed decision, aware of the potential consequences of their responses.

62. What was done then may seem of little importance today, but it was a valuable initiative at that time. The end result of this initiative was that many prisoners realized what was in store for them. We were very lucky that they [guards] did not realize we were communicating the information to other prisoners. Obviously, those who did communicate were selfless individuals and put themselves at great risk in a very difficult situation. Behnam Karami was a brave comrade. All political prisoners know him and remember him with deep respect. Unfortunately, Behnam died a few months ago in a mountain-climbing accident. I cherish his memory. I heard that three to four hundred people attended his funeral, many of whom had survived [the killings], thanks to him.

63. On 1 September, the Death Committee started to work again. The remaining prisoners of Gohardasht were tried in sessions lasting only a few minutes, and many political prisoners, including Homayun Azadi, were hanged in the Gohardasht amphitheater. It is worth noting that of the five prisoners who had nearly completed serving their sentences, three were executed; I remember the name of only one of them: Behzad Omrani. Two survived, and I am one of them. Those who survived were tortured and beaten with a cable.

64. When the Death Committee ended its work, the guards continued the atmosphere of death by forcing the prisoners to participate in collective prayer sessions every day. Even non-Muslim prisoners were forced to participate; they were told to say their own prayers.

65. Around the end of September, I was transferred to Evin and, after four weeks of solitary confinement in the Asayeshgah section of Evin, I was released on bail.

Frankfurt, July 2009

Maryam Nuri

ARRESTED: November 1985
DETAINED IN: Moshtarak Committee Detention Center, Tehran, and Evin
             and Gohardasht Prisons
RELEASED: August 1990

1. My name is Maryam Nuri. I was a political prisoner in Evin during the 1988 massacre of political prisoners. My husband, Rahmat Fathi, was one of the victims of this mass execution.

2. I make this statement in support of an investigation into the mass execution of political prisoners in 1988 in Iran.

3. This statement is true to the best of my knowledge and belief. Except where I indicate to the contrary, I make this statement on the basis of facts and matters within my own knowledge. Where the facts and matters in this statement are within my own knowledge, they are true. Where the facts and matters are not within my own knowledge, I have identified the source or sources of my information, and I believe such facts to be true.

Political Activities

4. When I was a student during the Shah's regime, I knew one or two people from the Guerrilla Organization [FKO]. This continued until the time of the Revolution, when I got closer to the organization and, for a period of time, I was a member of the FKO. As I was a teacher at the same time, I used to work in the teachers' department of the organization. After graduation, I worked in a factory as a simple laborer for some years because, as an intellectual, one should undergo proletarianization.

5. In 1984, I married Rahmat Fathi, who was in charge of FKO publications distribution in the organization. I was not really active with the organization at the time. I was told by the person in charge of Rahmat in the organization (who was also responsible for me) not to object constantly to the organization and instead to engage in a six-month ideological debate with him. I did not accept that, as working in the factory had taught me a great deal.

6. At that time, I used to read only one or two of the government papers, listen to the

radio, analyze the news, and make summaries for the FKO. I was not a member of the FKO, just a supporter, and I did not want to have a real job [in it]. The contradictions within the FKO between their theories and actions, the lack of consistency between the reality and the actions, and the disorganization during the previous couple of years had made me tired and hopeless. Due to the lack of a proper program, circumstances were such that we could have easily been arrested. Prior to our arrest, neither Rahmat nor I had engaged in any political activities, because we had fled our home in Tehran and were living somewhere outside of the city.

7. Around March 1985, we moved to the outskirts of Tehran, to a house on Saveh Road. We were both unemployed so we had to find jobs. In Iran there were and still are no social safety nets. The organization did not provide us with financial protection when we were going from place to place, and neither did our families. Consequently, we had to find jobs for ourselves, even though the people in charge of us at the organization or other members were in prison and there was a possibility that they would turn us in, and we had to organize meetings in the same houses that were under surveillance by the authorities. It now seems idiotic that we had to proceed in this fashion, but [at the time] we had no other choice.

8. I was a sociology graduate from Tehran University and was able to find a job as a social worker at the Behzisty (Welfare) Organization, which was a governmental organization. I was not hired on a full-time basis, since, because of the economic crisis, they only hired part-time people. Rahmat, who had started a housing construction company with his brother, began working there, even though he knew the company was under surveillance.

9. Under the Shah, there was a neighborhood for prostitutes called "Qal'eh" (Fortress), which was destroyed after the Revolution. Some of the prostitutes, including old and disabled women, young runaway girls, or girls without guardians, had been transferred to the Behzisty Organization, at a place called "Shafaq," located on Karaj Road or Saveh Road (I don't remember exactly.)

10. There was a 14-year-old girl who lived at Shafaq and had run away, only to be arrested by the Horr (a neighborhood in Tehran) Committee Revolutionary Guards for not observing her *hijab* (Islamic garb), two of whom had raped her during the night that she spent at the Committee. One of them had raped her promising to marry her. [Before the Revolution] my boss at Behzisty had been a social worker to prostitutes at Qal'eh, and as such he used to issue them permits after they had undergone a medical examination; a red permit meant that they were not in a condition in which they could continue to work, yellow meant they had to be under medical supervision, green meant they could continue to work. This same person [my boss] informed me that the young girl had run away and I had to find her.

11. I contacted some of the committees by phone and found her at the Horr

Committee in the south of Tehran. They had kept her there longer than the legally allotted 24 to 48 hours. I went there and took her with me but she ran away again to the Horr Committee the next day, and again I went and got her, this time finding out that one of the Guards had promised to marry her. All she wanted was to have a normal life, that's all. I pressed charges against the two Guards for rape but nothing came of it. Consequently, I wrote 15 letters of complaint to various authorities, including Khomeini and Rafsanjani, as well as the judiciary branch. My immediate boss had taught me that, as a legal social worker, I had the right to press charges, even at the judiciary branch, and defend my client.

12. The head of the Behzisty Organization at the time was Mr. Yarigarravesh. He summoned me and after praising my work said that he wanted to hire me [full-time], contrary to the law [that barred any employee hiring], because I was a competent social worker. Then he said, "Regarding this young girl, don't you think it's the *monafeqin's* doing?" I said, "No. She was at the Horr Committee and was raped by the Guards and this has nothing to do with any organization. That's why I brought charges against them." He praised me again and said: "You have done your job. We will take it from here." "I'm her social worker and have a right to pursue this and I will." He kept insisting on his stance and showed me to the door. Later, his secretary called me and said that they had received a call from Mr. Rafsanjani's office and had talked to Mr. Yarigarravesh, who had instructed him to silence me.

13. At the time, the Revolutionary Guards were the light of the regime's eyes, and any complaints or insults directed at them would have severe consequences. Bringing a complaint against them was taboo. The secretary told me, "You had a lot of courage talking to Mr. Yarigarravesh the way you did." After this episode my immediate boss who had, until then, advised me to defend my client using legal means, said to me: "I have a wife and kids and I'm afraid to do anything else and go any further. I'm out. And you, you're pregnant (I was seven months pregnant at the time); think about your child and your husband. Forget the whole thing." When I told my husband, Rahmat, the story, he said, "I fully support you. Do what you think is best." That's why, at the time of my arrest, I did not know whether I was being arrested for my political activities with the organization, or for the Behzisty affair; a court date had been assigned for that case and I was arrested a few days prior to my patient's court session.

14. In the Fadaiyan Khalq Organization (FKO), I was referred to as *taghouty*, a term used by the IRI regime to describe anti-revolutionaries. The Minority Organization believed that I was part of the well-to-do "petite bourgeoisie" that allies itself with the bourgeoisie and revolts against the proletariat, and that I was therefore an anti-revolutionary!

Arrest

15. My husband would call me several times a day, and when one day I did not get a call, I was sure that he had been arrested.

I thought I would also get arrested if I went home, and no one would know that we were both arrested. So I waited for my father to go home with me. It was six o'clock in the evening when we opened the door, and there were some men with beards sitting there in my home. They showed us an ID so fast that we could not even read it. They claimed to be from the central committee or prosecutor's office. I do not remember exactly. They said, "We only have a few questions." I told them, "Yes, I know. A few questions means a few years in prison." One of them said, "Oh, so you know what you've done."

16. They arrested me in November 1985, three to four weeks before my son was born. They took me to the Moshtarak Committee. This is an important fact—when we were arrested, a large number of FKO activists were also arrested. There were around 70 people.

Trial

17. I was there for around 12 or 13 days. As I was not really active, I was there a very short period of time. I was then transferred to Evin. After a few days I had my trial. I was taken in and I did not even know that it was my trial. I was blindfolded, but I could see a bit from under my blindfold. There was a bearded cleric in front of me. There was also a guy standing behind me.

18. The charges against me were: living in hiding, attacking the interrogator in the Joint Committee, and attacking the Revolutionary Guards. But I had not attacked anyone. I had heard that they raped people, so whenever they came near

me I would push them away, in a preemptive action. But this was held against me. It was also in my file.

19. When I was transferred to the ward, another prisoner told me how the interrogator had gotten some information from her by lying to her. The interrogator had told her, "Maryam Nuri has been arrested and has told us everything. You should tell us everything, too." That woman had told them whatever she knew about me from the time we were at the factory in 1980. The interrogators never told me directly that they knew everything. They only said: "Do you really think that you cannot talk about your issues in the factory? So what is the Islamic Association for then?" I realized that a person from the factory had been arrested and had given them information. The judge said, "If you were not doing anything wrong, why did you move from your home?"

20. I received a four-and-a-half-year sentence. I was released after four years and nine months. The sentence was issued very quickly. I did not sign the sentence when I was given it because I hadn't done anything. The Revolutionary Guard said that I had to sign, even if I had a complaint: "You have to sign first." But finally I signed the sentence. My husband was sentenced to ten years.

Prison Conditions

21. When I was first taken to the prison in the fall of 1985, I was surprised that all of the leftists were praying except for one. They all used to pray and believed that they

should pray and tolerate [the situation]. The Guards continually called on me and talked about praying and consequently I decided to pray. The first thing they did in prison was send me the things I needed to pray. They forced you [to pray]. I tried and I washed and I stood there, but when it came to bending I could not—I could not take it. I threw the prayer rug away and forgot about praying altogether. Mojtaba was the deputy director of the prison at that time. I was sent to Gohardasht Prison for six months, and the rest [of the time I] was in Evin. I spent six months in Gohardasht as punishment because I had been on a hunger strike.

22. My son was born at Evin Prison. About 24 hours before his birth, I was taken to the infirmary of Evin Prison. I received several shots from one of the repenters who had taken midwifery courses but had no practical experience, to induce labor. They gave me four shots and, while doing an internal examination, tore the water pouch. My doctor had told me that because of my body shape, I would not be able to give birth naturally to the child. I had told them this was the problem but they kept giving me these shots. Finally after a lot of shouting and when they realized they could do nothing for me, they sent me, with a Revolutionary Guard, to a hospital in Tajrish [north of Tehran]. At the hospital reception desk, my husband was supposed to sign the paperwork, but he was not there. The Revolutionary Guard wanted to pretend that he was my husband. I found out and screamed and told them he was a guard and I was a prisoner. The attention of the doctors, nurses, and other staff in the hospital was drawn to me, and my son was born by C-section.

23. I had my baby with me for three months and then I sent him to my parents to be taken care of. After a few months my mother came to visit and said that she no longer wanted to take care of my baby. She said, "You gave birth to him, you must take care of him yourself." I had a sense of responsibility toward my child, and although I was a *sar-e moze'i* and it was shameful to ask the head of prison for a furlough, I did so for the sake of my son. I had to tolerate the reproachful look of the inmates as well.

24. I asked for a 24-hour leave, and they gave me the leave. When I went home, my mother said, "I am not giving you back the child so you can take him to prison." [She confessed that] the head of the prison had asked the family to come and say these things [about refusing to take care of the child], in order to save me, but they never intended not to take care of my son and force me to take him to prison with me. We had a huge argument at home; it had been very difficult [humiliating] for me to ask for a leave. My son, then ten months old, did not want to go with me—he was afraid of my black chador. At the prison gate he would cling to my mother and would not leave her. I took him away from her by force. He cried constantly and passed out. I didn't even have any water to give him and had to bring him around using my own saliva. At that moment I was cursing and insulting everything and everyone, the Islamic Republic, my husband, Rahmat, but the guards didn't react,

seeing the condition I was in. They had been victorious.

25. I kept the baby in the prison for another three months. During these three months the atmosphere in prison was terrible, repenters would cause physical clashes. I was a *sar-e moze'i*, so not only did we have to bear our captivity, but also we needed to protect ourselves from the repenters' persecuting us. They would chant slogans, and create an atmosphere of intimidation and terror. It was winter. We had no carpet on the floor because we were in the *sar-e moze'i* ward. There was no hot water, the water was freezing cold. It would be warm just for a short time and become cold very quickly. On top of this my son developed a skin allergy, his face got rashes and he would scratch himself and it would bleed, and they would not let me take the child to the doctor. His condition deteriorated alarmingly. So I went and put the baby in the guards' room and said, "Now, you will be accountable for his health." So I left him there and returned to the ward. A few hours later, they called me on the loud-speakers and told me to take him to the doctor. But the doctor was not much help.

26. There were problems with food as well, and they would not give us food because of the hunger strikes [prisoners' protesting]. And there was no baby food at all. During one of our hunger strikes, when the assistant prosecutor of the prison came to give a speech to us, I gave my son to a friend and started protesting to him. I knew that the guards would beat you if you protested so I gave my child to someone else to avoid

getting him injured. Eventually after that incident, they called my family to come and take my child back. My mother took my son the next day.

27. We had no hot water, no food, and no hot tea. I had two or three visitations with my husband behind the glass partition and in the presence of Revolutionary Guards. During one visitation, Rahmat taught me how to make an electric kettle with a spoon and a plastic bin. The whole ward learned how to make hot water and use it to make tea. The spoons were melted and their number decreased every day. Even now when I think of it, I'm filled with joy.

Events Surrounding 1998

28. In the wards where I was held previously, people who had been arrested prior to 1985 prayed. The new arrivals in the prison (I was arrested in 1985) were much more energetic about resisting the authorities' demands that they should pray. The older prisoners had become tired of being beaten and so had started to pray. Many leftist prisoners were telling me to pray as well. We had a different experience of the out-side world, from both the experience of the organization and the experience of being in society. The issue of whether to pray or not was a big one among the leftist prison-ers. Personally, I was surprised that some of them were praying. This was in early 1986.

29. In the spring of 1988, before the execu-tions, there was a period when the MKO people were very active. There was a lot of discreet talking among MKO prisoners. The news was that the Mojahedin would

come into the country, that there was good news. We could hear the MKOs talking to each other. One day some authorities that were higher in rank than the usual prison guards came to ward 3—I do not remember who—but they were high-ranking [officials]. They asked the Mojahedin only about the organization they were affiliated with. They only asked that of the MKO people. They wanted to see whether they would say Mojahed or *monafeq*. They had different questions for the leftists, such as, "Do you believe in God?" It was a very specific question. They would ask and take notes.

30. Back then the subject of God was prevalent. I mean, even among ourselves there was a question as to what positions we should take. We were in ward 3 at the time and there were only leftists there, no MKOs or repenters. Prisoners in our ward were steadfast and in constant conflict with the guards. One day a Revolutionary Guard came to our ward and said, "We are going to make sure your laughter stops." After this questioning, we no longer had a television. We had no tools of communication. We guessed that there was something happening but we did not know what. We did not know that the war had ended. We only heard of it later.

31. I was in ward 3 (the *sar-e moze'i* ward) at the time of the executions. They would call MKOs in groups from the loudspeakers in ward 3 and would take them out of the ward. There were a lot of MKOs in our ward. When they took them, their absence was noticeable. An MKO girl who was

taken away came back. She said: "They are executing the men. They put them into two groups: those who say they believe in the Islamic Republic and those who say they don't. They execute those who do not believe." We could not even believe her. We asked ourselves, "How could the Islamic Republic make such a mistake to execute some and send back one person to inform the others?"

32. And yet all the changes such as closed doors and lack of facilities were evidence of an important event occurring. The Revolutionary Guards told us that even if someone was dying, they would not take her to the infirmary. For three months, we were completely cut off from the outside world. And then, at night we would hear single shots. And that was how we knew that people were being executed. We would hear the Revolutionary Guards marching in the garden chanting "Death to *monafeqin*, death to Communists." That is when I would hear single shots and then the sound of marching in the courtyard. I remember counting the single shots and that's how we could tell how many people were executed, although it wasn't an exact count. It would usually be at around three or four in the morning.

33. The doors of the prison remained closed. [As for the date] when they cut us off, we, the survivors, do not agree with each other. I have a letter from my husband dated 5 Mordad [27 July 1988]. It means that we were not cut off before 27 July, and that the men from Rahmat's ward had not been executed at that time. It was a normal letter; there is nothing unusual in that letter.

34. During the very last visitation we had with our relatives, we heard that the MKOs were supposed to come to Iran—the men's ward must have also heard something similar. But no one would believe such things. Rahmat had asked his brother during their last visit to plant a red rose in the garden at their home if he was executed. Others also had their last visits.

35. One of my cellmates, Nazli, had a brother in the men's ward who was a Peykar supporter. His brother had told her during a visit that there was a big storm on the way that could not be stopped. I remember we were doubtfully telling each other whatever we had heard during our visits. We were wondering what had happened. We realized only later that it was to be our last visitation.

36. After 90 percent of the MKOs left and never came back, we were confident they had been executed. Then they [the guards] came back and called the leftists in groups of one, two, or three. They started flogging the leftists. They flogged the leftists to force them to pray. The floggings continued. Those who were flogged were in the cells, but we would get the news. They were flogged at each prayer time. No one could tolerate more than five to six days of this. Two Tudeh or FKO Majority members were flogged for 20 days. They were almost in comas, but they were still being flogged five times a day. Some said later that it was worse to be flogged several times a day with fewer lashes rather than to receive a large number all at once.

37. I was the last prisoner taken to be questioned. I was blindfolded and taken to court. Someone asked me if I prayed and I said that I didn't. My response was very clear-cut. I may have been asked other questions in the same vein. I don't remember exactly what but the session was very brief. They took me to the hallway where all the solitary cells were and, there, the prisoners said the flogging had stopped.

38. I do not believe leftist women were only flogged and not executed for religious reasons. If they [the authorities] wanted to kill someone they would kill this person without minding any religious rule. Unlike the leftist men, the female leftists were never able to ally with each other and work or act as a group. The leftist women were always disagreeing, having disputes over every small thing. For instance some FKO (Minority) affiliates wouldn't speak to Tudeh or FKO (Majority) affiliates. Some like me and others would talk to them but some wouldn't. But the MKO affiliates were united and connected to each other. Their organization outside prison was functioning. But we were not united. The understanding was that, because of religious law, the punishment was not death for the leftist women; but maybe the reason was more because they were just not as organized as the others. The MKO women were organized and acted together, and they were executed. This was not about religious law and punishment. Based on my experience and the experience I had overall with them, they [the authorities] do not necessarily do what is based on the law; they do what is best for themselves as circumstances require it. This was not based on law.

39. After the flogging stopped, there was silence. No one was taken from ward 3 anymore.

40. After the executions, the guards had a very kind attitude. But I was transferred to solitary for a minor issue. [While in the solitary cell] I heard this from the female guards themselves. I overheard one particularly unpleasant Revolutionary Guard telling her friends how tightly the Mojahedin women had gripped each other while they were waiting to be executed and how they had peed on themselves in fear. She thought this was a great joke. I was in a solitary cell and I did not think they knew that I could hear them—though they know now that we have written our memoirs. It [my cell] was near the office.

41. After three months, the doors were opened and we were allowed visitations with our families. My mother was crying and told me that my husband was on the list of executed people. I do not remember what was said exactly but I seem to remember there was a list somewhere. Rahmat was executed in August 1988.

42. Before the executions began, the Revolutionary Guards had said, "We are going to make sure your laughter stops." The laughter certainly had stopped. Everyone was hiding from each other and went to bed early. We still had no idea of the scope of the executions but each time we had another visit from our families, we found out that more and more people had been killed. The environment was really very sad. Leftists who were steadfast were not crying. They were not supposed to cry.

43. We had two visits per month. I did not cry about my husband in prison, but I was very, very sad because he was younger than I was. He was 28 years old. I was not crying, but I cried when I saw my husband's mother. She was the only person I cried with. She was telling me that now that he was dead, I had a son and therefore I had to get out alive. I was very impressed at how she was holding up. She used to be very protective of Rahmat. She used to stop him from distributing flyers, offering to go on his behalf. Not that she believed in it, but she just wanted to help Rahmat. I never cried with my own parents, but I did with my husband's mother.

44. My mother-in-law asked the prison authorities for my husband's wedding ring and asked where he was buried. The prison governor refused to tell her unless she agreed to sign a paper saying that he had committed suicide. The family kept following up on Rahmat's case. During the three months that no contact was allowed between the prisoners and their relatives, Rahmat's parents had been trying every possible means to obtain a visitation with their son. They had contacted a regime insider to help them visit their son. They [later] told me, this person had told them that Rahmat was among those prisoners who had been flogged and was currently in the infirmary. He had told them that if they wanted to save their son they should pay a bribe of five million rials, which was a huge amount at the time, and they had not been able to find that amount of money.

45. Later the family [Rahmat's parents] got a telephone call instructing them to go to the prison. They thought they could visit him but it wasn't for a visit. They just got back a bag of his possessions, three sweaters, which I had knitted for him, and a book. In the bag, there was a hidden compartment. There, inside it, was a political book about the Revolution. I looked in the book to see if there was a message hidden in it, but there was nothing.

46. In the spring of 1989, I was in a cell in ward 209 when I heard the big gate to the ward open and I heard great screaming and sobbing. I realized something had happened. The guards were telling each other that Khomeini had died. Using Morse code, I told the person in the cell next to mine, "Imam is dead." It was the first time I had used the word Imam to identify Khomeini because it took less time [to tap out in Morse code].

47. My sentence was four and a half years but I was kept three more months in prison and was released after serving four years and nine months. We were not released, but we were given leave, which I didn't accept. We were all in solitary confinement but information was exchanged between the prisoners in the cells. We noticed that prisoners were being released. I was in the second group of people who were being freed based on leave. They came to see me and they told me, "We want to send you on leave." I said, "I want to be released officially. I don't want to just be on [temporary] leave."

48. They got in touch with our families to put pressure on them to come and get us.

Once I was released, my father told me that he and my mother had been waiting outside the prison from 10 a.m. until 4 p.m., that my mother had gotten tired and left. They had been waiting because I did not want to go out and I never asked for leave. They had to give me official papers attesting to the fact that [my sentence] had been served. Second, I was scared that they would release me, and then shoot me in the back and say that I had been killed trying to escape from prison. Third, in spite of all the disagreements among us, I felt linked to my cellmates [and couldn't leave the prison knowing they were still there]. We were pressured by the regime, but we also put pressure on each other; yet I felt connected to my cellmates. I was uneasy leaving, feeling as if I had not accomplished my goal. I mean after five years in prison, I should leave? Just like this? So that was it? To release me they wanted me to sign my release paper and I refused to sign; that is why it took me so long to get out of prison. Actually they kicked me out. And there I saw my father. I got upset with my father and I thought my parents had done something to get me released.

After Release

49. My mother-in-law was very depressed; she died two years ago [2007]. My mother-in-law used to go to Khavaran [Cemetery]. After I was released from prison I went with my mother-in-law to Khavaran Cemetery. The first day I was released, I went to my in-laws' [house]. The same day or a day later we went together to Khavaran. It was very important for us to

go there. For the first time I retreated from my own positions. I always thought that having a grave was ridiculous—when you die, you die—it does not matter that you have grave or where you are. But I needed Rahmat to have a grave—I needed to see what we had heard was his grave, even though it was a common grave.

50. Khavaran was a common, mass, grave, but I needed a single grave for Rahmat. I could not be a revolutionary who agreed that [all the victims] would all be buried together. I needed him [my husband] to have an individual grave. When there were many of us [at Khavaran], at the gravesite, the plainclothes agents would come. They would scream and swear at us and would trample the flowers that we tried to plant and would arrest some of us and usually try to disperse us. They did not want us to be there together. The families had contact with each other. After several trips to Khavaran with Rahmat's family, we decided to dissuade his mother from going there again, for each time she went there, she would come back depleted of all energy. After a while, I too stopped going.

51. I had to think about my son and I had to find a job; I had to make money. I wanted to have my own place; I did not want to live with my parents. After I had been let out of prison on leave, I would be taken back to prison by my family. They would call from prison [and ask that I be taken there.] One of my sisters had heard my father talk on the phone with the head of the prison. It was their policy to release us from prison, on leave, so we would get used to living on the outside, then bring us

back so that [prison would be even more unbearable than before, and] we would be more prone to make pledges [of allegiance to them] and declare our hatred [of our political organizations.] And they were successful. Some of the prisoners who were taken back and forth signed statements. I did not.

52. The Islamic Republic never bothers you *per se*, as a prisoner; it always gets your family involved. After I was released on leave, I was taken back three or four times—maybe after three weeks or one month. This game went on for months. They wouldn't call me because I wouldn't agree [to go back.] They would call my father and say, "You have to bring her back to prison." And at that point my father and I would get into an argument. I would tell my father, "You shouldn't take me; they have to arrest me if they want to take me." I would fight with him and resist him but, as these are your parents—you are not in prison and can't go on strike or stop talking—you have to give in at some point. So I tried to tell them so they would understand the logic of it. Each time, I went in with all my belongings, my clothes and a bucket to wash my clothes in (because I went in prepared to stay).

53. The last time, which was the fourth time my father took me to prison, they took us into a room. My father sat on a chair and I sat on the floor. The head of the prison (who is called Meysam and is known as a reformer) came in. My father got up because ordinary folks acted very cautiously with these people. So they shook hands and greeted each other. He told my father,

"Look, you know, your children are so arrogant they won't even get up when I, the head of the prison, come in." I said, "For me, you are all the same, warden, guard, you're all prison guards to me. I am not your employee and, you're not my boss." [He told my father], "See, if we didn't execute your daughter, it is because she was a woman and we took pity on her because she has a son, otherwise we would have executed her like her anti-revolutionary husband." I snickered and said: "Women?! You killed so many MKOs, you killed so many women. You lost the will to kill any more women. That is the only reason I am still here."

54. Meysam said to my father, "That is it. We are going to execute her today." He threw my father out. And my father went home, thinking that he had given his daughter to the executioner with his own hands. Other family members reproached him for having taken me to prison where I would be executed and told him that he would forever feel guilty for this. There was an argument between my parents and they kept weeping. I, myself, thought that I'd be executed for real this time. They took me to solitary confinement again, but I was released at 7 p.m. or 8 p.m. I took a cab to go home but I wasn't sure if they had changed their mind about killing me. I was worried that they might shoot me in the back.

Additional Information

55. Upon my release, I worked as a reporter, and also as an expert on social matters for urban development companies. My sister lived in Bolivia. I left Iran in the winter of 1996, one day before the New Year. I had promised the lady who worked at the German embassy in Bolivia, who facilitated my transit visa, that I would not claim refugee status in Germany while I was in transit in Frankfurt. So I didn't do anything during my time in Frankfurt and went to Bolivia to stay with my sister. In the five months and twenty-three days I was there, I was a temporary refugee (until I was able to go to Germany with the help of that same lady at the embassy).

56. I went to UNHCR in Bolivia, and tried to obtain asylum in the United States, but it didn't happen. So I had no choice but to return to Iran.

57. I went to the German embassy to get a transit visa again so I could go back through Germany and [the same lady at the German embassy] was very surprised that my situation had not been resolved. She issued a visa to me, and I entered Germany in the summer of 1997 and I have been here since then. I didn't know what to do at first but after making a big effort, I was able to finish a three-year nursing program, and I am currently working at a retirement home for the elderly.

Cologne, June 2009

OFFICIAL STATEMENT • 16

اطّلاعات

Subject: Eligibility requirements for pardons
The official: Prosecutor General Mohammad Musavi Kho'einiha
The occasion: Press conference
Date: 27 January 1988
Source: *Ettela'at*, 28 January 1988

Prosecutor General's comments regarding amnesty for prisoners on the occasion of the [9th] anniversary of the Revolution:

". . . An Amnesty Committee selected by Imam [Khomeini] is reviewing prisoners' amnesty. It has devised a comprehensive program so that a list can be prepared containing the names of those who prison officials and other relevant authorities believe are fit to be released, will no longer commit a crime, and deserve to be pardoned. Such persons will be pardoned or their sentences commuted. A prisoner should feel that the more he repents and the more he prepares himself for a healthy and dignified life after his release, the more he will be considered by the judiciary for amnesty. The judiciary takes notice of such actions and pardons these types of prisoners from time to time. . . ."

Ebrahim Rastak

ARRESTED: October 1982
DETAINED IN: Evin and Gohardasht Prisons
RELEASED: February 1989

1. My name is Ebrahim Rastak.* I am 49 years old. I was a political prisoner in Iran for six years and four months, from 1982 to 1989. I was in Evin Prison, and I was released just a few months after the executions in 1988. I came to the United Kingdom in 2001. I am now a British citizen, living in Cambridge.

2. I make this statement in support of an investigation into the mass execution of political prisoners in 1988 in Iran.

3. This statement is true to the best of my knowledge and belief. Except where I indicate to the contrary, I make this statement on the basis of facts and matters within my own knowledge. Where the facts and matters in this statement are within my own knowledge, they are true. Where the facts and matters are not within my own knowledge, I have identified the source or sources of my information, and I believe such facts to be true.

Arrest and Torture

4. I was arrested on 28 October 1982. At the time I was a student at the University of Science and Technology of Iran, Tehran, where I was studying chemical engineering. But because for almost seven years I was in prison, where I was not allowed to continue my formal training or studies, I never completed my degree. When I was arrested I was in front of my apartment near the university gates, talking in a telephone booth with some friends. The Revolutionary Guards suspected me of being a political activist.

5. I had links to the Fadaiyan Khalq Organization (FKO [Majority]). I was not a member, but I agreed with their policies and had read their political material.

6. I was tortured for three days. The Revolutionary Guard interrogated me, while beating the soles of my feet with a cable. They call this *ta'zir* [discretionary and corrective punishment]. I was given it twice; 75 lashes each time. They wanted to know whom else I knew.

Trial and Pre-trial Detention

7. I was tried before an Islamic Revolutionary Court and held in prison for seven years without any specific sentence. It was only after two years that I was taken to a court. One day, without notice, I was taken from my cell, blindfolded, and taken to a Revo-

*The name of the witness and some details in his testimony have been changed to protect his identity.

lutionary Court. I could not see the judge or anyone else in the courtroom, but from their voices it seemed as if there were two [other] people in the room.

8. The court officials told me that I had to say, "I am sorry," and that I must repent. They did not have any specific allegations against me, but they still insisted that I just say "sorry" and sign a letter that was put before me, and they said, "If you don't sign this you will remain in prison." The letter said, "I declare my opposition to and hatred of all the following groups and parties in Iran and condemn them." They had listed by name several political groups, including the FKO (Majority). I refused to sign the letter. I refused to sign it because I believed it to be illegal—at that time the FKO was supposed to be a legal party. The FKO had supported the Islamic Republic.

9. It was clear to me they had no proof of my membership in the FKO. I told the court that I was merely a sympathizer reading their newspapers and that I had never been a member of the group. The court officers told me, "You will stay in prison until you die and until you go to Hell."

10. Throughout my imprisonment I was periodically taken before a revolutionary court. I had no specific sentence [other than] "until further notice." Basically this meant that I had to stay in prison until they made a decision about me. During my detention, I was taken before a court at least four times, about once a year, but I was never sentenced. It was the same thing every time. They asked us to sign a letter denouncing our organizations. Those who signed the

letter were released. But I refused to sign. Even though I was not affiliated with the FKO in any formal way, I felt very strongly that I was entitled to my beliefs.

11. I was never provided access to a lawyer, nor was I given any information about my sentence.

12. I had visits from my family every two or three weeks during this first two-year period. My father was a retired teacher. I was able to see my brother only once because they generally did not allow us to have visits with our siblings. During this period, my mother had two heart attacks and was kept in the hospital because of the stress and anxiety caused by my situation. My mother had a third heart attack and passed away two years after I was released.

Prison Conditions: Evin and Gohardasht Prisons

13. After my trial in 1984, I was held in ward 3 of Evin Prison, an area designated for political prisoners. They called it the Amuzeshgah. The prison conditions were terrible—there were 34 people in a room that was only 4 x 6 meters [approximately 13 x 20 feet]. It was very cramped. Sometimes there would be as many as 58 people held in each cell.

14. Any form of organization or association among the prisoners was illegal. Because I had refused to sign the letter I was kept with the other prisoners who had refused to renounce their political views. At that time, they kept us apart from those who had repented, or who pretended to

have done so. I was kept in the ward with those who were considered to be *sar-e moze'i*, those who "stood by their ideas."

15. We were not permitted to continue our education inside the prison. But because so many intellectuals were arrested and held as political prisoners, among ourselves we did maintain our own educational activities. I was very interested in science and math, and so I began studying and learning from other prisoners, even though this was illegal. Pen and paper were illegal as well so we had to write on the wall, using whatever we were able to find. During this time I studied mathematics and genetics. This study and knowledge helped me obtain my present employment in England.

16. We were allowed to exercise in the yard for only 20 minutes a day. Apart from that, we organized ourselves within the cell, where we kept one section of the cell available for people to exercise individually. We created a list and took turns, in the order listed.

17. We were not forced to work. But we invented and built many things for ourselves from whatever materials we could find. For example, we made pens. At one point we learned how to calculate the radius of the earth and so many other things from the history of science and technology.

Events in 1988

18. In 1987 we went on a hunger strike to protest prison conditions. At that time I was in Evin. There were so many different problems during this period, but this particular strike was about the lack of food in prison. Two representatives of Montazeri came to meet with us and interview us about our concerns. For example, at that time we were kept in closed wards with 38 to 50 people in each room. We explained our problems to Montazeri's representatives. Later the wards were opened up so that we were able to move around the prison. It was cause for great celebration among the prisoners. But after a few months, they began to separate us. I was separated because I refused to repent. In late April 1988 I was moved to Gohardasht.

19. There are many terrible episodes to report from my time in prison. For example, when we were transferred from Evin to Gohardasht, we were moved into ward 13, which was a large ward that had separate rooms. One day, in early summer 1988, the guards came into the ward and made sure all the doors of the ward were closed. It seemed as if they started a big fan that was circulating some sort of gas. All of a sudden everyone in the ward became sick. We were coughing, vomiting, and sneezing. Because I had had some experience with tear gas, I could recognize that this was much worse. It was really horrible, but no one died and there did not seem to be any side effects afterwards. They were clearly not trying to kill us because we all recovered and no one died. They were just torturing us. Some of my friends were taken to the prison hospital because they became very ill. When they were asked why they were ill, they told the doctors what happened—that they had started coughing because of a strange, foul-smelling gas—but the doctors did not believe them.

20. In late July 1988 we heard that Khomeini had accepted the UN resolution and cease-fire. We then heard about the Mojahedin attack. All of a sudden, the prison guards stopped providing us with newspapers and stopped broadcasting the radio news inside the prison. They cut off all communication between prisoners and the outside world. We had no access to any news. We tried to get news by communicating with each other using Morse code, but no one had news from the outside.

21. However, through this communication we learned from prisoners in other wards that there was trouble inside the prison. We were told that the prison guards were coming into the wards each day with a list of names, or that they would select people at will, who would be taken away to the court. Prisoners in other wards told us, through Morse code messages, that people were being executed after their court hearings. We had heard that people were being executed en masse by hanging in the Hosseinyeh or the auditorium, which was a large space like a warehouse and was normally used for prayer.

22. It was about two weeks after Khomeini accepted the [UN] resolution that our turn came. A group of us were taken from our cell, blindfolded, and taken to the court. We were taken to a large hall, and made to queue. I counted, and there were 142 people in line waiting to be tried.

23. When it was finally my turn I was taken into the courtroom, my blindfold was removed, and I recognized four people in the room: Nayyeri (the religious judge),

Eshraqi (Tehran's Islamic Revolutionary Prosecutor), and two prison officials—Naserian (head of Gohardasht Prison), and Lashkari (the prison warden). I could recognize them because they were either well known in the prison or because I had seen them on television. Eshraqi was the prosecutor I had dealt with. Nayyeri was a very well-known cleric. I had seen him on television and in newspapers. He asked the questions during my hearing and it was clear he was the most senior person in the room.

24. In addition to Nayyeri, Eshraqi, Naser-ian, and Lashkari, three other people were there—I did not recognize them and I did not speak with them. Two of them were clerics and were recognized by my friends in prison—one of them was Karaj City's religious judge [Gohardasht Prison is located in Karaj] (I don't know his name), and the other was Purmohammadi (an official of the Ministry of Information). Five people were sitting (the four clerics and Naserian) and two were standing and taking notes (one of them was Lashkari). I am very unclear on who exactly was there and how many people because the numbers changed.

25. The questioning from Nayyeri went as follows:

You are Ebrahim? Yes.

Do you accept the Islamic Republic? No, I do not.

Do you believe your organization and its ideas? Yes, the FKO.

Do you believe in God? No.

Have you ever believed in God, even during your childhood, even for one second? No.

What about your father and mother? Do they pray? No.

Why don't they pray? They are from Kermanshah, Kurdistan. They are Ahl-e Haq.

26. I was honest in my answers. I come from a region in Kurdistan where there is a branch of Islam called "Ahl-e Haq" and no one in this group prays. At this point, another member of the committee spoke to Nayyeri and said "They are Ahl-e Haq and the Ahl-e Haq do not pray." Nayyeri said, "Take him to the left." They took me out of the room into the corridor. Those on the left of the corridor were the "unbelievers" or the "voluntary apostates."

27. To give some context and to describe the significance of this classification, I need to explain that there are two kinds of apostates. The first are those who have always been non-believers. The second are those who were once believers but have since renounced their faith. That is, those who come from a Muslim family, but who nevertheless renounce Islam (innate apostates). I am Kurdish and therefore I was already recognized as an enemy. My parents are from Kurdistan and practice a mystic form of Islam, which does not really believe in God. That made me an apostate, but in the category of those who have always been non-believers. Nevertheless, many Ahl-e Haq people were executed at that time. I knew it was dangerous for me, but I answered honestly. I do not consider myself Muslim. I did not and I do not agree with the Islamic Republic because they held me without charge for seven years. They held me because of my political beliefs. I was not in any way involved in any political activities. I believe in science and nothing else. I describe myself as a scientific materialist.

28. Outside in the corridor, there were 142 people on the left side. We were all whispering to each other, trying to figure out what was going to happen to us. We were brought a trolley with bread and cheese, and we called it the "last supper." We said goodbye to each other because we thought we were going to be executed. We had already heard so many stories, through Morse code communications from prisoners in other wards, about people being executed. We had also heard the screams of people being tortured. We knew we were going to be either executed or tortured—there was no other possibility.

29. The prison guards then started calling our names from a long list. All of the 142 people were called, except for me and three other people. The other 138 people were taken to the Hosseinyeh, the place that we knew from other prisoners was used for executions. I wanted to know what was happening so I asked the guard, "Why are you keeping us here?" He asked for my name. When I told him he just said, "Sit down here." It was then I realized that the three other people with me—Siamak Amini, Kaveh Etemadzadeh, and Fereidun Fam Tafreshi—were all "non-believers" like me. None of us had ever been Muslim. They were from Communist families and

their fathers were Communists. They had never been Muslim or considered Muslim. We were all voluntary apostates.

30. We were then transferred to another place in prison where they tortured us in order to make us become Muslim. They tortured us five times a day, at each call to prayer. They flogged us on the soles of our feet while telling us that we had to accept Islam and become Muslim. It was so painful I can barely describe it. They beat us with electrical cables of different thicknesses. They would tie us face down to a low-lying bed made from metal and wood. My hands and feet were tied to the bed and guards would sit on my back to hold me down. My head would be covered with a blanket and sometimes they would put something in my mouth so no one could hear my screams. Then they would beat us. At each call to prayer I was given 15 lashes.

31. As far as I am aware, all 138 people who were taken away were hanged because we never saw them again. In Gohardasht Prison they executed people by hanging. I have heard that in Evin Prison they also executed people by shooting them. Also, while we were tortured, we were held in prison cells, where we could read many things written on the walls by prisoners who had obviously known they were being taken for execution. Some of the prisoners were hanged right away, but because there were a limited number of ropes with which they could be hanged, many of the 138 people were taken into a large cell where they were able to lift up their blindfolds. In that short period of time before their execution, many of the prisoners wrote on

the walls of the cell. Some wrote, "We are not blindfolded and we can see what is going on." A friend of mine, whose name was Kasra Akbari Kordestani, wrote his name on the wall of one cell. Another friend of mine wrote something on the wall that to this day continues to cause me intense grief. He wrote, "I offer my little heart to all the workers and hardworking people of Iran."

32. I also saw the corpses of executed people. In one of the prison halls in Gohardasht there was a window from which we could see out into the prison yard. We could see two guards wearing strange, unusual clothing. They were wearing boots, not army boots, but rubber boots. Neither of them had beards, and they wore strange things covering their hair. Together they were carrying bodies to a large truck parked outside. We could tell they were carrying dead bodies because we saw the head of one woman as they were carrying her body away. I could not estimate how many bodies I saw but the truck was large—it had 18 wheels. From what I had seen of the guards' work and from the size of the truck, there must have been many, many dead bodies.

33. After discussions with the surviving prisoners, we put together the information that we got from prisoners from the various groups on how they were treated. The people who had been transferred to the right of the corridor were those prisoners who had admitted to being Muslims and said that they would pray. It was a question of whether you were a Muslim—if you said you were, you were placed on the right and you were not tortured. But if you said

you would not pray, you were sent to the left and you were tortured.

34. As leftists, we were treated differently from the Mojahedin. They were Muslims who sought to blend Muslim beliefs with Communism. So the questions for each group were very different. For the leftists, the questions were purely about our belief in God and in Islam, and our willingness to pray. The Mojahedin were Muslim and so they were not asked questions about their religious beliefs.

35. I understand from my wife, who was also a political prisoner but who was released two years before the 1988 killings, that former political prisoners were also being asked similar questions at this time. When political prisoners were released from prison in Iran in the 1980s, they were released on condition that they report periodically to the local revolutionary committee. She told me that the reporting was different around July and August of 1988. All of a sudden, the revolutionary committee called her late in the evening and requested that she report immediately to the committee. She refused, saying she had already reported as required the week before and, in any event, it was late and she needed to be escorted by her father. When she reported the next morning, she was subjected to intense interrogation. This was very different from her previous meetings with the committee. She said it was as if they were interrogating her all over again. They asked her the same questions she had been asked when in prison, and they tried to force her to sign a letter that indicated her support for the Islamic Republic, renouncing all political groups, and in which she guaranteed never to take part in any political activities. My wife did not understand why this was happening at the time, but later when we talked about it we realized how this fit into the broader context of what was happening in Iran, both inside and outside of the prison.

36. Inside the prison, I tried to kill myself three times after these events. The first time was on 1 December 1988 at 10 p.m. This was during the period that I was being tortured for refusing to pray. The guards were coming and flogging us on the bottom of our feet five times a day at the call to prayer. This was our religious sentence. But the guards would also come intermittently to beat us for no reason, using whatever they could lay their hands on. It was under the pressure of this terrible treatment that I first attempted suicide. But because I did not know how to do it properly, I slit my wrists in the wrong direction. I tried this twice more, and, each time, the bleeding would stop after a while. The prisoners found me later that night. I had lost a lot of blood, but I was still alive. Committing suicide is forbidden in Islam. One of my fellow prisoners who was a doctor treated my wounds and gave me antibiotics for the sores. The doctor and I are still friends today.

37. I was released on 15 February 1989.

London, June 2009

جمهوری اسلامی

Subject:	On pardon eligibility requirements for prisoners
The official:	The designated successor of Ayatollah Khomeini, Iran's Supreme Leader, Ayatollah Hossein-Ali Montazeri
The occasion:	Meeting with the head of Iran's prisons and the members of the Pardon Commission designated by Ayatollah Khomeini
Date:	29 January 1988
Source:	*Jomhuri Eslami,* 30 January 1988

. . . [Montazeri] emphasized that if relevant officials and prosecutors, based on their own knowledge or through received information about the mini-groups, ascertained that an individual had been disciplined [punished] and had repented, such person should not remain in prison, even if condemned to a lengthy prison sentence. "The criterion for amnesty or commutation of sentence should not be [a person's prior condemnation to] longer or shorter imprisonment, for a person condemned to a short prison term may not be disciplined yet, or, on the contrary, a person condemned to a long prison term may be disciplined and repent after a short time. This principle [pardon or commutation of sentence] should be implemented on the basis of an investigation, consultation with prosecutors, and information about the mini-groups, to conform to the views of the Imam [Khomeini]. If it is deemed that a person has been disciplined and has repented and there is no need for him to remain in prison, the Pardon Commission should begin the amnesty process for such individuals. God willing [for the anniversary of the Islamic Republic and other such occasions], persons deserving of pardon and freedom should be released and pardoned; they should either be freed [from prison] or their sentence commuted."

Mihan Rusta

1. My name is Mihan Rusta and I reside in Berlin, Germany. When my husband Reza Esmati was executed in 1988, I had been living here for a few years.

2. This statement has been prepared based on my interview with the Boroumand Foundation. I make this statement in support of an investigation into the mass execution of political prisoners in 1988 in Iran.

3. This statement is true to the best of my knowledge and belief. Except where I indicate to the contrary, I make this statement on the basis of facts and matters within my own knowledge. Where the facts and matters in this statement are within my own knowledge, they are true. Where the facts and matters are not within my own knowledge, I have identified the source or sources of my information, and I believe such facts to be true.

Political Activity Prior to Arrest

4. My husband, Reza Esmati, was born in Tehran in 1950. Upon graduating from high school, he studied sociology at Melli University of Iran. He obtained his bachelor's degree in 1974 and, that same year, he was arrested and sentenced to three years' imprisonment for political activities against the monarchy.

5. In 1977, having served his sentence, he was released from prison and started working as an accountant in a company in the city of Bushehr. He then continued the same line of work in Tehran until 1979.

6. After the Revolution and until his arrest, Reza was active in a Maoist left-wing political group that supported the Komala Party or Organization. Studying Marxist texts, and printing and distributing the Komala Organization's leaflets, were part of the group's activities. The group also had a workers section that operated in the north and south of Iran, in which intellectual activists who worked in factories were, in a manner of speaking, active in mobilizing workers. For instance, the workers section would stage strikes demanding higher wages or the right to form councils (in place of Islamic associations). That is the kind of work they would engage in most often. They may have done other

things for the workers, but I really do not know because I was never active in the workers section. I do know that the activists in that section were part of leftist [groups] whose members had been imprisoned under the Shah.

7. Nothing of any particular significance had happened prior to Reza's arrest. One of our blessings, or misfortunes, was that we did not have a telephone [line.] We never got a phone, nor did we have any intention of acquiring one. Reza used to say that a telephone was a means through which security forces could very quickly trap a person. I should mention that we tried very hard to give the appearance of a very normal family life. We sought to ensure that our lives did not arouse too much suspicion. Compared to many of the leftist activists we led a pretty comfortable life. I was 27 years old and more experienced. I knew the activists in the group. They knew me too. Our home was a meeting place. They tended to use the amenities in our home. Having a family was also useful at the time because [a family's] comings and goings seem like a normal thing.

8. From a security standpoint, we had more possibilities [and resources] than single people had. Hence, more gatherings tended to take place in our home. But ultimately, from a security perspective, that proved very detrimental for Reza. Everyone was aware of the facilities that our home provided. The assistance and collaboration of one of the group members—who frequented our home and had been arrested ten days previously—resulted in Reza's and Rostam Bahmani's arrest on that summer evening.

9. In general, a climate of siege, persecution, and arrest reigned throughout the country. All those who had been somewhat publicly active had either been arrested or had gone underground, which is why we felt in danger. Incidentally, the night Reza was arrested, Bijan Chehrazi, a well-known leftist figure (who was executed in September 1983) came to our house. He said to me, "I don't feel safe in your house. Don't stay here." I remember that a friend, who was spending the night with us, and I spoke to Reza, urging him to leave. Physically, I was still not in a condition to be able to move, because of the birth of my son by Caesarian section thirteen days earlier. Reza said, "Tomorrow, we will all leave together." I told him, "You leave tonight, we all will leave tomorrow." I did not want him to spend that night in the house. For about an hour and a half to two hours, we discussed the issue of whether we should stay in the house or leave. Finally, we gave in to Reza. Perhaps we should have been more persistent.

Arrest

10. When they arrested Reza on the night of 8 September 1981, we first saw two Revolutionary Guards at the door. They rang our bell at around 2:30 in the morning. We knew they had come to arrest us. When Reza opened the door, they immediately grabbed his arms and tried to drag him out of the apartment, but because I started to scream they instead came in. One of them carried a hand gun and the other a rifle. They acted as if we were armed. A friend who was visiting us that night and had

gone to the door was staring, with eyes wide open in astonishment, at the person accompanying the two Guards. At the time, I did not have a chance to ask him what the matter was. Later that night, however, our friend told me that the reason for his astonishment was that the man who had come with the Guards to arrest Reza was a member of our group, arrested ten days earlier. I knew him; we had worked with him. Apparently it was he who had guided the Revolutionary Guards to our home after he had been arrested. He had also spent five years in prison under the Shah. He, Reza, and several others who were arrested that same night had all been imprisoned under the Shah. That person has since been released and is currently roaming about freely.

11. Three decades later I still remember the scene. I have not forgotten their [the Guards'] faces. They were wearing ordinary [civilian] clothes. One of them looked more southern [Iranian]; he was dark, olive-skinned, with curly hair, and he was tall and thin. The other one was wearing sneakers; he looked like the religious type; he was fat, with stubble, salt and pepper hair, and light-colored eyes.

12. My son, who was only 13 days old, began to cry. It seemed as if he felt that something had happened because, ever since we had [brought him] home [from the hospital], he had always slept well. I had given him his milk, and his diaper had been changed. So normally he should have been asleep. Reza had sat next to me the entire time I was breastfeeding him. I had said to Reza, "You are tired. Go to bed." He had replied, "No.

I want to stay up with you as long as you are awake. I want to enjoy and keep these moments [in my heart and mind]." At the time, the circumstances were such that we believed everything would soon change. We all felt that perhaps such moments would not come again.

13. They did not show us an arrest warrant. All they had were their machine guns. They walked into the room with their shoes on. If I had to describe them, I would say that they were afraid of us, that they were somewhat apprehensive, as if they were expecting to be attacked. They were just standing in the middle of the room, neither sitting down nor looking us in the eye. They were acting somewhat strange. The baby was crying in the room. They told me to bring Reza a pair of trousers and a shirt. I asked, "Where are you taking him?" The one with the salt and pepper hair replied, "We are going to ask him a few questions." I said, "Where are you taking him? He hasn't done anything." The man replied, "It's nothing. Don't make a big fuss." I was groaning, and walking up and down looking for Reza's glasses. I do not know why I was not afraid, or why I did not wonder why they were not taking me. I kept asking, "Where are you taking him? You must tell me where you're taking him," but I did not ask whether they had an arrest warrant or not, or demand to see one. We had accepted not having such expectations. They said, "We will ask him a few questions and bring him back." Reza's eyesight was -4.00 [myopic], which means he couldn't see anything without eyeglasses. We kept looking for his glasses

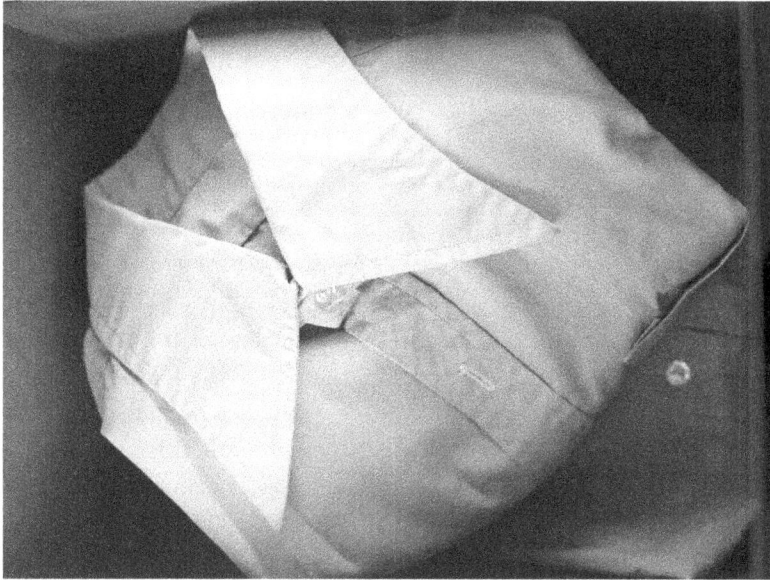

Reza Esmati's shirt, which he wore in prison for years. It was part of his belongings that were returned to his father after his execution.

but could not find them. We were afraid that they might go to the other rooms because we had a stencil (photocopying) machine in the backroom, and I did not want them to go there.

14. They did not search the house at all. They were afraid. We did not find Reza's glasses, so he left without them. Our house was at the end of an alley and had a gate through which a car could enter. It had a big yard that led to a parking garage. Our apartment was on the second floor. After they left, we quickly found the glasses. I stayed upstairs but our guest rushed down to give Reza his glasses. He described the scene to me: armed Revolutionary Guards had surrounded the entire building and the area around it. They were under the impression that they were raiding a team home, and therefore they expected resistance. The two who had come up carrying their G3 [rifles] were, in fact, ready to shoot because they had expected resistance. According to our guest, the Guards had taken over the courtyard of the house with an army. They were even wearing sneakers so as not to make noise. We had only a photocopier at home. We were not armed, though our group supported Komala, (which was waging a guerrilla war against the regime). We were not involved in any armed struggle, we were only disseminating the news about the ongoing armed struggle in Iranian Kurdistan. In any case, we managed to give Reza his glasses, which was the most

important thing at that moment. All of
this lasted maybe about an hour and a half.
During that time, the only words they
uttered were, "Go and fetch his clothes,"
or "Get dressed and let's go." They really
did not say anything else. After they left,
we waited a little while. We had to tell the
others.

15. They did not tell us where they were taking
him. That period corresponded with the
period of the daily summary executions.
Names of those executed were announced
on the television news, and in the *Kayhan,
Etella'at,* and *Jomhuri Eslami* daily newspapers. We would first buy the papers and
look for Reza's name and then listen to the
news. We would not go look for him. In
the early days, when arrests and imprison-
ments were widespread and the climate was
one of fear and repression, we would not
look for our loved ones. Now, I ask myself
how we could never have gone to look for
him, to see where they had taken him. I
think we were thinking that they were
executing everyone. At a time when they
would announce the names of 100 [people]
who had been executed in a single day, you
could not even imagine the number of
arrests they were making. All you can
think about is that one of these days your
loved one is going to be executed. Therefore, I was not thinking at all about looking for him. We felt helpless and we were
in a state of shock.

Prison Conditions

16. After a few difficult weeks, we began to
use every possible means to find a trace of
Reza. During those years, every household

had someone in prison. We had a neighbor whose 14-year-old son was arrested
on charges of supporting the Mojahedin
Khalq Organization. The mother spent
every day in front of various prisons in
the hope of finding out something about
the fate of her son. She was the one who
told [us] about the gathering of families in
front of Luna Park. From that day on, I
set out for Luna Park at 6:30 every morning. Luna Park was where the office of the
revolutionary prosecutor is now located.
But back then, there was no official building or office. It was just a building that
had been closed off with a railing. It had a
section like a watchtower where an armed
Revolutionary Guard was constantly
keeping watch. There was always a large
crowd there—around 200 to 300 people.
We did not have a specific agenda. We
were families who had no information
about our imprisoned loved ones. We did
not even know whether they were in Evin
Prison or not. We would gather in the hope
of obtaining news of them [and learning
something about their whereabouts]. There
were families who had several members
imprisoned. These families did not gather
solely in front of Evin Prison's revolutionary prosecutor's office. They would also
bring us news from other prisons.

17. One day when I was on the bus to Luna
Park, I could not help but listen to the
conversation of two men sitting behind me.
I looked at them very cautiously, from the
corner of my eye. They were two young
men who could certainly not have been
more than 18. They were talking about the
situation at the prison and how much they
hated the prisoners. They were complain-

ing about why no one would issue an order to shoot them all. They were saying that they were awaiting orders to "deal with them." Listening to them sent shivers down my spine. The picture they depicted of prison turned every hope into despair. The armed guards I saw during my visits to prison were no more than 14 to 16 years of age. They all carried G3s.

18. There were crowds in front of Luna Park every day, from early in the morning until around one or two in the afternoon. Those who had come earlier in the morning would get tired and leave for work (or for whatever reason) and another lot would take their place. There was a mother who had come from Shah Abdolazim [located in the southernmost part of Tehran while Evin is in its northernmost part]. It was December, and she did not have an overcoat. She had come in her sandals. Mothers would exchange news about various prisons. These mothers would inform each other about executions. We would stand in groups of five or six, exchanging information, and the guards would aggressively disperse us with threats such as, "Don't stand next to each other. If you speak to each other we will arrest you." We were not allowed to form a gathering. They would say, "You are not allowed to assemble here," and push us. They swore and cursed at us saying, "Shut your mouths, you filth! Break it up! Don't speak to each other!" Their behavior was extremely violent and aggressive. They considered us as part of the enemy, even though we had assembled there out of desperation. We were desperate for some information.

19. Certain days, [the authorities] would read out the names of some of the prisoners. Their families would form a line to be given their loved ones' last will and testament. We would often see bodies trembling, eyes wide open in shock and disbelief, and mouths open in astonishment. Often mothers would cry out and beat themselves on the head, while fathers would bite their lips; some younger people would try to lead them away from the scene, pleading with them not to cry in front of the executioners. It was on such occasions that the police would forcibly remove from the scene mothers who resisted and screamed, and would throw them into minibuses and take them to Evin. We heard that these mothers were generally released after a couple of days.

20. In November 1982, for the first time, we were allowed to give 200 tumans [for our detained relatives] to the revolutionary prosecution office. In February 1983, when visitations started, the space in front of the revolutionary prosecution office was reorganized. They put up fences we had to go through, on visitation days. Before every visit, though, Haji Karbala'i would tell families that they could each give 200 tumans and blankets and warm clothes to their imprisoned relatives. Well, this was a [good] sign. If you could deliver all this for the prisoner, it meant that he or she was still alive. There were families who had no money. We would all chip in to make the payments for families of prisoners who either did not have the means, or were not aware that they could give money to their loved ones, and had therefore come

unprepared and were not carrying enough money. I remember some mothers used to take off their sweaters to be delivered to their sons.

21. No one among those who gathered there had any idea what the affiliation of the imprisoned loved one of the next person was, whether [the prisoner] was Mojahed, leftist, or nationalist. No one would ask about the prisoners' political affiliations. This was not the families' concern. During the Mojahedin protests of 20 June, many of those arrested were merely passersby who had no connections to the protests whatsoever. The group that I was part of for months, however, was comprised mainly of families of political prisoners. I believe that in that period they had allocated Evin Prison to political prisoners. The prison was full. If you were not able to provide money or winter necessities to your prisoner within the allotted time, you lost your chance. After two weeks, they gave us a form receipt stating "200 tumans paid for prisoner." On the back of the receipt, the prisoner had confirmed, in his own handwriting, receipt of 200 tumans. When I saw Reza's handwriting, I breathed a sigh of relief. The entire crowd that had gathered there, and had not heard a word about their prisoner for weeks and months, was relieved once they saw their loved ones' handwriting. It was a sign that the prisoner was alive and was being held at Evin Prison.

22. Our first visit took place four and a half months after Reza's arrest. It was in the last week of January 1982, on the 24th or the 26th. I had gotten ready to go for the visit even though a few days earlier I had received a message from a friend advising me not to go. Apparently, one of the members of our organization, who had been arrested the same night Reza was arrested, had sent one of his cellmates who had been freed that week to my father-in-law's office to warn me that all information concerning us [the group] had been compromised, [that the authorities knew everything], even about me. He said I should not go to visit him. I said, "I'm going." At that moment, I didn't care if they arrested me. All I wanted was to see him. I really don't know why. Perhaps I thought seeing me would boost Reza's morale—it was no longer about missing someone and what not. You live in circumstances where you cannot think clearly. Your only wish is that your loved one live, that they don't kill him. In other words, you are constantly preoccupied with thoughts of death and execution.

23. I went for the visit. The visits were organized in alphabetical order. We would stand outside Luna Park and be told [of our turn] then and there. I was always there. [Prison authorities] would say, for example, those whose names start with such and such letters can come for a visit on such and such date. Then you would go and take a number, and the next day, the families would go for the visit. On those cold winter nights, families of prisoners would line up around one or two in the morning to receive a numbered ticket because they all wanted to meet with their loved ones on that day. The crowd was large and the visitation time was between 8 a.m. and 4 p.m., and it was possible that you would

not get a ticket for that day, and would have to come back again the following day. Everyone was worried and uncertain and did not want to lose their opportunity. Those who had spent the night at Luna Park would secure a visit for that day. Those who came later, would get later visiting times or, once the prosecutor's office closed at 4 p.m., they would lose the opportunity for a visit on that day.

24. They took my son Sa'id and me around five or six in the morning. It was a cold January. We had to take photographs with us for the visits, as each person was issued an identity badge. We had to attach these orange-colored badges to our clothing. They would check the photo on the card to make sure it was us, and then they would frisk us. Everything was done in silence. And if someone talked, he or she would be insulted. It was an oppressive atmosphere. Any remarks they made were along the lines of, "Put your bag here. You cannot take this with you." They never used the formal word for "you." They addressed us only with the informal word for "you."

25. When it was our turn, a minibus took us from Luna Park to Evin, which doesn't take long, maybe five minutes. The guard who was at the wheel of the minibus drove very fast and would suddenly put his foot on the brake. Since the minibus was filled with people seated and standing, everyone kept falling on each other, which would prompt him to curse us. The prison gates opened automatically as the minibus approached. To confuse us, he would drive round and round. In fact, the visitors' building was

the closest building to Evin's main gate. That was easy to determine.

26. When the minibus stopped in front of the visitors' building and we were let out, we were taken through a corridor with a wall on one side and a makeshift wall on the other. We had no way of seeing outside. The wall they had built was made of iron railings stretching from the ground to a person's waist, and above that it was made of iranite. Iranite was a type of green fiberglass roofing material, which looked like plastic, hard plastic. We would go through this tunnel and reach the stairs that took us to the first floor of the building where there was a small waiting room. We would wait there so that they could bring the prisoners from the back. In the waiting room there were televisions, which, for instance, broadcast Qur'anic verses or an interview.

27. Then we would enter a long hall, where approximately 10 to 50 prisoners would be standing behind glass partitions. The first couple of times, the phones did not work. We could communicate only through gestures. We had also taken Sa'id. During our first visit in January, they took Sa'id from us and gave him to Reza on the other side of the glass partition. Sa'id was four months old. I then gave two of Sa'id's photographs to the guard who had taken Sa'id to Reza to give to him. Reza had not seen Sa'id at all [since his arrest]. Until that day, he didn't even know what name we had given the baby.

28. There was a winter cap next to every prisoner. Later we learned from reports that came out of prison that the prisoners had

to wear the cap with its rim covering their eyes to prevent them from seeing where they were going. They did not blindfold them because they did not want us to see them blindfolded. Under these conditions, we would have had to shout to make sure that they heard us. Behind us there stood a row of male and female guards. The guards outnumbered the prisoners and their visitors. They kept marching behind the prisoners and were watching their every move. The female guards were, in addition, in charge of ensuring the observance of the Islamic dress code. At the end of the visit (which was supposed to be ten minutes but I don't believe we ever had ten full minutes) the young, or I should say child, guards would shout, "Out. The visit is over. Hurry up! Faster, faster!" We would watch each other until the very last minute, for as long as we could actually see each other. They would keep the prisoners there until all visitors had left. We [on the other hand] would be pushed out aggressively.

29. We would then get back on the same minibus. Most mothers would be crying and the guards would yell, "Are you crying for those dogs? For the filth? You are filth too! They are filth and they must be killed! They are dogs." And so it would continue for the entire five-minute ride back to Luna Park. That was the connection they established with us. No one among the families dared utter a word, except for instances where they would inform a family of their loved one's execution, at which point these families would wail, scream, and curse. The old people would not answer back for fear of getting us young ones arrested [and

in trouble]. I personally never responded, because I was afraid I might provoke them and be detained as a result.

30. During my first visit with Reza, I made him understand through signs and gestures that our friends were against my going there. He responded with gestures that there was no danger for me. In any case, those were dangerous moments and circumstances; every visit felt like entering the mouth of a lion. I was not the only one at risk; my arrest would also put all those who were in contact with me at risk. Of course, I did not have any organizational contact with anyone, but I had friends in the movement with whom I still met. I knew many of the activists. Our home was a meeting place. Yet none of that prevented me from going on those visits.

31. We had four visits. Two days after the fourth visit, the Revolutionary Guards came to arrest me. Probably at that time the revolutionary prosecutor's office was still not well organized. Or, I should say that they were at the stage of developing a structure, because had they been after me (which they were), they should have arrested me at the time of my first prison visit.

32. I had been at my mother's home for some time when [colleagues] at the finance ministry where I worked (I was on maternity leave) informed me that agents had gone there looking for me. I was a student and I worked at the same time, but in the final months, that is, from around May 1981, I did not go either to work or to the university. In any case, my colleagues had

been calling my mother from 2 p.m. until sometime past midnight, individually and possibly without telling one another, to save me from impending arrest. I packed my bags and left my mother's house. My baby was my whole life, and I had never imagined being separated from him. I went to [a friend's] home for a short time while trying to find a place. I left that same day. On the evening of the day I left [my mother's], they had gone to the home of Reza's father looking for me. I do not know what they talked about but I know that they did not have my mother's address.

33. My mother lived with one of my nephews who was 14 years old at the time. Before the Revolutionary Guards arrived, my mother had been alerted that they were on their way. She had tried to send my nephew away [because] in those days the elders did whatever they could to protect the young. Although my nephew was very young, my mother, who was a very intelligent woman and had heard that they were arresting activists' family members, feared for his safety. But my nephew did not want to leave my mother alone [and on her own]. Consequently, he stayed until the Revolutionary Guards went there. Three or four Guards had gone there and had asked my mother for my whereabouts. My mother, who was angry about the whole situation, told them, "You're the ones who know where my daughter is, not me." They had not shown her any arrest warrants. My mother asked them, "What has my daughter done that you want to arrest her?" The Revolutionary Guards told her, "She has killed someone," to which my mother replied, "You are the murderers, not my

daughter." My mother kept talking to them, making comments such as, "You are those very same people who until recently used to loiter on street corners teasing young girls. Now you think you are somebody and have turned up here!" They threatened to arrest my mother too. When they gave up hope of finding me, they took my nephew, they took him hostage.

34. I saw my mother the day after this incident. I did not go to her house but met her outside. At the time I had no idea that they had gone to my mother's house looking for me. We had already arranged to meet up earlier. My poor mother, she looked blue in the face. She kept imploring me, "Leave the baby with your mother-in-law and get away. They will kill you if they catch you." She was very frightened, particularly for me. I had no choice other than to leave the country.

35. It took nine months from the day they arrested Reza until the day they came after me. And it took another nine months for me to leave the country. In other words, Sa'id was exactly 18 months old. I left Tehran for Rezaiyeh on 19 April 1983. From there, I had a seven-day journey to Turkey. I stayed in Turkey for two months and left for Europe on 30 June 1983.

Trial

36. My husband, Reza Esmati, was tried three months after his arrest. Apparently, he had initially been sentenced to death for being associated with the anti-revolutionary [elements] (Komala), which sentence was subsequently reduced to twenty years' im-

prisonment. All these years, Reza's letters were ostensibly written to his sister, and she would forward copies to me. In September 1988, when all prisoner visitations had ceased and there were rumors of mass executions, protests were held outside the country. I, along with a number of other political activists and their families, held a one-day sit-in at the Berlin Cathedral, with the support of the city's cardinal.

Execution

37. Even though we had gotten word, here and there, of the execution of prisoners, it was only on 5 December 1988 that Reza's family and I obtained definitive news of his execution.

Berlin, October 2008

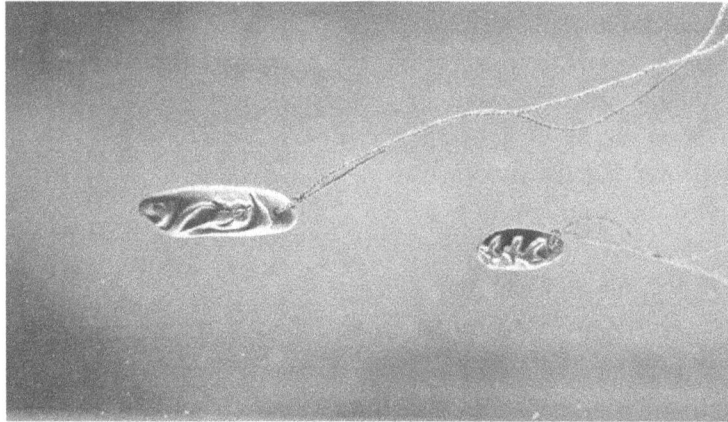

Two pendants offered to Monireh Baradaran by two of her cellmates on the anniversary of her brother's execution. Carved in stone, the one on the left is a flower and the one on the right is three little birds. The latter was given to Baradaran by Ashraf Fada'i, a high school student who was arrested in the summer of 1981 and executed in 1988.

اطّلاعات

Subject:	On confronting the deviant mini-groups and on campaigning against corruption and drug addiction
The official:	Islamic Revolutionary Prosecutor of Tehran, Morteza Eshraqi
The occasion:	Press conference
Date:	13 July 1988
Source:	*Ettela'at*, 13 July 1988

In a news conference, Haj Aqa Morteza Eshraqi, Islamic Revolutionary Prosecutor of Tehran, answered reporters' questions on the recent overhaul of the Islamic Revolutionary Prosecutor's Office and its campaigns against corruption and narcotics, the Val'adiat Project [Qur'anic verse on raiding the enemy; also a code name for an anti-drug operation in Iran] and its plan to increase the punishment for crimes related to procuring, distributing, selling, and transferring narcotics. . . .

On the issue of confronting the mini-groups [banned dissident groups], Tehran's Revolutionary Prosecutor stated that since these individuals are *mohareb* or outlaws, the Islamic Revolutionary Prosecutor's' Office continues its efforts to pursue and investigate their acts, in which regard it has hitherto issued many verdicts. . . .

Banoo Saberi

ARRESTED: July 1986
DETAINED IN: Moshtarak Committee, Tehran, and Evin and Dastgerd Prisons
RELEASED: January 1987

1. My name is Banoo Saberi. My husband, Abbas-Ali Monshi Rudsari, an FKO affiliate, was executed during the mass killings of political prisoners in 1988.

2. I make this statement, based on my interview on 18 October 2009, in support of an investigation into the mass execution of political prisoners in 1988 in Iran.

3. This statement is true to the best of my knowledge and belief. Except where I indicate to the contrary, I make this statement on the basis of facts and matters within my own knowledge. Where the facts and matters in this statement are within my own knowledge, they are true. Where the facts and matters are not within my own knowledge, I have identified the source or sources of my information, and I believe such facts to be true.

Pre-arrest Activities

4. My husband, Abbas-Ali Monshi Rudsari, was born on 3 February 1961 in the village of Bibalan Rahim-Abad in Gilan Province in the north of Iran. He was 28 at the time of his execution and [before his arrest was] a medical student at Esfahan University of Medicine. He was very intelligent. He ranked fifth from Gilan Province on the university entrance exam (the *konkur*). He became politically active during the 1979 Revolution. From the start, he was a member of the Fadaiyan Khalq Organization (Majority) ("FKO") and a member of the central provincial committee of Esfahan. He was engaged in its propaganda/promotional division. His responsibility was to oversee the organization's main publishing efforts. He knew Persian poetry quite well. He told me that he was always drawn to literature. But because his nephew had died of tetanus, he opted for medical school.

5. Before my marriage, I was a member of the Tudeh Party and my husband was with the FKO. From the beginning, the Fadaiyan were not on good terms with the Tudeh Party. Consequently, my husband and I decided that one of us would switch sides. So I agreed to join the Fadaiyan.

6. After the Cultural Revolution they [the authorities] did not hand my husband an "expulsion order" [expulsion from the university], but rather a "contingency order." It meant that you had to talk to them—you might be expelled or you might convince them otherwise. I used to teach at a school in Qadrehjun in Esfahan Province. I was assigned to do administrative work and was not a classroom teacher. After the first wave of arrests of Tudeh Party leaders in 1983, I decided not to return to work. By then, whoever had any doubts about being in danger or felt that he might have been identified had made a personal decision not to go back to work. Two weeks later, I received many letters from the school's human resources office summoning me, but because I had guessed that the intelligence administration of the Ministry of Education was behind it, I did not respond to those letters. Much later, in 1992, I received a letter stating that I had been expelled for being absent without presenting a valid reason.

7. Subsequent to the arrest of, and television interviews conducted with, the leaders of the Party, and the blow to the Party, the lives of many people like us fell apart. We decided simply to leave, forgetting about our living conditions, the university, and everything else. Even following up on such issues could have been risky. There was always the possibility of arrest. But still, there were many who did try it. One of my husband's friends who had been suspended had gone to Tehran to follow up on his suspension but was arrested in one of the random searches that were conducted by the revolutionary committees' agents. He spent many years in prison.

8. We were married on 4 May 1983, and immediately began a clandestine life. Initially, we had planned our wedding for June, but since it coincided with the arrest of the Tudeh Party leaders, we married quickly; I left my job and my husband stopped pursuing his case with the university. We went to stay at a friend's home for a while. Later, we left Esfahan altogether.

9. We went to Tehran because we were active in the Fadaiyan Organization. In Tehran, we had a small house near the Karvansara Sangi, on the Jadeie Karaj (Karaj Road.) We had bought the house under false names. Later, they confiscated the house and never gave it back to us. It was a very small house, but we bought it because it had a basement where we could do our printing and typesetting work without worrying about the noise being heard outside.

10. The organization had assigned us part of the printing responsibilities for a particular region and its towns. But this was not much work. We would send the stencils to various towns and they would publish *Kar*, the FKO (Majority) publication. We had a mimeograph (stencil duplicator) machine and a copy machine, which hardly worked. We did not have the capacity for large printing jobs. At most, we could print 100–200 copies. And this was mainly for small towns or minor outfits that needed about 20 publications each. As for the rest, we would send them just the stencils. I was not personally in touch with other towns but my husband might have been. Usually,

a number of people would come to take the publications, but he himself might have sent some of the publications directly to various towns; I think that was the extent of the contact.

11. Everyone expected us to get arrested. For example, I remember we had just rented a house when the law of landlords and tenants was passed and the landlord evicted us. I remember one day we were passing by a notary public office in Monirieh and my husband said, "Let us go in so that I can give you my consent for divorce and custody of the children. . .because we are in danger at all times, and I do not want you to face difficulties over such issues later on." At the time of our arrest, we had lived together for only three years. We had two children: my daughter was two years and four months old and my son was four months old.

Arrest and Interrogation

12. On 31 July 1986 armed agents came to our house to arrest us. From the window, I saw a few people outside in the yard. We saw two people standing in the corridor. They said they were from the revolutionary committees, or maybe they said they were from the Ministry of Information. I do not really remember that part. I asked, "Why did you not ring the door bell?" to which one replied, "We did, but your laughter was so loud as to prevent you from hearing the door bell." We were talking about the children and laughing. I protested, asking why they were taking us. He replied, "You had

turned your lights on as a way of signalling to the Iraqis."* I understood that he was making fun of me. I went to the smaller room to get dressed. One of them followed me to the room and stood there. I said, "I have to get dressed." He said, "It does not matter. I am standing right here waiting. Get dressed." Since he was standing there, I could only pull my long Islamic cover over the shirt I was wearing, and then put on my socks. He said, "It is not necessary to bring anything for the children, because we do not have much business with you." I had asked if I needed to take anything else along because I suspected they might keep us there a while. But when he said no, I did not take anything, which caused a lot of trouble afterwards. I even left dinner on the stove. My mother said everything went bad because it had been left there for months.

13. They put us into a car escorted by two other cars—one in front and one behind. The car was a Buick. There was a Revolutionary Guard sitting in the front and one in the back seat, next to Abbas and me. I was sitting by the door and Abbas was sitting in the middle. We kept going until we arrived at Lashkar ("Army Division") Crossroads, where they told us to close our eyes and lower our heads. They took us to a place which I learned afterwards was the Joint Committee in Hassanabad Square. We entered through a very large iron gate, which we could hear opening. Then, a very strong light was shined in our eyes. From there, they directed me to a place that was

---

*A reference to the Iran-Iraq War years, when Tehran's city lights were turned off at night to prevent Iraqi bombers from targeting the city.

separated from the structures next to it by plywood and had no door. Instead, its entrance was covered by a curtain.

14. They brought a towel and asked me to wrap it around my head to cover my eyes. I was holding my daughter's hand while holding my son in my arms. Somebody asked what my name was. I gave my false name. Next, he asked what my husband's name was. I also provided his pseudonym. Then he inquired about my husband's level of education. I said high school diploma. It was at that point that he said, "We know your husband has higher education." At that time a man entered the room and asked one of the guards about me, "Who is this woman?" He replied, "She is Abbas's wife." Then he laughed and said, "No, she is Ali's wife." This is because I had said I was Ali's wife. At that point I realized that, most probably, they knew our identities quite well.

15. Right after this exchange, I was asked to remove my blindfold. Somebody took my picture and handed me something like a number and said, "Put this around your neck." He took a picture and put my blindfold back on. Another person took a piece of plastic from the floor, handed me one side of it, and while holding the other side in his hand [so that he would not touch my hand], told me to follow him.

16. The prison conditions were really bad. When I was in the Joint Committee, the ward was packed. There was a fluorescent light in the cell that was always on. We were not able to get fresh air. My children and I were allowed to spend only ten minutes in a cell with a ceiling that was made

Photo courtesy of Banoo Saberi

of horizontal and vertical bars. It was a large, grated, open ceiling [without a roof]. Because it was open, the sun would shine through it. There were no books and, after lunch, they would just turn on the radio, which broadcast religious programs.

17. My son had just been circumcised. He had to be regularly cleaned with alcohol, but I could not do that for him in prison. He developed a severe infection and cried constantly. There were no diapers back then and I did not have enough cloth to change him. I had no choice except to tear my shirt into pieces and use it as changing cloth. When you needed something in prison, you would slip a note with a request under the cell door, but they usually ignored you. Finally after ten days, they came and took my son to the doctor and gave me some medication that I needed. Moreover, there was not much [food], and I had no milk to breastfeed. I would collect the bread that other inmates left in the bathrooms, and moisten it with my own

saliva, and then feed it to my son, which caused him to develop diarrhea.

18. My daughter was constantly anxious as well. She was hungry. The food they provided in the morning consisted of a piece of cheese, the size of a third of a finger, and two or three pieces of lavash bread (a very thin kind of bread), each the size of the palm of a hand. Beginning in the second week, they also provided some tea, which I would save for my son. The main food consisted of squash with a few tomatoes thrown into some sort of a broth. From our cell, because we could hear the sounds of flogging and cries, I had to keep my daughter busy. She heard everything but quickly learned not to ask me any questions. We could count the lashes. Every time she went to see her father, she would be restless upon returning and would keep asking for him. The one lucky thing for me was that there were a bunch of ants and mosquitoes that were tearing up and taking away, piece by piece, a lizard that had died in a corner of the cell. This was my child's entertainment. All night long I would tell her to go look at that scene.

19. Before we were arrested we were often in touch with our families and close relatives. They [the authorities] told my husband to call them [our relatives] because they wanted to give them the impression that everything was normal, and so that they would not find out we were in prison. They wanted to arrest my brother-in-law, and our home phone in Esfahan was tapped. They especially did not want my sister and my brother-in-law, who were living in hiding, to realize that we had been arrested. The first time my husband called

my mother, my sister, who happened to be there, asked him where I was. "Where is Banoo," she repeatedly asked, and he kept saying "Banoo is not here."

20. On another day, they told me to speak to my family on the phone. When I went there, Abbas was there too. They dialed the number, and first gave the phone to Abbas to speak, and then to me. My sister asked, "Where are you? Where are your children?" I said, "I'm here and I left the children with the neighbors." I never used to leave my children anywhere. Since they knew we lived a clandestine life, my sister asked if there was anything I needed that she could bring to me. I said, "I'm not well, my blood sugar level has dropped." When my cousin was arrested two years prior to this, this was how my sister had given me the news, by using this code [that her blood sugar level had dropped]. After this phone call, my sister realized that we had been arrested, and she called everyone from her home phone and informed them of our fate. After that, I was taken to be interrogated and the interrogators were really angry at me for having messed up their plan, as they said. Finally, they arrested my brother-in-law on 24 September in Tabriz.

21. In the first two weeks after our arrest, and after my constant protests, I was allowed to talk to my husband. He talked to me a bit. I talked about one of the interrogators we used to call "Seyyed." He told me, "When he hits you with his finger tips, you cannot breathe anymore!" After that I did not see my husband during the detention until my brother-in-law's arrest. Then I saw him once at the Joint Committee and once in Evin Prison. I will never

forget that meeting. My husband was tall, and he was handsome as well. He had a large build. After the visit, when we were instructed to leave, I stood up and waited, on purpose, so that Abbas could pass in front of me. When he did, [when he was] standing at the top of the stairs, by looking from beneath my blindfold I could see his entire body. I saw him from behind. I felt that he had grown very weak and that his knees could not easily support him. He had grown really frail. I will never forget that scene. I was like that myself, but my frailty was due to constant hunger, since I was breastfeeding and there wasn't much food for me to eat.

22. I do not know much about the conditions of my husband's detention but I heard from his cellmates that he was a strong, high-spirited man who helped others. Abbas's cellmate told me that the inmates were moved around to prevent them from developing strong connections with each other. He remembered Abbas always reading Hafiz's poems aloud and interpreting them. He always talked about literature, so much so that the cellmate thought that he had a degree in literature.

23. In October, after my brother-in-law's arrest, my children were taken from me and were given to my parents. I felt relieved. In November, I was taken to Esfahan with my husband to be interrogated. They had found out that I too had been politically active in Esfahan. They took Abbas with me just because they did not want to take a woman alone, without her being accompanied. They wanted two people. After two weeks, they returned us to the Joint Committee in Tehran. In December I was

transferred to Evin. While they took my fingerprints, I told them that I had not heard from my husband for a long time. They made a few phone calls and said that he had not been brought to Evin. After 17 days, I was transferred to Dastgerd Prison in Esfahan. I was released in January 1987.

Trial and Verdict

24. I did not have a trial but my husband did. I do not know the exact court dates but, in one of the letters that I received from him in February 1987, he had written, "I went to court today, and the verdict was that I would be separated from you for six years."

25. Judgments were issued very quickly. The reason for this was that all those who had been arrested had children, and their families constantly went to inquire why no verdicts had been issued. My husband told me, "There are no standards for issuing these verdicts. They could be for a day, for ten days, or for ten years. Unless they decide to set you free, you are not going to get out." Actually, the manner in which they issued their verdicts caused enmity among some families outside the prison. For example, one person would look at another with disdain and say, "Your husband had greater responsibility than my husband. Why is it that he received a lighter sentence than mine?"

1988 Executions

26. After being released, I would go from Esfahan to Tehran to visit Abbas. It was wartime and there were not many buses running. The last bus leaving Esfahan was the one at six in the evening. I would arrive

Abbas-Ali Monshi Rudsari's letter to his wife, Banoo Saberi, from prison, 29 March 1987: "My sweet Banoo, . . . Life is beautiful in my eyes. . . . I love life, I love the beauties [of life]. . .beautiful [Banoo] you represent life for me. I love you. In you I see the beauty of the ocean and the freshness of the forest. . . . Your Abbas. Evin Prison, Martyr Kachu'i's Education Center, ward 6, room 88."

Left, top to bottom: An envelope addressed to Banoo Saberi in Esfahan; on the inside of the envelope: "Evin Prison—Amuzeshgah ward 6 room 83 Abbas-Ali Monshi Rudsari, son of Farajollah"; on the back of the envelope: "Tehran, Evin Prison" and a "Controlled" stamp around 1 or 2 a.m. but the bus terminal did not open until 5 a.m., the time for morning prayer. So I had to spend all this time outside in the cold. To purchase my return ticket, I would have to go to [a government office called] the Special Unit Bureau (Edareh-e Yegan e Vijeh) to explain why I had come to Tehran and why I needed a ticket [to go back to Esfahan], so that they would issue me a travel permit. Only then would one of the bus companies give me a ticket.

27. I would go to Tehran once every two weeks. Even when they said that visiting rights were temporarily suspended, I would still go. Regardless of what they said, I went there every two weeks, because each time I went I would make a payment for him at the prison. I thought that as long as I was making the payments and they were accepting them, it meant that he was still alive, and they had not executed him. They would give me a receipt. In 1987, Abbas's visitations were suspended for three months. When I asked why, they said that he was among those being punished. Some prisoners had complained and protested [the conditions] and there were about 50 people whose visitation rights had been suspended. Whenever I showed up and said that I wanted to visit my husband, they would say, "No, visits are suspended, as punishment."

28. My husband used to send me letters and poems he wrote. His letters were written on very thin paper. I still have all of Abbas's letters and poems. On the envelopes, someone has written that the letter was "controlled" or "inspected." At the bottom of Abbas's last letter is written: "Ordibehesht

67 (April–May 1988) Education Center Hall, ward 8, room 87." Our last visit took place on 17 July 1988 and he didn't say anything in particular then.

29. You know, Abbas was a very calm person. Moreover, he was very concerned about me. He would not talk to me about the pressures he was experiencing in prison, he would simply say that they were increasing. One time I told him that there was a guard who treated our daughter badly when we were at the prison to visit him. He said he knew what I was talking about and added, "If you only knew what he does to us. . . ."

30. I remember that during our last visit he was wearing a shirt that I had bought him on the occasion of our anniversary in the month of May—a navy blue checked shirt that looked very good on him, because it complemented his light-colored eyes. He was trying to be in a good mood and raise my spirits. He also made a reference to his brother-in-law, saying that his prison term had come to an end. He said, "However you can, put up the bond [in the form of a deed or title to our house] and take him away. Banoo, tell them to follow up on his case. The less he stays here the better." Well, he too was executed in 1988.

31. The next visitation date was on the occasion of Eid Qorban [or Eid al-Adha, the Feast of the Sacrifice, an important Muslim holiday], and they said not to come for visits because they were going to move the prisoners around. [The visits being allowed twice a month,] Abbas's family and I had agreed that I would go once every month, and his family would visit at the end of the following two weeks.

32. On 19 November 1988, my father-in-law and my sister-in-law had gone to see him. They had told him [my father-in-law] to return the following day. But his father insisted and said he could not come back the next day because he had come from up north and had to return the same afternoon. The guard then told him to go to Evin Prison. So they went to Evin. They saw the families of the other prisoners. The families were called in one by one and were each given a bag. The families returned as though they had been crushed. One of those who exited was a mother who was holding up two bags, saying, "These two bags are all that remains of my child." My sister-in-law was the one who retrieved Abbas's bag. Afterwards, I heard from his cellmates that, of the 400 inmates in his ward, that is, ward 6, only 25 survived.

33. That day, I was returning from work. Because Abbas's visiting rights had been suspended, I had taken two of his pictures to be enlarged to put on the wall. The news was delivered to me by neighbors, friends, and my mother. We went to the north of Iran for the memorial the following day. Although my father-in-law had not announced the ceremony because of pressure from the security forces, everyone had found out about it. When I arrived, there was a big crowd. I held my own wake on Abbas's birthday in Tehran, and it was also very crowded [then]. On 1 September 1989, the first anniversary of the 1988 killings, we all went to Khavaran Cemetery. They arrested all of us, took us to various committees, kept us until the evening, and questioned us. Later we found out that they had kept ten people for a while and had then released them.

34. Before my children went to school, I used to go to Khavaran Cemetery once a week or once every two weeks. Every time I went to Khavaran, I also stopped at Evin Prison. The guard would ask what my business was, and I would say that I was there to see why my husband had been executed. He would make me wait while he called here and there. I would be waiting until he would finally say, "We are closed now." I would also go the prison's assistance office (*ta'aminat*).

35. Once when I went to the prison's assistance office, I did not say that my husband had been executed. One of the people in charge asked what I wanted. I said I was there to inquire about my husband. He asked my husband's name, and I said it was Abbas-Ali Monshi Rudsari. When he went to bring his file, another person came over and asked what I was doing there. He told the other man that my case related to those who had been executed. When he heard this, he took the file away. I said, "Why not show me the file you brought?" He said, "No." I said, "At least give me his last will." He said, "Some of them never wrote a will. They crossed out the form we gave them and returned it saying we have no will." I said, "Give me the crossed-out sheet." He said, "We don't have that either; get out of here."

36. The families of the victims had agreed to go to Khavaran the first Friday of every month. The security forces would bother us and ask questions such as, "Why have

you come to the cemetery of the apostates (*mortad*)?" I would reply, "I am here because you say my husband was an apostate, so you must have brought him here." He would say that he was not there. I would say, "Tell me where he is then, so that I may go there." But they never gave us an answer. Covert agents took our pictures too but ultimately no one cared. We went to the prison's assistance office (*ta'aminat*), to the joint committee's headquarters, and to the Ministry of Justice so many times. We went everywhere. We went to the State General Inspection Headquarters and had a sit-in and asked that someone meet with us. We gathered a petition, and still nobody gave us an answer. The truth was that every family went there. I think one of the things that gave Khavaran its importance was the relentless resolve of the families of the 1988 massacre.

37. The year [UN Special Representative on the situation of human rights in Iran, Reynaldo] Galindo Pohl came to Iran [January 1990], they [the authorities] had hung a very large banner from a hotel near Argentina Square (a public square in Tehran) on which they had written, "We are the families of those who were executed. Because our children committed acts of terrorism, we have no grievances against those who executed them." We had gathered in Argentina Square when a number of people arrived on minibuses, attacked us, and took many of the women's handbags. People said that a box that was placed there and announced by UN officials to be used as a depository for public grievances was compromised. Many people complained. The following day, those who had deposited complaint letters in the box were summoned, and photocopies of their letters were placed in front of them. I do not know if any of our letters ever reached Galindo Pohl. No one was able to meet him.

38. The government did not allow us to go to Khavaran. They would prevent you from going, especially if you were young, but it was easier for my mother to get around because she was older and would not raise their suspicion. The land in Khavaran had been sectioned off with cords to make it look like they were cultivating something there. All the signs that people had placed there to enable them to identify the location of the graves had been destroyed.

39. After being released, I used to be summoned for different reasons. Our telephone was always bugged. I could not let Khavaran go; that was why I stayed in Iran. But in my last summons they asked me to bring my son as well. He was only 11. I took my daughter too. In this session, they asked me some very private and insulting questions. They also asked me to contact my other brother-in-law, who was in Germany and was politically active. They wanted me to introduce, as my friend, someone [a regime agent] to his group in order for them infiltrate the group. Because they had wanted me to bring my son with me, I regarded it as a threat. That was why, three days later, I escaped Iran.

Georgia, October 2009

OFFICIAL STATEMENT • 19

اطّلاعات

Subject: Courts to act with greater resolve in confronting *mohareb* and drug traffickers
The official: Member and spokesperson of the Supreme Judicial Council, Morteza Moqtada'i
The occasion: Press conference on the latest session of the Supreme Judicial Council
Date: 1 September 1988
Source: *Ettela'at*, 1 September 1988

Mr. Moqtada'i briefed the press on the Supreme Judicial Council's latest session: "Addressing the first session of the Supreme Judicial Council after a one-month recess, Ayatollah Musavi Ardebili, the head of the Supreme Judicial Council, highlighted the belief in the [Rule of the] Guardianship of the Supreme Religious Jurist [Velayat-e Faqih], which is the basis of the Islamic Republic of Iran's political system, and stressed the need to obey the Supreme Leader and Jurist [Khomeini], and accept the United Nations Security Council Resolution 598. Moreover, on behalf of the Supreme Judicial Council, he called on the dear, heroic, and revolutionary nation of Iran to remain prepared and the fronts to remain fully supplied [with soldiers]. And he called on the dear and brave combatants to be alert and vigilant so as to maintain their superiority and power on the fronts, because as Imam [Khomeini] has said, our enemies are the enemies of Islam. Thanks to the steadfastness and endurance of the divine system of the Islamic Republic of Iran, their [the enemies'] image of arrogance has been shattered and their fake respectable façade

is undone, even as they continuously strive to destroy or weaken the Islamic Republic. In particular, our criminal enemy Saddam, whom we know well as someone who does not honor his pledges or international regulations, is now feeling wounded. Therefore, our people should understand that our acceptance of the resolution does not signify an end to the war and its resultant problems. People must continue to remain vigilant. . . ."

During the remainder of the session, the Supreme Judicial Council called on all the Revolutionary Courts and Prosecution Offices to act with the utmost determination in confronting apostate and *mohareb* mini-groups, as though they were "strictly confronting heathens" [Qur'an: Surat Al-Fath (Verse 29)]. These groups have proven their opposition to and animosity toward Islam and the brave and martyr-nurturing people of Iran. . . . They have also demonstrated their all-embracing cooperation with Global Arrogance [the United States] and the enemies of the Islamic Republic through military attacks and/or spying for foreigners.

Fariba Sabet

ARRESTED: May 1983
DETAINED IN: Evin, Adelabad, and Qezel Hesar Prisons
RELEASED: January 1990

1. My name is Fariba Sabet and I am an Iranian refugee living in Paris. I am from Shiraz, Iran. I was a political prisoner held in Evin, Shiraz, and Qezel Hesar Prisons between 1984 and 1990. In Shiraz, I was a cellmate of Fatemeh Zare'i [a sympathizer of the Mojahedin who was executed in 1988—see the statements of her husband, father, and daughter below].

2. I make this statement in support of an investigation into the mass execution of political prisoners in 1988 in Iran.

3. This statement is true to the best of my knowledge and belief. Except where I indicate to the contrary, I make this statement on the basis of facts and matters within my own knowledge. Where the facts and matters in this statement are within my own

knowledge, they are true. Where the facts and matters are not within my own knowledge, I have identified the source or sources of my information, and I believe such facts to be true.

Arrest and Detention

4. I am originally from Shiraz. I was in my final year, studying agricultural engineering at the University of Shiraz, when the Cultural Revolution took place. I had completed all of the degree requirements except for my final thesis. I was not able to complete my degree because of the Cultural Revolution.

5. At the time of my arrest, I was 26 years old and was married and had a ten-month-old daughter. I was arrested in May 1983. I do not know why I was arrested. The Revolutionary Guards arrested anyone who did not agree with the policies of the Islamic Republic. It was nothing new. I was arrested while visiting a friend's house. My daughter was with me and they would not let me give her to my family. We were both taken directly to Evin Prison.

6. I was taken to ward 209 of Evin Prison. The guards took my daughter from me and took me to the interrogation room. The house in which I was arrested had been

identified as a site of political activity so they wanted to know who I was and what I was doing there and whether I had any political affiliation. Since they could not identify me, they flogged me on a regular basis to force me to confess my identity. During the first days of my interrogation I was severely tortured. They gave me a terrible beating with electric cables. It was so bad that I began bleeding heavily. But as the interrogations progressed the violence subsided.

7. A group of prisoners who had repented had joined the interrogation team. Based on the detainee's confessions, they would draw hierarchical charts and diagrams of the organization and try to figure out the prisoner's position or rank in the organization. I was interrogated by a group of people, including some prisoners who had repented and who were experts on leftist organizations. We were always blindfolded during interrogations, but we could tell that it was repenters who were collaborating with the guards because of the way they spoke and what they knew. I remember one former leftist and repenter in particular—he had spent some time in the United States and could use computer profiling to help the interrogators to determine what people looked like and he could use statistics to draw charts. He was very useful to them. But I heard that he was nevertheless executed in 1988 during the killings.

8. Despite the pressure, I did not give them my real name. I was scared for my husband, who had also been involved in political activities. For the Revolutionary Guards, the first week or so was the most

important. It was in the first week or two that they were the most vicious. In most of the interrogations they tried to exhaust the prisoner; for instance they would take my child away from me during the day and would take me to the interrogation room where I could hear the screaming and moaning of prisoners who were being tortured. I was blindfolded during the interrogations. They wanted to break political prisoners in that first week because they knew the political groups were organized so that if a member did not make contact for over a week, he was assumed to have been arrested, and all subsequent meetings that that person had been involved in organizing would be cancelled. Because of this precaution, if they wanted to catch other political activists, they had to get information from prisoners in the first week or so. After a week or two had passed, the guards knew the window of opportunity for additional arrests had passed.

9. In total, they interrogated me for over a year and a half. I was held in solitary confinement in ward 209 of Evin for the first three or four months. They let me keep my daughter with me in the cell. I could not give my daughter to my family because that would mean revealing my identity and putting my husband at risk of arrest. My daughter became ill and suffered a lot.

10. Finally, they took me to the ward with the other political prisoners. One of the prisoners in that ward—a repenter—was an old friend of mine. She recognized me immediately and told the guards my real name and my husband's name. She did not know anything about my political activities or why I was there, but she was able to give

the guards my real name. I was taken immediately to solitary confinement for more interrogation. They asked me angrily as to why I had not given them my real name. I replied, "I was scared you would arrest my husband." But fortunately they still did not know much about me. I was kept for about two more weeks in solitary confinement.

Trial

11. I was taken to court for the first time about 18 months after being arrested. I was blindfolded and taken before a religious judge. He did not introduce himself or give his name, but I believed it was Mobasheri, and this was confirmed by the others in the ward. It sounded as though there was another person in the room, but I could not see from under the blindfold. I was never offered the opportunity to have legal representation, nor was I provided advance notice of my hearing.

12. The religious judge then read the indictment and gave me a very brief opportunity to respond. The hearing lasted no longer than five or ten minutes and went as follows:

    Judge: You lied to us and so you prevented us from catching your husband who is an anti-revolutionary. You are a member of the Rah-e Kargar [the Workers Party] political organization. Do you accept these charges?

    No, I do not accept them. I used to be a member of that group but I was not a member at the time you arrested me.

    Judge: In your interrogation paper you said that if you are lying to us you should be executed. How do you respond?

13. At this point he got very upset at me. He threw his stapler at me and shouted, "You are apostates!" He then continued, "Anyone who has Muslim parents has no right to be a leftist."

14. After two or three months, a representative from the prosecutor's office came and took me from the ward into another room to advise me of my sentence. I had been sentenced to ten years in prison. But the prosecutor's representative told me that I could be re-tried at any time. So this was not a definitive sentence. The prosecutor's representative told me to sign the sentence. I wrote, "I don't accept this sentence because I didn't do anything."

Prison Conditions

15. In the ward, my daughter would run around and play. But she was frightened by what was outside the ward. As soon as she would reach the ward's barred door, she would become silent and go back inside the ward. She was certainly affected by the atmosphere in the ward and the behavior of the other female prisoners. For example, one day Moqtada'i came to the ward [Moqtada'i was a member of the Supreme Judicial Council]. The prisoners were running to find chadors to cover themselves. My daughter was scared, and she took a blanket and put it on her head.

16. The conditions in the ward were hard. The ward was L-shaped. Most of the doors were open so the prisoners could circulate. There were three rooms in which we could move around. Each room was 36 square meters [118 sq.ft.], but in each of those

rooms there were 60 or 70 people. When I was there, there were three or four children in each room with their mothers. It was so cramped that we had to take turns sleeping because there was not enough room for all of us to lie down. Even then, we could not sleep on our backs, only on our sides, and our legs could not be straight. We had to give the children in the ward more room. We were worried that we would roll onto them or bump them in the night.

17. We did have time outside, but only if we were not being punished. If we were not being punished, we were allowed outside for two hours a day in an internal courtyard that was in the open air but was surrounded by buildings. When we were being punished, only the women with children were allowed outside to wash the children's clothes and let them dry—the guards were watching us all the time.

18. There were 22 children in the ward at that time. Their ages ranged from newborn to five years old. I do not know why the children were not allowed to go and live with the families of the prisoners. The children quickly became very articulate for their age because they were speaking to many adults every day. Every morning the children would be awakened by the call to prayer. My daughter could recite the prayers. She had learned them by heart because she heard them all the time. One of the children's problems related to the fact that they had no idea of the outside world; they could not make sense of the duality of the carceral world they lived in and the world they saw on television. For example, there was a garbage bin in the ward that had a cow drawn on it that the prisoners, as a joke, called "the cow." When my daughter saw a real cow on television, she asked me what it was. I told her that it was a cow. But she did not understand. She ran over to the garbage bin and said, "If that [cow on television] is a cow, what is this (garbage bin) then?"

19. [In Iran children call the women they know and who are close to them "aunt," even if they are not related]. Because my daughter had known only the women in the prison she called everyone "aunt." But she had never known any men other than the guards. She even called the guards "aunt" because that was all she knew. She had never known any other men.

20. As she grew older she became more nervous. For instance, when I was taken away for interrogation, she would beat me and tell me, "You must not go." She knew there was another world outside. She had seen minibuses in the streets on the television and she would ask me, "Why can't we go and catch one of the minibuses like the other people and go away from here?"

21. One day a woman came back to the ward severely wounded. She looked terrible; her feet had open wounds and she was very weak and bent over. My daughter came running to me asking for a bottle of milk. As soon as she got it, she ran over to the woman who had been flogged and shoved the bottle in the woman's mouth. Then she said we must take this prisoner out of the prison by minibus.

22. One night my daughter became so sick that we really thought that she would not

survive the night. We kept calling and pleading with the guards to come, but they did not come until the morning. In the morning, the women of the ward tossed her in the room of the Revolutionary Guards and said, "We can do nothing more, you look after her now!" The guards finally took her to the prison infirmary. She was kept there, breathing with an oxygen mask, for three or four days. She was given so many drugs and injections that she could not walk for days. They had had difficulty finding a vein in her arm. After a week, I requested permission to give my daughter to my family.

23. At about the same time, some foreign journalists had visited Evin and had asked why there were so many children inside the prison. Lajevardi said, "to allow children to stay with their mothers in prison is a sign of Islamic kindness so that the children wouldn't be separated from their mothers." I think this was broadcast abroad in France in late August or September 1984, and people [around the world] saw the children in prison. Soon afterwards an order was issued directing us to turn the children over to our families.

24. My daughter, who was then two years old, was given to my husband's family—a family that she had never known and had never seen before because most of them lived in provinces and were not allowed to visit me in prison. My daughter was happy. She was so happy to finally leave the prison that she took her things and said, "Bye, I'll send you pictures." But later my mother-in-law told me that she had cried a lot when she left and for a while she still called

everyone "aunt." At first she would not come to visit me in prison because she was afraid of the prison and the guards. It was a full year after she left the prison that she came to visit me for the first time.

25. It was very difficult to let my daughter go but I was very happy that she was leaving the terrible prison environment; it was no place for a child. I was very concerned that the guards would not give her to my husband's family. I thought that they might have lied and instead given her to an orphanage. It was not until two months later that I received a photo of my daughter with my husband's family that I knew that she was safe.

26. We were provided with only three bathrooms for all of the prisoners in the ward. There was warm water only two nights a week. Bathing time was from 7 p.m. to 6 a.m. the following morning. During the time we had the warm water it was impossible for everyone in the ward to wash. They were able to wash only once a week. Wounded prisoners and mothers with children had ten minutes to wash, while other prisoners were given six to seven minutes.

27. There was always a line at the toilet. When everyone in the ward came down with food poisoning, it was just terrible. People had to use the bathrooms. There was no way that all those sick people could cope with just three toilets. It was hard enough when we were well.

28. If we were very sick, we had access to the infirmary. If the tortured prisoner had only a swollen foot, the healing would be fast. The electrical cable used for flogging had

metal in it and the strokes were so strong that the skin on the soles of the feet was cut open. For those who had open wounds as a result of torture, it would take more than a year to recover from the wound and the ensuing infection. Even worse, some women were flogged so badly that there was no skin at all left on the bottom of their feet. Some women had to have the doctors graft skin to the bottom of their feet from, for example, their thighs or their back.

29. In Evin Prison, steadfast prisoners had been segregated from other prisoners. However, for a while the MKO steadfast prisoners were allowed to choose not to stay with us [leftist/non-Muslim prisoners]. In 1983 and again in 1984, I was sent to Qezel Hesar Prison for a while.

30. In the winter of 1986 I was transferred to Shiraz's Adelabad Prison. I had been politically active while I was a student at the University of Shiraz, and they wanted to complete the hierarchical chart of student activists in Shiraz. I was interrogated again about the students and what was happening at Shiraz University—who was who. Shiraz Prison was reputed to be very tough. I think they moved me there to scare me about how bad it could be. It was really, really bad.

31. The section I was held in had two rooms. I was told that I was prohibited from talking—I did not know what that meant. Later I understood that it meant I was not allowed to say a word and no one was allowed to talk to me. I asked someone for the time and the person did not respond.

I was held like that for a month. Every day I was interrogated. There it was the opposite—the interrogator had a mask on, but we did not wear a blindfold. You were sitting down and he was sitting somewhere higher up. The questions were mostly related to the time I was a student in Shiraz. The last day, my interrogator took his mask off and said, "Now do you recognize me?" It was one of my classmates from the university, so he knew that everything I said was a lie; he even knew all my relatives. Each interrogation session lasted two to three hours, and it was always with the same interrogator, my former classmate.

32. What was very sad was that a lot of my friends from the University of Shiraz were in other rooms, and almost all of them had become repenters. What I heard is that these repenters had been beaten so much that they had broken. If they [the prisoners] had said to them [the guards] that they are repenting, then they [the prisoners] were forced to beat other prisoners so that they would be broken forever. Another method [of breaking a prisoner] consisted of putting the prisoner under such physical and psychological pressure that she would try to commit suicide. At this point they [the guards] would intervene and save her, only to tell her, "God saved your life." In such an atmosphere, many would break.

33. I never heard of women being raped in Shiraz [Adelabad] Prison. But in Tehran there were many cases of rape. There was a young woman in our ward who was 18 or 19 years old. She had been raped while she was kept in solitary confinement. She had reported the rape to her relatives during a visit, and the guards had retaliated by

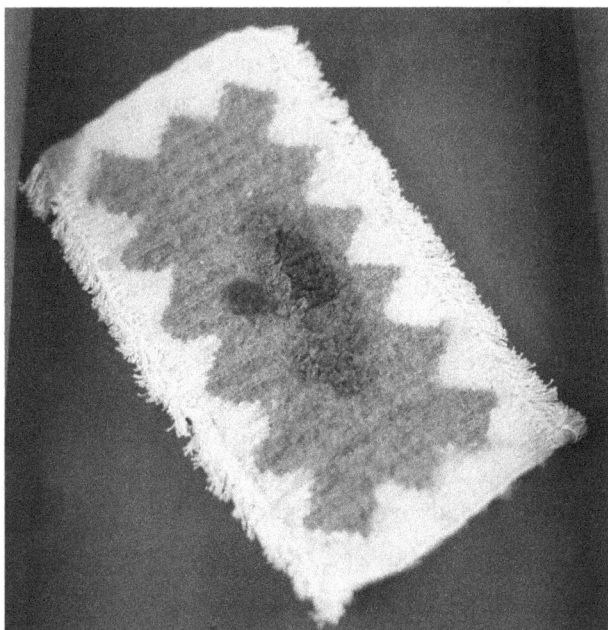

This kilim (11 x 18 cm. [4 x 7"]) was woven in the summer of 1988 in the women's ward (ward 3) of Evin Prison. One of the prisoners had the idea of using the horizontal parts of a three-tier bunk bed as a loom, and used it to weave this kilim.

trying to kill her by pushing her down the stairs.

34. In Shiraz I was a cellmate with Fatemeh Zare'i, but it was when I was not allowed to speak. Fatemeh was also prohibited from speaking. We did not have the right to speak to each other. She used to spend her time praying. [Fatemeh Zare'i, who expected to be released in the summer of 1988, was killed during the prison massacre of the summer of 1988.]

35. In Shiraz's Adelabad Prison, there were two toilets for 40 people. Except for me, everyone else was either a Mojahedin sympathizer or a repenter. I was a leftist and thus considered to be "'unclean'" and so could not use the same toilet as the Mojahedins or the repenters. Therefore there was one toilet for me alone while the other 39 people had to use the other toilet. On the door of toilet stall number 2 the word "Special" was written. My slippers were also separated from other inmates' slippers. And my dishes were kept in a plastic bag separate from other dishes.

36. My interrogation in Shiraz was completed, and I was supposed to be sent back to Tehran. But I made the mistake of saying that I was not a prisoner of Shiraz, and to teach me a lesson the prison warden decided to keep me one more month, sending me to an open ward of prisoners. [In an "open" ward, the inmates could see and talk to inmates from other wards.]

37. In the open ward, praying was mandatory and I was not praying. One of my cellmates was a very young woman. She told me, "If you don't pray here you will be beaten by the prisoners [repenters]." She said, "If they ask you, 'Are you praying?' you don't say anything. I will tell them you have just prayed or you cannot pray [an allusion to women's menstruation that dispenses them from praying]." This young prisoner taught me how to behave to avoid being harassed. She told me that if I did not follow her advice, I would not be allowed to use the shower and I would be attacked and beaten during the night once the light was off.

38. One night at 9 p.m. when the lights were turned off, I heard a very loud noise in the hallway. Some of the die-hard repenters were accusing some of the prisoners of being "'fake'" repenters and were beating them badly; three or four people were seriously beaten and one had teeth broken. Later one of my cellmates told me, "I am afraid you will be the next victim." I was so scared that I hid under my blanket. The following day, it was forbidden to speak about what had happened during the night. This was in the spring of 1986. This was in the public, open ward in Shiraz.

39. I was told that to torment political prisoners they [the guards] would, for example, bring into their ward a common criminal convicted of theft and sentenced to having a hand amputated. They would then force the political prisoners to watch them carry out the amputation on the convict. But I myself did not see this.

40. The atmosphere was more intense than it had been in Evin where, in the beginning, they tried to force us to pray, but then later on they would leave us alone. In Shiraz they would keep broadcasting prayers through a loudspeaker. At first glance, I thought everyone had repented. But then I realized that in fact a lot of people had not repented deep inside, they were just trying to protect themselves by faking repentance and allegiance to Islam. They were still loyal to their political organizations. Many had repented just to protect themselves. Some of the prisoners were praying to avoid being tortured. In our ward there were women from 16 to 70 years old.

41. I was taken back to Evin, ward 325, in the spring of 1987. I was kept there for three months. It was like a two-story apartment building from the time of the Shah, with individual rooms and a very nice garden; there were trees and the doors were open from 6 a.m. until midnight—even [the doors] to the garden. We were locked in the building only at night. My interrogations were completed.

42. However, they had put a crazy person in with us. She was in very bad shape. She could not hold herself—she would pee on herself and we had to wash her clothes and her blankets. We also had to watch her because she would beat others, and so every night someone had to stay awake and make sure she did not attack anyone. They took care of her only when her mental health deteriorated so much that the prisoners went on a hunger strike to have her taken

to the hospital. I think she was transferred to an asylum.

43. I was kept in ward 325 for three months. By the end of September 1987 I was transferred to the Amuzeshgah section of Evin Prison. For two days, the doors were closed in this section. They opened the doors after two days. There were nine rooms in this section and 30 inmates were allocated to each room. We were on the third floor. The prison guards would leave the food on the first floor and tell us to come and pick it up ourselves. But the pot was too heavy and we could not carry it to the third floor. We went on strike in protest but to no avail. We were starving, and we finally managed to take the food upstairs by ourselves. Two days later the guards brought the food to us upstairs.

44. Our only link to the outside world was a television that was located at the end of the Amuzeshgah section.

Events Surrounding 1988

45. In early April 1988 we were again interrogated. They came from the Ministry of Information to question us. There was a separate building [within the prison] allocated to the Ministry of Information—they took us there. Zamani was the interrogator. He liked to behave as an intellectual, as if he wished to debate with us. It was Zamani or his assistant, I do not remember. They would say, "Speak your mind, the Islamic Republic is a democracy." Then they would ask, "What do you think about the Islamic Republic? Do you still believe in the organization you were affiliated with?" Most of the questions were political. They inquired about the prisoner's opinions: "What do you think about current events? What do you think about the war?" We thought these questions were related to the amnesty. My fellow detainees would say they did not believe in the Islamic Republic. I said, "I have been away from my organization for a long time. I have no idea what their ideas are now; therefore I have no opinion about them." The interrogator would then ask me, "You do not have any opinion or you do not wish to talk about it? It is not the same." I responded, "I have no opinion." I had never been interrogated by agents of the Ministry of Information before 1988. In fact, with these questions, they wanted to see if I was still a steadfast prisoner. They never pardoned me. After this nothing noticeable happened. They took me once to the room [allocated to the Ministry of Information], and they came once to our ward and they said, "All inmates must say what their profession was before being arrested. Were you [university] students, teachers, physicians, high-school students?" The second time, they were guards [questioning us]—we did not know if they were questioning on behalf of the Ministry of Information or on behalf of the prosecutor's office. Both questionings happened in the spring of 1988.

46. An inmate, my best friend, Goli Abkenari, committed suicide, and I was interrogated about her suicide and realized that the interrogators were from the Ministry of Information. They had no sympathy for my friend; they were only curious. Goli drank cleaning fluid to kill herself, and all her

digestive organs, including her mouth, had been burned. She could not breathe. Afterwards, to enable her to breathe, she was subjected to a tracheotomy and she lost her voice. [She subsequently died in prison.]

47. There was a loudspeaker that broadcast radio news in the ward. It was 25 or 26 July 1988, and from the loudspeaker we heard that the government had accepted the UN resolution. The same day, in the afternoon, female guards joined by male guards came to the ward and took the television with them—female guards were never left alone in the ward. We were in a separate building. On the ground floor, where the ward's doors were closed, were prisoners who had completed their sentences, but were kept in prison because they had refused to sign a loyalty oath [to the Islamic Republic]. The repenters were kept on the second floor, and we were on the third floor. It was an isolated building.

48. The same day or a day later, they confiscated all our books and newspapers. We used to receive newspapers every three days. There was no more newspaper delivery, and visitations were suspended. I rarely had family visits because I was from Shiraz and my family had to come from a distant city. I think my last visit was before the second half of July.

49. After this, the guards came to our ward and called and took with them four of the MKO members who had received heavy sentences. It was a horrible atmosphere. Everyone was upset. It seems to me that the MKO prisoners had a premonition that they were going to be executed, because they made their farewells with all of us.

50. That night one of these four came back to the ward and talked to her own people and from them we heard that this woman had said, "They are now killing everyone." After a while, the guards came back and took her again. Perhaps they brought her back to the ward so that she could let the others know what was happening.

51. From the next day to approximately the last week of August, they came every day and would call the names of the MKO prisoners from a list that they were consulting. And they would take these prisoners with them. Then at night we would first hear voices chanting, "Allaho Akbar [God is great]" and "death to the *monafeqin*," and then we would hear shooting. I think they took 70 MKO prisoners, or perhaps there were 70 of us all together. I do not remember precisely. But they would call them every day; they would not take them all together. So the remaining prisoners would come and stand by the hallway and say goodbye to them. They would take their belongings with them. Then there was only one MKO prisoner left. She was very upset and wished they would also call her name. Her name was Mahin. The day they called her, her eyes twinkled. She said goodbye to everyone, she cried, and she left. She was called alone. Prisoners would leave never to return. We could hear the shooting every night.

52. We did not know what to do—we just walked around the ward and during the night told each other stories, trying to distract each other. We had all packed the bags to give to our families—we even discussed packing smaller bags of belong-

ings because if the bags were too big they might not give them to our families. One would say, "I am putting this thing in my bag so that my family will see it;" another would say, "I am putting this in my bag for my daughter to see it." We lived in these conditions for two months.

53. When all the MKO prisoners had left, the guards started to call the leftists. For the MKO they took them away and asked them to bring their bags, but for the leftists they did not ask them to pack. Once the leftists were taken away, they [the guards] would come back later and ask the remaining prisoners to pack the belongings of those who had been called. They first started with the Tudeh and FKO people. Some of those came back to the ward and said they had been asked several questions—I do not know who was asking, the prosecutor or the Ministry of Information—"Do you believe in the IRI [the Islamic Republic of Iran]? Do you pray? Are you willing to repent or not?" And then they would say, "If you don't pray you will be flogged every day." Right away they would issue a sentence of flogging five times a day, each time with five lashes. This punishment would go on until the prisoners agreed to pray. They explained that female apostates were not to be killed but would be beaten until they would pray, whereas male apostates were to be killed, and we were aware of this rule.

54. But those who were returned to the ward were again taken away. They also started to take the *mellikesh* from the lower floor. We would try to communicate secretly with those prisoners downstairs. We would write

notes and send them to the people below with a thread, and they would respond and send back the note attached to the same thread. We had pen and paper at the time. There were windows from which we would send the notes. We would first alert them with Morse code. We had our [audible] code and also used light to send Morse messages. We would specify the time for communication, and we would send the thread down. Each day they would take a new group of people for questioning. They had started with the more moderate [and moved] to the more radical leftist members.

55. In the morning before the call to prayer, they would open the door and would beat the prisoners one by one in the hallway so everyone could hear. They had hardly returned to their rooms when the time for the noon prayer came, and they were beaten again. They would beat them five times a day. In the first few days it was not that bad. But then [because the skin is already swollen], it is nerve-wracking because you feel like it is never going to end. When it finishes you are just waiting for the next time, you cannot do anything else. But if a woman had her period they would let her alone [because prayers are not allowed when one's body is soiled with blood]. Someone had tried to commit suicide and we later heard that Sorur had committed suicide the very first night using her chador. I do not remember her last name. The continued flogging had resulted in someone giving up: "Ok, I will pray." This person was returned to the ward downstairs. Other inmates had communicated with her and she had told them, "It seems

that they are killing the MKO members every night." She had heard something or she had read the names and the dates on the walls written by those who were in her cell before her—meaning such person was executed on such and such a date.

56. They took three groups from our ward. Some were only interrogated. All the Tudeh and FKO members were already finished with the interrogation. Those taken from our section had gone on a hunger strike in protest. They had started to beat them in retaliation. As a result they all had "agreed to pray" except for two people who had endured 22 days of flogging while on a hunger strike. They had lost consciousness in their cells. They did not remember what happened; they opened their eyes and realized they were in the prison infirmary.

57. As far as I remember, the people who agreed to pray were not brought back immediately. They would come back gradually. After that they did not take anyone else. The two prisoners on the hunger strike were kept in the infirmary for a few days. They were brought back to the ward along with the remaining prisoners. They were in very bad shape. They were very weak, they had lost a lot of weight, they were very tense and nervous, and their bodies were covered in lesions. One of them remembered that she had tried to commit suicide but was too weak to do so. During the first few days they could not even concentrate enough to talk—they were too disoriented; they could not remember anything. All they could think about and focus on was that they would not say, "I want to pray." One of them now lives in Germany and the other is in Iran.

58. By late September, they [prison authorities] allowed us to contact our families and let them know they could come to visit us. Until that time we had no idea of the scope of the killings of political prisoners. Some of the victims' relatives were informed of the executions of their loved ones over the phone, and the phone call would end abruptly. Some of the relatives were asked to persuade their detained relatives to repent to avoid being executed. After the phone calls to our relatives, they brought the television and the newspapers back to the ward.

59. On the first day of visitation, the first group of prisoners who had visitors came back in tears. They had just learned that all the other prisoners had been executed. The families had told them they had come to the prison time and again to see them but they were not allowed in. One day they were told to separate into two lines. One line was much longer than the other. This [longer] line was for the relatives of the executed prisoners who were summoned to take their loved ones' bags. That night [after the first visitation], we realized that all those taken away from our ward had been executed. These were people sentenced to five to ten years of imprisonment, some of whom had already finished their sentences. Some of them were people whose husbands had been executed earlier and so their children were left with no one.

60. During the second visitation after the killings, my daughter came to visit with my mother-in-law. My daughter was not [technically] allowed to come in, but she lied and said she was only six so she was able to

see me. During the visit my daughter told me, "You should do whatever they want so they don't kill you. Grandmother told me we should pray so they wouldn't kill you. So I put my chador on and I prayed a lot so they won't kill you." Then she asked me what we did after all the executions—did we cry? I told her I will tell her when she grows up. She also told me, "They have told my grandfather that you are in prison because you don't love me. But I know you love me."

61. Some families were exhorting their children to repent, to avoid execution and come out. But my in-laws never said anything. They told me I should do what I considered to be right.

62. I was held for two more years after the killings. They would give prisoners leave from prison, but they would not release us because we refused to repent. They kept asking if we agreed to repent. Only 70 of us were left. So they took us to another place with two rooms, and the doors were closed.

63. After a while another group was released; 30 of us were left in prison. Then, to annoy us, they brought ordinary [non-political] prisoners and put them in our rooms with us. We thought that by doing so they wanted to say that there are no longer any political prisoners in Iran; and they wanted to kill us as well. So we went on a hunger strike. Some of our fellow political prisoners thought that we might offend the ordinary prisoners, who would not understand the meaning of our hunger strike or our protest. Some would say that we should clearly explain to them why we are going

on a hunger strike. Some of us [not all] went on a hunger strike.

64. We were together with those ordinary prisoners for a month. This cohabitation had a profound effect on me. Some of them had been arrested for writing bad checks; one had had a fight with her husband; another had murdered someone. There were some inmates with small children. There were also young women there who had had relationships outside of wedlock or women who were married and had had adulterous relationships and who were awaiting stoning—to be stoned to death.

65. The daughter of one of the ordinary prisoners behaved like my daughter. She would become very agitated, and her mother would beat her. This really saddened me. This baby was very pretty; her name was Neda. We [political prisoners] loved the kids and would make clothes for them. The prison guards would drive a wedge between ordinary prisoners and political prisoners. They would encourage the ordinary prisoners to harass us. Cohabiting with them had completely disrupted our life in prison. They would not respect any hygienic rules in the toilets and bathrooms. So we decided to separate our bathroom from theirs. In response they made a point of using our facilities. At night when we were asleep they would use our toilets and our bathroom. Sometimes they would chant slogans against us, such as, "death to Communists" and "death to the *monafeqin.*"

66. One of the ordinary prisoners in our ward was pregnant. She kept crying and saying,

"What am I to do with this child? I am a wretched woman and I don't want this child to have a similar fate." One day [after the young woman gave birth to a little girl] the head of the prison and the guards ran into the ward and closed all the doors. And then we did not see anything but we heard something fall very heavily. After a short while they reopened the doors. When the ordinary prisoners brought us food, they told us that the mother of this pretty newborn baby had taken her to the bathroom to bathe her but was hitting her head on the bathroom floor to kill her. I believe she wanted to kill her out of love because she kept saying, "My life is so miserable; I don't want her to end up like me." She then had tried to kill herself by throwing herself from the stairs. Both her legs were broken, and the mother and the child were transferred to the infirmary. One of our cellmates was an MKO prisoner who was a repenter and had not been executed. All her relatives—her husband, her four brothers, and her sister—had been executed. She agreed to take care of the child and became her surrogate mother. I think she named the baby Shaqayeq (Poppy). She took care of the baby until the day she was released. At the time of her release, she asked permission to adopt the child. They did not authorize her to do so and said, "You need to ask permission from the religious judge." She had begged them, "I love this child. You will send her to an orphanage. Why don't you let me take her with me?" But the religious judge had told her, "Since you are a *monafeq* you may not be entrusted with this child."

67. I was kept in detention until 1990. I had spent seven years in jail. In the last few months I was in solitary confinement. Most of the releases would happen in the following fashion: they would give leave to the prisoner and if after the end of the leave the prisoner did not show up, they would not go after her. A great number of the prisoners were never legally released; they were always worried they would be arrested again.

Paris, June 2009

OFFICIAL STATEMENT • 20

اطّلاعات

Subject: The danger from the hypocrites has not been completely removed
The official: Deputy Intelligence and National Security Minister Ali Fallahian
The occasion: Friday Prayer ceremony in Rudbar-e Qasran and Lavassanat
Date: 23 September 1988
Source: *Ettela'at*, 26 September 1988

During this week's Friday Prayer ceremony in Rudbar-e Qasran and Lavassanat, the Deputy Intelligence Minister announced: "...While describing the types of treason the hypocrites [reference to the Mojahedin Khalq Organization] have been engaged in, Hojjat ol-eslam Fallahian, the Deputy Intelligence Minister [under Mohammad Reyshahri], said, if we remain quiet, the Arrogance [reference to western powers, in particular the U.S.] will try to dominate us. Therefore, we must try not to allow foreigners to rule over us." He added, "The hypocrites have now aligned themselves with the two superpowers of East and West, and when Iran reestablished relations with France, they left France and obtained asylum in Iraq. [There,] during the war that Iraq imposed on Iran, the hypocrites recalled their forces from other countries and convinced them that they would be able to advance onto Tehran through a [military] operation. In order to realize this foolish dream, the hypocrites deployed ten thousand of their forces, who were then captured by the combatants of Islam." Hojjat ol-eslam Fallahian noted: "Under present conditions, the hypocrites are trying to save Saddam from his deadlock, and re-engage the Baathist enemy into war [with us]. Currently, the forces of the hypocrites do not even equal the size of an Iraqi brigade; their leaders, however, protect and maintain themselves by deceiving the youth of our country [into joining them]." He stressed that the danger from the hypocrites has not been completely removed, and people must explain this to their children. He added, "We must constantly maintain our anti-arrogance and anti-blasphemy stance, and continue to fight the agents of mini-groups and hypocrites."

Reza Shemirani

ARRESTED: July 1981

DETAINED IN: Tohid (Moshtarak Committee Detention Center), Evin and Qezel Hesar Prisons

RELEASED: July 1991

1. My name is Reza Shemirani and I was a political prisoner in Evin during the 1988 massacre of political prisoners.

2. I make this statement in support of an investigation into the mass execution of political prisoners in 1988 in Iran.

3. This statement is true to the best of my knowledge and belief. Except where I indicate to the contrary, I make this statement on the basis of facts and matters within my own knowledge. Where the facts and matters in this statement are within my own knowledge, they are true. Where the facts and matters are not within my own knowledge, I have identified the source or sources of my information, and I believe such facts to be true.

Events Prior to His Arrest

4. I was born in Tehran on 6 December 1959. In 1978, I passed the general examination for entering university and was admitted to Tehran University's Medical School. My family was not politically active. I became politically active during the Revolution. From the beginning, I was involved with the Mojahedin Khalq Organization.

5. As a university student, I was influenced by the 1979 Revolution in Iran. Naturally, during the Revolution the atmosphere was political. Young people, and, in particular, students, who spent time in the academic environment, were interested in various issues. At the time, the issue of the day was politics. In an environment that was free and democratic, many, including me, became active.

6. Our activities at the time were mainly political. We had publications, talked to people, attended political gatherings, and campaigned in favor of our organization's candidates in the parliamentary and presidential elections. The situation was normal, and each political group, including

the Mojahedin, was active in promoting its political views. Supporters of various groups were politically active, and most students had political leanings.

7. During the same time, Khomeini's speeches and actions regarding women, cultural issues, and various religious beliefs and schools of thought became increasingly radical. He responded to peaceful actions and political threats with clubs and fascist acts. Sometimes I sold publications. I was 17 years old at the time. I remember, in Khazaneh Square, we had a table with books. Some of these plainclothes people, the club-wielders of those days, attacked us with cables, knives, and axes. As an individual observing all this, I naturally reacted to it and opposed it.

8. Mas'ud Rajavi was a candidate in the presidential election. He was lawfully registered by the Ministry of Interior, and his participation in the race was legal. I, like everybody else, was putting up posters and campaigning. One night around 11 p.m., seven or eight Revolutionary Guards and plainclothes individuals attacked me and beat me up. I was taken to the hospital and got eight stitches on my head. I was taken to the Hezar Takhtekhabi Hospital. The scar is still on my head. This is one specific example [I can tell you about].

9. At the time, the Mojahedin believed that we should use the relatively free post-revolutionary atmosphere to promote our views and grow. [They thought] that we should avoid actions that might lead to harsh military rule; that our only weapon against clubs was denunciation [of the violence].

Up to that point, we had not resisted by fighting back.

10. If you remember, many of our people were martyred at the time because we fought back only with words, our publications, and our activism. Nasim Rostami was martyred in Shiraz. Abbas Amani and one of our sisters [fellow female militant], whose name I do not recall, were killed in Bandar Abbas. Reza Reza'i was killed in Reza'ieh Square in Tehran. Many more were badly injured. The organization was not in a position to tell us what to do if we were attacked with daggers, for instance. One way, naturally, was to run. We did not do anything else because we were scared. We called for help. In reality, in every neighborhood we went to, we attracted some people who would come [to help us].

11. On 20 June 1981 (30 Khordad 1360), I was in Tehran and participated for a short while in the demonstration planned by the organization [MKO]. Many were killed that day, and many were injured and arrested. I saw people who were injured and arrested and beaten by the Revolutionary Guards as they were being dragged away. The demonstration was peaceful, but the regime started shooting and arresting people and turned it into a bloody protest.

12. The newspapers wrote the next day that a number of people were executed. No injuries or deaths among the regime's forces were reported on television. After 20 June I too became a fugitive because they were executing people every day. They set traps, closed both ends of a street, and arrested every young person. At the time, they were

sensitive about certain items of clothing. It was dangerous even to wear sneakers. I had changed the way I dressed and wore ordinary [nondescript] clothing.

13. I was in the streets because I had nowhere to go, and that is why they arrested me. Today, with my experience, I could do many things, but I was 20 at the time. I had read and sold a couple of political publications in a revolutionary atmosphere. Now, suddenly, we faced a military situation. I was not prepared and could not imagine that the situation would become what it did. We wandered around and slept in the streets. At the time, dying or being executed was not our main concern. All we cared about was not losing our connection with the [Mojahedin] Organization. At the time of my arrest I was in contact with the organization, but we did not do much. All we did was meet.

Arrest and Detention

14. I was arrested on 20 July 1981 by the Revolutionary Guards. I was walking on Takht-e-tavus Avenue at about 11 a.m. when I was arrested. They may have been following me. I was crossing the street when someone said, "Excuse me, brother. Can you come for a moment?" When I turned around, I saw that he had a gun. Then he hit me on the back of my neck with his gun and pushed me into a car. They pushed my head down and blindfolded me, and I did not know where they took me. I think they may have taken me to the Bonyad Shahid [Martyr's Foundation] building in Reza'ieh Square because it was not far from where they arrested me.

15. I was kept there all day. At night (it was also the 19th of Ramadan), they came and asked a few questions—nothing much. They gave us [food to end the fasting]. Then they drove me to the Tohid Committee [Moshtarak], (called the Joint Anti-Sabotage Committee under the Shah). I believe there were three or four other detainees there, in the Moshtarak Committee.

16. They first subjected me to a mock execution at the Moshtarak Committee. They told me that I was about to be executed, blindfolded me, and tied me to a tree. They pulled the muzzles of their guns. They wanted to crush me. Then they took me to Branch 2 [to be interrogated]. They tortured me a great deal. At the time, I was not blindfolded and it was my interrogators who had masks that showed only their eyes and their mouths. Later, however, I was the one who was blindfolded and they showed their faces.

17. They took me to be interrogated at dusk and beat me until dawn the next morning. They wanted me to reveal [details] of the meetings planned with [contacts] in the organization. But I would not admit to anything and I told them that I was not a Mojahedin sympathizer. A person arrested at the same time as I was had apparently told them that we were [both] Mojahedin sympathizers, but I kept denying it. When it was almost morning they told me, "From now on, we will beat you until you give us your information." As they were beating me, they mentioned a few names, and I understood that they knew that I was a Mojahedin sympathizer.

18. They tied my fingers together and my toes together, and they tied my hands to the bed and they beat me with an electric cable. I was either on my back or on my stomach. Three people were involved in torturing me, but only one of them was the interrogator. One was sitting on me and holding a pillow on my face, the second one was lashing my feet, and the third person was walking around the bed yelling and insulting me. They were insulting me really badly. I was lashed with an electric cable all night. If I had something to say, I was told to lift my finger. But what valuable information could a 20-year-old like me have to deserve so much flogging?

19. In the Moshtarak Committee, they gave us food, and it was very good. They had released me from the bed and left food to eat at dawn before the start of the day's fasting. But I was unable to eat [this food] because of the torture. They also gave me watermelon, and I ate a substantial amount of it because I was sweating. Usually, you are not supposed to have [fluids] after torture to avoid dialysis, but I ate the watermelon.

20. My interrogator was called Taqi and was a student at the time of the Shah. From what he said, I gathered that he had been imprisoned under the Shah and had been with the Mojahedin or the non-religious groups and had a good knowledge of them. He seemed to be open-minded and tried to get information during the exchanges we had. Usually, he did not beat me himself. He would leave the room and tell the others, "Beat him."

21. Then they threw me in a cell and said that they would be back in half an hour. In fact, they took me to the cell at 5 a.m. and did not come back until 5 in the afternoon. I had lost all notion of time. For me, it was still 5 a.m. I was half-awake and living a terrifying nightmare. I kept thinking about what would happen if they came back and forced me to give them a couple of names and those people would also get arrested.

22. Two days later, I was sent to Evin along with a few other people. But we could not communicate in any way. I could tell from the sound of feet and people getting in and out of the car that I was not alone. I do not know who they were and whether they were men or women. I was taken and kept in ward 209.

23. I was held in 209 for three months and interrogated the entire time. However, the interrogations were sporadic. When they first arrested you, they cared about getting the time-sensitive information from you, or figuring out when or with whom your next meeting was scheduled. But after a while, once you did not go to your meetings [your fellow organization members would know you were arrested and would change the meeting places and schedule at this point], there was no more time-sensitive information that could be useful for them. Also, at that time, the prison was very crowded. They had five to six people in every cell. The hallways of ward 209 were full of prisoners and we had to walk over their legs with our injured feet.

24. They would give me a piece of paper and take me to the interrogation room. There, I

would sit facing the wall. The interrogator would come and check my paper and beat me if I had not written anything. Sometimes they would take me to the basement and tie me to a bed and beat me. In the basement of 209, there were rooms similar to showers or bathrooms, small rooms with a bed. They usually wanted our organizational chart and any information I had on safe houses, sympathizers' names, and similar information.

25. They beat me with a cable. There were hangers with cables that had various thicknesses and forms: thick, thin, knitted etc. . . . The tin wires in the cables broke into pieces when they hit the prisoners' bodies during the torture sessions. The floor was covered with pieces of broken copper wires and blood. The room was very dirty and the light was very weak. The [torture] bed was an old wooden one. At the time, to terrorize and subjugate me, they would take me to the room with my blindfold on but would take it off in the room so that I could see the cables and the torturers. They had their faces covered with black masks, and they sometimes were in only their underpants and undershirts. This [sight] was torture in itself.

26. The interrogation lasted three months. I was held in solitary cells in wards 2, 209, 9 and 5. [The wards] looked alike. They just moved me around. We were not alone. There were a few of us in each solitary cell. My feet were injured up to my knees as a result of the torture. Most of the other kids were in the same situation. Sometimes, the interrogators had to drag prisoners who could not walk to take them to the interrogation room. Many moved around in wheelchairs. Some who could not walk were carried by others, and some walked on all fours because their feet would not fit into shoes or slippers. After 10 or 15 lashes to the soles of your feet, the swelling does not allow you to wear shoes. In 209, I fed or cleaned some of my cellmates after they used the bathroom. In each cell, there were three or four prisoners like that. Their hands were numb, injured, and swollen as a result of being pulled and tied behind their backs—*qapani*.

27. Prisoners were not all treated the same way, and some were tortured more severely than others. It depended on the case. For example, someone had been arrested at night in the middle of an operation, whereas someone else was only suspected of having participated in a military operation. I was arrested 29 days after the 20 June [protest]. The interrogation of someone who was arrested during the 27 September [1981 MKO armed street demonstration] was different than for me or someone who was arrested before the 20 June [1981 peaceful demonstration]. The pressure on those arrested after 27 September was naturally more intense than it was on us. Usually, they put us together [in the cells] in a way that we could not help each other [by exchanging information].

28. One night, I was taken for interrogation at 10 p.m. After interrogation, I asked my interrogator, who was reciting a Molavi poem to himself, what would happen to me. He said that it depended on who the Shari'a judge for my case was: "If you are lucky and get a good Shari'a judge, then you will be fine. If the judge is not

good, then it is not good." I said, "Isn't Gilani the Shari'a judge?" He said, "Judge Gilani has brought in some of his students to help here." This was a few days before my trial, and the interrogator told me that my interrogation was over and that he was sending me to court. My interrogation lasted three months. I was in 209 until my court date.

Trial

29. The 2 p.m. news could be heard through loudspeakers when I was taken to court. They took my blindfold off and seated me facing the wall. From the sounds, I could tell that the Shari'a judge, the interrogator, and two or three other people were sitting behind me. From his voice, I could tell that the judge was 25 or 26 years old. Because of the loud noise, neither he [the judge] nor I could hear each other. He told someone, "Go and tell them to lower the volume of the loudspeaker. We cannot hear anything." By the time they lowered the sound, my trial was over. It took five to six minutes.

30. I was charged with participating in the 27 April 1981 protest on Taleqani Avenue, sympathizing with the Mojahedin, acting against national security, and reading and selling publications that favored the Mojahedin. There were no charges related to any military action. They had arrested me in the street, but they knew that at that time I could not have been involved in military operations and that whatever I did was political. The regime talked about armed demonstrations to justify [its repressive actions], but at the time no one carried arms. If anyone was armed, at least one Revolutionary Guard would have been killed, but none of them were killed. The 27 September protest was armed but not the one on 20 June.

31. Before my trial, the interrogator told me, "Let me tell you something. If you want to stay alive, don't defend yourself when the judge reads your charges. Just say, 'Whatever you say, Haj Aqa.'" That is what I did. In those days, because of the overcrowded prisons, the trials were like court-martials and did not take more than a few minutes. Some of those arrested were executed merely for having two-rial coins in their pockets. They were accused of intending to use the coins [in a public phone] to contact [other activists] and set up organizational meetings.

32. Two to three days after the trial, the guards told me to pack my belongings to go to the public ward. I asked, "How about my sentence?" I was told, "You should be happy because you will stay alive." I asked, "What am I sentenced to? Life?" He said, "No, ten years." Later, they showed me my sentence. It said ten years' *ta'zir*. On a smaller piece of paper, it was written: "Convicted to ten years for sympathizing with the *monafeqin*." It was a revolutionary tribunal document, I think. There was no name of the judge or signature.

Prison Conditions

33. I was transferred to room 3, ward 1 (downstairs). At the time, it was called ward 325. There were Forqan kids, the Fadaiyan, and the Tudeh. But more than 90 percent were Mojahedin. ["Kids" is a familiar way of referring to a group of people that the speaker feels close to.]

34. On 16 December 1981, they transferred me to Qezel Hesar Prison, ward 7—Mojarad. Anyone transferred to Qezel Hesar was kept there first, and then sent to the public ward. For four months, I was held in ward 7, Mojarad, which was meant to house 12 people but there were 500 people there. There were 40 to 50 prisoners per room, and we often had to stand for hours. Every cell had two beds and 20 people would sit on each bed.

35. I remember that one day, maybe around 11 or 12 February, Lajevardi came to the ward with the head of Qezel Hesar Prison. They told us to come out and stand in a row. There were very long hallways in Qezel Hesar. I remember that the line started in the ward, and the middle of the row reached the end of the hallway. The head of prison said to Lajevardi, "Have you noticed how many they are?" They had brought Lajevardi so that he could see the large number of prisoners and authorize the use of unit 1. [After Lajevardi's visit] we were the first group to be transferred to unit 1, ward 4.

36. I was in Qezel Hesar Prison in 1985. In the summer of that year, a more moderate faction replaced Lajevardi's group. In fact, Lajevardi was removed and instead Majid Ansari—and generally Montazeri's group—took over [control of the prisons]. One summer day, Meysam came. Then Ansari came and gave a speech. He described Haj Davud and his people as anti-revolutionaries who were responsible for our skepticism about Khomeini. At some point in 1982–83, they would organize *komeil* prayer, and it was mandatory for all

to go. [But since the pro-Montazeri group took control of the prisons] they were no longer looking to do cultural work and came only to turn us into repenters. They wanted to do ideological work, but no one attended [their programs].

37. When Meysam came to Qezel Hesar, he organized several book fairs and sold a variety of intellectual books. I remember that they even brought excerpts of the Mojahed magazine. They wanted to create an intellectual environment. Meysam also brought some color televisions that they installed in every ward and said that these were a gift from the Ministry of Commerce. We had normal television programs, but they did not let us see movies. There were also newspapers.

38. Around late spring in 1986, they closed Qezel Hesar. Some [prisoners] went to Gohardasht and some to Evin. I was transferred to cell 5 in the Amuzeshgah at Evin. The prison atmosphere was heavier and scarier there than in other prisons. At Evin, one was close to the interrogators who could kill you whenever they wanted. Such was not the case in Qezel Hesar. What made Evin terrible was the memory of the executions of 1981. When they opened fire on prisoners, it was as if they were unloading iron bars. Then came the single shots. Each shot meant that one person was killed. In our cell, we used to count the single shots every night.

39. In Evin, prisoners from all groups were held together. I was taken back to ward 5, room 9. Before the 1988 executions, the atmosphere in Evin had changed a lot. One person was responsible for each room. In

Qezel Hesar, the repenters were in charge of the rooms, but in Evin, they gave us the responsibility. In ward 5, Mohammad Farjad (Najar) was representing the prisoners. Mohammad was one of the Mojahedin kids, a student who had studied in Italy. I was second-in-charge. Of course, we did this through an election, and we voted [to elect the ward's representative]. This was the process through 1987. Mohammad was hanged in the executions of 1988.

40. In mid-1987, prisoners were separated and grouped based on the length of their sentences. Prisoners with sentences longer than ten years were sent to one ward, and those with fewer than ten years to another one. I went to ward 1 (upstairs) where they held all those sentenced to ten years.

41. Prisoners of various beliefs were held together [in our ward]. Room 5 in ward 1 belonged to non-religious groups, and the other five rooms housed the Mojahedin. We had no problems with each other. We coordinated what needed to be done through voting. I remember Ali-Reza Zomorrodian, one of the Peykar kids who had been in prison in the previous (the Shah's) regime, was the person in charge of communication between the non-religious kids and us. He was a nice kid with character and was very effective. He too was executed in 1988.

42. At the end of the summer of 1987, I was sent to solitary confinement in Asayeshgah because of organizational activities inside the prison, and was tortured and interrogated. Before prisoners were divided based on the length of their sentences, we had a lot of hunger strikes. In fact these were not hunger strikes, they were boycotts of the [prison] food. The atmosphere was more open. The situation was the same in ward 1.

43. I was the ward's assistant. Another person, Eskandar Nazemolbaka, was in charge of food and sanitation in the ward. He was a Mojahed from the north, and he was also executed. At that time, I was coordinating the ward's contact with the outside [other wards]. In other words, when we had a political position that needed to be communicated to those outside [of our ward], I was in charge of doing it. That is why I was in solitary confinement and interrogated and tortured from the end of the summer of 1987 until the 1988 executions.

44. The interrogations were the same as before—and even worse. They called me every day at 7 a.m. and I was interrogated until 7 p.m. Sometimes they only called me and left me alone. But the very fact that I had to sit by the door of the [interrogation] branch in the prosecutor's building in Evin was the worst torture. They took me there at a time when I could hear the voices of those who were being tortured, and this was psychological torture.

45. Increasingly, [prisoners] took actions to protest. The Montazeri group had taken over the prison, and we had more freedom. I have to specify that the prisoner could in no way confront the guards physically. We were prisoners, and we could not get into [physical] fights, but we confronted them politically. We did not do so openly, but, as days went by, we openly had heated discussions and things had changed significantly.

46. When there is opening, resistance is stronger. Prisoners who were not religious openly refused to fast, as opposed to a time when they even would pray. In 1986–87, they would tell [the guards], "We don't pray, and we don't fast." They would refuse the food [left at the door at dawn when those who fasted ate] and they asked for fresh food.

47. The Mojahedin kids also refused to write "hypocrite" when asked about their charge. They would write "the organization." When [the guards] asked them, "Which organization?" They would answer, "You know which organization." We would assess the environment and conditions and make decisions about our position. At some juncture, we would say "hypocrite," and at another juncture we would not. At some juncture we lived with the repenters, and at another we did not allow them to be in our rooms. The organization [Mojahedin] managed to send messengers into the country to recruit people and take them [to Iraq]. These messengers would be arrested and imprisoned, and they brought news of the resistance, which boosted prisoners' morale.

48. So then, in this freer atmosphere, [the Revolutionary Guards] were trying to figure out who was suggesting the food boycott or who was in charge of the organizational work [among the prisoners]. In Branch 7, the interrogators were the old ones. But I did not know the interrogators of Branch 13. Of course, I had a blindfold on. In comparison to 1981, when the questions were very clear, in 1987, the questions were about the organization inside the prison. The interrogators were more sophisticated.

They had the experience of six to seven years of interrogation and, unlike before, they would not tie you to a bed quickly and beat you on the soles of your feet with a cable until the skin exploded and prevented them from beating you more. They used much more sophisticated psychological methods.

49. For one of us, they [the interrogators] had resorted to continuous light [exposure] and sleep deprivation. They threatened and tempted us. In the case of Ali Ansari in the winter of 1987, they had put him under this kind of pressure. When they sent him to the ward and told him to think until they would call him the next day, he committed suicide, saying that he refused to let them make a traitor out of him. Ali had a seven-year-old daughter called Zeinab. He had been in prison under the Shah and had a lot of experience. But the psychological torture used on him had been so serious that he ate broken glass mixed into depilatory cream, and he died right there behind the door.

50. In the fall of 1987, when I was in Branch 13, my interrogator told me that they had a plan for prisoners, and this plan was being carried out. In return for my cooperation, he said, "I will send you somewhere where you wouldn't be with your friends and you could save face." He did not tell me what these plans were, but around the same time, in the fall of 1987, they had taken Masoud Moqbeli to the Moshtarak Committee. They had made him listen to Radio Mojahed. They told him, "Go back to your ward and tell the prisoners that we don't want prisoners anymore; that we

have categorized prisoners into red, yellow, and white. We will execute those categorized in red and release the whites and will make a decision about the yellows." They had also taken one of the Tudeh kids and told him the same thing.

51. In my opinion, the executions of 1988 were not triggered by the attack of the Mojahedin. From a year before, the regime had a plan. It is possible that, at that juncture, they just accelerated the process. There were signs indicating that the regime intended to move toward executions: taking me or the Tudeh prisoner for interrogation, or what happened in ward 1 (upstairs) and the ward of prisoners sentenced for life.

52. Being interrogated about internal prison issues is much harder than interrogations related to the outside. When you are questioned about the latter, some meetings will be cancelled or [safe] houses will be abandoned. But inside prison, if you give a name the person's life is on the line. Thank God, I came out proud. My conscience is at ease when I sleep at night.

53. They wanted to know about the organization within the prison. They asked, "Who suggests the hunger strikes? Who is in charge of organizing? How is the ward organized? What is the organization's hierarchy?" I told them, "I am not in every room to know who initiates it; when there is decision-making, I am informed of the result." Therefore, I would start to list prisoners room by room in alphabetical order. The interrogator would tell me, "I have the room's list. Who is making the scheme?" I told them that I did not know anything about a specific person, and I would give them general answers.

54. The interrogator would write a question on a form and put it in front of me. He would say, "Fill it out," and I would have to write and sign the bottom of the page. Then he would leave for two or three hours and come back again. The interrogation about the prison organization was very harsh. I resisted as long as I could. I was taken for interrogation between 5 a.m. and 7 p.m. every day, and I would go back to my cell at the end of the day with swollen feet. They either beat me or kept me next to the torture rooms in order for me to suffer and hear those who were tortured.

55. After a while, I reached a point at which I realized that my body was giving in. One day in November, in order to protect the information I had, I finally told the interrogator that I would give them all my information the next day. I told the guard that I wanted to take a shower and asked him for some depilatory cream. I went back to my cell and into the bathroom and ate the cream in order to kill myself. Five minutes later, I threw it up. It was horrible. I was throwing up in a sink in the cell. I ate it again but they heard the noise and came in and took me to the infirmary. My insides were burned. I was in critical condition for ten days. The interrogator came to visit me and asked me why I had done this. I said, "I told you that I knew nothing and you kept beating me and I had no information to give you." He said, "You could have given me spuriously the list of the ward's prisoners; we had the list anyway [it wouldn't be betraying your cellmates], and you would get away with it." Luckily this episode ended my interrogation.

Events of 1988

56. After the interrogations, they took us to ward 6, room 99. We were there for a month. There were 13 of us in that room. All of us were Mojahedin sympathizers and had been under interrogation. Every one of us had been in solitary confinement for internal prison matters. I had not had any visitations in three to four months. After being transferred to ward 6, I had a visit once every two weeks. There was no news and nothing particular was happening at the time. This ward was public, but the room we were held in was closed and we could not mix with the others. They gave us newspapers, and we managed to communicate via Morse code with other prisoners to talk about what was happening and exchange news.

57. On 18 July 1988, they told us to pack our bags, which we did, and they took us to the Asayeshgah. We were in cells next to each other in groups of two or three prisoners. After 18 July 1988, we had no visitations.

58. On 24 or 25 July, one day after Eid Qorban, the guards gave us a form to fill out. It was an A4-sized form with a few questions. They asked for information such as our [first] name, last name, address, our charge, the length of our sentence, and past criminal record. They also asked about the number of siblings we had, and whether any family members or relatives were political prisoners and such. They told us that we could write "sympathizer of the Mojahedin" instead of *monafeqin* ("hypocrites") if we liked, in response to the question about our charge, which we did. At that juncture, we all wrote "Mojahedin" as our charge because we had suffered and paid such a high price for it already. Then they took the forms.

59. We did not sense any danger and did not think that things could get worse. We thought that [the worst] had already happened to us. We had no knowledge of the events outside of prison regarding the war [the Iran-Iraq War] or the Mojahedin's activities. [In Room 99], we found out about the signing of the [U.N. Security Council] Resolution ending the war from newspapers, but we were not aware of the Mojahedin attack. At the time, the person in charge of the prison was the cleric Seyyed Hassan Mortazavi.

60. On 27 July, they came to our cell, called for Amir Abdollahi, and took him away. Amir and Abolhassan were brothers. Abolhassan was in the cell next to us, and Amir was in our cell. They took him [Amir] out of the cell in the afternoon, at 3 or 4 p.m., and brought him back at midnight or 1 a.m. to pack his belongings. As he was packing, he told us that he had been to court and had received a death sentence, and that they wanted to execute us all. The guard was at the door, so he could not talk much. Amir was sure that he was going to be executed that very moment. He wanted to leave his blanket behind but the guard told him to bring it as he would need it that night.

61. That night, we did not sleep at all and we tried to understand what was happening. What did it mean that they were executing everybody? We could not understand it. Amir was young, 22 or 23 years old, and

had a life sentence. What was happening? At the time, we did not know about the Forugh Javidan operation.

62. The next day, in the afternoon, they took me and Mas'ud Abu'i to the prosecutor's building. The hallway was filled with people, boys and girls. Slowly, it became clear to us that they were executing prisoners. So, whenever we could, we told others Amir's story because the guards were saying that these courts were in charge of implementing the Imam's pardon order. Those who were tried were not allowed to return to their wards and were taken to solitary confinement and executed that same night. It seemed to me that there were more than 100 prisoners in the prosecutor's building. We had blindfolds on, but our hands were free and so we could adjust the blindfolds a little and see from underneath.

63. We stood there for a while, and then they took us back. I saw Mortazavi, the prison warden, in a Revolutionary Guards' outfit, and he looked very happy. They took me to the Asayeshgah and half an hour later, around 7 p.m., they took me to ward 209. There I saw all the kids I knew from ward 1 (upstairs). They took them back to their ward, and I did not get a chance to talk to them. I do not think they had any idea about what was happening. I was in 209 for half an hour, and then they took me back to the Asayeshgah.

64. On 30 July, a Saturday, they called me and took me to the prosecutor's building again. The hallway was again filled with prisoners. And in the management building, there were 80 or 90 girls, Mojahedin sym-

pathizers. It was about 4 or 5 p.m. when they took me to court. Nayyeri, the Shari'a judge, as well as Lashkari and Eshraqi, the prosecutor, and two or three Revolutionary Guards were present.

65. This was, in effect, the second or third day after the start of the executions. I had agreed with the others that if we were asked about our charge, we would say, "sympathizer of the hypocrites," but if they asked us to do an interview, we would not agree to it. Nayyeri asked me what my charge was and I told him, "sympathizer of the hypocrites." He did not think that I knew about the executions. He told the guard, "Give him [paper] to write his *enzejarnameh* [letter of expression of disgust and hatred of the Mojahedin] and sign it." The guard said, "Sir, ask him where he is coming from." Nayyeri said, "We have no time. Let him write the *enzejarnameh.*" The guard said again, "But sir, he is one of those group leaders and was brought from solitary confinement and has been interrogated. Ask him what he has done." Nayyeri said again, "We have no time. Give him the paper to write." The guard came out with me and said, "Write down the ward's organizational chart," and then went back in. I wrote two or three sentences [to express] hatred and gave the paper back quickly and left.

66. During those two or three minutes, another guard said, "Those who have been to court, come this way." And he took us to the Asayeshgah. The place was so crowded that no one could watch every single prisoner. During the transfer in the minibus, I talked to some of the sisters and realized

that no one was aware of what was happening, and that they did not know about the executions. I informed them of what I knew, and they, in turn, told me about the Forugh Javidan operation. In fact, it was only then, around 29 or 30 July that I knew that something had happened outside the prison. There were about ten of us on the minibus, mostly sisters. One of the sisters who was in the back of the minibus said out loud, "The fact that the Mojahedin have attacked is none of our business." And I said, "What is this situation, where everyone is being executed?" In this way, we exchanged the information we had.

67. They took me back to a solitary cell in the Asayeshgah where I was alone. Those who had gone to court were not taken back to their own cells so that they would not be able to inform the others. We were lucky that Amir Abdollahi had been brought back to the cell. It may have been a mistake or the stupidity of the guard who brought him back to pack his belongings. The guard's name was Javad, and he was really mean. I was in the Asayeshgah for nine days. One day when I was in the hallway, I heard Haj Hassan, who was in charge of the Asayeshgah, talking on the phone. He said, "We don't have space. We have to move some people from here." That night, they moved 70 or 80 of us to ward 3 upstairs.

68. I was in solitary confinement until 8 August. That night, they came and took all of those who had already been to court on foot from the Asayeshgah to ward 325. We had an armed military escort—a car preceding us and a car following us. I was transferred to ward 3 (upstairs). Mojtaba Halva'i and Mohammad Elahi were among the guards. Evin was under martial law. This was very unusual. Even the guards could not go out after midnight and had to stay where they were. Those kids who were at the prosecutor's until 12 a.m. were kept there overnight. Any movement was forbidden after midnight.

69. By September 1988, they had executed everyone [the religious prisoners] and had started the trial and execution of the non-religious kids. We were taken to ward 3 (upstairs), which was public, and we were together. Those non-religious kids could not accept or believe what we told them. They believed that a wave [of freedom] had come from the Soviet Union and had reached us as well and that liberty was at hand. They were referring to events in the Soviet Union under Gorbachev. They refused to accept what we told them about the executions. They believed that freedom was on its way and that Iran also would evolve, especially the [Fadaiyan] Majority kids. When [the prison authorities] took the non-religious kids to court, they gave them a hard time over issues such as praying, but [the non-religious prisoners'] analysis [of the situation] did not include executions. They simply could not believe it. For us, too, it still was unbelievable. Each time we went out, we tried to look in every corner with the hope that we could find [those who were executed].

70. There were two groups of solitary cells: those in the Asayeshgah that had been built by Lajevardi in 1981 and those of ward 209 that dated from the time of the Shah.

Ward 209's solitary was next to the clinic building and ward 325. In fact, the clinic was between wards 209 and 325.

71. They took us to 209 to be tried. The Office of Sentence Enforcement had been established in the basement of 209 and the executions took place right there. They took the prisoners there and informed them of the fact that they had been sentenced to death. They would hand prisoners a plastic bag to put their belongings in and a piece of paper on which to write their will. Then they would also give prisoners a marker to write their names on their left hand. There was a room there with five nooses attached to a horizontal bar that resembled a goal post (*tir darvazeh*). There, they executed boys and girls at the same time. The bodies were removed in containers through the basement of 209. We did hear noises of cars moving around, but nothing out of the ordinary.

72. One of the kids from the north was taken to see the executions. Nayyeri wanted to save him from being executed because he had several children. He had said, "Take him to see the room." They had taken him to show him the executions. When he came back to the ward, he was in very bad shape and was not saying anything to anyone because he was so scared. He told only one person he knew from before who was very close to him. He was released later. That person also told another friend and the news came to us, but we did not spread the news widely because it was dangerous and it could have put him in danger. This was in ward 3 upstairs of the ward 325 building.

73. On 27 September 1988, they came and called 12 people, including me. It was 2 p.m. We said goodbye to the others and they took us to ward 209. In fact, we were the 12 people who had slipped through the cracks, and they wanted to execute us. They put us in cells in groups of three. Seifollah Mani'eh and I were in the same cell. The light bulb in our cell was not working. That same night, Zamani, head of Tehran Province Intelligence Administration [in charge of Evin's intelligence], came to our cell and asked what we were doing. He was involved in our interrogation. We told him that we had no light in our cell. He said, "Fine," and he left.

74. We were left there for two days waiting for them to come and take us to be executed. On 29 September they came and told us to pack our belongings and took us back to our other cellmates. When they wanted to take us back to the ward, one guard would not let go of us. He made a phone call and was told to let us go back to our ward. It seemed that there was no longer a question of executing us. The guard in our ward who thought we had been taken to be executed was surprised to see us. After a phone call, he told us, "You are lucky!" When we entered the ward, all the kids were in shock to see us alive, and they celebrated our return.

75. When we returned to the ward, the atmosphere was very bad. From the entire prison population, there were only 120 to 130 of us left alive, including some Forqan guys, some [FKO] Minority guys, and us. I felt that the prison was unfamiliar to me, as if I had gone to a prison in another country. It was very hard to accept and to adapt to

the new situation. Conditions had changed drastically. Many of the guards tried to avoid taking responsibility for what had happened. Some were saying that they were on holiday at the time.

76. One night, Zamani, who was in charge of intelligence at Evin, called me and Mohammadreza Ata'i, whose brother was among those executed in 1988. It was September–October (Mehr) and there were four of us: me, Seifollah, Moham-mad Hassan Mofid, and Mohammadreza Ata'i. Zamani knew all of us from before. They took me and one guy one night and Mani'eh and the other guy the next night. The discussion lasted about two hours.

77. He asked me what I thought about the executions. I asked him whether it was safe for me to talk. He said, "Yes, you can say what you want." I still did not feel secure and told him, "You executed people who were mentally ill." He said, "Unfortunately, yes. In any major action, individuals make mistakes." I told him, "These people had already been sentenced. If you accept the legitimacy of your own courts, why did you execute them?" He said, "Because they were steadfast." I said, "Why were they steadfast? Wasn't their steadfastness encouraged by the behavior of Haj Davud and Lajevardi?" I knew that he had a con-flict with Haj Davud and Lajevardi. Zamani said, "Yes, anti-revolutionaries such as [them] led the prison situation to be what it became." I asked, "If you know that, why did you kill them?" He said, "This is none of your business. His Holi-ness the Imam [Khomeini] had given the order." He did not refer to the attack of

the Mojahedin in the conversation. He wanted to know what we thought of the executions.

78. A month or two later, we again had visita-tions; I'm not sure but I think it was in October–November (Aban). I was released when I had served my sentence. I had been arrested on 20 July 1981 and sentenced to ten years. I was released on 20 July 1991. They required bail and someone to sponsor me. They also made me sign written com-mitments in which I promised that I would inform them if the organization got in touch with me; that I would inform them if I heard anyone say anything against the regime; that I would not engage in political activities; and that I would not try to join the organization. I signed the papers.

79. After my release, I had to report to the committee on Vesal Avenue every month. Each time, I was interrogated for an hour. The interrogations were about whom I had seen, whom I had been in touch with, and whether I had contacted the organization and vice versa. They wanted to know what I was up to.

Release from Prison

80. After my release, I was self-employed. I tried to continue my education, but the documents they required made it impos-sible for me to do so. My documents included my military service certificate that has a red stamp saying "banned from serving." I have a letter from the office of criminal records stating that I was arrested for sympathizing with the Mojahedin and was in prison [no university would accept a

student with such record]. When you want to get a job in Iran, you need a letter from the criminal records office. It took two or three months of misery before I was able to get the letter from the prosecutor's office.

81. In 2001, I left Iran. I stayed for ten years before deciding to leave. I knew that whatever happened, they were going to come back to get us because we would be suspects forever. I was always controlled.

82. We were always in danger, and I always felt endangered. Throughout the years, several people were arrested again. I know a couple of people who are fugitives. In 1988, they re-arrested people who had been released and executed them. When the regime wants an execution as a warning to others, who would be better than we? They even arrested people who were not in touch with the organization—for example, the sister of one of the kids in Hamedan. Her name was Zahra. Or for example, Reza Mirza'i—he was out and they called him and put him back in prison. His two brothers had been executed previously, but Reza was out and was busy with his life. They did not execute him, but they brought him in. I knew Abbas Mohammad Rahimi. His brother Hushang was released with me, and after our release I used to see both brothers. Hushang disappeared, and I think they killed him. I do not know how, but I think he is dead. His body was never found.

83. I am not happy to be alive. If I could go back to the past, I would prefer to be among those who were executed. In Iran, we were strangers to society after our release. I felt like I belonged to a generation that was alive years before and had been catapulted a century forward. We were living among people we did not know. My only relief is that my conscience is free because I did not cause anyone to be killed and I did not betray anyone. Even in 1988, I did not give any information. Some of us stayed alive, but it could have been others and not us. It is very difficult. We lived with the same people for eight years, and we built honest and genuine friendships while living in the worst conditions. We had gotten over our differences and created a sort of unity, and suddenly they were all gone and I was left behind. Then I came into a society where relationships are so different from ours. One feels like a stranger. At least outside of Iran, you associate with intellectuals and people who have the same political leanings as you do. But it's very difficult in Iran. There are times when these things occupy your mind and sadden you, but you have to face them [and fight them] and fill the emptiness. Personally though, it is so very difficult, and it's hard not to be sad.

Switzerland, October 2009

رسالت

Subject:	The students' question and answer session with the president regarding human rights, the difficulties experienced by students, and economic issues
The official:	President of the Islamic Republic of Iran, Ali Khamene'i
The occasion:	Meeting with a group of students
Date:	Last week of November 1988
Source:	*Resalat*, 7 December 1988

Last week, in a warm and friendly gathering with students, Hojjat ol-eslam val Moslemin Khamene'i responded to the most critical questions that circulate in student environments.

Mr. Khamene'i said: "Students and the clergy (whether of junior or senior rank) have certain points in common. This commonality plays a fundamental role in preserving the Islamic system." . . . In replying to the first question on why Iran had accepted the Resolution [598, the UN Resolution ending the Iran-Iraq War], the President said: "Perhaps if the war [with Iraq] had continued, we might have been able to achieve our objectives in the long run. However, certain shortcomings caused us to accept [the resolution]. Of course, some of these reasons were mentioned in the Imam [Khomeini]'s letter to the government authorities. But because we are still in a state of neither war nor peace, and the enemy is still on our soil, mentioning these [reasons] here may be problematic. We shall leave this for when I can speak more freely.". . . [The President] was asked about the reasons for the Islamic Republic's lack of

attention to human rights issues, and not permitting the United Nations' human rights experts to carry out their investigations in [Iran]. [He was also asked] about the reasons for the widespread executions in all the provinces of Iran. . . . The President replied: "Your tone of questioning is the same tone as that adopted by foreign radio. However, it is still a question and I will answer it. We are not indifferent to human rights. Nowhere in the entire world will you find a situation similar to the one we have here, where the leaders of a country, like the President, Prime Minister, or others in charge of the most important [state] responsibilities, enjoy such an [excellent] relationship with their people. You will find few countries where freedom of speech and freedom to express your views are as [encouraged] as they are in Iran. For example, if someone were to insult me right here and now, he would not be prosecuted. In fact, I would not even press charges [against him]. Those who speak against us by raising human rights issues are the same people who want the *monafeqin* (Mojahedin) and others who wish to subvert this regime to have complete freedom of action in this country. And they want the regime to show no reaction against these groups, whatsoever. . . . Regarding the executions, the same [unjustified] approach that foreign radio takes to them is now being adopted here. In fact, the *monafeqin*'s radio says the very same things. But did we ever say we had abolished the death penalty? Like many countries in the world, we too have capital punishment, but only for those whose crimes are deserving of it. Whoever commits such crimes will be executed, irrespective of family ties or where they come from. In your view, must those people who plotted with the *monafeqin* while in prison, and also plotted with foreigners to carry out atrocious actions on Iranian soil—such as those that took place in Islamabad—be rewarded? If a person's connection to that traitorous organization becomes known, what are we to do with him? In our view, such a person must be condemned to death and we will certainly execute him and we will not keep it a secret. Of course, when I say we, I am referring to our regime; I am not in charge of the judiciary. It goes without saying that if a person is executed whose [crime does not call for] a death sentence, then his executioner must be put to death. He must face *qesas* [retribution—the law of an eye-for-an-eye and a tooth-for-a-tooth]. Our logic is clear. We are not hiding anything."

A newspaper photograph of an anti-Shah demonstration at the time of the Revolution

Shahab Shokoohi

ARRESTED: May 1981
DETAINED IN: Qom Prison
FURLOUGHED: September 1982
RE-ARRESTED: June 1983
DETAINED IN: Evin and Gohardasht Prisons
RELEASED: March 1989

1. My name is Shahab (on my birth certificate Abdolreza) Shokoohi and I am 50 years old. I was a political prisoner in Iran for eight and a half years. I was held in Evin and Gohardasht Prisons. In 1988, I was held in Gohardasht. I was affiliated with the Marxist-Leninist organization Rah-e Kargar. My brother was a member of the same organization and was executed in 1983. I left Iran in 1999. I am now a political refugee in England.

2. I make this statement in support of an investigation into the mass execution of political prisoners in 1988 in Iran.

3. This statement is true to the best of my knowledge and belief. Except where I indicate to the contrary, I make this statement on the basis of facts and matters within my own knowledge. Where the facts and matters in this statement are within my own knowledge, they are true. Where the facts and matters are not within my own knowledge, I have identified the source or sources of my information, and I believe such facts to be true.

Arrest and Torture

4. My older brother had been a political activist and a member of a small Communist guerrilla group, The Red Star (Setareh Sorkh) in the late 1960s. He was arrested in 1971, accused of armed opposition to the Shah's regime, and sentenced to life imprisonment. I was a young boy and the story of my brother had deeply affected me. So as I grew up, I too was drawn to political activism and joined the Marxist-Leninist guerrilla organization Fadaiyan Khalq. I was first arrested in 1974. But because I was only 15 years old at the time, I was sentenced to only one year in prison. My

brother was released during the Revolution in the amnesty that was declared for political prisoners who had opposed the Shah.

5. My brother and I both supported the Revolution. The Revolution was a wonderful opportunity for the people of Iran. But the Mullahs took that opportunity from the people. We were all very happy because we thought that Iran would finally be a democracy and that people would be free. But a few months later the new government started arresting those former political prisoners who were criticizing it. The new government was an Islamic government. The regime was far from tolerant and democratic. They began arresting us because we were opposed to an Islamic state.

6. In May 1981, while I was on my way to the front (of the Iran-Iraq War, 1980–88) I was arrested because I was carrying leftist leaflets. I was affiliated with the Marxist-Leninist Workers Party (Rah-e Kargar) and opposed the government. At that time I was sentenced to only three months and was held in the city of Qom prison. While I was in prison, supporters of then-president Banisadr and the Mojahedin organized a big demonstration against political repression. As a result, the president was impeached by Parliament and dismissed by Ayatollah Khomeini. The Mojahedin then turned against the regime and took up arms against the Islamic Republic. After the bombings affecting the Islamic Republic Party (a pro-regime political party), the government engaged in a policy of terror. The authorities were executing many of the people they arrested, especially suspected Mojahedin, without trial.

7. While I was in prison in Qom, I met a young boy by the name of Ali Shari'atmadari (or Shari'ati), who was only 17 and was the son of an important Qom cleric. In the wave of daily executions in Qom—they would execute five or seven every day—they took him and some of the other young people to court, and, the next day, we were informed he had been executed on suspicion of being an MKO sympathizer. He was not affiliated with the MKO. He had told me that he was not a member of any political group, but that he only liked chronicling the events he witnessed, and that is why he had been arrested. They found a notebook on him where he had been writing what he had seen in the streets of Qom. Public opinion in Qom was outraged, all the more so because his father was an important cleric with a following in the city. There was public outrage about the fact that a young, innocent boy could be executed so easily. The judicial authorities acknowledged the mistake and in the Friday sermon that week in Qom (*namaz jom'eh*) the head of the High Judicial Council, Musavi Ardebili, acknowledged publicly that there had been some judicial errors that were being investigated.

8. In these circumstances (in Qom)—and although I had already been tried and sentenced—I, along with five other defendants, was again taken to the court (in late August 1981) and charged with being opposed to the regime. The fact that I had refused to vote for the new president (Raja'i), and that I had written hostile slogans on the walls of the prison (that was before the Great Terror), was considered

as evidence against me. In fact, I had been denounced by a repentant Mojahed. Judge Andalib—responsible for all the mass executions in Qom, including the execution of Ali—sentenced the five of us to death. The court session lasted only a few minutes. I was lucky because the Revolutionary Guard Heidari, who took us to the court, was kind and denied the veracity of the former Mojahed's denunciation. He said these are lies. In any case, Judge Andalib told each one of us that he was sending all of us to the other world, and it would be up to God to decide if we were guilty or innocent. They brought us back to our cells to take us to be executed the next day. In the early morning, they came to take us and we were ready to be executed. The guard Heidari came to the cell, and told us to go to bathroom. We asked him, "Why the bathroom, aren't we going to be executed?" and he said, "Thank God, they have not come for you yet." Later in the day, we were informed that the execution was suspended because our cases had been referred to the High Judicial Council for revision. Fifteen days later we were notified that the verdicts had been commuted to life sentences.

9. I had been in prison in Qom only a year when Khomeini introduced new prison reforms (in mid-1982). They allowed many political prisoners to leave prison if they provided financial bail, in the form of the deeds to their parents' houses or deposits of money, as a form of a good behavior bond. I told the prison authorities that my mother was in the hospital and not well because I was worried that they would not let me go.

They required some documentation. My older brother, who was a teacher, arranged for documentation from the doctor and hospital, and so I was released. My brother told me that I should never go back to the prison and that I should leave the country. My brother left and moved to Germany.

10. I stayed in Iran, but did not go back to prison. I lived in a safe house. It was during this brief period of freedom that I met my wife. We were married, but had no ceremony or certification of our marriage. We had to live underground. My wife was also politically active at that time.

11. About nine months after I was released they came to arrest me because a member of our organization had been arrested and, under torture, had denounced me. I heard the guards coming and I tried to escape, by climbing out of the window and running along the roofs of the adjoining homes. But there was a guard sitting, waiting, and hiding in a car at the end of the street. He saw me and shouted, "Stop." But I did not stop. He shot me, hitting me in the elbow. My elbow was shattered. As a result I still suffer from pain and limited mobility in my elbow.

12. I was taken to Ward 3000. It used to be a prison, or a detention center, but it is now a museum in Tehran. I was beaten very badly. For three or four days running they continued to give me lashes to the soles of my feet and all over my body. My arm, where I was shot in the elbow during my arrest, became infected because I was not provided any medical treatment. I became very weak because I had lost a lot of blood and I could not eat anything.

13. The infection in my arm became worse and worse. The smell was terrible. Eventually they took me to a special hospital outside of the committee, the name of which was Najmieh Hospital. I was held in a separate room from the other patients and chained to a bed. The guard told the doctors that they should cut my arm off because the bone was becoming diseased (becoming black). The doctor refused, saying it was possible that my arm could be saved with proper treatment. The guard became very angry and yelled at the doctor, "Do what I say!" The doctor (boss of hospital) was very brave and responded firmly, "I am the doctor here and I will do it my way. I do not tell you how to do your job. Do not tell me how to do my job." The prison guards called the Revolutionary Guard center to discuss the doctor's advice and they decided to let the doctor do his work, and that doctor saved my arm.

14. The doctor was the head of the hospital and he was a very good man. He operated on my arm and put it in a cast to heal. The doctor also treated the wounds I had incurred from the lashings. I was in hospital a total of three days. The doctor complained that I was not properly healed and that I needed more time to recover, but the guards ignored him this time.

15. When I was returned to the prison they began with the lashes again. They would leave me on the side of the corridor during the nights, before bringing me back for another session of several lashes, and so on. This continued for a month and a half. From under my blindfold I could see down the corridor. It was full of people. There

were maybe 50 people being held there. But no one could speak to anyone else. The one time I tried it, I was beaten so badly I would not risk it again.

16. After I had been in Evin for about one month, I was taken out of the cell by the prison guards. They would ask me questions. They would say, "Tell the truth. If you don't tell the truth we will kill you." My interrogators names were Morteza and Mas'ud. Mas'ud was a member of the student group known as the Student Followers of the line of the Imam [Khomeini], who had occupied the U.S. embassy and taken the U.S. diplomats hostage. I could not see them because I was blindfolded the whole time, but I knew their voices and could recognize them easily. I kept saying to them, "I don't know what you want."

17. After this I was taken to solitary confinement (ward 209) in Evin Prison for seven months. I thought I was going to go crazy. It was awful.

18. My wife was arrested at the same time as I was. We were both held in the committee [Moshtarak Committee] for six weeks before being transferred to Evin. It was only after one year in Evin that I discovered where she was, and that she had survived but was in prison.

19. When I refused to talk they took me to ward 209, which had eight corridors for torture. Because all of the small torture rooms were in use, they tied me upstairs at the basement entrance by the window to wait my turn. It was awful sitting and waiting for my turn to come when I could hear the pain they were inflicting on the

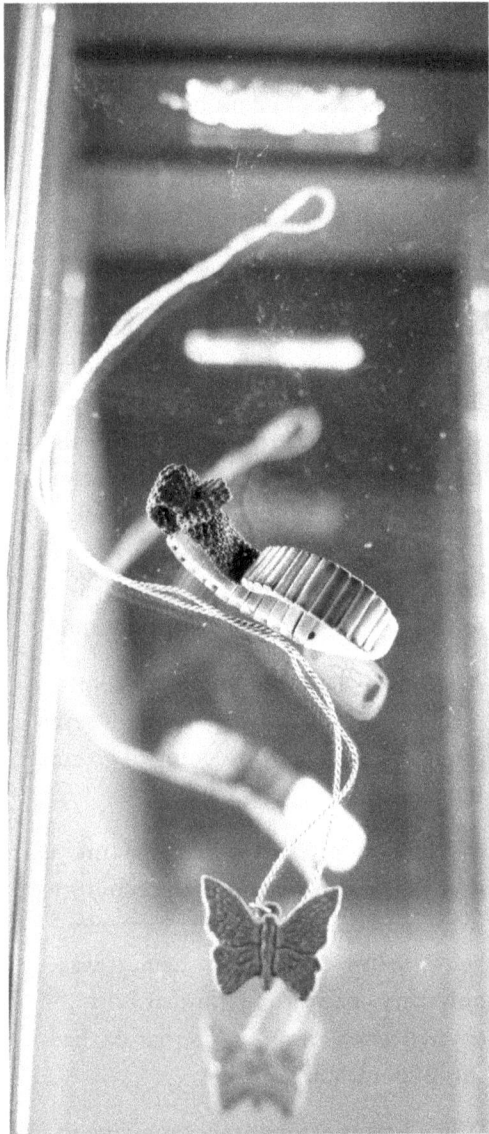

Jewelry that Shahab Shokoohi made while in prison for his wife, Shohreh, who was also a political prisoner. The butterfly is carved in stone. The other two pieces, parts of a bracelet, are made of bone from food they were served and from date pits.

people before me. I could hear them giving one man lashes and so I started to count—as a way to distract myself, and partly because I was trying to work out in my mind whether I could take what was coming. They gave this poor man over 350 lashes in one sitting. I could not see, but it was clear from the noises I was hearing that he was in excruciating pain. Several times the man fell unconscious and the guards would be frustrated, so they would splash him with cold water so he would wake up, and the torture could continue. Finally, they stopped lashing the man. From under my blindfold I could see them dragging a wounded, bloodied person past my feet. It was a horrific sight—there was blood everywhere and his flesh was gashed so badly I could see his leg disintegrating. When they got very close, I got a glimpse of the man's face and he let out a sigh of agony. It was then I realized that this man was my brother. At this point, even though I had already survived almost three months of torture and solitary confinement, I felt completely broken. Seeing my brother like that just broke me.

20. In the late afternoon the guards ended their work and left me alone there for hours and hours on end. I thought they had forgotten me there; I asked a guard but he said the interrogators wanted me to be tied there. I was forced to stand up all night, handcuffed to the door, with one hand tied up, the other cradling my injured elbow. They allowed me to go to the bathroom three times, but I was forced to stay in the torture chamber by myself overnight until the guards returned to duty the following morning.

21. In the morning the caseworker came to see me. He asked me, "Are you human now!!!?" and "Will you collaborate with us now?" I said, "What are you talking about?" He simply replied, "Okay, fine. If that is the way it is." And they left me there in that position for 13 days, but they would not let me sleep. After five days I was very disoriented and faded in and out of consciousness. I could not tell if I was awake or asleep. I was dreaming that I was under the sea and drinking too much water, as if I were drowning. After five days I could not understand anything. Sometimes, still hanging from my hand, I would fall asleep and my head would drop, but the guards would wake me up by kicking my feet.

22. After 13 days of sleep deprivation they took me to a cell, and I slept for four straight days. I could not get up. When I finally woke up, I had no idea what time it was or where I was. They had put me in solitary confinement. For seven months I had no contact with anyone except the guard who would come to my cell to ask me the same questions. Food was pushed through the door. Every now and then they would take me for interrogation and I would receive lashes. During the lashings the guards would say to me, "You have to be on our side and tell us everything you know. If you tell us what we want to know then we can do something so that you are not executed. If not, we will kill you." During these seven months, as punishment, my food ration was half a normal ration, which left me hungry all the time and was extremely difficult.

23. After seven months, they lost hope and took me into to a large cell with 25 or 30 people. In 1986, Ayatollah Montazeri [Khomeini's designated successor] had just implemented some reforms in the prison system, so the doors to the cells were open and we could mix with other prisoners in the ward. We had pens and pencils for writing, and there was a small shop where we could buy basic items with money provided by our families. We also had visitors.

24. After two and half years in prison I was allowed my first visitation with my wife. We were allowed only ten minutes together. She told me that for a long time she did not know whether I was alive or dead. We were not even allowed to kiss each other. In the six years that I spent in prison, I had only three or four ten-minute visits with my wife. But I was able to have visits with my family every month. I saw my mother and sister regularly. During that time I had to go to court, and the judge (Nayyeri) in charge of my case told me he would send me to my brother. I realized my dear brother had been executed and he [Nayyeri] gave me the date of his execution. Then he sentenced me to death as well. My sentence, however, was commuted to 15 years' imprisonment because a relative of ours was connected to a powerful cleric, a member of the High Judicial Council, and through bribes he succeeded in changing my sentence as well as some other friends' sentences. But he had not been able to do anything for my brother because my brother was among the leadership of his organization and his resistance in prison had become legendary; they did not spare him.

25. These Montazeri reforms stayed in place for a year or so. 1986 was the best year to have been in prison. The man in charge of the prison was a reformer and so he was good to the prisoners under his administration. His name was Meysam and he was a reformer like Montazeri. He himself had been a political prisoner during the Shah's regime. I think he knew how to treat the prisoners and how to neutralize them. He was an intelligent administrator and avoided useless, brutal violence.

26. A year later, Montazeri's people were removed from the prison administration and conditions became much worse. In 1987 conditions became so bad that the prisoners began striking all the time and fighting with the guards.

27. Throughout that time I was in Evin Prison. However, in the fall of 1987 I was transferred to Gohardasht Prison. I was transferred along with a large group of prisoners from Evin because the guards were concerned about how regularly we were going on strike to protest prison conditions. They decided to separate the prisoners in Evin to stop us from organizing together. I was among those transferred to Gohardasht. They separated us on the basis of the length of our prison terms.

28. Those with heavier penalties were separated out first. The first group to be transferred to Gohardasht was made up of those who had sentences of between ten years and life imprisonment. Later on they sent the short-term prisoners [to Gohardasht], and even those who had finished their sentences but were not being released because they had not repented or renounced their political views. These prisoners were known as *mellikesh*.

29. As soon as we entered Gohardasht Prison they attacked us and started beating us very harshly. Then they shaved off our mustaches. This was our punishment for striking in Evin. We were then thrown into cells of two or three people. They wanted to keep us separate from each other so we could not organize as a group.

Events Surrounding 1988

30. In 1988 the atmosphere in society was changing. This affected the mood in the prison. Family members would tell prisoners during their visitations that society was very much against the regime and that people were beginning to think it would end. Because of this, the prisoners became very audacious. Sometimes they would even [verbally] confront the prison guards. Sometime in July the prison officials stopped allowing family visits.

31. Around 15 August 1988 we heard on the news that the Mojahedin had attacked the country. At that moment, we were cut off from information. The guards came into the cells and took the televisions. They told us there would be no visits, no television, no newspapers, and no shopping. All of the prisoners' privileges were removed. Any contact with the outside world was cut off.

32. From other prisoners, communicating between cells in Morse code, we had heard there was a court that was determining the fate of the prisoners. Sometimes we also heard the guards talking about it among

themselves. But we could not bring ourselves to believe it.

33. Around 20 August 1988 they came into the cells in my ward and told us to put on blindfolds. In my ward there were Mojahedin and leftists. When we were outside, the guards separated all of the Mojahedin. They took us out of our cells and into a large corridor. There were 72 of us who were taken out of the cell and ordered to stand in line. The Revolutionary Guards said we would be asked some questions. When we asked them what was going on and where they were taking us, they did not tell us that we were going to court; they told us we were meeting with an amnesty delegation. We did not understand the significance of what they were telling us at the time.

34. For those of us that who were leftists, we were basically asked only two questions by the guards: "Are you a Muslim?" and "Do you pray?" Those who responded that they were Muslims were immediately returned to their cells.

35. The Mojahedin were asked a different question. They were asked, "Which group do you belong to?" If they answered *monafeqin*, they were left in their cells for the time being. Those who answered "Mojahed" were taken to court, to be executed afterward.

36. It was only afterwards that we were able to bring together all of these stories. At the time we had no idea what other prisoners were being asked or how they were responding. We did not know what was

happening. There were 72 prisoners taken out of my ward. Of those 72 people, only nine came back (after the prison killings ended). The others were taken out into the main corridor and, as we discovered later, they were taken to be executed.

37. I was kept in the corridor several hours before my turn to go into the courtroom. The corridor was full of people, including prisoners I did not recognize from other sections. The courtroom was just a normal room that had been changed into a tribunal room. When it was my turn, a guard accompanied me into this room and told me to remove my blindfold. Inside the room I recognized only Nayyeri and Eshraqi. Several people were sitting at the side but I was told not to look at them. I managed to see one of the people at the side of the room, but I did not recognize him.

38. Nayyeri questioned me as follows:

Are you a Muslim? No.

Since when have you have not been a Muslim? I never remember having prayed or having said "God."

Were your parents Muslims? Yes.

How can your parents be Muslim, but you are not?

39. They asked me this question to trap me. Because if I said I had been a Muslim at some point in my life, but I now proclaimed I was not, then I would be deemed an apostate and they would kill me. So I responded, "I am going to introduce you to the Mullahs of our neighborhood

who drink alcohol and dance on Friday." Nayyeri got very annoyed. He shouted, "Take him away and give him lashes until he becomes a Muslim!"

40. The guards took me away to be flogged. They gave me 50 lashes. After that, it was sunset and they were not sure what they were supposed to do with me. The guard went to find out. He came back shortly afterwards and took me to [the amphitheatre]. When the door was opened he was surprised and talked to himself, "Why is it so dark and quiet?" He shouted at me, "Stay here, don't touch your blindfold and I'll come back."

41. Of course, as soon as I knew he had gone, I took off my blindfold. It was really dark. Around the stage there was a little bit of light. I could see a huge pile of prison shoes lying at the foot of the stage, as well as piles and piles of clothes. Without thinking, I looked up. It was then I saw six ropes hanging across the stage. I finally realized how serious this was. They were executing everyone. At that point the guard came back and yelled at me again "What were you looking at?!" I said, "Nothing, it is too dark in here, I cannot see anything." Fortunately for me, it was so late that the executions had stopped for the evening and so they took me back to a cell where I was held alone. I could barely sleep because of what I had seen. I worried what would happen next. It was a very long night.

42. The next morning I was taken back to court. While I was waiting in the corridor, Eshraqi came out of the courtroom to speak to me. I had my blindfold on but I could recognize him because of his clothes and his voice. Eshraqi said, "Why don't you just say the word you are a Muslim? Then everything will be okay." I replied, "Are all the people of Iran Muslim? There are some people who are not. Consider me as one of those." Eshraqi then said, "You are Muslim or nothing. Put this in your head." He turned and went back into the courtroom.

43. A few minutes later I was taken into the courtroom before Nayyeri and Eshraqi. I knew Nayyeri because he had been the president of the tribunal that had handed down my original conviction. The questioning went as follows:

If we release you, what will you do? Iran is an Islamic country and you are not a Muslim. I am a citizen and I am going to live my life. I don't care what religion anyone is—whether they are Jewish, Christian, or Muslim. I am just going to live my life.

Who was the Prophet of Islam? He was a man in history; he had some ideas and some followers.

What are the fundamental principles of Islam? I know there are five principles, but I do not know what they are.

44. I knew what the five principles were, but I would not say them. I knew they were asking me religious questions to trick me into admitting that I was, in fact, an apostate. They were trying to trap me into saying something to demonstrate I was in fact a Muslim and that I was denying my beliefs. Eshraqi seemed to be trying to be fair and said to Nayyeri, "Look, it is obvious he has never been a Muslim." But Nayyeri kept pursuing the questioning in this way, try-

ing to trick me. At some point Nayyeri got frustrated with me and shouted, "Take him away."

45. Eshraqi pleaded with him, "Please Mr. Haji, let me ask one more question." Eshraqi turned to me and asked, "If you go into an Islamic society, will you abide by the laws of the society?" I replied, "Yes." It seemed to me as if Eshraqi knew that they were going to execute me, but that he did not agree with that many executions and he was searching for a way to save some of the prisoners' lives.

46. Eshraqi said, "Look, Mr. Haji, he is a Muslim because he is willing to abide by our laws." They then declared that I had never been a Muslim; I was a non-believer, but not an apostate. Nayyeri ordered that I be sent away to be flogged for three days. "We will give you three days to become Muslim. If not, you will be executed. Take him away," he said.

47. They took me to a small cell and left. I heard some noises through the window. I tried to see through the small gap of the window. I saw a big truck (like those that have refrigeration systems) was there, and some guards, who were wearing special white clothes, covering them from head to toe, were carrying the bodies and putting them in the back of the truck. Some of them also had capsules on their backs as if they were spreading chemical powder or something similar. Oh my God! They killed so many people. I could not sleep that night.

48. The next day I was taken to a large ward called ward 6. There were 11 others in my cell. We were all leftists. Some Revolutionary Guards came into the ward. But they looked different; they had shaved their heads and were wearing large black, rubber boots. They assaulted us so badly that it seemed like they wanted to kill us. It was the worst physical beating I ever received in prison. While they were beating us, one of the guards said, "Our reward for killing each one of you apostates is 40 days in paradise!" As they were beating us I saw them hit one of the younger kid's [prisoner's] head against the radiator. His head was cut open and there was blood everywhere. He had a tremor and they dragged him out of the ward. I think he died because I never saw him again. I had my ribs broken, as did another one of the prisoners. I remember lying on the floor in agony, my ribs broken, and a guard jumped on my back. I was so badly injured that I had to have a back operation years after I was released from prison.

49. After one hour of beatings they took us to another small ward. We were all bleeding and had broken teeth and bruised faces. A cleric came into the room and said to us, "Now are you ready to pray?" One of our cellmates said, "Let me reason with him." We were all desperate for the beating to stop, but we did not want to pray. One of the prisoners said to the cleric, "We are all bleeding and so we cannot pray in this state while we are unclean." The guards agreed and left us alone for the time being.

50. That evening we started to confer with each other to decide what to do. Some of the prisoners would say, "We won't pray— let them execute us." But the majority of

the prisoners agreed that we should pretend that we were praying. One or two prisoners thought it better just to commit suicide. We did not want to give in to the guards and give up our beliefs. I found a piece of glass and I resolved that I would kill myself if the conditions became worse.

51. The next day they came back to the cell and asked, "Are you ready to pray?" The same prisoner said to them, "We cannot pray in this state. Look at us! We are covered in blood and in dirt. We are so injured we cannot even stand up and bend." The cleric who was there at the time was not accompanied by the guards. So he said to us, "Fine, I am going to tell the guards that you have accepted so they will not give you any more problems."

52. On the third day they took us all into a ward with other survivors. When we were first brought into the cell and saw some of our friends, we began hugging each other, excited to see each other again. But then it dawned on us that we were the only ones left in the prison. We quickly did the math and estimated that of the nearly 5,000 prisoners in Gohardasht and Evin only about 800 prisoners remained. There were only 800 in the adjoining cells and we were all leftists. There were no Mojahedin. It was only later when I went back to Evin that I discovered that some Mojahedin, maybe 250 prisoners, had survived there.

53. As the magnitude of the killings sank in, we went into a state of shock and depression. My friend Ali Mohebi, who was one of the 12 people in my cell, took it really badly. When he realized that there were

only 800 prisoners left in Gohardasht, he had a heart attack and died.

54. At first we were so depressed and shocked that we did not speak to each other about what happened. No one wanted to talk about it or to volunteer information about what had happened to him in order to put the pieces together.

55. In prison my best friends had been two brothers. We had lived together in such close quarters for so long that I knew their smell; we knew everything about each other. I remember the guard saying to Naserian, "they are brothers," and Naserian responded by saying, "it does not matter— take them away!" So my two best friends had been killed. I found a piece of metal in the prison, and I remember thinking to myself that if I were to see Naserian again I would kill him or die trying.

56. Although I had survived the executions, I figured my execution was certain and that they had just postponed it for a later date. I never believed that I would ever be released. For two months we stayed in Gohardasht in that cell, waiting to be called for execution. Suddenly one day the guards came into the cell and read a list of names. My name was on that list. We were told to bring our belongings. I thought I was going to be executed like the others. But we were transferred to Evin Prison.

57. In Evin I was put back into solitary confinement, where I was kept for a month. I really thought that I was just waiting to be executed. After a month passed, the guards came in and told me to come out with my belongings. I remember it was

winter and very cold, and I had to walk a mile in my prison slippers and light shirt to the courtyard. It was freezing. Usually they would transfer us by car. I was taken for a visitation with my sisters. They were wearing black and could not stop crying. I asked them what was wrong but they would not stop crying—they were hysterical. Soon after, I was taken out of solitary confinement and put into the normal cell. It was then I discovered that I had lost my mother—she had passed away that winter while I was in solitary confinement.

58. Then, the whole time until the prisoners' release, there was a trial of will between authorities and the prisoners over whether to sign a confession and accept the regime. The regime did not want to have any more political prisoners, but refused to let them go until they signed confessions. The prisoners, on the other hand, having been through so much, refused to give up their beliefs and sign confessions. But, group by group, they signed the confession and were released. Eventually the prison guards separated the prisoners because they knew it would be easier to get individual prisoners to relent and sign a confession if they were on their own, not bolstered and supported by being in a group.

59. Finally I was alone in the cell. The guards forgot about me and left me in the dark with no food. Finally I called out to a guard who was passing by my cell, but the guard became scared and ran away—there were not supposed to be any prisoners left in the cell. The guard thought I was some kind of ghost or something. Finally, one of the orderlies discovered me and reported it to the prison authorities. I was then released. I think I was the last prisoner in Evin.

60. I spent a total of eight and a half years in prison. I have lost so many friends and I lost my brother. My wife was also held in prison for many years. This is only a tiny part of my story. There is so much more to tell about what happened in those prisons.

London, June 2009

OFFICIAL STATEMENT • 22

اطّلاعات

Subject: Divine government, non-divine or human governments, and due process of law
The official: Chief Justice of the Court of Cassation, Head of Supreme Judicial Council, and the
                Acting Friday Prayer Leader, Ayatollah Abdolkarim Musavi Ardebili
The occasion: Tehran Friday Prayer
Date: 20 January 1989
Source: *Ettela'at*, 21 January 1989

In the first sermon of this week's Friday Prayer, in Tehran, Ayatollah Musavi Ardebili compared divine government with non-divine or human governments and referred to the great advantage of Islamic government, which is the Guardianship of the Supreme Jurist [Velayat-e Faqih]. He said, "In human governments, where all laws and regulations are drafted and established by individuals, many an impasse occurs in practice, which leads those in power to resort to authoritarian rule. In Divine government, however, the main framework of the legal system and major laws are established by God, and when a problem arises, the Guardian Jurist [Vali-e Faqih] can, by relying on his guardianship, his intelligence, and divine law, promptly resolve the issue." Regarding this subject, the provisional Friday Imam of Tehran said, "In the last ten years, the Islamic government of Iran has been confronted with numerous difficulties created by domestic and foreign enemies and has had to deal with many conspiracies. In all these matters, his holiness, the Imam [Khomeini] has used his Guardianship prerogatives in a very appropriate

manner to resolve obstacles." In another part of his sermon, he highlighted the problems caused by the cumbersome rules and regulations of the judiciary. "While the infallible imams [the twelve Shi'a imams after Prophet Muhammad] deemed even a one-hour delay in the enforcement of 'Hadd,' the punishment of a *mohareb* [one who wages war against God] as a crime, many of our criminal cases take years to be decided." Tehran's Acting Friday Prayer Leader gave examples of such cases and said, "Seditious elements conspired in Sabzevar [the northeastern region of Iran] and brought their associates from Tehran and other cities in order to ignite unrest in the region. They armed them with handguns, hand grenades, and other weapons, and in one night they caused about 400 to 500 residents to fight each other, and as a result some were killed and some were wounded." He added, "If we investigate this case within the framework of current judicial rules and regulations, it might take us five years before we are able to reach a conclusion. By then many people would have forgotten this case and they might feel pity for those seditious elements and their families." Mr. Musavi Ardebili said, "When the Imam [Khomeini] was informed that carrying out God's sentences takes such a long time, he lectured judiciary officials and scolded them in a fatherly way. Within seven or eight days, the Imam's admonition produced the desired result and cleared the way for concluding criminal cases." He said, "More than a year had passed since two blacksmiths in the provincial city of Doroud, assisted by other thugs, attacked the home of one of their colleagues. They killed him, raped his wife, and stole his belongings. Yet [because of] due process these criminals could not be punished anytime soon." The head of the Court of Cassation added, "Thanks to the Imam's fatwa, in two days, four people were executed, two hands were amputated, and three people were sentenced to prison terms. Regarding the Sabzevar incident, I was informed today that the commission that was sent to Sabzevar from Mashhad to investigate this incident has found the offenders guilty of corruption on earth and enmity against God. I instructed them to issue two death sentences for these individuals, so that, in case they obtain the next of kin's forgiveness to prevent *Qesas* (retribution) they can still be executed for *Moharebeh* (enmity with God). . . ."

Soraya Zangebari

ARRESTED: August 1985
DETAINED IN: Evin Prison
RELEASED: May 1989

1. My name is Soraya Zangebari. I was a political prisoner in Iran from August 1985 to May 1989. My husband, Qorban'ali Shokri, was also in prison during the same period. He was executed during the 1988 mass execution of political prisoners.

2. I make this statement in support of an investigation into the mass execution of political prisoners in 1988 in Iran.

3. This statement is true to the best of my knowledge and belief. Except where I indicate to the contrary, I make this statement on the basis of facts and matters within my own knowledge. Where the facts and matters in this statement are within my own knowledge, they are true. Where the facts and matters are not within my own knowl-edge, I have identified the source or sources of my information, and I believe such facts to be true.

Pre-arrest Activities

4. I went to the United States of America (U.S.) to study in 1976. I was a member of the Confederation of University Students of Iran in the U.S., where I started my po-litical activism by joining the United Com-munists of Iran. I returned to Iran after the Revolution in early 1979 and continued to militate for the United Communists Party. For a short while I enrolled in Reza'ieh University to continue my agricultural studies. But I was more into political activ-ism [than studying]. We [the party] had an office in the university. After a while I had to flee and return to Tabriz. Soon I met my husband in our organization and we got married in 1981.

5. My husband was an elementary school teacher in our hometown of Tabriz. He was born in 1950 and was a university student before the Revolution but did not finish his degree. We were both involved in non-violent political activism; we were not involved in any kind of armed struggle. Our activities consisted of attending meetings, doing propaganda work, and

distributing party leaflets. In the winter or the early spring of 1982, we heard the Tabriz Friday Prayer Imam, Malakuti, who later was killed in a terrorist attack, say that some teachers were teaching Communism instead of teaching from the school textbooks. Actually he was alluding to my husband. My husband was once arrested in Tabriz in 1982. The authorities arrested him. They thought he was a Tufan Party sympathizer because he was at a friend's house who was a Tufan member. He was incarcerated by mistake and they did not discover his real political affiliation.

6. [During that first incarceration], on 20 December 1982, our first wedding anniversary, I visited my husband in prison for the first time since his arrest. He did not expect to see me there. He thought that I had escaped and was a refugee. He forgot that we were in the prison and that our conversation might be taped. He asked me what I was doing in the prison, and why I had not escaped. I told him, "Why should I have escaped? I did not do anything." I tried to get his attention. I asked him if it was true that he had engaged in political activities. He denied any such activities. He said that he had done nothing and expected to be freed soon.

7. But I could see he had been badly beaten. He was in bad shape though he was very self-composed and, even if he was in pain, he wouldn't say anything about it. In fact, the friend, in whose house my husband had been arrested, had a fugitive brother-in-law who had been an army officer and one of the leaders of Tufan. They tortured my husband because they thought he was

this fugitive officer and they wanted him to confess his identity. But since none of the arrested Tufan affiliates knew him, nor could they identify him as a fellow member, he was released after a two-and-a-half-month detention.

8. In 1984, during the post-New Year picnic festival, Sizadah Beh Dar (2 April), my husband and I went to visit the family of a friend who had been arrested a year earlier. This friend was also a teacher, and after the picnic festival on 3 April 1983 he had returned to school, and his colleagues had told him that the school administration had been looking for him [in fact they had come to arrest him and did arrest him at school]. After hearing that story I convinced my husband not to return to work the next day. The next morning [just after the school opened], one of his colleagues called and told us very cautiously that the "brothers" [security forces] from the "administration" had been at school looking for my husband. We left our house immediately and never went back.

9. The Tabriz branch of our organization suffered a blow and was dismantled. My husband's friend (in whose house he had been arrested in 1982) was supposed to connect us to the southern branch of our organization, but he was re-arrested before connecting us. My husband and I, along with a couple of other friends, moved our furniture and equipment, such as the copying equipment.

10. We were trying to reconnect to our organization and reorganize the last of the people who had not been arrested. To do so, we

planned a meeting in Iranian Kurdistan in May 1983. I attended this meeting, but my husband couldn't attend. There were about 35 of us who attended.

11. We moved to Tehran, where we stayed at my parents' house. We started looking for jobs. Finally, we found a house and jobs in private companies. It was not easy to rent a house because, by law, the landlord needed to have a copy of the tenant's Basij ration booklet, issued during the Iran-Iraq War to each family by each district's revolutionary authorities. These booklets helped both with controlling the population and with distribution of the food and clothes rations. Many people were scared to rent their homes.* Naturally we didn't have a Basij booklet, but we finally managed to find a home, and we stayed there for about a year.

12. Those were daunting days. The more scared we became, the more we felt the necessity to continue our resistance and work to change the [political] situation. We lived for many years in a constant state of alert. We incessantly checked our escape routes. Expecting imminent arrest and in order to be ready to escape [at a moment's notice], we slept in our day clothes. This unrelenting pressure convinced us that life should not be like that. We had to change the situation through more political activism.

13. My sister, who had cancer, was insisting that we should leave the country. However, we refused to leave Iran. We thought it unethical. [We thought,] it wouldn't be fair for us to leave while most people were in such a difficult situation. We ought to stay and change the situation.

Arrest and Interrogation

14. The day we were arrested we were in a [political] meeting. My husband, my cousin, and I, along with my 53-day-old son, were in our apartment in Shahrara, expecting our organization's officer for a meeting planned for that day. Our officer was late. He had missed the meeting the previous day as well. Originally, we had agreed that, for security reasons, when one person did not show up at a meeting, the rest of the group would assume that the person had been detained. Our mistake was that we still planned another meeting the following day and we still waited for him the following day. And when we saw that he didn't show up, my husband went to pick him up, and we didn't realize [that something was wrong] when my husband didn't come back. We even waited for my husband at home. That was our mistake.

15. We had no electricity (which was common in those days, due to the war). My cousin and I were sitting on the bed, eating grapes and playing with my son. I heard a sound at our apartment door. The moment we opened the door, six or seven armed Revolutionary Guards rushed into our

---

*To get a Basij booklet, one had to have a few co-signers to confirm his or her identity, place of birth, and residency. The co-signers could be neighbors, people at the mosque, the mosque's Imam, the revolutionary committee or their members in the neighborhood. A new landlord and tenant lease agreement law had been executed by the Sepah and the prosecutor's office. The landlord and often his family too would be imprisoned if he did not follow the law.

apartment. They separated my cousin and
me and searched the apartment thoroughly.
One of them, whose name was Ebrahim,
pointed his gun at me. He became my interrogator afterwards. He told me, "Come
on! Get dressed! Hurry up!" I said, "So go
out of the room and let me get dressed!"
He turned his head away so that I could get
dressed. He was looking in the closet and
under the bed. Except for a few banned
books, we had nothing illegal in our house.
The Revolutionary Guards confiscated the
apartment key so that they could search
the place more thoroughly later on.

16. I asked one of them for how long I should
pack things for my infant child. One of
them said, "It won't take longer than an
hour. Your husband has been arrested for
drug possession. We want to take you for
some blood tests. You must not talk to
anyone in the hallways and if they ask anything, just tell them that it is nothing and
you will be back soon." From bursting into
our apartment to putting us in their car, all
this lasted only a few minutes. They took
my key to the apartment to return it
to my brother-in-law after they had completed their search. They told us in the car
that we were going to Evin.

17. In prison, we found out that our organization's officer had resisted torture for 24
hours, before giving them any information,
so that we would have 24 hours to leave
and hide. Thus we were arrested in August
1985. A large group of our organization's
affiliates had been arrested, and we never
found out how we had been identified. We
probably were in the prosecutor's trap.

18. They drove us to Evin Prison. There, at the
guards' office in Evin Prison, they blindfolded us and took us to the interrogation
chamber. The interrogation building was
an office space. It consisted of many rooms
with numbers on their doors. Each room
was used for a specific group (political leaning). For example, room 6 was used for a
branch of the Communist groups known
as the "third line" [it opposed Soviet impe-
rialism]. This is where they took me. There
were many men and women in the hallway.
I could see their legs. Their feet and their
legs were wrapped in bandages and their
feet were bloody, swollen, and larger than
normal.

19. After [I waited] a short while at the door of
room 6, my interrogator called me in, and
asked for my name and personal information and sent me out again. I sat in the
hallway all day, blindfolded, with my child.
Because I was told we would stay only one
hour I had brought only one additional
change of clothes and a half-pack of Pam-
pers for my baby. In the evening, we were
all transferred to the ward. A female guard
threw me into a cell. When I removed my
blindfold, I realized that I was in a restroom.

20. The solitary cell in ward 209 was, in fact,
a restroom. It was a 6 square-meter [2 x 3
meters, 6.5 x 10 feet] cell with a toilet and
a small sink. There was a plastic plate, a
plastic cup, and one spoon in the cell. A
small carpet partially covered the floor.

21. Early the next morning, the guard told
me to get ready for interrogation. My
outfit was a cloak [a long coat-like dress of

thinner fabric] and a scarf. The guard told me that my veil was not appropriate. She gave me a very long chador. It was heavy and slippery. I did not know how to keep it on and hold my baby at the same time. The guard found a solution. She pulled the veil down on my forehead and put on my blindfold over it. She took my shoes and gave me rubber flip-flops (slippers) and took me to the interrogation in a car. I spent the whole day in the interrogation building. Sometimes they took me to the room again and asked for my personal information.

22. For the whole week, I was taken to the interrogation building every day in the same fashion. They would again ask my name and information and make me wait blindfolded in the hallway with my infant, and then in the evening they would return me to the solitary cell again.

23. When we were waiting in the hallways to be interrogated, the guards were watching us to make sure the newly arrested people did not communicate with each other. One day as I was getting off the bus to go to ward 209, I saw Mohammad Tavakkoli, our officer in the organization, sitting there. I could see him from under my blindfold. I was on the step of the bus and he was sitting on the ground. One of the guards asked him to move. Mohammad asked the guard to let him move on all fours. He had been tortured on his feet, and he could not walk. I recognized his distinct voice. This became invaluable information. My interrogator did not know the extent of my information. He kept asking me what Mohammad looked like.

He was testing me to see if I was telling the truth. Knowing that he was arrested, I told him what he looked like. But when the interrogators realized [that I knew he was arrested], they beat me up.

24. I was not taken to the torture room and was not flogged. But once in a while, during the interrogations while I was blindfolded and had my baby in my arms, they would hit and kick me, in my head and my body. In the interrogations, you should answer the interrogators no more or less than is necessary. One of their methods was to repeat constantly the same questions to see if you were contradicting yourself and thus they could interrogate you further on the contradiction. They wanted us to write everything down. At night, in my cell, I used to repeat what I had written during the day in order not to forget it.

25. Once my interrogator asked someone to come to the room and take the baby away. I had a blindfold on. He sat me on a chair facing the wall. Suddenly, someone put a cable around my neck like a noose and started pulling up. It felt as if he were trying to hang me. I was shocked. That man said, "She needs to be taught a lesson!" The interrogator replied, "Not now, wait." Then the interrogation began.

26. My interrogator asked me about my connections within the organization. During the first week [after my arrest], when the interrogations were not long and difficult, I had had time to gather very limited but important information. When they asked whom I knew [in my organization], I would give the names of those I had seen

in prison and knew were already arrested. I occasionally bumped into people of our group in the ward and they would say to me, "Why are you here? You were not politically active!" This helped me a lot. I tried to convince the interrogators that because of family reasons I had stopped any political activities long before my arrest and knew nothing of [recent] political activities.

27. My sister had passed away three months before my arrest [I did not have anyone to leave my baby with]. I had just had a Caesarean section. In prison I soon ran out of diapers and food for my baby. I was hungry, I did not have milk to breastfeed my baby, so he was hungry and was crying all the time. In the evening I used a piece of fabric that I had as a diaper. In the morning, I used my headscarf as his second diaper and washed the fabric and tried to dry it by spinning it with my hand. When the fabric was dry I would wash my headscarf and wear it immediately [while it was still wet], because, when taken for interrogation, we needed to have both a headscarf and a chador. Also, during the interrogation if the chador would open, my neck could be seen and you know this would put Islam in peril. While in prison I saved Islam from peril many times. One morning I washed his cloth and used my headscarf for his diaper as usual. As I was about to change him and wash my headscarf, I was called for interrogation. So I had to save Islam by putting on the dirty headscarf on which my son had peed. After a month or two, they informed my parents of my whereabouts. My family brought some clothes and a blanket and stuff like that for the baby.

28. My health was very poor after my Caesarean, the scars of which were still hurting. My sister's death after five years of struggle with cancer was a huge blow to my morale. My physical pains remained with me for years. I used to wake up after two hours of sleep because of a pain in my body. I could not move at all. First I could manage to move my hands and then gradually the rest of my body. All of my bones were hurting. A doctor said it was because of lack of sunlight. We could get fresh air, but it was in another cell that had an open ceiling [no roof]. They used to leave me there for hours and because, in that cell, there was no place for my child to sleep, I had to hold him in my arms for hours. This gave me great pain in my back. That was why I preferred to stay in my own cell.

29. During all these times, I tried to present myself as a woman with little education. By doing so I made my interrogator feel reassured. For example, I intentionally made a lot of grammatical and spelling mistakes when I was writing my answers for the interrogators and I used very childish handwriting. Sometimes the interrogator looked at my writing and corrected me proudly. He was so happy that he knew more than me; I believe that I played my role well until the end and it did me a great deal of good. It is well known that from an interrogator's point of view, the smarter and more educated you are, the more dangerous you can be, [and that is] especially true for a woman. That is why, if you know less, you may survive.

30. Anyway, by the time I was arrested, in 1985, the pressures in prison had decreased.

For example, they did not force us to say our prayers. Other prisoners who were in the prison before me used to say jokingly that the prison looked like paradise then (in 1985).

31. My son and I remained in solitary confinement for six months, the time it took for my interrogation to be completed. Then came the time for my trial.

Trial

32. I couldn't wait for the interrogations to be completed. During the interrogations, one feels degraded and humiliated, as if one is a fly that could be crushed at any time by a flyswatter. But the thought of my forthcoming trial would give me self-esteem. The only image I had of a trial was the one I had seen in the movies: a jury, a judge, and a lawyer. I was wondering if they would designate a lawyer for me or if I could pick a lawyer myself; I was debating with myself about whether I should accept or reject the lawyer they would designate for me. For a few days before my trial, my mind was absorbed with these thoughts, until, one day, I was called for my trial.

33. It was a funny court. The guard said, "You will go on trial today." He took me to the prison's administrative section and left me waiting behind an office door. Someone called me in. I went in, and a voice told me to lift up my blindfold. It was just an ordinary office room. A mullah and an old man were sitting at a very small desk. I just burst into laughter. Then, I panicked and quickly covered my mouth. The guard who had taken me to the court jumped

in front of me and angrily asked what was going on. "Nothing," I said, "I just stepped on my veil and I was afraid of dropping my baby."

34. Nayyeri was the religious judge. He read the charges to me. Membership in our organization (Ettehadieh Komonist-ha) was one of the charges against me. The most incriminating charges I remember were "attending my organization's congress [the Ettehadieh's fourth congress was held in Kurdistan], and "traveling to Kurdistan without my husband's permission." My husband and I had previously agreed that he would deny any knowledge of my Kurdistan trip, and I would say I had lied to him and told him I was visiting my parents.

35. The whole trial session took less than half an hour. Among other questions, Nayyeri asked if I still believed in my organization. I responded to some questions by yes and to others, no. Then he asked if I had something to say. I said, "Yes, I need to feed my baby." He told the guard, "Take her out so that she can feed her baby." I breastfed the baby for half an hour in the hallway, and was called into the room again. The old man sitting next to Nayyeri instructed me to sign a paper. I asked to read the content before signing it. He said that the content was what was said in the court. I insisted on reading what I was going to sign. But he told me that it would make no difference whether I read it or not. I don't remember if I signed it or not.

36. After my trial ended, Nayyeri asked me if I wanted anything. I said, "Yes, I have

no news of my husband, I request a visit." Nayyeri said, "Keep her outside [in the hallway] until her husband's trial is completed and then let them meet."

37. My husband was sentenced to five years in prison. His sentence was lighter than mine, because I had committed the crime of traveling to Kurdistan without my husband's permission. Or at least this is how I explained to myself my seven-year sentence versus my husband's five-year sentence.

38. My husband and I met after a long time for one hour, in one of the rooms in the same building. It seemed that the room was used as a prayer room because the floor was covered with a small carpet. My son was with me and he was about six months old. During this meeting, my husband was mainly focused on our son. We talked about our son, the organization, and our fellow militants who had been arrested. I did not have an opportunity to find out about my husband's physical condition.

39. We were careful not to be overheard because we thought they were listening to us. We even thought they might be filming us. As we were talking we made sure that our conversation was very vague and unclear. We whispered and communicated through signs and allusions. I think the interrogator knew little of our background and past activities in Tabriz and in the university. He did not know about my having lived in the U.S., because living in the U.S. could be a crime.

Prison Conditions

40. One evening, near the end of my solitary confinement, another prisoner was brought to my cell. It was my cousin who had been arrested with me. The last few weeks with her were really fun. We sang and joked and played the game of 20 questions, and laughed all the time. Once in a while the guard came in swearing at us and ordering us to shut up, but she could not control us.

41. I learned how to use Morse code while I was in solitary confinement. That learning process is one of my best memories from prison. One night, while in my cell, sitting behind closed doors, worrying about my child, I heard some taps. I got angry, wondering why they were doing construction in the middle of the night, which would wake my son up. But the tapping stopped and another began. Then I understood that they were talking via Morse code. That was very nice—two live persons, under similar circumstances as mine, were near and they were talking. It was like life was flowing again. I started counting the taps. Later on, on the wall of the cell or on the bathroom wall, I found a chart showing the numbers for Morse code. I tried hard to learn it and finally I did. Once my cousin came, we tried to practice it together. It was so interesting.

42. After a while, they told us to pack and go to the public ward. My son and I were taken to ward 216. Ward 216 had four sections. Nowhere else in the world could I find the intensity of good things that I felt and saw in prison. Despite bad prison conditions and solitary confinement, I found invalu-

able friendships in prison. During the time I was in Evin, in the wards you could find *sar-e moze'i*, repenters, MKOs, leftists, anyone! I was constantly being moved from one ward to another.

43. A few months after I was issued my sentence, the Executive Office of Judgment called me. At the office, I was told that I was eligible for clemency and that my term had been reduced to three years in prison. I asked why I had been convicted for seven years in the first place. The officer replied, "So you would behave." I asked, "Why has it been reduced now?" He told me that was none of my business. My son and I were in prison for four years.

44. My sister had passed away before my arrest and my mother had a heart attack after our arrest. So I did not have anyone outside of prison to give my son to. He had no contact with children of his age. During his four years in prison, he learned to talk, and, since he had a good memory, he learned the names of 200 inmates in our ward. He would help me remember their names. The first word he [my son] said was "havakhori, " which is recreation in the prison yard. Once when he saw his own face in a mirror on the fridge of the ward, he got really scared. It took him a long time to get used to his own face. He could not see his father often because I could not meet my husband regularly. Later, I noticed that he was afraid of his father. He was afraid of men in general. I thought if he could see his father every week, he would get used to him.

Events Surrounding 1988

45. In the summer of 1987, all four sections of ward 216 were combined and transferred into two sections in ward 325. Apparently monarchist inmates used to be held in that section. It had a very big, nice yard. It was a beautiful ward. We spent the summer there. At the end of the summer, all of us were transferred to the Amuzeshgah ward. They divided us, according to our political positions, into repenters, *sar-e moze'i*, etc., and sent us to different places. In the Amuzeshgah, there were about 200 inmates. Two wards were allocated to *sar-e moze'i*. I was not there. I believe I was in ward 3, but I am not positive about that.

46. In the spring of 1988 (Persian date 1367), the prison authorities announced that we could get prison furloughs and stay with our families. It was at the prisoner's request. Before that only repenters were allowed to request a furlough. I immediately asked for it. I wanted my son to see the world outside of prison. We were allowed to go for eight days. My family had to submit their house ownership documents (the deed) as security for the visit.

47. After the furlough, in late spring of 1988, they allowed a lot of visitations between imprisoned couples and immediate family members in private rooms for long periods of time. It was strange and unprecedented. The visits were every other week and lasted more than an hour. A Revolutionary Guard was always present at the visits and we were told to speak Farsi so that the Revolutionary Guard could understand our conversations. But still it was much better

than before. Past visits had taken place in a kiosk with glass partitions and lasted for only fifteen minutes.

48. Before each visit I would prepare my son for seeing his father. When I saw we had regular visits, I put in a request to visit my husband more often but for shorter periods, thinking this would help my frightened son become more comfortable with his father. They agreed and we had a few weekly meetings until they stopped completely. In our last meeting, he sat on his father's lap for the first time. Noticing that nothing bad happened and being full of amazement, he started to touch his father's face and head. He said, "Mom, see! He has ears. He has eyes. He is like us!" This was our last visit.

49. After a while, suddenly, all the visitations were suspended. I do not remember the exact dates. But it was after Iran accepted the UN resolution 598. A few days later they took the televisions out of the room. And the following day they didn't bring newspapers. The next day, we were supposed to have visits with our families. But the authorities announced that there would not be any visitations. We were cut off from the outside world. All of the prisoners were curious and puzzled about the changes, but none of the guards answered any questions. We would ask, "Where are you taking these [prisoners], where are you taking them?" They would respond, "It is none of your business, don't be nosy."

50. After the suspension of the visitations, the guards changed completely and became aloof and acted like robots. Unlike before,

they didn't come to the ward to beat us or to search the room. They kept their distance from us and looked at us differently. Before they would at least talk to the repenters, but during these two months they ignored the repenters too in the same way. They totally ignored us.

51. One day, we were in the prison yard and heard a loud explosion. The guards were nervous and sent us back inside. They disappeared for a while and when they came back they did not respond to any of our questions. A few days later, we were in the yard again. The Friday Prayer was being broadcast on the speakers. I think Rafsanjani was the prayer Imam on that day. We could not quite hear what he said in the sermon but we could hear the crowd who attended the prayer. In support of the Imam, worshipers yelled, "*Monafeqin* (MKO) prisoners should be executed!" That alerted us. We realized something was happening.

52. Two guards soon came through the ward with pen and paper in hand. They looked at the prisoners inside the cells. They paced to the end of the ward, looked inside the cells, took some notes, and then left the ward slowly and quietly. A few minutes later, the loudspeaker called the names of some of the prisoners. We knew that those prisoners were going to their executions. I am not sure how we knew it, but those who were called knew it too. At first we could not figure out how they selected the prisoners. After a few days we realized that they called only the MKO prisoners. None of them ever came back.

53. One of the MKO sympathizers in our room, before she was called, became very pale, like a ghost. She knew her name would be called. And they did call her. No one said anything. The whole section was wrapped in silence. Everyone was shocked. That they took someone out of the ward was not unusual, but this time we knew they were being taken to be executed. They called at least 100 MKO sympathizers from our ward. They even took the repenters.

54. This situation continued for two months. On the last days of the second month, the guards would come to the entrance to the cells. They would call us one by one and ask inquisitively about our beliefs. One of them called me and asked me if I believed in God and I said yes. Then, she asked if I did my prayers. I said, "No." She asked, "Why?" I said, "I do not know. I have never done it from my childhood. My parents never did it either." I knew those questions were going to determine if I lived; that is why I said I believed in God. She was an ordinary guard and took notes on the prisoners' answers.

55. A short time after the massacre, they stopped calling prisoners' names, and we got in-person visitations with people from outside the prison. There were 200 people in our ward before the massacre. After two months, there were 100 of us left. The visits took place in the prison yard. The yard was crowded and everybody was sitting on the ground. I was confused and still in shock. My mother and sister came. My family kept asking questions. I did not know what or how to answer my family's questions. I remember very little.

56. After that visit with our families, visits inside the prison resumed. Months passed and I had no news about my husband. I asked the guards repeatedly about my husband. They told me to ask my family about my husband. Many times I asked my family about my husband, but they would not tell me anything. My family was keeping it from me. They denied having any information about him. That situation upset me, and I told my father that he did not care about my husband and that was why he had not made any inquiries about my husband. My father became very upset and said that he had asked about my husband. The authorities had told him that my husband was in exile and nobody knew where.

57. When I came back to the ward, I told my cellmates about my father's response. Everyone was surprised. I was told that there was no possibility of exile. Either prisoners are alive or they are executed. I wrote a letter to Hosseinzadeh, the second-in-command of the prison, and requested a meeting. Hosseinzadeh himself was xvery uneasy. His face was red, his head was lowered, and he would not look at me. I asked him for my husband's will. He referred me to the Executive Office of Judgments, the office where they enforced the sentences. In agony, I started screaming, "Why did you kill him? Why did you kill him? Did you not say that you would kill only murderers? He was not a murderer." Hosseinzadeh said that my husband was not a murderer. He told me that he had advised him to change his ward from *sar-e moze'i*, but he refused. Afterwards, I

thought maybe his execution was because of his ward. I knew him; if he knew that the questionnaire would determine his life, he would not say he didn't believe in God. The Executive Office told me that my husband did not have a will. I asked for his grave number and the plot. "Was he an MKO or a leftist?" "A leftist," I said. "He has no grave number."

58. My husband's belongings were returned to the family. They consisted of a few pieces of clothing and a mirror. One day my son dropped the mirror. In back of the mirror was a note. On the note he had written our son's birthday and described an imaginary birthday party for him in the prison yards. He wrote about the party in great detail, mentioning who had brought the cake and who had brought presents. Surprisingly, all the names were correct. I don't know how he had learned the names of my ward-mates.

59. I have two official documents concerning my husband, both issued by the authorities. The first one is a letter that was issued when I wanted to get a Basij booklet. In that letter they indicated that my husband had been executed. The second document is his death certificate. This document maintains that my husband died from natural causes. But the date of his death and the date of his burial at the registry office of the Behesht Zahra Cemetery do not match. The registry office also states his death was registered several months after his actual death.

60. In order to be freed, I had to sign a letter expressing my hatred for my organization. The letter was drafted by them, I just signed it. My family had to turn over the deed to their house as a bond for my release.

61. Around May 1989, I was released. I had spent all my time in prison at Evin. I stayed in Iran for four years. I did everything I could to get by. I could not get a job or a place to live. To have a permanent job, I had to go through background checks to show that I had a clean criminal record, but I could not give the companies that. These documents were necessary when the companies wanted to hire me as a regular employee. Once the employers found out about my imprisonment, they fired me. I never told them voluntarily about my past. I was applying only to private companies, and they were scared that their properties would be confiscated if they offered me employment. This situation was repeated with every job that I took. It was also very difficult to rent a place as a single woman, especially with my background. Once a month, I had to report my whereabouts and answer questions such as, "What do you do? Where do you live? What do you read? Etc."

62. After a while, I heard from a few of my ex-prisoner friends that they had applied for passports. In one of the monthly report visits, I asked if I could apply for a passport. He asked me if I wanted to leave the country. I said no, I was just asking. He told me to go to the passport office and apply and if I got a passport it would mean that I was allowed to travel. I went to the passport office and I applied; they issued a passport for me the same afternoon. I was surprised and I knew there was a mistake.

Before applying for a passport, prisoners had to have a letter from the prosecutor's office on Mo'allem Street, which was the case for my friends. The prosecutor's letter would define whether a prisoner was eligible for a passport or not. I got the passport without the letter. The next day, early in the morning, the passport office called our home and asked me to bring the passport back. The clerk at the office took my passport, put it in the safe, and gave me a letter.

63. I took the letter to the prosecutor's office on Mo'allem Street. They said to call back one week later. I called every week for five months and never received an answer. Then I decided to buy a fake passport. When I got the passport, I realized that it was my real passport that the smuggler had obtained by working with someone at the passport office. The reason [I knew it was my real passport] was that when they issued my passport, the clerk used a green stamp. Then when I returned it, he crossed out the stamp. The passport that the smuggler gave me was re-stamped over the old one. The smuggler told me that I was still forbidden to leave the country legally.

64. I had to meet with the smuggler at the Bazargan border (near Turkey). The smuggler kept my passport. At the border, he waited until the next shift for a police-man who was cooperating with him. Once his friend came, he stamped my passport and I crossed over the border. That was in November.

Sweden, October 2009

OFFICIAL STATEMENT • 23

Subject: Ayatollah Khomeini's classified death fatwa against the Mojahedin
The official: Former warden of Evin Prison
The occasion: Interview with Iranian Students News Agency (ISNA)
Date: 21 August 2004
Source: ISNA

ABF EDITOR'S NOTE: In this interview, Ali Amani, prison warden in 1984 and deputy prosecutor under Assadollah Lajevardi, in the course of alluding to factional rivalry, mentions Khomeini's decree against the MKO prisoners and confirms the veracity of Ayatollah Montazeri's allegations. His statement is important, because he was a political enemy of Ayatollah Montazeri and a high-ranking member of the very influential and currently powerful Islamic Coalition Party, Hey'at hay-e Motalefeh.

Describing the Imam as the greatest supporter of martyr Lajevardi, Amani noted: "The Imam [Khomeini] was Lajevardi's biggest supporter. But he adopted silence owing to the ever-increasing attacks upon Lajevardi. . . . But with his Fatwa regarding Mojahedin prisoners after the Mersad Operation, the Imam demonstrated his displeasure about the performance of the judiciary and the freeing of the *monafeqin*. Of course, for security reasons, the content of this Fatwa remains classified and cannot be discussed here."

Fatemeh Zare'i: *Three Witnesses*

The following three testimonies concerning Fatemeh Zare'i, who was executed during the 1988 prison massacres, are by her husband, Hassan Makaremi; her father, Aziz Zare'i; and her daughter, Chowra Makaremi.

Hassan Makaremi

1. My name is Hassan Makaremi and I am the husband of Fatemeh Zare'i. My wife was arrested in 1980 and was executed during the 1988 prison massacres.

2. I make this statement in support of an investigation into the mass execution of political prisoners in 1988 in Iran.

3. This statement is true to the best of my knowledge and belief. Except where I indicate to the contrary, I make this statement on the basis of facts and matters within my own knowledge. Where the facts and matters in this statement are within my own knowledge, they are true. Where the facts and matters are not within my own knowledge, I have identified the source or sources of my information, and I believe such facts to be true.

Fatemeh Zare'i's Political Activities Before the Revolution

4. Fatemeh Zare'i was born in November 1950. We were married in the city of Shiraz in 1974. Our two children were born in 1977 and 1980. In the early 1970s, Fatemeh Zare'i became active in politics for a short period of time. She was then studying at Pars College in Tehran and started to attend Ali Shari'ati's talks in that city. My wife did not wear *hijab* (a covering on her hair) before the Revolution in Iran. When she became familiar with Shari'ati, she wore a *hijab* for a short time. When we got married she did not wear it. A few months before the Revolution she started wearing it again. She always said her prayers. Her mother always wore a *hijab*, but her sister never did.

Connections to the MKO and Political Activities Before Her Arrest

5. After the Revolution she joined the Movement of Muslim Teachers, which was

an association affiliated with the MKO [Mojahedin Khalq Organization]. One or two months after the Revolution they opened a chapter in Shiraz, which she was involved in. She was a full-time physics teacher of senior high school students. The high school was named after Reza Shah, but it was renamed after the Revolution—I cannot remember its new name. In 1980, during the Cultural Revolution, she received a letter stating that she did not abide by the principles of the Islamic Republic and therefore she was dismissed, without pension. I also was purged the same year, a few months later. Her political activism increased after she was purged during the Cultural Revolution.

6.   Fatemeh and her sisters were sympathetic to the MKO; I was not. I was a more seasoned political activist; I had been involved in politics since the time I was a student at Polytechnic University. I had met the MKO and FKO leaders in prison. During that period, I suggested we should leave the city of Shiraz, but Fatemeh was reluctant to do so. All her family members who were MKO militants were in a combative mood at the time. Fatemeh had been instrumental in recruiting her sisters and her students for the MKO; it was understandable that she could not suddenly leave them and move to another city.

7.   [At that time] if there was any debate within the MKO about armed struggle again, Fatemeh was not aware of such debate. At the time some [members] even argued against the rifle on the MKO's flag. The Mojahedin probably had two types of members and sympathizers: [first,]

those who, I think, would obey without questioning the organization's orders, and accept them and accept without posing any question that "when the day comes they would join an armed demonstration organized by the MKO"; and [second,] those like Fatemeh who, I think, would not accept such a thing. I think there is no possibility that Fatemeh knew of this [possibility of armed resistance] or was somehow involved in it. She was not a person to follow such a path. That was not her nature. Taking up arms requires a particular outlook and motives that were uncharacteristic of Fatemeh.

8.   In Iran back then there were two types of religious associations: one was Islamic, the other was Muslim—for example, the Islamic Students' Association [supporting Ayatollah Khomeini], and the Association of Muslim Students [pro-MKO]; the Islamic Teachers' Association and the Association of Muslim Teachers. First, Fatemeh was a founding member of the Association of Muslim Teachers, then [she was involved in] the Association of Muslim Mothers; she was in charge of the latter. And between these two periods, she was a candidate in the parliamentary elections [May 1980]. During her campaign, which lasted five or six months, she spoke at different meetings about the Mojahedin's programs that she would promote if she were elected. In a nutshell, and as far as I know, this was the core of her political activities. The political action [of these two Muslim groups] may have had a clandestine component, but publicly their activities were limited to union types of activities. For example, at

the Association of Muslim Mothers, they would gather, read, and analyze MKO magazines. As far as I know, from what I have seen, these were their activities. They analyzed the articles, taught each other about the articles, recruited, held meetings, and distributed leaflets. This was the core of their activities. At first, programs were about how we, as a society, should progress, and gradually they became more radical. The more the government put pressure on them, the more defensive they became; they would attack what they called the "reactionary" [regime].

9. Fatemeh was very active and before her arrest she would organize public protests and demonstrations; it happened that demonstrators were stabbed during the demonstrations. Approximately 80 people had been killed by the Hezbollah militants [during the demonstrations] before the 20 June 1981 demonstration. One time Fatemeh's office was attacked by the Revolutionary Guards (government paramilitary forces), but they could not arrest her. Throughout the country they [Hezbollahis] wanted to take over their [the MKO and their affiliates] headquarters. These attempts were at times successful. But people would defend them [the MKO affiliates]; their family members went to defend them as well. They [the MKO] had the ability to mobilize support. I would go too, along with some respected elderly citizens of Shiraz and some nationalists [moderate liberals] and some others; we would go there whenever they asked. We would stand there [in front of the MKO/Union's headquarters]; we would not go inside, but we would say: "Don't attack them;

they're not doing anything illegal. If they're doing something illegal, bring the police, go inside and arrest them. But who are you as Hezbollahis [members of the Party of God] coming here with batons?" I did this twice. The last time they came to take over the MKO headquarters, it was protected by a metal mesh. They were attacking and beating them [the MKO], but they [the MKO] defended themselves well. The Hezbollahis would throw stones; someone threw a rock at me, which hit me in the arm, and it still sometimes hurts.

Arrest

10. We were known in Shiraz because we were both politically active. I was not affiliated with the MKO, however. We did not have many financial problems since I worked at a private company. Our problems mostly concerned our daily lives. One day, some unidentified people broke the windows in our house. We did not know who they were. We changed the windows, reinforced them, and covered them with a protective metal mesh. Some bookstores also had their windows broken [by Hezbollahi assailants]. It was an oppressive atmosphere.

11. My wife was a candidate in the parliamentary elections [for the first Majles]. There were only three MKO candidates and she was one of them, for she was well known because of her activism; therefore our problems doubled. I started thinking about leaving Shiraz. But we had bought a house along with Fatemeh's parents and it was difficult to pick up and leave. She knew of the danger but at the same time she was excited. In the three months prior to her

arrest, she did not sleep at home at night. When she was arrested, one of her former students recognized her. She was arrested on 15 June 1981. The following day, the women who had been arrested with her called me on the phone and told me that she was arrested. I did not go to visit her [in prison]. I left the children with our parents and fled into hiding.

12. One or two days later, Fatemeh's parents took some clothes for her to the prison. That was the first visit in prison. One of my friends knew the religious judge and told me that Fatemeh would be released in a few days. She was in good spirits in prison. The women who had been released said that she consoled other prisoners. She wanted to preserve herself [not go to either extreme]. She did not want to repent, but neither did she want to be executed.

Trial and Sentence

13. She was tried less than a week after her arrest and condemned to five years' imprisonment for distribution of counter-revolutionary papers. But three days after the 20 June 1981 MKO mass demonstration, Fatemeh was tried again, and this time she was sentenced to ten years' imprisonment. Eighteen months later, based on rumors according to which the MKO was recruiting and organizing four-member cells within the prisons, Fatemeh was transferred to Tehran's Evin Prison for interrogation and was charged with the new crime of recruiting and organizing within the prison. Three women had said that Fatemeh was in such a network, but she never confessed. Our children

went there to visit her every two or three months. There, she was tried [for a third time] and condemned to execution. But in those days, the Qom Supreme Court had to approve all execution sentences. In Fatemeh's case, the death sentence was rejected based on the fact that there was no evidence to support the charge except for the confessions of the three prisoners and also the fact that Fatemeh herself had not confessed. The delegation formed by Ayatollah Montazeri [to investigate prisoners' families' complaints] examined her case and commuted her sentence to ten years' imprisonment. In 1984, she was again transferred to Adelabad Prison in Shiraz.

Prison Conditions

14. She was thus reassured about her chances of survival, and thought she would henceforth have to serve her ten-year sentence. According to what I was told, Fatemeh was aware that networking was not possible within the prison. It was not possible to trust anyone, be it a repenter or a steadfast prisoner. She had decided to be prudent. This meant that when she was under pressure to criticize the Mojahedin she would refuse to do so on the grounds that, having been in prison for years, she had no idea what they did and thus could neither criticize nor praise them. And when asked what she thought of the Islamic regime of Iran, she would give a similar response, refusing at once to criticize or to praise the regime. She would reply, "I am here in prison to serve my sentence and after that I want to go out and raise my children." I also heard that Fatemeh was teaching in prison. She probably taught physics. I have this

Fatemeh and her son (Chowra's brother), in 1981

Photo courtesy of Chowra Makaremi

information from several sources. As far as I know, visits were conducted from behind a glass divider and through telephones. "In-person" visits [without the use of the phone and glass dividers] took place only once a year.

15. After seven and a half years, they [the Adelabad Prison officials] had told her that she would be pardoned for good behavior after having served eight years. That would have been 1989. Twice she was allowed to go home for weekends. Prison officials would call and tell her not to leave the house. They took the title of the house as bail [to ensure Fatemeh's return to prison].

16. During her two home visits, it was apparent that she suffered from spinal injuries and had vitamin deficiencies. She had lost her hair and had developed skin disease. She was not physically strong, she had a small body. When she was arrested at age

30, she lived under a lot of pressure; the prison was damp. She possibly suffered from malnutrition. It was emotionally painful, being away from her children. Naturally she had become weak. And her last picture, taken the last time she visited home, reflected that. She had told her father that she had been tortured; the issue came up mostly about the year and a half she spent in Evin Prison.

17. In 1983, I came to France. In 1985, our children came to France. We expected her to come to France for Noruz [the Iranian New Year, 21 March 1989]. I had made an appointment for her to have surgery.

Events Surrounding 1988

18. Sometime before the prison killings all visits stopped. Fatemeh's parents went to the prison several times and took money and clothes for her. Prison officials would accept the money and clothes but did

One of the dolls that Fatemeh made for her daughter during her imprisonment

not allow visits; they told her parents to leave and return at a later time. Every week Fatemeh's parents would wait at the door of Adelabad Prison, in Shiraz, to hear from their daughter, but would leave with no news.

19. The last meeting occurred in late August 1988. Her parents did not know she was to be executed. This visit took place in the presence of the religious judge. This was completely out of the ordinary. As far as I remember, during the last visit, Fatemeh was dry, bitter, and tired. If there was anything else, they [Fatemeh's parents] did not tell me. They said that they went there with so much joy, and she did not feel the same. Today we can guess that she [Fatemeh] probably knew it would be her last visit, but did not say anything.

20. For a while after this meeting, her parents had no news from the prison. Finally they were summoned to prison; they were even told they could bring stuff [for Fatemeh]. I would call two or three times a day; I was worried because they had started to inform the families about the executions. People had been informed earlier in Tehran. So I became suspicious as to why so many people were calling and asking the same thing: "What is going on?" So I started calling them [Fatemeh's parents] frequently. But I felt that Fatemeh's family members were cold and did not tell me everything. So one day I called my mother. I remember that day; it was in December. I asked my mother, "Why is it that so many people call me, what is happening?" She told me. She told me what had happened.

21. They all knew; they did not want to tell us right away, my mother told me. So then I immediately called her [Fatemeh's] father. Her father was trying to console me, and his words gave me strength. He said, "Aqa

Hassan, I have seen 300 names." And they [prison officials] had given him [Fatemeh's father] a location in the Shiraz cemetery where she was buried. They [Fatemeh's parents] went and saw that there was a grave with no stone. They made a mental note that this was Fatemeh's grave. Then they [the authorities] agreed and authorized the family to put a gravestone [on Fatemeh's grave]; I have a picture of this gravestone.

22. Fatemeh's mother told me that she went there every week. One day she was sitting there, washing the gravestone, when an elderly woman approached her and asked her, "Why are you visiting my child's grave?" Then Fatemeh's mother explained that this was her child's grave, and the elderly woman smirked and said, "That's what you think." Whether this was an emotional aggravation that [the government] wanted to cause or someone else used to be buried in the same plot, nobody knows. There is no evidence. But at least for the family to believe she was buried there was a comforting fact.

23. As time went by, they [her relatives] gradually brought us her belongings. We store them in a nice custom-made cabinet that we call "Mother Fatemeh's Museum." That is where we keep all of her belongings; we took pictures of them. Some of her be-

longings, all the pictures and biographical information, documents, all the books that mention her name, the two or three articles that I have written about her—they are all stored in there as well as her last clothes. The two or three dolls that she had made for her daughter. I have not heard of any will being written by her; we did not see any writing from her.

24. We were all proud of Fatemeh. Her parents told us a lot about her. Besides her parents, her friends who were in prison with her also confirm the same thing: she had a strong character and was well respected— both before her arrest and during her imprisonment. My daughter wrote in her article, "To those who say, 'Why did your mother leave her two children to pursue political activism?' I say that she loved all the children. And we were two of them."

25. All these enthusiastic women and men who were so knowledgeable and had so much love to give have been eliminated since 1981. They were all burned. The whole society was burned. When a society is burned and no man and no woman are left to rise and build the country, then of course individuals like Ahmadi Nejad [Mahmoud Admadinejad] come to the fore. This is a great calamity to which the opposition pays no attention.

Paris, April 2009

The Notebook of Aziz

CHAPTER 9

Plot such and such; Row such and such; Number such and such
Execution of Fatemeh Zare'i, 1988

Photo courtesy of Chowra Makaremi

Aziz Zare'i, passages from whose notes are excerpted below, was the father of Fattaneh (1954–1982) and Fatemeh (1950–1988) Zare'i. Both Fatemeh and Fattaneh had been nominated by the Mojahedin Khalq Organization [MKO] of Iran as candidates to serve in the first Islamic Consultative Assembly of Iran [Majles], and they were actively participating in the election campaign. Fattaneh was standing as a candidate for Gachsaran; and Fatemeh, for Shiraz. As pressure on opponents, in particular members of the MKO, intensified, Fattaneh and her husband, Ali Mohammad Ghanbari, uprooted themselves and moved to Bandar Abbas. In April 1982 the Revolutionary Guards located their hiding place. Fattaneh's husband was killed in the course of clashes with the Revolutionary Guards, and Fattaneh herself was arrested. After months of pressure and torture, Fattaneh, who was eight months pregnant at the time, was executed on 17 October 1982.

Fatemeh Zare'i, the eldest daughter of Aziz Zare'i, was arrested in Shiraz, on 15 June 1981. Her interrogation and trial took place at Sepah [Revolutionary Guards] Prison in Shiraz. In the winter of that year, she was sentenced to five years' imprisonment and transferred to Shiraz's Adelabad Prison. In the summer of 1982, the judicial authorities in Shiraz transferred Fatemeh back to Sepah Prison and began new proceedings against her. Throughout her detention in Sepah Prison, Fatemeh was subjected to intense physical and psychological pressure to repent, cooperate with the security forces, and give a television interview. She neither demonstrated any affection for the MKO nor agreed to cooperate with the authorities. Finally, in January 1984, a second verdict—a ten-year sentence—was approved, and she was transferred to Adelabad Prison. Three months later, in April 1984, Fatemeh's family heard that she had been transferred to Tehran. After enduring a harsh period of torture and psychological pressure, Fatemeh was sentenced to death, on the charge of recreating an MKO network inside the prison. Fatemeh rejected the charge, and the Supreme Court in Qom overturned the verdict. She was once again transferred from Evin to Adelabad Prison, in Shiraz, to serve out the ten-year sentence. In the spring of 1988, judicial authorities in Shiraz informed Fatemeh's family that after serving eight years of her prison term she had been included in an amnesty, owing to her good behavior in prison, and that she would be freed in a few months' time. She was even allowed to go on a couple of prison furloughs to visit her family. Fatemeh Zare'i was executed in the summer of 1988 during the mass execution of political prisoners. What follows is an excerpt from notes written by her father, Aziz:

> *To release this pent-up pain that is weighing heavily on my chest, I have decided to leave a note to my grandchildren to tell them about my beloved departed ones, Fatemeh and Fattaneh, because [otherwise] they would have no knowledge of the why and the how of what took place. And I know no other way of releasing myself from this incurable pain. . . . There is no doubt that Fatemeh's children would wish to know who their mother was and why she was executed.*

With such an intention, a 70-year-old grandfather with little education leaves behind one of the most valuable documents about state violence in the decade of the 1980s to be registered in the history and the collective memory of his nation. In simple language, these extraordinary notes illustrate the crushing impact of state violence on the victims' families, and expose the shocking psychological tortures meted out by the authorities covertly and without the knowledge of the prisoners' relatives.

Aziz Zare'i's notes were translated into French by Chowra Makaremi, the daughter of Fatemeh Zare'i, in 2011. They were published in France by Gallimard Press under the title *The Notebook of Aziz*, with explanatory footnotes, some of the correspondence of Fatemeh and Fattaneh prior to their arrests, and an account of how the notes were discovered by Chowra. Excerpts from chapter 9 of *The Notebook of Aziz* are being published here, in an English translation by the Abdorrahman Boroumand Foundation, with the kind permission of Gallimard Press. The extraordinary significance of this text lies in the fact that Fatemeh Zare'i's parents were granted exceptional leave to visit their daughter in Shiraz' Adelabad Prison after she appeared before the death board. And Fatemeh related to them her experience there.

The Notebook of Aziz: Excerpts from Chapter 9

During a prison visit in early July 1988, Fatemeh appeared uncharacteristically distraught. I asked the reason for her distress. She said, "They have twice put pressure on me to cooperate with them and they have again brought out my file from 1984. But I will not do the wrong thing, even if they cut up all the flesh on my body and feed me with it, because for me an honorable death is far better than a disgraceful life, which the regime wants. For my children, I will never trample on the pure blood of my sister Fattaneh and hundreds of other sisters like her, for the sake of a few disgraceful days of life in this world. Let them do whatever they want and can. We have a God too." From around early July 1988, the prison atmosphere totally changed. Every week when we went for our visit, they made more difficulties. We heard that these difficulties were made mainly with respect to the Mojahedin prisoners throughout the country. The situation had become such that all convicts had lost their spirit. And the parents of prisoners were instinctively in a state of fear and hope. This deadly situation continued until 31 July of that year, which was 1988. It was noon and we were having lunch when the blasted telephone rang. It was again that foul voice that sounded like a death bell. After asking some identification questions, the voice said, "Since Sister Fatemeh Zare'i is to go on a journey, you may not be able to see her for some time. So come and visit her at four o'clock this afternoon." We had already visited her on Saturday, 30 July, and now they were telling us to visit her on Sunday, 31 July as well? What did that mean? What has happened now? What is wrong? But, being gullible, we accepted what they had told us. As usual, her poor mother and sister began to beat themselves; we did not know anyone in Shiraz at the time. But even if we did, they would not dare approach the home of a Mojahedin member. They [the authorities] had created such fear that people were even afraid of their own shadows.

Finally, at 4 o'clock we took some fruit and clothes, and the three of us, her mother, sister, and I went to Sepah Prison. They led us to a little room and a dejected Fatemeh was brought in. Perhaps Fatemeh knew what was happening but did not want us to know her fate. The four of us sat in silence staring at each other, until the prison official broke the silence. He repeated what he had said earlier, which was that Sister Fatemeh Zare'i was going on a journey and that we had been summoned to bid her farewell. But I noticed that Fatemeh was giving him a meaningful look. After the prison official had finished, Fatemeh began to speak. She said: Last night, at 11 p.m., when everyone was asleep and there was total silence in Adelabad Prison, they woke me up. Without telling me what was going on, they blindfolded me and took me to a room where several gentlemen were seated, including the Shari'a judge, prison chief, prosecutor, interrogator, head of executive affairs, several intelligence agents, and a few others whom I had never seen before. First, the judge looked at me and said, 'We have learned that you are a supporter of the *monafeqin*.' I responded, 'If you are still not convinced, there is nothing more I can do; I am not a supporter [of the MKO] and I don't know what else I can do to change your opinion.' Then they asked, 'What is your perception of the Islamic Republic?' I responded, 'I have been in prison since the Islamic Republic declared its existence just over seven years ago. I have not been part of society to have any opinion on the nature and performance of the Islamic Republic.' Then the judge ordered them to take me away. It was around midnight when they brought me here. As to what their intention is, I have no idea."

Then the prison official responded, "The intention is what we said earlier. They want to send you on a journey. As for the destination, I have no idea." Then I, Fatemeh's father, asked the prison official how much money she could take with her on the journey? He replied, "She can take any amount she wants." I had 500 tomans on me, which I gave to Fatemeh, as well as a few pieces of clothing that her mother had brought. Of course, it was all clear to Fatemeh, while we, owing to our naïveté, did not want to see the reality. Fatemeh kept asking us to look after her children and kept giving her little sister advice.

Then I asked the prison official when we would be able to find out how Fatemeh is doing or where she is? He replied, "You can come back in 15 days time. Perhaps by then it will be clear."

Then, on the instructions of the prison official, I and Fatemeh's mother went toward the prison gate where, unexpectedly, we saw parents of many other prisoners who had gathered there. I made inquiries from many whose children had been released a few months or a few years previously. They said that they did not know; that they had come, as usual, to report but had not returned home afterwards. It is customary that those who have been

released must report to prison officials twice a week and sign a registry.

On that day, which was the last day of July, there was a huge crowd outside the prison walls. Security guards armed with machine guns were standing along the length of the prison walls and would not allow anyone to approach. There were also several armed guards in front of the courthouse, which is close to the prison entrance, to prevent the crowd from getting close. There was also a notice on the wall, which said that owing to the large volume of work they regretted that they could not let in any visitors. The parents were in a state of terror and apprehension. Moreover, no one dared make inquiries of friends, acquaintances, or persons in the same situation because they had heard that they would be accused of being spies or informants. In fact, these immoral individuals had installed some of their agents among the prisoners' relatives to spread these rumors so that they would be afraid of exchanging even a few words with fellow sufferers. That chaotic day was like all other days; by the end of the day the crowd would disperse and we would all go our separate ways. I could say that we had all utterly changed. We had lost all will and wisdom. That week, and subsequent weeks, somehow passed by in that manner. Among the 80 or 90 female prisoners, some 25 of them were mothers, each with one to three children—and often the fathers had already been executed. Some 50 of these female prisoners were 12 years old when they were first arrested, and were now about 18 or 19 years of age. There was also a 60-year-old mother among them, called Mrs. Ayatollahi, whose son had been executed already. Her daughter and brother were also among the inmates. Anyway, every Saturday we would congregate outside the prison walls, while a Revolutionary Guard would yell from above: "Don't waste your time. Your children are banned from having visitors. Nor do they need anything, because we have everything here already." In any case, that appalling situation, which had started on 31 July, continued until late October of that year. Only each time the number of prisoners, both boys and girls, would increase. It was in late October when, one day, unexpectedly, they opened the prison gate. They told us to enter. We felt elated. We were all regretting not having brought some fruit with us or wondering why they had not told us earlier, so that at least we could have brought some clothing for them. However, after waiting for some hours, they distributed some forms among the relatives of each prisoner and told them to fill them out with their own and their prisoners' details, including home and work address, source of income, how they met living costs, and number of household members. People could fill out their own forms; and anyone who was illiterate had to rely on the help of others. Once the forms were completed, they collected them, and, if there were any problems, they made the corrections themselves. Then they opened the gate and told us to leave. And we all went away disillusioned. I hope that God does not forgive them their sins, cruelties, and brutalities, and what they have done and continue to do to this oppressed nation.

A couple of weeks after we had filled out the forms, rumors began to circulate. One said that all those for whom forms had been filled out were massacred en masse. Another said that they had put them all in a tunnel and exploded it. While another said that they had taken them all to Eslamabad and buried them alive in Bakhtaran. And so the rumors continued. But no one believed any of it. The relatives believed that the prisoners had completed their sentences and some had even been released, so there was no need to execute them. Or that even if there had been executions, it was probably at the most just 10 or 20 or so who had been executed, but not all of them. That state of fear and hope continued. On visitors' days, we would congregate outside the prison gate only to leave in vain. Until one Saturday in early December, when, while I had gone to the prison gate myself, they telephoned my home, saying: "Tell Fatemeh's father to go to Adelabad Prison at 8 a.m." When I returned home, Fatemeh's mother, who thought I knew what had happened, asked, "What has happened now?" I did not know anything about the telephone call and replied, "Nothing, like other times." She would not believe me until, after a few exchanges, I learned about the telephone call. My heart suddenly sank and my voice started to tremble. I thought something must have happened. We, that is I, Fatemeh's mother, and Fatemeh's younger sister, spent the rest of the day in a state of mourning awaiting news. The next day, as instructed, I went to Adelabad Prison at 8 a.m. There were others at the gate who had likewise received the telephone call. On seeing them I felt slightly comforted. Everyone had their own opinions. One believed that they were going to let us visit them; another believed that they wanted to tell us why the prisoners had been banned from having visitors. In any case, one thing we all agreed upon was that whatever the reason it would end that indeterminate state. For five months we had received no news about the dead or the living. Every so often, we asked prison officials if they knew why we had been called there. They told us to wait as some intelligence agents were coming to answer our questions. On that day, there were about 100 of us there, representing some 30 prisoners. After hours of worry and anxiety, they called the first person, an old man, like me, of 60 to 70 years of age. We were all holding our breath. Why had they called in just one person? We were waiting for the old man to return to question him. It was not long, perhaps just ten minutes, before the old man reappeared holding a piece of paper 20 x 30 cm [8 x 12 inches]. We all rushed toward him. The old man was illiterate and did not know what the letter said. He said, "They gave me the paper and told me to get someone to read it to me; and then they asked me to print my finger on another piece of paper. They told me not to make a scene as otherwise they would imprison all family members. They repeatedly told me not to lose the letter." The content of that letter, which was the same as myriads of other letters given to the other old men, was this: "Plot such and such; Row such and such; Number such and such." Then the old man sat in a corner and burst into tears. The second and third persons also went in and came out in the same way. I was the fourth. And this was how it went: An intelligence agent would come to the prison gate and call out someone's name. Then, after taking him through the twists and turns of prison corridors, they would take him from one room to another. After a thorough frisking, they would take the person into a room where a young man of no more than 30 years of age was seated behind a desk flanked by two Revolutionary Guards. After greeting the individual, said young man would ask the person, in a charming manner, what he thought of the Islamic Republic? Or what his memory

was of the martyrdom of the 72 allies of the Imam? I don't know how the others responded. But my responses were very frank. Then they would present the person with a typed letter telling him to read it. The letter was a written directive that said: "You are not allowed to organize any kind of mourning ceremonies; you are not allowed to arrange a funeral, neither in a mosque nor at home or a cemetery; you must refrain from crying loudly and from reciting the Qur'an." Then he would read you the letter telling you that violation of any of the mentioned points would be deemed as opposition to the system of the Islamic Republic and offenders would be severely punished. I was given the letter and told to sign it. I instinctively tore up the letter and scattered it on his desk. Then after a couple more questions, two persons came in and took me out through the other prison gate and put me in a car. They drove the car to the environs of the airport and threw me out. They left a piece of paper in my pocket, which read: "Cemetery, Plot 25, Row 5, Grave number 2." In that plot and other plots in the cemetery there were, sure enough, a large number of prefabricated concrete slabs. The more inquisitive have proven that those graves were old graves on which they had placed some prefabricated concrete slabs. There they would send hapless families who had lost their beloved ones and would then secure a written agreement from them not to sob by those empty graves. As to where these cold-hearted owls had taken these families' dearest ones, or indeed the elite youth of society, God only knows. According to a prison official, the remaining 400 male and female Mojahedin prisoners in the two Shiraz prisons of Adelabad and Sepah were transported overnight by a special group in several big trucks. They were blindfolded and driven from 1 a.m. to 3 a.m. [The prison official said that] no ordinary prison guards were involved in the event. God only knows where they took them and what they did to them. Sure enough, there were many rumors. Some believed that they had been taken to a remote area, where they had first poisoned and then buried them in a mass grave. Some were of the opinion that they had taken only the Mojahedin to Eslamabad and disposed of them there. As told by relatives of prisoners in other towns and cities around the country, the chilling massacre had taken place simultaneously in nationwide prisons in early August 1988. The correct information I have concerning a few of the towns and cities is as follows: 400 [prisoners] in Shiraz, 38 in Fasa, 28 in Bushehr, 50 in Behbahan, 25 in Gachsaran, 75 in Masjed Soleiman, 50 in Kazeroun, over 500 in Bandar Abbas, and it is said that there were many in Ahvaz, although no one knows the precise number. Most of the executed were males. In all prisons, the inmates had been simultaneously banned from having visitors, and the news relating to them was also announced simultaneously. In other words, from 31 July 1988 to 31 December of that year, prisoners' relatives were suffering the agony of not knowing what had become of their dear ones. Meanwhile, those bloodsucking executioners were taking pleasure in what they had done. In their words, they had carried out acts of *qesas* [eye-for-an-eye retribution]. As the saying goes, "A blacksmith had committed a sin in Balkh, but instead they beheaded a coppersmith in Shushtar."

I will now highlight some of the tortures they meted out to my prematurely killed daughter, Fatemeh, in Ward 3000. As to where this Ward 3000 is, I have no idea. I remember the name clearly because Fatemeh, our daughter, used to mention it as the place where she was tortured. But I did not know its location. Fatemeh said that the tortures she had been subjected to included flogging her with cables, throwing her in ice water, throwing boiling water over certain areas of her body, attaching electric wires to her breast and neck, applying electric shocks, pulling out her hair with their hands, burning some of the sensitive areas of her body, breaking her teeth, putting her in a capsule, dubbed the Apollo [allusion to the American space capsules], and hanging her upside down for long periods. As a result of the latter, Fatemeh broke her spine and was subsequently unable to stand on her feet. . . .

However, my Fatemeh, that devout, pious, and devoted woman who held everyone in high esteem, who could not even hurt a fly, spent seven and a half years in the worst possible conditions in the dungeons of the unknown soldiers of the Lord of the Age, where she was subjected to the most advanced forms of torture. The day they arrested Fatemeh, she had a five-month-old daughter* and a three-year-old son. She had a brother who was also imprisoned at the time for being related to her. And her sister-in-law was on the run, out of fear, with a two-month-old baby. One of her sisters was also on the run in fear, while another, having graduated in France, was too afraid to return to Iran, lest she meet the same fate as her two sisters. She also had a 10-year-old sister who was constantly fearful, expecting something to happen at any moment. As for Fatemeh's two innocent children, it is evident

*According to Chowra Makaremi, she was eight months old when her mother was arrested.

what they were going through. Meanwhile, our friends and relatives were too scared to even phone us to see how we were doing. Because our home telephone remains tapped, even though some time has passed since Fatemeh's execution, anyone who calls us, friend or acquaintance, would be summoned immediately and asked by the Revolutionary Guards what the nature of their relationship is with the Zare'i family. Even letters sent to us from far or near end up at the intelligence headquarters. God knows what kind of prodigy they considered Fatemeh to be or how much of a threat she posed to the regime. All I know is that in the five years that Fatemeh's two innocent children were with us, we used to take them to the front of the courthouse or the prison gates several times a week, in the summer heat or winter chill, in the hope that they [the authorities] might let them see their mother for at least an hour. However, our appeals and endeavors were to no avail. Although I knew that our pleas would have no impact on their callous hearts, we were not dissuaded, because every time we saw the state the children were in, yearning for their parents, we would simply forget everything and rush the children to the courthouse. Alas, there was no father, mother, relative, or acquaintance about. They had all been blown away by the storm of the Revolution, leaving only a broken and bewildered old man of 70 years of age and an old woman of 60. Even sparrows do not dare fly in the direction of our house lest they be ambushed by the Revolutionary Guards. In any case, they were so sensitive about Fatemeh and her family that they even monitored the activities of similar families. I have an older brother and an older sister. My older brother lives in Tehran and my sister in Abadeh. Neither of them have children. My poor brother, who suffers from a lingering illness, naturally could not come to our house. However, when they announced Fatemeh's martyrdom, he came to Abadeh, and was immediately summoned by the Revolutionary Guards of Abadeh. They asked him to swear that he would not arrange a memorial service or allow anyone to sob loudly at home. Fear caused his health to deteriorate even further, and he ended up being hospitalized. He subsequently suffered a minor stroke, which left him paralyzed in one arm. Fatemeh's sister and brother also do not dare breathe a word because they know that they face an even greater danger. Dear God, you are witness to how this bloodsucking regime acts ruthlessly and brutally in the name and under the pretext of safeguarding dear Islam. For over seven years, my innocent Fatemeh, despite having two adorable children and elderly parents and a brother whom she worshipped, endured so much suffering, including physical and psychological torture, that I cannot bring myself to describe it. Yet she did not yield to the inhuman behavior of the regime. The day they arrested Fatemeh, her little daughter was five months old and her darling son was three. Although from the day of her arrest Fatemeh was not permitted to embrace her innocent children for even one day, nevertheless, from those very first days, whenever we went to visit Fatemeh, her little daughter would try to break the dividing screen to go to her mother. But those cold-hearted security guards would not even allow them to meet for a few minutes. God only knows how many times, when Fatemeh's children were with us, I and their grandmother, who had become paralyzed owing to grief, took them day after day at the crack of dawn, in the summer heat and winter chill, to the front of the courthouse or the prison gate in the hope of getting permission for them to visit their mother for perhaps a couple of hours a week. We appealed to all sorts of institutions and to individuals of all ranks and positions. We would plead with them. Sometimes we would be kept waiting from 5 a.m. to 2 p.m., only to leave without success.

As I mentioned earlier in my notes, I am not so educated. Moreover, my hands shake, hence my reluctance to leave behind any notes—and because I believe that my martyrs and other innocent and blameless martyrs, whose pure blood was shed when they were not guilty, will be avenged in this world and in the hereafter. [But] I thought that in this way [by writing these notes] I would be able to keep my mind occupied, because, indeed, Fatemeh was everything to me. Life after losing her has no purpose or meaning for me. When I recall her character, or the weight of her words, I boil with rage and I suddenly see the world as a dark place, especially whenever I see mothers who are holding their children's hands or carrying them in their arms. Yet for seven and a half years, my Fatemeh, who had not committed the slightest sin, endured the kinds of torture in prison that the strongest men would die of. That courageous woman endured all that, both psychological and physical, for seven and a half years. And the worst and hardest of them all was the fact that, during all that time, they did not allow her to hold her loved ones for even an hour. They would only bring her blind-folded to the telephone behind the screen once a week to talk for about three minutes, which would be cut short, and then she would be banned from having visitors for a week, if her

words inadvertently went beyond mere greetings. [I'm haunted by] the woe and wretchedness of those visiting days, from the moment of seeing our loved one's sunken eyes, scorched and compressed lips, shivering body, and in particular shaking hands, owing to which she could not even hold the telephone receiver properly. And how we wished to God to die, yet death was not to follow and it is still shying away from us. How many parents have endured the tragedies that we have endured, particularly with the fate of two innocent and desolate kids: their mother incarcerated and their father on the run.

As far as I know, that poor woman was subjected to mock executions five times, and in the middle of the night. Moreover, they strangled three inmates in her cell during the night, one of whom was no more than 14 years of age and was her parents' only daughter; that innocent child's two brothers had been executed earlier. She had an old mother who went blind; I don't know if she is still alive or has been released from further grief and torment. Again, I would like to stress that I am, sadly, not highly educated, hence my inability to write about what I had observed in the prisons I was a frequent visitor to. Perhaps luck will strike and, upon God's will, one day this calamitous storm, which is more horrific and devastating than Noah's storm, will subside. And anyone who emerges unscathed from this divine calamity will learn about what this generation suffered and endured—from the day they embarked on arresting their so-called opponents, to the day they massacred all of them, guilty or innocent. And where and how they took their lives has never come to light.

Chowra Makaremi

National Center for Scientific Research, Iris, France

Most of the things I know about the imprisonment, torture, and execution of my mother [Fatemeh Zare'i] and my aunt [Fattaneh Zare'i] come from a memoir my grandfather wrote in the last years of his life, after the massacre of the summer of 1988, when my mother was executed. It took me six years to translate those 80 pages of testimony. During those years, I had a memorable dream.

I dreamt that I was with a lot of other people, a whole population, locked in a large cave made of small stone cells. Mine had a window overlooking the sea; others, like those where my Iranian family lived, were saturated with smoky air and their inhabitants were suffocating. All of a sudden, a fierce explosion expelled us all from the cave. I walked and found myself in a camp where a small food stall was set up. At a table, my mother and my late aunt Fattaneh, executed in 1988 and 1982, respectively, were sitting in their prison suits, wearing the prisoner's *maqna'eh* and chador. They were young and smiling, with bright eyes and pink cheeks. Their sister—another aunt who now lives in Shiraz after ten years in hiding during the 1980s—was sitting there too, wearing the same uniform. Surprised, I asked her why she was with them. She stared at me and answered, "But I have been with them all along." I sat at the table, smiling back at them. But I soon noticed that my mother and my aunts were exchanging anxious looks, trying to protect me from a difficult truth: the watch on my Aunt Fattaneh's wrist—the one

the guards gave back to my grandfather along with her wedding ring, to inform the family of her execution in October 1982—the watch was marking the end of my visit. They knew it was almost time for me to leave, but they did not have the heart to tell me so. I caught their furtive looks and wondered what was going on. Suddenly my whole body began to shake furiously and endlessly, and I was surrounded by their healthy faces trying to calm me down. Their youngest sister, with whom I grew up at my grandparents' house, was coming for me; she pushed a wheelbarrow. As we walked back together, she told me we still had plenty of work to do. "What work?" I asked, and there we were on the site of the explosion of the cave: the cells and the thousands of people buried by the explosion. Nothing remained but a cliff over the sea, but the earth was as grey as ashes and an arm was lying there.

I was eight months old when my mother was arrested and imprisoned in Adelabad [Prison], in Shiraz, on 15 June 1981, and my father went into hiding. First, my grandparents, who were in charge of me, spent hours queuing and begging in vain for a daily visit permit so that my mother could breastfeed me. We were finally able to see her after she was tried and sentenced to ten years' imprisonment. We visited my mother once a week from when I was one to almost six years old, when my brother and I joined my father, who had been granted refugee status in France.

The situation of others was worse. Some children were kept in prison with their parents. Aunt Fattaneh was pregnant when she was arrested along with a fellow Mojahed, who was also pregnant. My aunt was executed when she was seven to eight months pregnant. We never knew what became of the baby. Was he born? We cannot know.

Her friend Zahra, who was also sentenced to death, gave birth to her baby in prison and kept her baby with her in the ward until the little girl was two. The baby was then given to the family, and her mother was executed. For years, the girl, named Zahra like her mother, shouted and ran away whenever she saw a man —for her they were a race of torturers and guards.

During her almost eight years in prison, my mother spent long periods in the Sepah (special detention center) or Ward 3000 of Evin Prison, in Tehran, where she was tortured and kept in solitary confinement. We did not know where she was or if she was even alive. But when she was in Adelabad Prison we had a weekly visit in person. When I turned three and my brother six, the age at which children can start hiding things and lying, our visits were restricted to phone calls behind a window [through a glass partition]. The blindfold she had to wear used to terrify me and make me scream, my grandfather wrote. One of her cellmates, whom I spoke to, recalled how my mother's palms were always bloody when she returned from these visits: she had been clenching her wrists, digging her nails into her flesh. Unfortunately, I have no clear memory of those hours in prison—I remember the dust and the hallway where families were waiting, I remember being escorted with my brother into a back-door office where a tiny woman in chador took our hands, but I have no memory of her face.

My mother was supposed to be released in March of 1989—my father hoped she would exit the country immediately, and he had booked a room in a hospital so she could recover and rest. In July 1988 my mother had her last visit with her family. Then the prison closed and prisoners and their families entered the blackout of the summer of 1988. In early December, the families were gathered in Adelabad Prison and received the news of their relatives' executions. My grandparents were given a paper indicating the location of my mother's grave in the Shiraz cemetery. However, my grandmother found out that another woman, who had died 30 years earlier, had been buried in that grave. Other prisoners' relatives had the same experience, and it appeared, as my grandfather reports, that ancient graves had been re-coated with concrete and presented to the families as the graves of their beloved ones. Families had been informed of their relatives' executions after the 40th day following their death, which marks the end of the period of mourning in Shiite Islam. They did not know how their children, siblings, or spouses had been buried; they did not know where the burial site was; and they were not allowed to organize mourning ceremonies or to tell their co-workers, their neighbors, or their schoolmates about what had happened.

I was eight years old when my father told us that my mother had died. I did not listen to a word of what he was trying to tell us that day in a train station in Paris. I understood that my mother died of a vitamin deficiency because there was no sun in her prison. I believed this story for quite some time, until around the age of thirteen—and it took me six more years to understand that my mother's execution was not an isolated case, but one among thousands during the mass killings of 1988.

As witnesses, we have to deal with a paradox: the memories that may serve as accounts refer to painful experiences, and while these memories are precious in a search for justice, they are sometimes erased or altered, or they lie somewhere out of reach, behind the screens we have erected to protect ourselves from the unbearable reality. But something else makes it difficult for me to be a "good" witness—and I am aware of the ambiguity this term implies. Living in France from the age of six, I did not grow up in a society where I had to bear the stigma that families of political prisoners in Iran in the 1980s had to bear, or the shame and humiliation of having to hide the reason for my mother's death. [Not living in Iran,] I did not feel excluded by a society that builds its identity by demonizing and annihilating the people I am supposed to love and respect—my parents.

However, there are testimonies that demonstrate how the mass execution of thousands of parents has weighed and continues to weigh on their children's experiences, personalities, identities, and fates. This was the case for Sarah Azad (not her real name, in order to protect her identity) and for Omid Montazeri, whose case has been publicly followed in the press.

Sarah was six months old when her mother and father were arrested in 1986. She was imprisoned with her mother, who was released two months after her arrest—although she stayed under the control of the judiciary. Her father was sentenced to 15 years' imprisonment and jailed in Evin [Prison], in Tehran. He was executed in the summer of 1988. For several years after that Sarah's mother was interrogated weekly by the Interior Ministry. Sarah grew up and learned to write "killed in a car accident" on the school forms that asked about her parents; she was forbidden to tell her schoolmates about her father's death. In time, she preferred to invent an imaginary father, who was always travelling for professional reasons. At the age of 14, she learned about the existence of the mass graves in Khavaran and, from then on, she took part in the annual commemoration and flower-planting there. When she entered university, where she majored in arts and photography, she was summoned to the dean's office. School authorities told her they "knew who she was," and warned her that she faced expulsion if she said anything about the circumstances of her father's death. In 2008 Sarah joined a student journal and collaborated on the arts and culture column. In early April 2009 the journal was closed by the Interior Ministry. However, the team carried on, organizing public conferences about the importance of voting in the coming presidential election. After the elections, Sarah and her mother took part in the protests against the electoral fraud. On 10 July, Sarah's mother was summoned to the Ministry of Education, which, as a high school teacher, she depended on. Her teaching license was revoked, and she was interrogated by an agent of the Interior Ministry, who said that she had been her interrogator during her prison time in 1985.

After the Ashura protests in December [2009], Omid Montazeri, one of the founders of the student journal on which Sarah collaborated, and a son of a prisoner executed in 1988, was arrested along with his mother. A few days later, the daughter of another prisoner executed in 1988, who had also taken part in the Ashura demonstrations and was active in the social networks, was arrested and accused of being a leader of the unrest following the elections. The same day, security agents went to Sarah's home while she was out and asked for her. Pressured

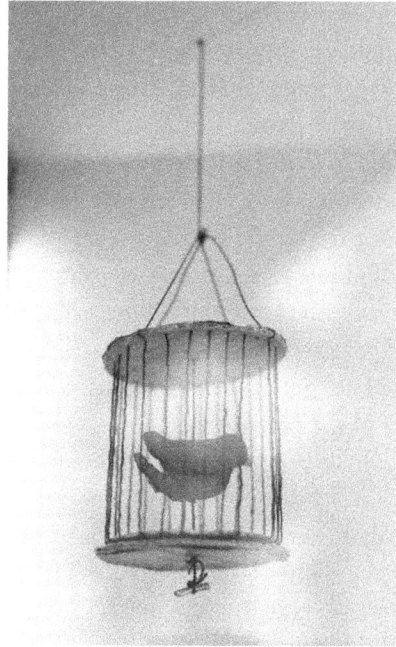

A bird cage made by Hamid Montazeri in prison. He used newspaper print, thin foil from cigarette packages, and threads from socks. The sculpture, easily folded, was smuggled out of the prison and given to his daughter, Shokufeh, and his son, Omid. Montazeri was executed in 1988.

Shokufeh wrote about the bird cage: "I have taken this cage with me all over the world.... It knows all my walls. I have carried it with me so that I would not forget, that I shall be born again in a land where there will be no spider and no fleas, no glass [partition] and no telephone."

by her mother, who was very worried about the fact that the arrests were targeting children of former political prisoners, Sarah and her mother left town that afternoon. At eleven that evening, four men and one woman from the security forces appeared at her home to arrest her; a warrant specified that she was accused of being a leader of the post-election unrest. They forced her grandfather, who lived downstairs, to open the door of Sarah's apartment, and they searched it for several hours. In the following weeks, they interrogated her relatives and friends. The interrogations, which aimed at identifying her as a leader of the protest movement, focused on the links with her father's fate and his past political engagement. ("How could she possibly not hate us after what we did to her father?" they asked her grandfather; the title of the file they kept on her was "Elements in Relation to Marxism.") Sarah's annual visits to the Khavaran cemetery had all been recorded and were of particular interest to the interrogators, who considered them to be proof of her guilt. In the spring of 2010 Sarah exited Iran through Turkey and later went to France, where she was granted refugee status. Sarah had taken part in many public demonstrations from the summer to the winter of 2009. However, the question for her remains: Why was she targeted after the election, despite the fact that her contributions to the student journal were limited to the arts and culture columns? Why did the security forces look for her rather than the more active contributors writing on political or socioeconomic issues? Why did they target her among hundreds of other protesters who demonstrated during those months? The interrogators in charge of her file made it clear that there was a method and a logic to their repression. They were targeting the children and spouses of those executed in 1988, as the case of Omid Montazeri publicly showed.

Omid's parents were arrested in July 1986, when his mother was pregnant with him. Omid's father was imprisoned in Evin and later executed during the massacre of 1988. On 28 December 2009, right after the Ashura protests, Iranian security forces entered Omid's home and arrested his mother, along with other friends and relatives. Omid was arrested upon his arrival at the Ministry of Intelligence, where he had gone seeking information about his mother and her guests. He was accused of being a leader of the post-election unrest, and imprisoned in Evin Prison, in Tehran, interrogated, and sent to solitary confinement. His public confessions were filmed and portions of them were shown on television. Interestingly, although the mass execution of political prisoners in 1988 has been denied by authorities and the families were pressured to keep it secret, Omid was presented in his trial as the "son of a prisoner executed in 1988." Omid received a six-year suspended sentence on 27 February 2010. He exited Iran in 2011.

Beyond the stories of Sarah and Omid, two children of political prisoners executed in 1988 who were themselves forced into exile more than twenty years after the executions, many press articles reported how, after 2009, families of political prisoners executed in the 1980s were summoned for interrogation, their phones were once again tapped, and their activities put under surveillance.

It is difficult to see clearly the motivations and procedures of a state apparatus that has taken form through 30 years of illegal violence, arbitrary practices, and secrecy. But a hypothesis, that further research and testimonies would have to confirm, is that the repression targets more specifically the children of prisoners executed in 1988 in at least two ways:

First, relatives of political prisoners have been followed and monitored throughout their school, university, and adult lives. This surveillance and the resulting files contributed to the blanket of silence surrounding the mass killings of 1988. And they [the authorities] did more, since they intensified their acts of repression whenever [they thought that] Iranian society needed to be silenced again, as was the case after the 2009 presidential elections.

Second, reports about the mass killings and many other testimonies show how state violence was based on marking enemies for annihilation. Sarah and Omid's experiences lead me to believe that the children of the enemies are in turn marked and perceived as enemies. The ideology of the enemy was carried on when security forces asked about Sarah: "How could she not hate us after what we did to her father?"

The injustice and violence that deprived us of our parents have opened a space where political issues and the most personal, intimate dimensions of our lives are merged, whether we like it or not. This is where I stand and where I am speaking from. And, like the Iranian security forces, I see that there is tremendous potential for agency and action.

Oxford, England, October 2011

APPENDICES

Appendix A
Brief Chronology

A brief chronology of significant events in Iran relevant to the witness testimonies

1963

January

Shah announces the "White Revolution," a six-point program of reform calling for land reform, nationalization of the forests, the sale of state-owned enterprises to private interests, electoral changes to enfranchise women and allow non-Muslims to hold office, profit-sharing in industry, and a literacy campaign in the nation's schools. Ayatollah Khomeini along with other senior Ayatollahs of Qom publishes a protest letter against Shah's reforms.

June

3 June: Ayatollah Khomeini launches a violent diatribe against the Shah and his reforms.

5 June: Ayatollah Khomeini is arrested by security forces; thousands of demonstrators take to the streets to protest the arrest. The violent suppression of the demonstrations by security forces results in the deaths of scores of demonstrators. A curfew is declared. Khomeini is placed under house arrest in Tehran and held for the next ten months.

1964

6 April: Ayatollah Khomeini is released and returns to Qom.

26 October: In a speech in Qom, Ayatollah Khomeini strongly criticizes the newly ratified law granting immunity from prose-cution in Iranian courts to the United States Advisory Mission personnel in Iran.

4 November: Khomeini is arrested in Qom, taken directly to the airport, and flown to Turkey. He is exiled from Iran.

1965

The People's Mojahedin Organization (MKO) is established, clandestinely, for the purpose of fomenting an Islamic revolutionary guerrilla movement in Iran. Activities consist of recruiting members and ideological and military training both inside and outside Iran. MKO militants are sent to Lebanon and Palestinian camps for guerrilla training.

1971

February

8 February: The attack and disarmament of a police station in the city of Siahkal in Gilan Province, by members of a Marxist-Leninist organization. This attack marks the creation of what in retrospect is considered the People's Fadaiyan Organization (FKO) and the beginning of guerrilla warfare in Iran.

27 February: Security forces' counterattack results in the death of six militants and the arrest of the remaining three.

March

17 March: Tried and convicted in a military court, 15 members of the Fadaiyan are executed.

1971 *(continued)*

APRIL–AUGUST

MKO leadership plans to disrupt the sumptuous celebration of the 2,500th anniversary of the Iranian monarchy scheduled for October.

23 August: The MKO plot is discovered through an infiltrator. Within two months, 120 members, or nearly 90% of its cadres, are arrested.

1972

Trial and execution of Mojahedin leaders.

1977

22 May: In a commencement address at the University of Notre Dame, newly elected US President Carter signals the direction he plans to take in foreign policy, rejecting America's "inordinate fear of Communism" and calling for a serious commitment to human rights.

NOVEMBER

15 November: The Shah visits the White House, prompting demonstrations by anti-Shah students in Washington, DC.

DECEMBER

President Carter visits Iran. In a toast to US-Iranian friendship, he emphasizes, "The cause of human rights is one that also is shared deeply by our people and by the leaders of our two nations."

1978

The Shah frees a number of political prisoners and grants limited freedom of action to peaceful opposition figures. Public dissent gains momentum.

SEPTEMBER

Breakdown of civil order as all sections of society protest against the Shah. Strikes and riots all demand the return of Khomeini.

8 September: "Black Friday." In the early hours of the day, the government declares a curfew in Tehran and other major cities. In Tehran, hundreds of thousands of demonstrators gather at Jaleh Square and for the first time demonstrators chant "Death to the Monarchy" and call for an "Islamic Republic." The army uses firearms to disperse the demonstrators. An estimated 90 people are killed that day.

1979

JANUARY

4 January: The Shah appoints his longtime opponent Shapur Bakhtiar as Prime Minister. Bakhtiar dissolves the political police, restores the freedom of the press, and calls for free and fair elections as the only solution to the country's crisis.

12 January: Ayatollah Khomeini entrusts Morteza Motahhari with the establishment of a clandestine Council of Islamic Revolution. The first nucleus of the Council is composed of clerics close to Ayatollah Khomeini who decide to co-opt a few religious nationalist figures. Headed by Motahhari, the Council meets secretly and takes over the leadership of the revolutionary movement, giving it its decidedly religious turn.

16 January: The Shah leaves Iran, never to return.

FEBRUARY

1 February: Khomeini returns after 14 years in exile and is hailed by the masses as the savior and new leader. He refuses to submit his mandate to elections and demands Bakhtiar's resignation.

5 February: Khomeini establishes the Provisional Islamic Revolutionary Government with Mehdi Bazargan as its prime minister.

5 February 1979 *(continued)*

Demonstrations continue in this period and clashes between security forces and demonstrators result in a number of deaths.

11 February: The army declares its neutrality. Bakhtiar's government is toppled by a popular uprising.

15 February: Summary executions of officials of the former regime begin.

18 February: The Islamic Republic Party is established by Ayatollah Khomeini's closest allies to defend the tenets of the Islamic Revolution and the principle of the "Guardianship of the Islamic Jurist."

MARCH

Political parties and organizations establish their headquarters and start organizing, recruiting, and publishing their newspapers.

1 March: Planning for a referendum, Ayatollah Khomeini declares, "What our nation wants is an Islamic Republic, not a Republic, not a Democratic Republic, not a Democratic Islamic Republic. . . . Do not be afraid of the word 'democratic'; do not be afraid of eliminating it. This is a Western form [of body politic]."

30–31 March: The referendum is held to determine the form Iran's new government will take. Voters are asked to decide whether or not they accept changing the "former regime" to an "Islamic Republic." They are provided with two ballots, one green (the color of Islam), on which "Yes" is printed; and the other, red, on which "No" is printed. Yes wins by an overwhelming majority.

APRIL

1 April: Khomeini declares victory in the referendum that establishes the Islamic Republic of Iran and declares April 1 "the first day of the Government of God."

MAY

15 May: Khomeini demands that the press conform to the principles of the Islamic Republic, further cementing the Islamization of the media that had begun in February. Both state-run and independent media are brought into line with Khomeini's policies.

24 May: Ayatollah Khomeini announces that "anyone whose direction is separate from Islam" is an "enemy" of the revolution.

JUNE

22 June: A rally of protestors calling for an elected Constituent Assembly to draft a new constitution is broken up by followers of the Ayatollah.

JULY

1 July: The correspondent of the *Los Angeles Times* is expelled from Iran for his paper's negative coverage of the government. He is the first foreign journalist to be expelled, but, in the following weeks, correspondents from the *New York Times*, the BBC, the *Financial Times,* and *L'Express* are also forced to leave.

2 July: The National Democratic Front (a coalition of leftist and nationalist groups) publishes an open letter to Khomeini calling his leadership a dictatorship and criticizing Khomeini for promoting unthinking obedience, burning books, dismissing teachers, and controlling the media.

11 July: A provisional Press Bill is implemented, providing for imprisonment for up to two years for anyone who defames Islam, the Revolution, or its leaders.

July 1979 *(continued)*

22 July: Khomeini bans the playing of all music on Iranian radio and television because music is "no different from opium" in its effects on people.

23 July: Foreign journalists are forbidden from interviewing Iranians when not in the presence of a Ministry of Intelligence official.

AUGUST

3 August: Elections for an "Assembly of Experts," instead of a Constituent Assembly, are held. Twenty political groups boycott the elections, calling them unfair. Khomeini accuses the boycotters of being "enemies of the Revolution." The Assembly of Experts is charged with drafting a constitution for the Islamic Republic of Iran.

7 August: Revolutionary Guards raid and close down the offices of *Ayandegan*, the largest newspaper critical of the regime.

9–13 August: Demonstrations against the government's growing authoritarianism take place. Clashes between the security forces and demonstrators result in hundreds being injured. Khomeini bans all demonstrations.

20 August: Twenty-two opposition newspapers, including that of the National Democratic Front, are ordered to close.

August–September: Violent clashes occur between Revolutionary Guards and Kurds protesting the failure of the draft constitution to grant them autonomy and equal rights.

SEPTEMBER

4–8 September: The Associated Press is ordered to close its Tehran bureau and withdraw its four correspondents from Iran. The government seizes all assets of the newspaper publishing groups *Ettela'at* and *Kayhan*.

OCTOBER

14 October: The Assembly of Experts approves a constitutional clause naming the Ayatollah head of the armed forces and giving him power of veto over the election of a president.

NOVEMBER

1 November: Khomeini makes a statement urging students to "expand with all their might their attacks against the United States and Israel" in order to force the return of the Shah to Iran.

4 November: Armed students protesting the presence of the Shah in the U.S. storm the U.S. Embassy in Tehran and take 100 hostages.

6 November: Bazargan's provisional revolutionary government resigns in protest against pro-Khomeini students who have taken over the U.S. Embassy. Khomeini orders the Revolutionary Council to assume control of the government.

DECEMBER

2 December: Voters go to the polls to accept an Islamic Constitution that gives Khomeini total control over the body politic.

6–27 December: Violent clashes oppose government forces to supporters of Grand Ayatollah Shari'atmadari protesting in Qom and Tabriz. The Ayatollah opposes the Constitution because it contains "an important fault" that is "contradictory to the sovereignty of the people."

1980

JANUARY

24 January: Khomeini urges Iranians to vote in the presidential elections. Abolhassan Banisadr is elected President.

1980 (*continued*)

APRIL

18 April: Khomeini gives a public speech attacking the "Westernization" of universities. Hezbollah militias injure hundreds of students.

22 April: The Pars News Agency announces that at least three people have died and more than 160 injured in clashes between Muslim fundamentalists and students at Tehran University.

JUNE

12 June: Universities are shut down and will not reopen for two years, during what becomes known as the "Cultural Revolution." Khomeini appoints a "Committee for the Islamization of Universities" to ensure that an "Islamic atmosphere" is taught in every subject.

SEPTEMBER

22 September: Iraq launches several strikes against Iranian airfields, starting the Iran-Iraq War.

1981

JANUARY

21 January: U.S. hostages released.

FEBRUARY

6 February: According to press reports, Hezbollah militias attack demonstrators from two Marxist-Leninist groups who are holding a rally in Tehran. At least 39 are reported injured.

MAY

2 May: The Mojahedin take to the streets to protest the closure of Iran's universities. Three persons are killed and 100 injured in clashes between the Mojahedin and Islamic extremists outside Tehran University.

JUNE

20 June: Massive street demonstrations by Mojahedin supporters in favor of Banisadr. Many killed.

22 June: Abolhassan Banisadr is dismissed and flees to Paris with Massoud Rajavi. The regime arrests and imprisons Mojahedin supporters.

28 June: A bomb explodes at the Islamic Republic Party headquarters; more than 73 are killed. "Reign of Terror" against Mojahedin begins.

OCTOBER

Rafsanjani calls for extermination of "hypocrites," i.e., the Mojahedin. Many MKO prisoners are executed. Ayatollah Mohammadi Gilani declares that *bastinado* when used as a religious punishment is not torture. Ja'far Nayyeri is appointed a religious judge in Tehran. Ali Khamene'i is elected President. Mir Hossein Musavi is nominated as Prime Minister.

NOVEMBER

15 November: Hojjat ol-eslam Musavi Tabrizi says that 6,000-7,000 prisoners have been jailed for political offenses since the fall of the Shah.

DECEMBER

13 December: Amnesty International deplores the execution of at least 1,600 people between June and September 1981.

1982

JANUARY

30 January: Guidelines are sent classifying Mojahedin prisoners with a view to releasing repenters.

1982 (*continued*)

FEBRUARY–MARCH

Revolutionary Guards raid safe houses, killing and arresting top leaders of leftist Peykar and Fadaiyan Khalq Organization (Minority).

APRIL

16 April: 1,000 people, including leading members of the Shi'a clergy, are arrested in connection with an alleged plot to assassinate Ayatollah Khomeini.

20 April: Grand Ayatollah Shari'atmadari is stripped of his religious title by faculty at the theological school in Qom for alleged complicity in a plot to assassinate Ayatollah Khomeini. (He was in fact opposed to the clergy's involvement in politics.)

MAY

Heavy fighting continues between Iranian and Iraqi forces.

JUNE

29 June: Iraq reports that the last of its troops have left Iran. Iranian officials reply that the withdrawal does not satisfy Iran's conditions for an end to the war.

AUGUST

Fighting continues between government and Kurdish forces.

NOVEMBER

Iran begins a major offensive against Iraqi troops.

7 November: Speaker of the Majles Hashemi Rafsanjani says the Communist Tudeh Party is a "disreputable party with a filthy record."

1983

FEBRUARY

7 February: Tudeh Party officials are arrested.

10 February: Iran's President Ali Khamene'i says the "punishment of the leaders of the Iraqi regime" is the main goal of the war.

MAY

On "May Day" confessions of Communist (Tudeh Party) leaders are televised. Regime begins to arrest pro-Soviet leftists and dissolves the Tudeh Party.

SEPTEMBER

21 September: Universities reopen throughout Iran.

1984

FEBRUARY

2 February: Sentencing guidelines for political prisoners are announced.

8 February: Amnesty International charges Iran with large-scale abuses of human rights, including over 5,000 executions since 1979.

MAY–JUNE

Heavy fighting takes place across the Shatt al-Arab waterway; Iran attacks Basra and Iraq shells Abadan.

1985

MARCH

Iran and Iraq continue fighting and shell cities and other civilian areas.

APRIL–MAY

Anti-government and anti-war demonstrations in Tehran.

1985 *(continued)*

OCTOBER

10 October: Khamene'i is sworn in for a second four-year term and asks the Majles to reappoint Prime Minister Mir Hossein Musavi.

NOVEMBER

23 November: Ayatollah Hossein Ali Montazeri is selected by the Assembly of Experts as Khomeini's successor.

DECEMBER

7 December: Bombs explode in two Parisian department stores, marking the beginning of a series of Iranian-sponsored terrorist attacks in France. Iran seeks to deter France from supplying arms to Iraq and to silence the Iranian opposition in France as well as to obtain the release of convicted terrorists linked to Iran who are detained in France.

1986

FEBRUARY

Pro-Iranian Lebanese Hezbollah organizes four terrorist bomb attacks in Paris. The bomb planted in the Eiffel Tower is discovered before it can explode.

MARCH

8 March: Four French journalists in Lebanon are abducted by the Revolutionary Justice Organization.

Fighting in Iraqi territory continues and cities in both countries are targeted.

MAY

20 May: A delegation headed by Iran's Deputy Prime Minister arrives in Paris, the first by such a high-ranking official since the 1979 Revolution.

JUNE

7 June: Rajavi and the Mojahedin are expelled from France. They move to an armed camp on the Iraq border, under the protection of Saddam Hussein.

20 June: Two of the French hostages in Lebanon are released.

SEPTEMBER

Second campaign of bombing in Paris, sponsored by the Iranian government, demanding the release of Anis Naccache, who was sentenced to life imprisonment for an attempt, in 1980, to assassinate opposition leader Shapur Bakhtiar. During the botched assassination attempt a Naccache commando killed a policeman and Bakhtiar's French neighbor.

1987

JUNE

20 June: The Mojahedin announce the formation of the Iranian National Liberation Army to overthrow the present regime.

JULY

7 July: UN Security Council Resolution 598 suggests terms for a truce in the Iran-Iraq War.

21 July: Iran calls Resolution 598 "null and void." Fighting continues throughout the year, including attacks on civilian targets.

SEPTEMBER

From September on the Ministry of Intelligence distributes questionnaires to political prisoners, testing their continued adherence to their political and religious beliefs.

1988

JANUARY
Government announces "pardon committees" to determine early release of political prisoners.

MARCH
The war of the cities continues with hundreds of casualties. Saddam uses chemical weapons against the Kurds in Halabja and in Iranian villages in Marivan.

JUNE
Ayatollah Khomeini appoints Majles Speaker Ali Akbar Hashemi Rafsanjani commander-in-chief of the armed forces.

JULY
3 July: USS *Vincennes* shoots down IranAir Flight 655, killing all 290 passengers and crew.

14 July: Rafsanjani chairs a leadership meeting that advises acceptance of a ceasefire agreement along the lines of UN Resolution 598.

20 July: Khomeini broadcasts his bitter acceptance of a truce with Iraq ("more deadly than drinking poison").

25 July: The Mojahedin launch their "Eternal Light" invasion.

28 July: Khomeini's fatwa orders the execution of all "steadfast" Mojahedin prisoners. Chief Justice Musavi Ardebili asks for and is given clarification.

29 July: Mojahedin army is defeated; it retreats to Iraq.

29 July: Death Committees convene to begin the "First Wave" of killings.

AUGUST
"Trials" and execution of Mojahedin prisoners take place in Evin and Gohardasht and at least 20 provincial prisons.

1 August: Judge Ahmadi complains to Khomeini and to Ayatollah Montazeri that he is being out-voted by prosecution and Intelligence Ministry members of the Death Committees.

4 August: Montazeri complains to Khomeini about the unfairness of the procedures.

6 August: Chief Justice Musavi Ardebili announces that the public demands executing them all "without exception."

13 August: Montazeri summons Death Committee members and tells them to suspend executions for the religious holiday. Nayyeri admits they have already killed 750 in Tehran.

15 August: Montazeri calculates that between 2,800 and 3,800 prisoners have been executed in the first ten days of the fatwa.

20 August: Iran's acceptance of UN Resolution 598 formally brings an end to the Iran-Iraq War.

26 August: The Death Committees reconvene to begin the "Second Wave" of killings.

SEPTEMBER
"Second Wave" of killings continues.

1 September: The Supreme Court reopens. Chief Justice Musavi Ardebili orders prosecutors to confront the "heathen" leftist groups.

2 September: Amnesty International issues "urgent action" in response to reports of the prison killings.

1988 *(continued)*

6 September: A second, secret, fatwa may have been issued approving the killing of leftist apostate prisoners.

6–8 September: In letters to Ali Khamene'i and Mir Hossein Musavi, the Supreme Leader relinquishes his power to impose Islamic punishments (*ta'zir*) to the Exigency Council. The latter would determine how much of this prerogative would be left to the government.

OCTOBER

Reynaldo Galindo Pohl, UN Special Rapporteur on the Situation of Human Rights in Iran, reports to the General Assembly that 200 Mojahedin were massacred in Evin Prison assembly hall and 860 buried in a mass grave in Tehran.

NOVEMBER

20 and 29 November: Pohl meets with Iranian ambassador to the United Nations Mahallati, who denies the allegation and says that the Mojahedin died on the battlefield.

DECEMBER

Prime Minister Mir Hossein Musavi implicitly defends actions against leftists and Mojahedin in an Austrian television broadcast.

1989

JANUARY

Rafsanjani admits that executions have taken place, but "fewer than 1,000." Galindo Pohl, the UN Special Rapporteur on Iran, reports to the Human Rights Commission and lists names of over 1,000 victims.

FEBRUARY

14 February: Ayatollah Khomeini issues a death fatwa on Salman Rushdie and his translators and publishers.

NOVEMBER

Professor Pohl's report to the General Assembly confirms (paragraph 110) that mass executions of political prisoners took place in 1988.

DECEMBER

Amnesty International report alleges "perhaps thousands" of executions of political prisoners.

APPENDIX B
Glossary

Entries identified with a single asterisk are drawn from Iraj Mesdaghi's "Prison Dictionary." Those identified with a double asterisk are based in part on that source.

Adelabad Prison Located in the city of Shiraz in central Iran's Fars Province, Adelabad Prison is the city's general prison, built under the previous regime. It is said to have carried out the largest number of executions after the Revolution.

Allaho Akbar Literally, "God is [the] Greatest," an expression used by Muslims in a multitude of situations, ranging from slaughtering an animal in the "halal" manner to chants on the battlefield. In the context of the Iranian Revolution, the phrase was first used as an anti-Shah, pro-Khomeini revolutionary slogan, and was taken up subsequently by executioners in prisons and elsewhere, prior to carrying out the act of execution. Since 2009, it has also been a chant used by dissidents against the Islamic Republic, cried out from rooftops during various uprisings against the regime.

Amuzeshgah A pair of interconnected administrative buildings at the Evin Prison complex in Tehran, which, after some minor changes were made, was used as a prison.*

Apostate, fetri or innate According to Iran's Islamic Penal Code, based on Shi'a Islam, an innate apostate is one who is born to Muslim parents (or a Muslim parent) who then leaves Islam. The punishment for a male innate apostate is death. The punishment for a female apostate, whether voluntary or innate, is life imprisonment, unless she repents, in which case she will be set free. (See also Shari'a)

Apostate, melli or voluntary According to Iran's Islamic Penal Code, based on Shi'a Islam, a voluntary apostate is one who has converted to Islam after reaching the age of maturity, but who then leaves Islam. The punishment for a voluntary apostate is death, unless he repents within three days after final sentencing for apostasy. (See also Shari'a)

Asayeshgah A building in the northern part of the Evin Prison complex, built in the early 1980s. Literally, "sanitarium" or "place of rest," it houses the Evin prosecutor's office as well as solitary confinement cells.**

Ashura A day of mourning on which Shi'a Muslims commemorate the martyrdom of Hossein ibn Ali, the grandson of Mohammad, at the Battle of Karbala in Muharram 61 AH (October 680 CE). On this day Shi'a wear mourning attire and refrain from music. It is a time to express sorrow and respect for Hossein's passing, and it is also a time for self-reflection, when one commits oneself completely to mourning Hossein. It is a public holiday in Iran.

Ashura protests in 2009 Protestors used the opportunity of the Ashura commemoration to organize a major anti-regime demonstration; many young activists were arrested on that day.

Boxes See Coffin

Boycott ("Food Boycott") One level below a full-fledged hunger strike, the prisoners would refuse to receive food for a specified period and would make do with what they had in the ward. Boycotting the prison store, visitations, and walks outside in the prison courtyard were other types of prisoner protest.*

Chador Traditional head-to-toe veil worn by Muslim women.

Closed ward A ward where cell doors were closed at all times and were opened only when prisoners went to wash or to use the bathroom. The ward was under special watch. Also called a solitary ward.*

Coffin A space with two wooden dividers on the left and right sides, a wall on the front side, and open on the back side—a box with one open side. These boxes, also called "coffins" and "graves," were in a section in Qezel Hesar Prison called "judgment day." "Steadfast" prisoners were sent there for punishment and were told, "This is a grave, and we want you to feel the pressure of the grave." Blindfolded prisoners were forced to sit on their knees in these spaces; they could not stand up and they were not allowed to move. They were forced to listen to the loudspeaker, which constantly played readings from the Qur'an and mourning songs.*

Committee 3000 See Moshtarak Committee

Death Committee A three-man delegation formed pursuant to Ayatollah Khomeini's secret fatwa (religious decree), probably issued in late July 1988. The delegation consisted of a Shari'a (religious) judge, a public prosecutor, and an intelligence chief; it was charged with ascertaining whether prisoners affiliated with certain groups remained faithful to the group, or had repented and expressed sorrow for such allegiance. The prisoners' answers determined whether they would live or whether they would be executed. Prisoners would later call this delegation the "Death Committee." Other delegations were formed throughout the country in various provinces, on the same basis. (See Eshraqi, Nayyeri, Ra'isi, and Forugh Javidan)

Development Corps "Sepah Tarvij." Along with the Health Corps and the Knowledge Corps, the Development Corps was established during the Shah's 1963 reforms to allow young people to perform their military service in villages, by helping with development projects. The Health Corps and the Knowledge Corps promoted health and literacy, respectively.

Eid Qorban Sacrifice Festival, also called Feast of the Sacrifice. This is an important religious holiday celebrated by Muslims worldwide to honor the willingness of the prophet Ebrāhīm (Abraham) to sacrifice his young first-born son, Esmā'īl (Ishmael), as an act of submission to God's command, and of his son's acceptance of being sacrificed, before God intervened to provide Abraham with a lamb to sacrifice instead.

Enzejarnameh Literally, "enzejar," meaning abhorrence and "nameh," meaning letter. An abhorrence letter, in which prisoners would declare that they abhorred the ideas, commitments, and positions of political groups to which they had belonged, was one of the requirements for freedom.**

Eshraqi, Morteza Tehran Public Prosecutor and a member of the "Death Committee" that handed down death sentences in the 1988 mass killings of prisoners. He was identified by many survivors as having been involved in their initial prosecutions. As of this writing, he is practicing law in Tehran. (See also Death Committee)

Eshratabad Revolutionary Committee Formerly a police station, it was located in central Tehran, adjacent to and part of the Eshratabad barracks. (See also Islamic Revolutionary Committee)

Evin Prison A prison complex in Iran, located in Evin, northwestern Tehran. It is noted for its political prisoners' wing, where prisoners were held both before and after the 1979 Iranian Revolution. Constructed in 1972 under the reign of Mohammad Reza Shah Pahlavi, Evin Prison is located at the foot of the Alborz mountains. Initially designed to house 320 inmates (20 in solitary cells and 300 in two large communal blocks), by 1977 Evin expanded to hold more than 1,500 prisoners (including 100 solitary cells). Under the Islamic Republic, the prison population expanded significantly.

Fatwa A religious decree pronounced by a high religious authority, usually a grand scholar of Islamic jurisprudence or "Mojtahed." In Shi'a Islam, fatwas can be binding, depending on the level of authority of the issuer, on all Muslims, or solely on the followers of the particular Mojtahed.

Forugh Javidan MKO's military operation, literally meaning "eternal light." Having been expelled from France, Mojahedin Khalq Organization (MKO) leaders and many of its members went to Iraq and founded the National Liberation Army of Iran in 1987. With the help of Iraqi leader Saddam Hussein, who provided the MKO with bases in Iraqi territory and logistics support, the MKO subsequently made several incursions into Iranian territory during the Iran-Iraq War, including Operation Aftab on 7 April 1988, Operation Chelcheragh on 18 June 1988, and Operation Forugh Javidan on 25 July 1988, the last and bloodiest of these incursions, when they were overwhelmingly defeated. In the wake of this operation, thousands of imprisoned Mojahedin supporters were killed during the mass executions of political prisoners in 1988, pursuant to Ayatollah Khomeini's decree.

Ghosl Literally, "washing" in Arabic, a prescribed method of religious (i.e., there must be a specific intent) washing, or purification, of the body. It encompasses acts ranging from washing after sexual acts to the ritual washing of the dead.

Gohardasht Prison A prison in Gohardasht (Rajai Shahr), a town in the northern outskirts of Karaj, approximately 40 km west of Tehran. Also known as Rajai Shahr Prison, it is considered one of Iran's harshest jails because of its many reported cases of torture.

Haji One who has performed the Hajj (See Hajj)

Hajj or haj Annual pilgrimage to the holy city of Mecca (in Saudi Arabia) and one of the five pillars of Islam. It is a religious duty that must be carried out by every able-bodied Muslim who has the financial means to make the pilgrimage at least once in his or her lifetime.

Hashti Prison hallway. (See also Zir hasht)

Hezbollahi Literally, Member of the Party of God, the name given to paramilitary pro-Khomeini pressure groups in the early years of the Islamic Revolution.

Hosseinyeh A place of worship for the mourning period of Ashura (see Ashura). A large, covered hall at Evin Prison that had once been the prison gymnasium, but was turned into a space used to conduct mourning rituals, as well as to give speeches and interview prisoners. At Gohardasht Prison there is a large space called Hosseinyeh at the end of each ward that had been used as a commissary under the Pahlavi regime. Some mass executions in 1988 took place in the Hosseinyeh of Gohardasht Prison.

Islamic Revolutionary Committee Paramilitary militia initially organized in every neighborhood mosque and school in the immediate aftermath of the Iranian Revolution. The committees were organized to function as a quasi-police force parallel with the Shahrbani (the official police force). Given the fact that by mid-1979 there were over 1,500 committees in Tehran alone, they were organized under a single command by order of Ayatollah Khomeini. Their duties included a wide spectrum of activities ranging from collecting thousands of weapons distributed to the general public during the Revolution, to confiscating property, fighting anti-revolutionaries, and preventing usury and bribery, among many other things. The committees served as "the eyes and ears" of the new regime, and were instrumental in establishing and maintaining an atmosphere of fear and intimidation. They carried out such illegal activities as arbitrary arrests and executions, unlawful searches of residences and persons, unlawful confiscations of property, and numerous other human rights violations and abuses. In 1991, the Islamic Revolutionary Committees were merged with the Gendarmerie and the Shahrbani to form a single entity called the Islamic Republic Police Force.

Islamic Revolutionary Tribunal (or Court) In the immediate aftermath of the Revolution, on February 13, 1979, Ayatollah Khomeini ordered the formation of an ad hoc tribunal, commonly referred to as the Extraordinary Revolutionary Tribunal, headed by Ayatollah Sadeq Khalkhali, to conduct what amounted to a court-martial of the high-ranking officials of the previous regime. No specific jurisdiction was defined, the Shari'a judge having broad authority and freedom to determine which cases to try and what charges to bring. Less than two weeks later, on 24 February 1979, a written decree was handed down by Ayatollah Khomeini appointing Ayatollah Khalkhali as Shari'a (see Shari'a) Judge and instructing him "to issue Shari'a-based rulings," thereby establishing the foundation of a system of special courts known as the Islamic Revolutionary Tribunal. Initially, no substantive or procedural rules were devised for these courts; their jurisdiction was as broad as that allowed by Shari'a rules interpreted by Ayatollah Khalkhali and other Shari'a judges in various provinces and towns, operating under his supervision. The revolutionary courts system was established in various towns and provinces, with a single Shari'a judge making the ultimate decisions. The rulings were final and not subject to review or appeal. The jurisdiction of revolutionary courts underwent several modifications over the years, each one expanding yet again the areas over which they had jurisdiction: "Acts contrary to Islamic Shari'a ('Monkerat' or

Islamic Revolutionary Tribunal (or Court) *(continued)*

forbidden acts/activities), and vile Western acts and acts of that nature, with a view to [disobeying and belittling] the [Islamic Republic] system and disrupting political and moral security" were examples of such additions. In 1994, the jurisdiction of revolutionary courts underwent its last change, as of this writing.

Jamshidabad Prison A military prison located in the northern part of Tehran in the Jamshidabad barracks. In the immediate aftermath of the Revolution, it was still run by the Army.

Jihad An Arabic term meaning "struggle," commonly misunderstood as "Holy War." Within the context of Islam it refers to either the spiritual struggle to fulfill one's religious duties ("greater jihad") or the struggle against the enemies of Islam, which can take a violent or a non-violent form.

Jihad ward A prison unit where the prisoners, mainly repenters (see Tavvab) volunteered to work in the prison's construction, gardening, and landscaping projects, for which they were not paid. These prisoners were called "Jihadi." (See also Labor ward)*

Khabith Evil

Komeil A specific Shi'a prayer conducted on Thursday evenings and in the mid-month of Sha'ban (the Arabic month during which it is said the Shia's twelfth Imam was born). According to Shi'a belief, the prayer disposes of enemies, increases wealth, and forgives sins.

Labor ward A ward where prisoners, mainly repenters, could do work such as gardening, carpentry, and tailoring, for which they would be paid a small wage. (See also Jihad ward)

Majles Shoraye Eslami The Islamic Consultative Assembly or the Iranian Parliament, the national legislative body of the Islamic Republic of Iran.

Majlis See Majles Shoraye Eslami

Maqna'eh A type of Islamic head wear that covers the hair, the ears, the neck, and the shoulders, and drops below the chest, leaving only the face exposed.

Mellikesh Convicts who had served their full sentences but were not released.

Mersad, Operation The Islamic Republic's counterattack, literally meaning "ambush," against the MKO's Eternal Light Operation. (See Forugh Javidan; see also Mojahedin Khalq Organization in Political Parties and Religious Denominations, below)

Mohareb [ba Khoda] Literally, "warrior against God," the person perpetrating the crime of "Moharebeh" (waging war against God), which is an Islamic concept that found its way into the laws of the Islamic Republic of Iran subsequent to the 1979 Revolution. It usually carries the death penalty. Article 196 of the Law of Hodud and Qesas (Islamic punishments) of 1982 defined Mohareb as one who "takes up arms in order to create fear and alarm and to deprive the population of its freedom and security." Article 198 further stated that "all individuals and supporters" of a group or organization that takes up arms against the Islamic regime "who have knowledge of the location of the group or contribute in any way to the advancement of its objectives shall be considered Mohareb, even though they have not participated in any of their regular branches." In the 1980s this concept was broadly interpreted by the Islamic Republic judiciary to encompass

Mohareb [ba Khoda] *(continued)* anyone associated with the MKO and leftist organizations. (See Islamic Revolutionary Tribunal)

Mojarad (ward) See Closed ward

Monafeq Literally, "hypocrite," defamatory epithet the regime used to identify MKO members. Monafeq refers to a person who pretends to be Muslim but is in reality an infidel.

Monafeqin Plural of Monafeq, hypocrites

Moshtarak Committee An institution in Tehran, also known as the Tohid Committee, Comité Moshtarak, Ward 3000, or Committee 3000, that was created in response to the armed struggle launched by MKO and FKO in the early 1970s. Its full name was the Comite-ye Moshtarak-e Zed-e Kharabkari (Joint Anti-Sabotage Committee). It was formed when the political police (SAVAK), the Police (Shahrbani), and the Gendarmerie collaborated in an effort to stop sabotage and dismantle the guerrilla organizations. Renamed the Tohid Committee after the 1979 Revolution, it was used as a detention center by the revolutionary security forces. In 2002, the Tohid Committee was turned into a museum (the Ebrat Museum) dedicated to the history of repression and torture under the Shah, with no mention of what the building was used for during the first two decades of the Islamic Republic of Iran.

Motahhari, Morteza (1920–1979). Iranian cleric, Islamic scholar, politician, and one of the high-profile ideologues of the Islamic Revolution of Iran. A disciple of Ayatollah Khomeini, he wrote several books on the tenets of Shi'a Islam concerning a multitude of topics. Khomeini entrusted him with the task of creating the Council of the Islamic Revolution, a secret body that was set up on 12 January 1979. From that date until his assassination on 1 May 1979, Motahhari headed this council, which led the Islamic revolutionary movement to victory and then acted as a "parallel government" that competed with the official post-revolutionary government. Part of Motahhari's intellectual output was dedicated to a critique of Marxist theories. He was assassinated in May 1979 by a member of the Forqan organization. His works were widely taught in prisons.

Namaz Jom'eh Friday Prayer ceremony

Nayyeri, Hossein'ali Shari'a judge and member of the Death Committee, named specifically by Ayatollah Khomeini in his 1988 fatwa. The Committee handed down death sentences in the 1988 mass killings of prisoners. He was identified as presiding over Death Committees in Tehran prisons by many survivors who had been permitted to take their blindfolds off when attending the committee, because he had presided over their earlier cases or was well known from television appearances. He admitted to Montazeri on 13 August 1988 that he had already executed 750 prisoners in Tehran. As of this writing, he is Deputy Chief Justice of the Supreme Court of Iran. (See also Death Committee)

Open Ward A ward where cell doors are open and prisoners are free to walk about in the hallways and use the bathrooms.

Prosecutor's Office After the establishment of the revolutionary courts, the Revolutionary Prosecutor's Office was also established in order to prepare cases for trial by the revolutionary courts. Designed to serve as a venue for questioning a person accused of a crime,

Prosecutor's Office *(continued)*
among other functions (within Iran's inquisitorial, as opposed to adversarial, judicial system), the Prosecutor's Office was used instead by interrogators/torturers inside prisons to extract information from the victims. The Prosecutor's Office of the General Courts, which was, and continues to be, a completely separate court system with jurisdiction over matters not within the jurisdiction of revolutionary courts, functioned in an entirely different setting, applying its own rules of procedure. (See Islamic Revolutionary Tribunal)

Public ward See Open ward

Qapani A type of torture consisting of being hung from the arms bent behind one's back.

Qesas The principle of an eye for an eye, the Islamic law of retribution.

Qezel Hesar Prison One of the largest prisons in Iran, it was built in 1964, in the Central District of Karaj County, Alborz Province.

Ra'isi, Ebrahim A prosecutor and the deputy of [Tehran Public Prosecutor] Morteza Eshraqi. He took Eshraqi's place on the Death Committee on occasion. He went on to become Head of the General Inspection Organization, and, as of this writing, he is Deputy Head of the Judiciary. (See Death Committee; see also Eshraqi, Morteza)

Rajai Shahr Prison See Gohardasht Prison

Ramadan The ninth month of the Islamic calendar, during which Muslims throughout the world fast.

Revolutionary Committee See Islamic Revolutionary Committee

Revolutionary Court See Islamic Revolutionary Tribunal

Revolutionary Guards A branch of Iran's military founded after the 1979 Revolution to safeguard the achievements of the Islamic Revolution. Its official name is "Sepah-e Psadaran-e Enqelab-e Eslami" (Islamic Revolutionary Guard Corps). One of the main roles it has played since its formation has been to quash uprisings throughout Iran. It has also been instrumental in preventing and silencing dissent. Its feared Intelligence Section has been responsible for detaining and torturing political opponents. It has its own detention centers around the country, and its own section within Evin Prison. (See Sepah Detention Centers; see also Evin Prison)

Sar-e moze'i Prisoners who remained steadfast in their political opinions.

Sepah Detention Centers Detention centers and prisons used by the Revolutionary Guards Intelligence Section to detain and interrogate dissidents. They are spread across Iran in various towns and cities, including Tehran, Tabriz, and Shiraz.

Shari'a The religious law of Islam, which is based primarily on the Qur'an and the tradition of the Prophet Mohammad ("Sunna") and which regulates most aspects of a Muslim's life. In Shi'a Islam, Shari'a includes the traditions and teachings of the Twelve Imams, successors to the Prophet.

Shari'ati, Ali (1933–1977). Iranian sociologist whose main focus was on the sociology of religion. He is considered to be one of the ideologues of Iran's Islamic Revolution. In his numerous writings he provides a modern revolutionary interpretation of Islam. His

Shari'ati, Ali *(continued)*
powerful and emotional prose, though theoretically weak, had an incalculable influence over the youth and the middle class in pre-revolutionary Iran and facilitated the loyalty of Iran's middle class to Ayatollah Khomeini. Ironically, Shari'ati opposed the political rule of the clergy.

Shari'atmadari, Hossein Known to many former prisoners as "Brother Hossein," he is the managing editor of *Kayhan*, a conservative newspaper close to Ayatollah Khamene'i, Iran's Supreme Leader, which regularly engages in publishing accusatory and slanderous stories. Shari'atmadari, who is said to have close links to the intelligence apparatus, was purportedly an interrogator at Evin Prison, something he has denied. He has, however, admitted to having actively interviewed and "conducted dialogues with [political] prisoners. . . and [to] having succeeded in bringing them back to the path of the people and the Revolution."

Shiraz Sepah Detention Center The Revolutionary Guards Intelligence Section's detention center, located in the city of Shiraz in Fars Province in central Iran. It is also known as Number 100, because of its location on Sepah Street. It is physically part of an Islamic Republic Army base.

Solitary ward See Closed ward

Supreme Judicial Council "Shoraye Ali Qaza'i." Established pursuant to Principle 158 of the Constitution and entrusted with managing and supervising all judicial, executive, and administrative affairs falling within the framework of the judicial system, it was the IRI judiciary's highest authority from 1982 to 1989. Composed of five members, including the Chief Justice of the Supreme Court

and the Prosecutor General, it was replaced by the Head of the Judiciary, a single person appointed by the Supreme Leader of the Revolution, in 1989.

Ta'zir Discretionary religious punishment

Tamshit Room The torture chamber of Unesco Prison, which was located in the basement. The word "tamshit" literally means to manage, while, figuratively, it connotes "taking care of business."

Tavvab Literally, "one who has repented" or "repenter," it was a term used to refer to those prisoners who, for whatever reason, had expressed regret for and cut off their past and did not stop at anything to escape execution or be freed from detention ahead of schedule.

Tohid Committee See Moshtarak Committee

209 Basement The torture chamber of the Revolutionary Guards Intelligence Section in Evin's ward 209. This was where some of the trials were conducted during the 1988 mass killings and where prisoners were hanged, then and there.

Ulema Religious scholars. "Ulema" is plural.

Unesco Prison A building located in the city of Dezful in southern Iran, which was established, in cooperation with Unesco, for cultural and educational purposes during the Shah's regime. After the Revolution it was transformed into a prison, with new construction in the early 1980s expanding its small capacity.

Ward A prison section composed of a number of cells. The six wards of the Amuzeshgah at Evin Prison and the 24 wards at Gohardasht Prison were called "salon" instead of "ward." (See also Amuzeshgah and Gohardasht Prison)

Ward 209 A building adjacent to the Evin infirmary ("Behdari") made up of 10 wards and approximately 100 cells. Prior to the formation of the Ministry of Intelligence, it was used exclusively by the Revolutionary Guards' Intelligence and Security Section, which played the main role in crushing political organizations in the 1980s. It was later taken over by the Ministry of Intelligence.*

Ward 3000 See Moshtarak Committee

Wards 5 and 6 A two-story villa with a nice view, located in the southern part of the Evin Prison complex, composed of the two wards. Older prisoners and prisoners not belonging to "mini-groups" (a derogatory term used to describe MKO and certain leftist organizations) were kept there, where there were more and better amenities.*

Wards 216, 240, 246 The common names for wards 1, 2, 3, and 4 in Evin, which were actually their phone extensions. "216" stood for wards 1 and 2, male wards; "240" and "246," for wards 3 and 4, female wards.*

Wards 311, 325 Solitary confinement cells at the old Evin Prison complex that were used by both male and female prisoners. They were also known as the "green cells."

Workers' ward The prisoners kept in this ward worked at the prison itself.*

Yazid Yazīd ibn Mu'āwiya ibn Abī Sufyān (23 July 647–14 November 683) was the third Caliph and the first through inheritance. He had been appointed by his father Muawiyah I and ruled for three years from 680 CE until his death in 683 CE. Yazid's army fought and killed Imam Hossein, the grandson of the Prophet Mohammad and the third Shi'a Imam, in the battle of Karbala (in present day Iraq) on 10 October 680. Imam Hossein's martyrdom, called Ashura and commemorated annually by Shi'a Muslims, is one of the most important events in Shi'a Islam. Yazid is regarded by Shi'a Muslims as the epitome of cruelty and ruthlessness. (See also Ashura)

Zir hasht Offices where prison guards and prison administrators were stationed. The administrative work of the detention centers and wards was also carried out in these offices. This expression is a remnant of the Shah's regime and Qasr Prison. The Qasr Prison office was located at the junction of eight wards and was therefore called Hasht ("Eight") or Hashti. This was also where prisoners were punished.*

Appendix C
Political Parties and Religious Denominations Referred to in the Witness Testimonies

The following list of political groups and religious denominations is not exhaustive and includes only those referred to in the witness testimonies. The summary descriptions are limited in scope and chronology.

Ahl-e Haq ("People of Truth" or "Yarsan")

Ahl-e Haq is a religious minority not recognized by the Iranian Constitution. It is a mystic religious school founded in the late 14th century in western Iran, the majority of whose members live primarily in western Iran and Iraqi Kurdistan. (There are Ahl-e Haq adherents in Turkey, Albania, Syria, and Afghanistan.) In Iran they are estimated to number around one million and are subjected to religious discrimination and prevented from practicing their faith communally. Though some adepts of this school still consider themselves Shi'a Muslims, the Ahl-e Haq tenets are distinct from the Shi'a doctrine. They believe that God has manifested Himself in human form several times and that man is given more than one thousand lives to purify himself and find proximity to God. For them, Shari'a is only the esoteric aspect of religion and the first stage of religious education. This first stage is to be followed by the second stage (the path), and the third stage (gnosis, knowledge of spiritual realities), and, finally, the fourth and last stage (the ultimate truth). The title of the Order, Ahl-e Haq, meaning "people of truth," implies that they consider themselves to have already gone through the previous stages and are now at the final stage. As such, they believe that they are no longer required to observe some of the rules of Shari'a.

Arman-e Mostaz'afin

Arman-e Mostaz'afin was a small political group opposed to the political role of the clergy, strongly influenced by the teachings of Ali Shari'ati, one of the major theoreticians of political Islam in Iran. Actually called Sazman-e Razmandegan-e Pishgam-e Mostaz'afin, the group came to be known by the name of its publication, *Arman-e Mostaz'afin*. It was founded in the summer of 1976 by Baqer Borzui and premised upon its own particular interpretation of the Qur'an, with strong leftist leanings. The group became active after the Revolution, mainly in the realm of theory and ideology, and in the course of two years published numerous books as well as articles in its publication *Arman-e Mostaz'afin*. To achieve its goals, the group's strategy was to draw the people away from the clergy. In the winter of 1982, the leaders of the group were arrested, and, although none were executed, Arman-e Mostaz'afin ceased to exist inside Iran in 1982.

Bahá'í (religious denomination)

The Bahá'í Faith was founded in Iran in 1844 and is now its largest non-Muslim religious minority. While reaffirming the core ethical principles common to all religions, the founder of the Bahá'í Faith, Bahá'u'lláh, was also said to have revealed new laws and

Bahá'í (religious denomination) *(continued)*
teachings to lay the foundations of a global civilization. The central theme of the Bahá'í Faith is that humanity is one family and the time has come for its unification into a peaceful global society. The authorities of the Islamic Republic have subjected the members of the Bahá'í religious community of Iran (approximately 300,000 members in 1979) to systematic harassment and persecution, depriving them of their most fundamental human rights. The Bahá'í religion is not recognized under the Constitution of the Islamic Republic, and Iranian authorities refer to it as a heresy. As a result, the Bahá'ís have been denied the rights associated with the status of a religious minority; they cannot profess and practice their faith and are banned from public functions. Discrimination under the law and in practice has subjected them to abuse and violence. The Islamic Republic Penal Code grants no rights to Bahá'ís, and the courts have denied them the right to redress or to protection against assault, murder, and other forms of persecution and abuse. In so doing, the courts have treated Bahá'ís as unprotected citizens or "apostates," citing eminent religious authorities whose edicts are considered to be a source of law equal to acts of Parliament. The Founder of the Islamic Republic, Ayatollah Khomeini, made execution a punishment for the crime of apostasy and decreed that a Muslim would not be punished for killing an apostate. Banishment from public functions has seriously damaged the Bahá'ís' professional, economic, and social lives. Soon after the Revolution, a Ministry of Labor directive called for the dismissal from public office and all governmental organizations and associations those "who belong to any of the misguided sects recognized by all Muslims as heretical deviations from Islam, or to organizations whose doctrine and constitution are based on rejection of the divinely-revealed religions." Finally, the mandatory requirement of specifying religion in application forms and official documents (lifted recently in some areas as a result of international pressure) has seriously limited Bahá'ís' freedoms and opportunities in all areas of their lives, including divorce, inheritance, access to universities, and travel. In practice, since 1980, thousands of Bahá'ís have lost their jobs, pensions, businesses, properties, and educational opportunities. By banning the Bahá'í organization, an elected spiritual body that administers the affairs of the faith at both local and national levels, the Islamic Republic has denied Bahá'ís the right to meet, elect, and operate their religious institutions. Furthermore, the Iranian government has executed at least 200 Bahá'ís and has imprisoned, tortured, and pressured to convert to Islam scores more. Because of the unanimous international condemnation of the persecution of this quietist (apolitical) religious community, Iranian authorities do not always admit that the Bahá'ís are being punished for their religious beliefs. Therefore, judicial authorities have often charged Bahá'ís with offenses such as being involved in "counter-revolutionary activities," supporting the "former regime," being "agents of Zionism," or being involved with "prostitution, adultery, and immorality."

Democratic Party of Iranian Kurdistan (PDKI)
The Democratic Party of Iranian Kurdistan (PDKI) was founded in 1945 with the objective of gaining autonomy for Kurdistan, in northwestern Iran. After the Revolution, conflicts between the new central

Democratic Party of Iranian Kurdistan (PDKI)
(continued)

Shi'a government and the mainly Sunni Kurdistan, regarding the role of minorities in the drafting of the constitution, designation of Shi'a Islam as the official state religion, and the autonomy of the region, resulted in armed clashes between the Revolutionary Guards and the Peshmerga (the militia of the PDKI). The PDKI boycotted the 30–31 March 1979 referendum on the establishment of the Islamic Republic regime. On 19 August 1979, Ayatollah Khomeini called the PDKI the "party of Satan" and declared it "banned and illegal." Mass executions and fighting broke out and continued for several months in the region. By 1983, PDKI had lost much of its influence in the region. Over the years, members and leaders of the PDKI have been victims of deadly terrorist attacks, both inside and outside Iran. The charismatic leader of the PDKI, Dr. Abdorrahman Qasemlu, was assassinated in July 1989 in Vienna, Austria. His successor, Dr. Sadeq Sharafkandi, was killed in September 1992 in the Greek restaurant Mikonos in Berlin, Germany. Although the Islamic Republic has never accepted responsibility for these assassinations, evidence in the Sharafkandi case directly implicating Iran's leaders led the Berlin court investigating the matter to issue subpoenas to a number of high ranking Iranian officials.

Ettehadieh Komonist-ha (EK)

Ettehadieh Komonist-ha (Communists Union) was the product of the August-September 1976 merger of two Marxist-Leninist groups, Sazeman-e Enqelabiun-e Komonist ("Communist Revolutionaries' Organization") and Puya, composed of exiled opponents of the Pahlavi regime who were mostly active in the Iran Student Confederation (an opposition student union based outside Iran, 1967–1983). They followed the teachings of Mao Tse-tung and did not believe in guerrilla warfare. They viewed the Soviet Union as a "socialist-imperialist" state and the Shah as a puppet of the United States and Great Britain. The group was marked by ideological divides during the periods preceding and following the 1979 Revolution, which caused it to split into several factions. One of the most important rifts was triggered by the decision by a number of members to take up arms and take over a city in Iran. The uprising plan—devised in the midst of an active and violent anti-Communist campaign by the revolutionary Islamic government—split the Ettehadieh into two factions, one believing in armed movement and the other opposing it. In the winter of 1982, armed members of the Ettehadieh hid in a forest ("jangal" in Farsi) in the north of Iran outside the city of Amol. This group, known as the Jangal Group, was involved in several clashes with the Revolutionary Guards and ultimately, on 26 January 1982, attacked the city of Amol, hoping to spark a general uprising. There were casualties on both sides as well as among civilians; the surviving members of the Jangal Group were arrested. Most EK members and supporters, including those who opposed the Amol uprising, were subsequently arrested and tried for belonging to the organization and for having participated in the Amol clash, and many were executed.

Fadaiyan Khalq Organization

The Fadaiyan Khalq Organization, a Marxist-Leninist group inspired by the Cuban Revolution and other Latin American

Fadaiyan Khalq Organization *(continued)*
urban guerrilla movements, was founded in 1971 by two Communist groups opposed to the Pahlavi regime. In 1981 the organization, which after the Revolution had opted for open political and electoral activity, split over the issues of armed struggle and support for the Islamic Republic and the Soviet Union. Three separate branches came into existence: the FKO Majority, FKO Minority, and FKO Guerrilla Organization.

FKO Majority supported the Islamic Republic as a revolutionary and anti-imperialist regime. The group renounced armed struggle. After the spring of 1983, however, the Islamic Republic targeted its members solely on the basis of their political beliefs.

FKO Minority opposed the Islamic Republic. In the summer of 1981, the FKO Minority announced the organization of combatant cells. However, based on available information, these cells never became operational. Though the group did not completely abandon the theory of armed struggle, its activities were mainly limited to the political arena and the labor movement. Many of its members and supporters were arrested and executed in the early 1980s.

FKO Guerrillas (Ashraf Dehqani Branch) did not renounce armed struggle and continued to promote it as part of its ideology. It strongly opposed the Islamic regime of Iran. The group was founded and led by Ashraf Dehqani, a high-ranking female member.

Forqan
Forqan was formed in 1977 by a group of Ali Shari'ati's followers who adhered to a modern interpretation of the Qur'an and Islamic ideology. It is not clear whether the group was armed or not, but it went underground soon after its formation. From the onset of the Revolution, this group opposed the involvement of the clergy in the government, as well as the particular interpretation of Islam later implemented by the Islamic Republic authorities. In the short period of its post-revolutionary activity, the group was accused of involvement in armed robberies and the assassination of several high-ranking regime officials, including two clerics, former students and close collaborators of Ayatollah Khomeini. Most of the known members of the group were executed or killed in clashes with Islamic Revolutionary Committee forces, resulting in the total elimination of the group by 1980.

Hezb-e Kar-e Iran ("Iran Labor Party" or Tufan)
Khrushchev's de-Stalinization policies in the Soviet Union led to a political crisis in the Iranian Communist party Tudeh, as in many Communist parties around the world. Hezb-e Kar-e Iran or Tufan (initially called the "Revolutionary Organization of the Tudeh Party," and subsequently the "Marxist-Leninist Organization of Tufan") was founded on 10 December 1963 as a result of a split from the Tudeh Party of Iran. The Party believes that after the death of Stalin, who had established the dictatorship of the proletariat in its true sense, the Soviet Union became a socialist-imperialist country. The organization changed its name after the 1979 Revolution, first to the Party of Workers and Farmers of Iran, and later to Iran Labor Party, Tufan. The Party supports the overthrow of the Islamic Republic and the establishment of a proletarian dictatorship. Its activities are concentrated mainly outside Iran. The Iran

Hezb-e Kar-e Iran ("Iran Labor Party" or Tufan) *(continued)*

Labor Party is a member of the International Conference of Marxist-Leninist Parties and Organizations and publishes the magazine *Tufan.*

Islamic Republic Party (Jomhuri Eslami Party)

The Islamic Republic Party (Jomhuri Eslami Party) was formed in 1979. It was the first political party to gather the most influential clergymen and laymen who shared Ayatollah Khomeini's ideology. The party was formed on the premise of strengthening, protecting, and exporting the ideals of the Islamic Revolution under the leadership of the Spiritual Leader and of fighting all "anti-Islamic" forces and political opposition. The *Jomhuri Eslami* newspaper was the Party's main publication. On 28 June 1981, an explosion at the Islamic Republic Party headquarters caused the death of about 72 party members, including its secretary general Ayatollah Mohammad Beheshti, then head of the Supreme Court. The Iranian authorities blamed the bombing on the Mojahedin Khalq Organization (MKO). The MKO, however, without denying involvement, never accepted responsibility for the bombing. In the next few years, several individuals who were affiliated with the MKO or accused of being Iraqi agents were charged in connection with the bombing and were executed. No other opposition group claimed responsibility. The Islamic Republic Party dissolved itself in June 1987 due to factionalism, divergences of opinion, and disagreements over policy-making among its high-ranking officials.

Komala

While in exile in Iraq in the mid 1960s, several remaining members of the Kurdistan Democratic Party of Iran established the Revolutionary Organization of the Kurdistan Democratic Party. Among its leaders were Esma'il Sharifzadeh, Abdollah Mo'ini, and Mola'avareh, who began an armed guerrilla struggle in Kurdistan inspired by the Cuban Revolution. The group was defeated in 1969 and several of its members killed or arrested. With the release of a number of the leaders in 1978, the Revolutionary Organization of Working People in Kurdistan (Komala) was established. After the Revolution, in accordance with Marxist theory, Komala opposed capitalists and landlords and encouraged workers and peasants in Kurdistan, in particular in the city of Sanandaj and vicinity, where they had strong support, to initiate an armed uprising against capitalists, landlords, and the central government. In 1982, Komala joined another Marxist group, Union of Communist Militants (formerly Sahand), an organization concentrating mainly on theory and ideology, and established the Communist Party of Iran. Komala subsequently adopted the name "The Kurdistan Organization of the Communist Party of Iran, Komala." By the mid-1980s the central government had succeeded in pushing Komala fighters out of Kurdistan and into northern Iraq. Years later, Komala split from the Communist Party of Iran and faced several schisms, each continuing to use the name Komala.

Mojahedin Khalq Organization (MKO)

The Mojahedin Khalq Organization (MKO) was founded in 1965. This organization adopted the principles of Islam as its ideo-

Mojahedin Khalq Organization (MKO)
(continued)

logical framework. However, its members' interpretation of Islam was revolutionary, and they believed in armed struggle against the Shah's regime. They valued Marxism as a progressive method of economic and social analysis but considered Islam as their source of inspiration, culture, and ideology. In the 1970s the MKO was weakened when many of its members were imprisoned and executed. In 1975, following a deep ideological crisis, the organization refuted Islam as its ideology and, after a few of its members were killed and other Muslim members purged, the organization proclaimed Marxism as its ideology. This move led to the split of the Marxist-Leninist Section of the MKO in 1977. In January 1979 the imprisoned Muslim leaders of the MKO were released along with other political prisoners. They began to reorganize the MKO and recruit new members based on Islamic ideology. After the 1979 Revolution and the establishment of the Islamic Republic, the MKO accepted the leadership of Ayatollah Khomeini and supported the Revolution. Active participation in the political scene and infiltration of government institutions were foremost on the organization's agenda. During the first two years after the Revolution, the MKO succeeded in recruiting numerous sympathizers, especially in high schools and universities; but its efforts to gain political power, either by appointment or election, were strongly opposed by the Islamic Republic leaders. The exclusion of MKO members from government offices and the closure of their centers and publishing houses, in conjunction with the Islamic Republic authorities' different interpretation of Islam, widened the gap between the two. Authorities of the new regime referred to the Mojahedin as "hypocrites," and the Hezbollahi supporters of the regime attacked the Mojahedin sympathizers regularly during their demonstrations and when they distributed their publications, leading to the death of several MKO supporters. On 20 June 1981 the MKO called for a demonstration protesting their treatment by government officials and the government officials' efforts to impeach their ally, President Abolhassan Banisadr. Despite the fact that the regime called this demonstration illegal, thousands came to the streets, some of whom confronted the Revolutionary Guardsmen and Hezbollahis. The number of casualties that resulted from this demonstration is unknown, but a large number of demonstrators were arrested and executed in the following days and weeks. The day after the demonstration, the Islamic Republic regime started a repressive campaign—unprecedented in modern Iranian history. Thousands of MKO members and sympathizers were arrested or executed during this campaign. On this date (21 June 1981) the MKO announced an armed struggle against the Islamic Republic and assassinated a number of high-ranking officials and supporters of the Islamic regime. In the summer of 1981, the leader of the MKO and the impeached President (Banisadr) fled Iran to reside in France, where they founded the National Council of Resistance. After the MKO leaders and many of its members were expelled from France, they went to Iraq, where in 1987 they founded the National Liberation Army of Iran. The National Liberation Army entered Iranian territory a few times during the Iran-Iraq War, but was defeated in July 1988 during its last operation, the Forugh Javidan

Mojahedin Khalq Organization (MKO)
(continued)

(Eternal Light) Operation. A few days after this operation, thousands of imprisoned Mojahedin supporters were killed during the mass executions of political prisoners in 1988. Ever since the summer of 1981, the MKO has continued its activities outside of Iran. No information is available regarding members and activities of the MKO inside the country. Notwithstanding the "armed struggle" announcement by the MKO on 21 June 1981, many sympathizers of the organization had no military training, were not armed, and did not participate in armed conflict.

Navid

Navid was the Tudeh Party's underground group that became active in the fall of 1975, before the Revolution. In late 1975 and early 1976, it began publishing a clandestine newspaper under the same name, which soon became a monthly publication, distributed in a clandestine fashion by the group's members, who were never made aware of the group's hierarchy. *Navid* ceased publication soon after the Islamic Revolution.

Peykar Organization for the Liberation of the Working Class

The Peykar Organization for the Liberation of the Working Class was founded by a number of dissident members of the Mojahedin Khalq Organization who had converted to Marxism-Leninism. Peykar was also joined by a number of political organizations, known as Khat-e Se (Third Line). The founding tenets of Peykar included the rejection of guerrilla struggle and the adoption of a strong stance against the pro-Soviet policies of the Iranian Tudeh Party. Peykar viewed the Soviet Union as a "socialist-imperialist" state, believed that China had deviated from the Marxist-Leninist principles, and radically opposed all factions of the Islamic regime of Iran. The brutal repression of dissidents by the Iranian government and splits within Peykar in 1981 and 1982 effectively dismantled the Organization and scattered its supporters. By the mid-1980s, Peykar was no longer in existence.

Rah-e Kargar ("Revolutionary Workers Organization of Iran")

Rah-e Kargar or the Revolutionary Workers Organization of Iran was established in the summer of 1979. The Organization was founded by individuals from various leftist groups who rejected the idea of armed struggle and believed in political action. They identified themselves as Marxist-Leninists, promoting a socialist revolution and the leadership of the proletariat. They differed with the pro-Soviet Communist party, Tudeh, in that they opposed the Islamic Republic and Ayatollah Khomeini's leadership.

Ranjbaran Party

The Ranjbaran Party of Iran was established in Tehran by a number of Marxist groups and parties in late December 1979. The founders of Ranjbaran were Marxist–Leninist and followers of Mao Tse-tung. They opposed the USA and the USSR and supported Ruhollah Khomeini as an anti-imperialist leader. During the massive repression of 1981, the party was banned and its leaders were executed. Its publication, *Ranjbar*, has occasionally been published outside Iran since 1981.

Rastakhiz Party

The Rastakhiz Party was established in 1975 as Iran's sole political party, upon the abolition of the multi-party system and the establishment of the single-party system in the country. The government announced membership in Rastakhiz to be the civic duty of all citizens. The main principles of Rastakhiz were: loyalty to the Constitution, to the Monarchy, and to the goals of the White Revolution. The latter was a series of reforms, launched in 1963 by Mohammad Reza Shah Pahlavi (1919–1980) with the goal of improving economic and social conditions in the country. Land reform and women's suffrage were at the center of the White Revolution. Among other reforms of the White Revolution were the establishment of the Knowledge Corps (to combat illiteracy), the Health Corps, and the Development Corps, which added a component of civil service in remote areas to the compulsory military service (see Development Corps in the glossary). The activities of the Rastakhiz Party ceased after the February 1979 Revolution.

Razmandegan Organization

The Razmandegan Organization for the Liberation of the Working Class was founded in the winter of 1979. Its activities were focused on the working class and factories. The founding tenets of Razmandegan included the rejection of armed struggle and the adoption of a strong stance against the pro-Soviet policies of the Iranian Tudeh Party. It viewed the Soviet Union as a "socialist-imperialist" state and believed that China had deviated from Marxist-Leninist principles. Razmandegan, like the Peykar Organization, was among the groups that became known as Khat-e Se (Third Line). By early 1981, disagreements concerning the Party's position on the Iran-Iraq War caused internal splits within Razmandegan. These splits, which coincided with the massive and brutal repression of dissidents by the Iranian government, caused the organization to disband.

Sahand Organization

The Sahand Organization (later Union of Communist Militants) was founded after the Islamic Revolution of February 1979, with the specific goal of focusing on theory and ideology. In 1982 the Union of Communist Militants and Komala, along with the remaining members of other Communist organizations such as Peykar, Razmandegan, and certain affiliates of the Fadaiyan Khalq, joined together to found the Communist Party of Iran. Later, the Union of Communist Militants was itself divided into a number of factions. Once the principal pillar of the Communist Party of Iran, Komala then separated from the Party. The Communist Party of Iran is now composed mostly of the members of the Union of Communist Militants. There is a Kurdistan organization affiliated with it, which also calls itself Komala.

Setareh Sorkh ("The Red Star")

Setareh Sorkh was a Communist guerrilla group established in 1970 by Ali Reza Shokuhi to fight the Pahlavi regime. Shokuhi was imprisoned from 1971 to 1979, along with some of his comrades. Upon Shokuhi's release, he and former Setareh Sorkh members, along with members of a number of other leftist parties, participated in the establishment of the Revolutionary Workers Organization of Iran, Rah-e Kargar.

Shi'a Esna Ashari (state religion of Iran)

Shi'a Esna Ashari ("Followers of the Twelve Imams") refers to the adherents of the branch of Islam, who believe that Imam Ali, the Prophet Mohammad's cousin, son-in-law, and the first Muslim, is his rightful successor and the first Imam, as are his descendants, ending with the twelfth, Imam Mahdi, who is in occultation (i.e., that he disappeared and will one day return to fill the world with justice). Infallibility of the twelve Imams and the eventual return of the Twelfth Imam Mahdi are the cornerstones of the Shi'a religion.

Tudeh Party

The Tudeh Party of Iran (Hezb-e Tudeh or the Party of the Masses) was founded in 1941 by a group of mostly Communist intellectuals. Its non-radical, reformist platform reflected the founders' hopes of attracting the larger religious population. However, the Party's Marxist-Leninist orientation and its anti-imperialist and anti-Fascist positions made it most influential among Iranian intellectuals. In the late 1940s and early 1950s, the Tudeh, with its country-wide organization, including active women, youth, and labor groups, as well as a secret military network (Sazman-e Nezami-ye Hezb-e Tudeh Iran), played a prominent political role in Iran. The Tudeh was banned following an attempted assassination of the Shah in 1949. Nonetheless, the Party continued its activities, as well as its publications, of which there would be many. Following the 19 August 1953 coup, the Tudeh's military network was annihilated and many of its leaders were arrested or forced into exile, mostly in the Soviet Union and Eastern Europe. Over the years, the Party's political influence was diminished, due in part to the various splits resulting from its pro-Soviet stand and its policies in periods of political tension in Iran. After the 1979 Revolution, the Tudeh declared Ayatollah Khomeini and the Islamic Republic revolutionaries and anti-imperialists and actively supported and collaborated with the government. Though the Party never opposed the Islamic Republic, it became the target of the regime's attacks in 1982. The Party's leaders and cadres were imprisoned, and some members, in particular those related to the new secret military network, were executed. The Tudeh lost scores of its members during the mass prison killings of 1988, though the Iranian authorities spared its leadership. The Party, which resumed its activities in the early 1990s in exile, is not openly active inside Iran, and the degree of its strength and influence there is not known.

Tufan See Hezb-e Kar-e Iran

Vahdat-e Komonisti (Communist Unity) Organization

The Vahdat-e Komonisti (Communist Unity) Organization was founded in November 1978 by Communist political activists, particularly students who were educated outside the country and returned to Iran, as well as like-minded activists inside the country. The history of its founding dates back to the Ettehadieh Komonist-ha (Communists Union), which was formed outside Iran in the late 1960s. The members of Vahdat-e Komonisti identified themselves as supporters of the "political-military struggle for the preparation and accomplishment of a Socialist revolution," and as leftists, opposed to Stalinism and Maoism. Among the

Vahdat-e Komonisti (Communist Unity) Organization *(continued)*

activities of this organization were critiques of the political and ideological viewpoints of political organizations in Iran via the publication of *Raha'i*, the main Vahdat-e Komonisti publication. During the massive crackdown on opposition groups in June 1981, the organization faced significant crises and split into various factions. Members of the organization outside Iran continued their activism until 1986 through the publication of *Andisheh Raha'i* and *Bultan-e Akhbar-e Iran* (the Bulletin of Iranian News).

ABF EDITOR'S NOTE: In the early 1980s, a number of militants from various leftist groups joined the ranks of the armed rebellion in Iranian Kurdistan, notwithstanding the official position of their respective organizations on armed struggle.

Victims who were remembered by name by the witnesses

(f) *denotes a female victim*

Photographs of victims' gravestones, from Iraj Mesdaghi's book *Raqs-e Qoqnus-ha Va Avaz Khakestar* (Dance of the Phoenixes and Song of the Ash). The photographs do not correspond to the names listed here.

Abbas Mira'ian

Abbas Reihani

Abbas Reza'i

Abbas'ali Monshi Rudsari

Ahmad Nuramin

Akbar Abdolhosseini

Akbar Sadeqi

Ali Akbar Bak'ali

Ali Mobaraki

Ali Na'imi

Alireza Haj Samadi

Ali Shahbazi

Ali Taikandi

Alireza Daliri

Alireza Zomorrodian

Amir Rashidi

Amir

Asghar Manuchehr Abadi

Behruz Yusof Purlazarjani

Behzad Fath Zanjani

Behzad Omrani

Bijan Eslami Eshbela

Dariush Safa'i

Davud Zargar

Eskandar Nazemolbaka

Faramarz Zamanzadeh

Fatemeh Modaress Tehrani (f)

Foruzan Abdi (f)

Gholam Reza Kashani

Hamid Mo'ayeri

Hesamoddin Savabi

Homayun Azadi

Hosein Haqiqat Talab

Hossein Bahri

Hossein Maleki Pur

Hossein Mirza'i

Ja'far Hariri

Ja'far Hushmand

Jahanbakhsk Sarkhosh

Jalal Fatahi

Jalal Maherolnaqsh

Javad Nazeri

Kambize Ata'i

Kasra Akbari Kordestani

Mahin Qorbani (f)

Mahmud Hassani

Mahmud Qazi

Mahmud Zaki

Majid Moshref

Majid Vali

Majid

Mansur Najafi Shushtari

Manuchehr Bozorgbashar

Mariam Golzadeh Ghafuri (f)

Mas'ud Ansari

Mas'ud Bakhtari

Mas'ud Mas'udi

Mas'ud Moqbeli

Mas'ud Rahmani

Mehdi Fereiduni

Mehdi Sa'idian

Mehran Hoveida

Mehrangiz Mohammad-Rahimi (f)

Mehrdad Ardebili

Mehrdad Ashtari

Mohammad Ali Behkish

Mohammad Bijanzadeh

Mohammad Farjad (Najar)

Mohammad Shahbazian

Mohammad Tavakoli

Mohammad Zamiri

Mohsen Rashidi

Mohsen Vazin

Mojtaba Motale' Sarabi

Morteza Abdolhosseini

Mostafa Esfandiari

Mostafa Mirza'i

Nasser Hassanpur

Ne'mat Eqbali

Parviz Salimi

Qorban'ali Shokri

Rahmat Fathi

Reza Abbasi

Reza Abbaszadeh

Reza Bahmanabadi

Reza Esmati

Roshan Bolbolian

Sadeq

Sa'id Mas'udi

Seifodin

Seyfollah Qiasvand

Shirmohammad

Sirus Adibi

Soheil Daniali

Soheila Darvish Kohan (f)

Soheila Mohammad-Rahimi (f)

Taqi Sedaqat

Zahra (Farzaneh) Mirza'i (f)

Many of those who tell their stories in this book gathered with other survivors for a group photo on 25 October 2011. On that day, the Abdorrahman Boroumand Foundation (ABF) hosted a symposium in Oxford, England, "The Massacre of Political Prisoners in Iran: A Quest for Justice," in conjunction with Geoffrey Robertson, QC (the author of the full report on the 1988 massacre, from which the Executive Summary in this book was drawn), and with Oxford Transitional Justice Research at the University of Oxford. At the symposium, for the first time ever, victims, eminent international legal experts, scholars, country specialists, and human rights advocates came together to talk about truth-telling and to explore possible legal and political avenues of recourse for the victims of the 1988 prison massacre. This event was, for ABF, a means to bring to the attention of the international community an unnoticed and and sometimes willingly neglected mass killing, the suffering of the survivors, and the pattern of impunity that continues to plague Iran.

For Geoffrey Robertson's full report, go to http://www.iranrights.org/english/attachments/doc_3518.pdf.

A video clip of the symposium can be viewed at http://www.youtube.com/watch?v=z10s4AGgBYU.
For a report on the symposium in the ABF newsletter, go to http://www.iranrights.org/english/newsletter-24.php.

www.ingramcontent.com/pod-product-compliance
Lightning Source LLC
Chambersburg PA
CBHW081147090426
42736CB00017B/3215